ALDOUS HUXLEY

SELECTED LETTERS

ALDOUS HUXLEY

SELECTED LETTERS

Edited with an Introduction by
James Sexton

Ivan R. Dee
Chicago 2007

www.ivanrdee.com

Frontispiece photograph courtesy of the Estate of Aldous Huxley.

Library of Congress Cataloging-in-Publication Data:
Huxley, Aldous, 1894–1963
  [Correspondence. Selections]
  Aldous Huxley : selected letters / edited with an introduction by James Sexton.
    p. cm.
  Includes index.
  ISBN-13: 978-1-56663-629-2 (cloth : alk. paper)
  ISBN-10: 1-56663-629-9 (cloth : alk. paper)
  I. Sexton, James. II. Title.
PR6015.U9Z48 2007
823'.912—dc22
[B]
                                                          2007019219

To Janice, Richard, and Ian

ACKNOWLEDGMENTS

I wish to thank the Social Sciences and Humanities Research Council of Canada for a research grant that helped make this edition possible. In addition I particularly wish to thank Ms. Laura Huxley, Dr. David Bradshaw, and Prof. Grover Smith for their encouragement and help during this project. I am also indebted to the following individuals and research libraries for their support:

Kent Bicknell, Robert Cowley, Valerie Eliot, Amerigo Franchetti, Philip Goodman, the late Matthew Huxley, Stan Lauryssens, Dr. Rolando Pieraccini, and Bronwen Welch.

Aberdeen University, King's College Library; Alfred University, New York, Herrick Memorial Library; Archives et Musée de la Littérature, Bibliothèque Royale Albertine, Brussels; Archives of American Art, Smithsonian Institution; City of Baltimore, Enoch Pratt Free Library; Bibliothèque de la Société des Auteurs et Compositeurs Dramatiques, Paris; Bibliothèque Municipale De Vichy; Bibliothèque Municipale De Versailles; Boston University, Mugar Memorial Library; British Library; University of California, Berkeley, The Bancroft Library; University of California, Los Angeles, William Andrews Clark Memorial Library, Charles E. Young Research Library; University of California, Santa Barbara; Cambridge University, King's College Library; Cambridge University, Marshall Library of Economics; Columbia University, Rare Books and Manuscripts Division; James S. Copley Library; Cornell University, Carl A. Kroch Research Library; University of Delaware Library; Duke University Library; Eton College Library; Frank Lloyd Wright Library;

Acknowledgments

Georgetown University Library; Harvard University, Houghton Library, Harvard Theatre Collection, James Schlesinger Library; House of Lords Library; University of Houston Library; Huntington Library; University of Illinois, Chicago, School of Living Records; Indiana University, Lilly Library; Keele University Library; Lambeth Palace Library; Leeds University, Brotherton Library; Library of Congress, Manuscripts Division; Liverpool University, Sydney Jones Library; London University, University Library; London University; Warburg Institute; McMaster University, Mills Memorial Library; University of Michigan Library; University of Michigan, Bentley Historical Library; University of Missouri Special Collections Library; National Library of Scotland; National Library of Wales; New York Public Library, The Berg Collection; New York Public Library, Rare Books and Manuscripts Division; New York State University, Buffalo, Lockwood Memorial Library; New York University, Fales Library; Nottingham University Library; University of Oregon Library; Oxford University, Bodleian Library; Oxford University, Merton College Library; Oxford University, Wellcome Unit For the History of Medicine; Peace Pledge Union Library; Pennsylvania State University Library; Pierpont Morgan Library; Princeton University, Department of Rare Books and Special Collections; University of Reading Library; Rice University, Woodson Research Center, Fondren Library; University of Southern California, Feuchtwanger Memorial Library; Southern Illinois University at Carbondale, The Morris Library; Stanford University Library; Sussex University Library; Sydney University Library; Temple University Library; Harry Ransom Humanities Research Center, University of Texas, Austin; Texas Woman's University; Thoreau Institute, Lincoln, Massachusetts; University of Victoria Special Collections Library; University of Virginia, Alderman Library; Warwick University, Modern Records Centre; Wellesley College, Margaret Clapp Library; Yale University, Beinecke Library.

For permission to quote from the published and unpublished writings of Aldous Huxley, I am grateful to the late Dorris Halsey and the Aldous Huxley Literary Estate.

J. S.

Victoria, British Columbia
August 2007

CONTENTS

ALDOUS HUXLEY
SELECTED LETTERS

INTRODUCTION

In a letter of 9 May 1929, Aldous Huxley advised that he was "not one of nature's letter-writers. Self-contained and placid misanthropists are bad correspondents." In fact, though, Huxley was a born epistolarian. Grover Smith, editor of the indispensable *Letters of Aldous Huxley* (1969), estimated that Huxley wrote approximately 10,000 letters in his lifetime; Smith published fewer than a thousand of the 2,500 he was able to examine. This present book adds hundreds more that have never been published—in particular a large cache of love letters, a type wholly absent from Smith's edition. Thanks to the passage of time and the lapse of the embargo on those letters with sensitive content, many previously unavailable letters may now be read.

The first letter in this new collection dates from 1901, when Aldous was nearly seven; the last was written fewer than two months before his death on 22 November 1963, the same day President John F. Kennedy was assassinated.

Huxley's writing life may be divided into two roughly equal parts, as illustrated by the letters that follow. The first period, from about 1914 until shortly before his departure for America in early 1937, reveals Huxley as the witty, satirical aesthete from a distinguished English family—his grandfather was Thomas Henry Huxley, the influential biologist and foremost advocate of Darwin's theory of evolution; his father, Leonard, was an author and editor; and his older brother, Julian, later followed his grandfather as a biologist and became a prolific author who was also briefly director general of UNESCO. Aldous first came to public notice as the protégé of Lady Ottoline Morrell of Garsington Manor, Oxfordshire. During this time the clever young Oxford grad with that kind of "hydroptic" thirst for knowledge peculiar to John Donne, one of Huxley's early masters, set out to establish himself as a professional writer.

Not long after Huxley became a more or less permanent house guest at Garsington, he met the woman he would eventually marry after a two-and-a-half-year separation from late 1916 to 1919: the eighteen-year-old Belgian refugee Maria Nys, who was then living under the aegis of the Morrells at Garsington. Although all the love letters to Maria were thought to have been lost in the 12 May 1961 house fire that destroyed Huxley's papers in his Hollywood home, five of them have been preserved by a private collector, and he has permitted me to publish the longest of them.[1] But by far the largest cache of Huxley's intimate letters is that addressed to his mistress, Mary Hutchinson.

In 1921 Huxley alienated Lady Ottoline by depicting the foibles of the Garsington circle in his first novel, *Crome Yellow*, a talky work of ideas set in an imaginary country house called Crome and consciously modeled on such novels as *Headlong Hall* and *Gryll Grange* by Thomas Love Peacock, a contemporary of the poet Shelley.

In a letter to his patroness, dated 3 December 1921, Huxley feigns shock at Lady Ottoline's outrage over his all-too-identifiable setting and cast of characters. Protesting his innocence, he writes:

> Your letter bewildered me. I cannot understand how anyone could suppose that this little marionette performance of mine [*Crome Yellow*] was the picture of a real *milieu*: —it so obviously isn't. You might as justifiably accuse Shaw of turning Garsington into Heartbreak House or Peacock of prophesying it in *Nightmare Abbey*. ... My error, I admit, was to use some of Garsington's architectural details. I ought to have laid the scene in China. ... [And] the characters are nothing but marionettes with voices, designed to express

---

[1] In the house fire Huxley was able to save the manuscript of *Island* and a few suits. His second wife, Laura Archera Huxley, managed to save her Guarneri violin. All the love letters to Laura, save one, were also destroyed. A few that he wrote to her after the fire are reprinted in her memoir of her life with Aldous, *This Timeless Moment* (1968). The fire prompted Huxley's observation a few days later, "It is odd to be starting from scratch at my age—with literally nothing in the way of possessions, books, mementos, letters, diaries. I am evidently intended to learn, a little in advance of the final denudation, that you can't take it with you."

ideas and the parody of ideas. . . . They have about as much reality as Dr. Opimian . . . in *Gryll Grange*.

Despite his spirited *apologia*, the correspondence between the two did not resume until 1927, notwithstanding Maria Huxley's tactful letter of 5 November 1923 to Lady Ottoline, which begins, "I received your letter with great pleasure; I distributed your love as directed. . . . I hope you will like Aldous's latest book—it is very good, and also much better—you know what I mean by this unpleasantly clumsy way of expressing my thoughts."

The Huxley persona in the letters from his Garsington days through the late 1930s is completely consistent with his own retrospective assessment in 1946 of his former self as "an amused, Pyrrhonic [skeptical] aesthete." *Jesting Pilate* is the title of a collection of his essays written in 1925 while he was traveling with Maria and dispatching many of his wittiest letters to Mary Hutchinson during a tour of India, southeast Asia, Japan, and parts of the United States. It nicely sums up the unattached, gadfly persona that Huxley wished to convey to his public: the title is taken from the first line of Bacon's "Of Truth": "'What is truth?' said Jesting Pilate, and would not stay for an answer." The letters of this period are cynical, merrily mocking human frailties.

The details of the Huxleys' unconventional love life are complex. The lives of Aldous and Maria were soon entered by Mary Hutchinson, another fashionable Bloomsbury hostess and wife of a prominent barrister, St. John Hutchinson. In a late, unpublished memoir, Mary wrote that of the two Huxleys, she loved Maria best. Both Maria and Mary were bisexual, and at least in her youth Maria was romantically involved with several women. According to Huxley's biographer Sybille Bedford, "Maria was bisexual and she did have a series of short-term passionate relationships . . . while she was married to Aldous. . . . They were sophisticated people who were not afraid to experiment." The three-sided relationship between the Huxleys and Mary reached its peak around 1925, but the physical element at least seems not to have survived into the next decade. To judge by a letter from Maria to her sister in 1947, her relations with Mary, if not Aldous's, had gradually tapered off into indifference. In the letter she refers to Mary, whom she had not contacted since the outbreak of the war, as a *"nymphomane"* and of their friendship as *"si passée"* as to be unrenewable.

5

Those accustomed to the Huxley wit will not be disappointed in the many letters and postcards to Mary, chiefly in the 1920s and 1930s. Theirs was certainly a more than platonic liaison, beginning around December 1922 and lasting until the late 1920s. The relationship was begun only after considerable thought, especially on Mary's part, given that she was already involved in an extra-marital affair with Clive Bell, husband of the well-known artist Vanessa Bell, Virginia Woolf's sister—all mainstays of the well-known Bloomsbury Group of artists and intellectuals. The letters to Mary depict Aldous in love. He wooed by the book—consciously adopting the role of conventional Petrarchan lover: his missives are frequently larded with quotations from French poets to catch the eye of his Francophile lady who had once sat for a portrait by Matisse. In them he complains of his mistress's cruelty, pleads lovesickness, and even admits to jealousy over Mary's favoring his rival, Bell.

The second, radically different phase of Huxley's career begins in the late 1930s when he was struggling with his autobiographical novel *Eyeless in Gaza*, shortly before he left Europe for America. This period is characterized by his gradual transformation from witty jester into a determined seeker of peace, both for himself and for mankind. In late 1935, under the influence of the charismatic Anglican cleric, Canon H.R.L. (Dick) Sheppard (portrayed in *Eyeless in Gaza* as a muscular Christian cleric, the Reverend John Purchas), Huxley joined the movement later known as the Peace Pledge Union, remaining a sponsor and member until his death.

Around this time—like his fictional self, Anthony Beavis, in *Eyeless in Gaza*—Huxley also underwent a kind of religious conversion. He soon became Sheppard's chief lieutenant. In a letter to him dated 9 November 1935, Huxley reveals for the first time a sincere humility. Rather than laughing at others, he can now laugh at himself.

> Ever since lunching with you the other day, I have been feeling very much ashamed for the glibness with which I talked of the project of organizing the peace movement. When one has been endowed with the gift of the gab, one is sadly tempted to make use of it for elegantly expressing ideas which one knows as ideas and not by experience. That I should have talked so much to you—the theoretician to the man who knows the business of dealing with people by the process of self-dedication—is frankly comic, and it is only by laughing at myself that I can take the edge off my shame.

In another pivotal letter, dated 30 July 1936, Huxley tells Mrs. Kethevan Roberts:

> I think a good deal can be done to modify oneself. It's a question of using the proper techniques: meditation, Mental Prayer, whatever one likes to call them.
>
> I had a bad time all last year with insomnia and consequent neurasthenia, but have now emerged again, thank goodness. Meanwhile the political nightmare seems to be growing worse and worse. Whether any of us will be alive three years from now becomes increasingly dubious. One can only go on with the old job of imploring people *not* to kill themselves. There are signs through the prevailing lunacy, that they would like to become sane—but the trouble is that they aren't yet prepared to take the necessary steps without which there can be no preservation. They want the end without going to the trouble of using the appropriate means.

Perhaps the key idea in this letter is Huxley's desire to modify himself through a disciplined adherence to technique. He had begun to practice Buddhist and Hindu methods of meditation, hypnosis, and yoga, and had become an enthusiastic follower of F. M. Alexander's self-help techniques. Later he experimented with the Bates Method of exercises to help improve the poor vision that had always vexed him. Later, in 1953, in *The Doors of Perception*, he famously described his controlled experiments with mescaline under the supervision of Dr. Humphry Osmond, striving to approximate the mystic's experience of enlightenment. Huxley used these techniques first to help him achieve inner peace; then he continued to write in support of such causes as world peace, birth control, the abolition of hunger, and environmentalism. The essential element in his new faith was that it must first of all be

> a personal ethic, a way of life for individuals; only on that condition will it come to be embodied . . . in forms of social and international organization. . . . It is easy to talk about a more excellent way of life, immensely difficult to live it. Five Latin words sum up the moral history of every man and woman who has ever lived: *Video meliora, proboque;/Deteriora sequor.* (I see the better and approve it: the worse is what I pursue.)

A futile attempt by the now public-minded activist to forestall war may have precipitated Huxley's move to America. Just months before his departure, he and Gerald Heard, through influential relatives, were able to suggest a plan to British Prime Minister Neville Chamberlain that might have seriously stalled Germany's military buildup. They proposed to corner the entire Canadian supply of nickel, a raw material that Germany desperately needed. But "the fatal Chamberlain . . . responded with . . . the pet word of the purblind, 'Impractical.'"

Soon afterward Huxley and Heard began an American lecture tour, which Maria described in a letter to a friend as "a Mutt and Jeff on war and peace and religion and so on." From then on, Huxley's writing grew increasingly didactic, the satirist giving way to the prophet. He became a self-styled "rational propagandist" for various reform ideas. In his next novel, *After Many a Summer Dies the Swan* (1939), Huxley used William Propter as a mouthpiece for some of the decentralist ideas of Ralph Borsodi, pioneer of the "back to the land" movement, whom Huxley had met in New York state in 1937. Borsodi persuaded Huxley that decentralized production in homes and small workshops was cheaper than centralized mass production, an idea to which Huxley returned in the revised foreword to *Brave New World* in 1946. Propter insists that Good is, on the lower level, "the proper functioning of the organism," and on the higher level "it exists as the experience of eternity . . . the transcendence of personality, the extension of consciousness beyond the limits imposed by the ego."

Huxley dealt with the same theme in the summer of 1945. To a correspondent who had lamented that the universe is such that "it is always easier to do harm than good," he responded:

> The reason for this strange paradox, is that people find it so enormously difficult to "die to self." . . . But that is what in fact the world is like, all the masters of the spiritual life—those whose purity of heart permits them to have insight into reality and to see God—are agreed. Many are called, few chosen. One can only suppose that this immensely stringent intelligence test is, in one way or another, on one level of existence or another, continued indefinitely until, as the Mahayana Buddhists insist, all sentient beings shall at last have chosen to be liberated from selfhood into the knowledge of the divine Ground.

In one apt metaphor, Huxley likens life to an intelligence test that continues indefinitely. The metaphor conveys the main theme of Huxley's novel *Time Must Have a Stop*, which appeared in the same year as the letter above. The plot describes the last day in the life of the unrepentantly sensual scapegrace, Eustace Barnack, who fails the intelligence test. After overindulging all day in rich food and fat cigars, he suffers a fatal heart attack. Huxley structured Barnack's after-death experience around a description of the three stages of the *bardo*, the intermediate state between death and rebirth that is described in *The Tibetan Book of the Dead*. Barnack, faced at first with the Clear Light of the Void or Divine Ground, fails to recognize the immanent Godhead because of his egotism and a lack of spiritual insight. He then falls into the equivalent in Christian terms of two lower purgatorial levels, thereby missing his chance to transcend.

Huxley explained this experience in his anthology of Christian and Eastern mystical writings, *The Perennial Philosophy* (1945): "For oriental theologians there is no eternal damnation; there are only purgatories and then an indefinite series of second chances to go forward towards . . . total reunion with the Ground of all being."

Huxley launched his final campaign as a Cassandra-like prophet in 1946 with his foreword to a new edition of *Brave New World*. His great cause gathered momentum in 1956 when he began *Island*, a utopian answer to his famous dystopia of *Brave New World*, eventually completing it in June 1961. In those intervening five years he warned against the coming of the brave new world and proposed an alternative to its soulless technological society. His letter of 10 January 1959 to the engineer Gilbert Perleberg describes the future he was determined to help avoid:

> The problem, it seems to me, is this: how far can individuals or small groups of individuals, who have opened themselves to the Good and feel impelled to work for an order of things that shall make the Good more accessible to more people, prevail against a system— Technology in every field of human activity, industrial, organizational, economic, political, psychological and mind-manipulative— which develops autonomously according to the laws of its own nature. . . .

Huxley's novel *Island* depicts such a society, one that uses technology but is not subservient to it. The novel's utopian elements are familiar to those who know his writings after *Ends and Means* (1937). On the fictional island of Pala, children are reared on the mystical teachings of the perennial philosophy, and the society as a whole is neither exclusively capitalist nor socialist. Instead Pala is a small, decentralized federation of self-governing units, some of whose solutions to economic and social problems result from the elimination of Huxley's familiar *bêtes-noires*: militarism, overpopulation, overorganization, and the *ersatz* religion of consumerism.

Despite his American publisher's efforts on his behalf, Huxley never won a Nobel Prize, though no doubt less worthy recipients have been awarded that prize in Literature or even Peace. In 1963, a year following the publication of his last novel, he died on the tumultuous day of the assassination of President Kennedy, and his passing went largely unnoticed.

Still, in due time accolades were expressed from around the world. T. S. Eliot wrote, "Huxley's reading was immense, his taste impeccable, and his ear acute . . . his place in English literature is unique and is certainly assured." Yehudi Menuhin called him "scientist and artist in one," and Isaiah Berlin described him as "a wholly civilized, good and scrupulous man, and one of the greatest imaginable distinction." Christopher Isherwood wrote: "Fearless curiosity was one of Aldous's noblest characteristics, a function of his greatness as a human being. Little people are so afraid of what the neighbors will say if they ask Life unconventional questions. Aldous questioned unceasingly, and it never occurred to him to bother about the neighbors."

PART ONE

1901–1937

Aldous Huxley, the third son of Leonard and Julia Arnold Huxley, is born in 1894 at Godalming, Surrey. The next year his grandfather, the eminent biologist and author, Thomas Henry Huxley, dies. In 1899 his only sister, Margaret, is born. In 1901 the family takes up residence at Julia's school for girls, Prior's Field, Godalming. In 1903, along with his cousin Gervas, Aldous becomes a "boarder" at Hillside Preparatory School (depicted as Bulstrode in the autobiographical novel Eyeless in Gaza*). There he befriends Lewis Gielgud, eldest brother of the actor Sir John Gielgud. Huxley attends Eton in autumn 1908, and in November of that year his mother dies. In early 1911 he leaves Eton because of serious eye trouble,* keratitis punctata, *and is nearly blind for eighteen months. He learns Braille, an advantage of which, he tells Gervas, is that one can read in bed without getting cold hands. In 1912 his sight improves and he writes his first (lost) novel on a typewriter. He spends May and June in Marburg, studying German and music. He enters Balliol College, Oxford, in 1913 and soon begins a correspondence with Jelly d'Aranyi, the violinist, about whom Julian Huxley says that he and his two brothers fell under her spell. She never married. In August, Aldous holidays in Scotland with Julian, and later that month he learns of his favorite brother Trev's suicide. In October 1914 he returns to Oxford, lodging with the Haldane family at Cherwell, where he befriends Naomi Haldane (later Mitchison). He first visits Garsington, the Oxfordshire estate of Lady Ottoline and Philip Morrell, in December 1915, and there meets his future wife, Maria Nys Huxley, and his future sister-in-law, Juliette Baillot, later Mrs. Julian Huxley.*

TO JULIAN HUXLEY[1]

May 1901

Dear Julian,
The weather is lovely hear. Baby is so mistchivas, she cant keep still for a moment now. We had one or 2 showers yesterday. The kitten can warlk now and go around room.

Aldous

TO JULIAN HUXLEY

Prior's Field
Godalming
Summer 1908

Dear Julian,
Thank you very much for the cyclopedia. I now know everything, from who invented dice to the normal temperature of the sea-cucumber. You will be pleased to hear that I am allowed up and a very good thing too. What *are* you going to lecture about????? Birds or what??? I expect mumps will soon cease as there are at present no more cases: of course it is possible that we may have another and third batch but we shall probably get off free after this.

Isn't this a nice violet? Bella sent me a bunch of them with some splendid carnations. I wonder if you know the language of the flowers? If you give peach-blossom it means "I am your captive." While hyacinth means "unobtrusive loveliness." White clover means "think of me." All this is out of my cyclopedia. Here is a fine puzzle. A square with nine divisions. 5 always in the middle. One has to make fifteen every way one adds. Up and down; across, or diagonally. I have got it out.

Your loving brother,
Aldous

[1] Julian Sorell Huxley (1887–1975), eldest of the three Huxley brothers. An eminent biologist and popularizer of science in books and lectures, he was the first director of UNESCO and a founding member of the World Wildlife Fund.

TO JULIAN HUXLEY

New Buildings
Eton College
Windsor
ca 1910

My dear Julian,
It was with abnormal surprise that I heard I had not written to you. I hear Trev is doing Reck-eck-eck the gay Lord Quex in the pantomime by Aristophanes at Oxford. I suppose you have heard that I have got the second holiday task prize. Fifteen bob's worth of books. I think I'll get a Matthew Arnold nicely bound. Trev tells me by telegram you had six Valentines. You ask if the head has done any floaters lately. Yes!

You cannot have seen the *Chronicle* or *Daily Mail* lately (for his floater got into that). Now having raised your expectation. The floater was giving a general order for great coats. Result indignant O[ld] E[tonian] letter in *Chronicle*. Up to kind Ashy this half. One and a half more minutes till post time.

TO TREVENAN HUXLEY²

ca Fall 1910

Dear Trev,
My eyes are less pink, so your wish came true. I enclose a few pictures, one of which is quite a new idea of an animal. It is very dull here, not being allowed to read—still drawing and Miss Milligan are better than nothing! If even sometimes you were here to play Bezique with me! That would be a little better than drawing! I have got some Plasticene which was lent me, but it is red and comes off on one's fingers so I have tried to use it for colouring but not with the best success, as you can see for yourself!

At the present moment I have been almost 9 days in bed, without being allowed to read. Frightful rot, *I* call it! I have to bathe my eyes every 1½ hours, or so. I do it like this:—first I pour some lotion into a glass shaped like this [picture of a glass] and coloured green, then I put my eye in it, lift my head and the glass up till it (the glass) is upside down, and open my eye.

---

² Trevenan Huxley (1889–1914). Second of the three Huxley brothers, he committed suicide in August 1914.

I hope Dobbin and Lena have made friends by now! You must tell me about the cats and dogs and rats, etc. when you next write which I hope will be soon, for it is very dull here (as remarked before, I believe). [what a very Mrs. Nicklebeian sentence!]

Goodbye from your loving brother.

TO JULIAN HUXLEY

48 Banbury Road,
Oxford
May 1913

My dear Julian,

After seven anxious days, sans communication with the outer world—or rather the inner circle of the HOME—we learn that you are in a safe asylum, far from human ken. Myself am well, and yourself, I hope, recovers—a pleasing point of grammar, what?

Swamped by slugs, inundated with reactionaries, this poor city mourns—but it is satisfactory to think that slugdom is preparing its own destruction by its monstrous actions . . .

But let that pass. . . .

T[rev] and I have been spending most of this term in acting Naomi Haldane's[3] Play [*Saunes Bairos*] . . . a drama in three acts of exorbitant length, complexity, and number of characters.

But let that pass. . . .

It is all over now—and the town mumbles still with it—*De mortuis cui boni. O extempore, O glores.*

Once Raleigh[4] lectures and I hear him—not without certain interests evinced—But let that pass.

Should I disturb your quiet with writing, or no?

Farewell,
Aldous

---

[3] Naomi Haldane (Mitchison) (1897–1999). Scottish novelist.
[4] Sir Walter Raleigh (1861–1922). Huxley's tutor at Oxford.

TO JELLY D'ARANYI[5]

Balliol College
Oxford
[1913?]

My dear Jelly,
Sunday! and the right day for an Englishman to write a letter! I'm afraid I was being very dull and stupid and grumpy, when I came to see you the other day—perhaps I always am—I don't know—but particularly so then. I apologise for it and I wish one could arrange one's moods and behaviour just as one wanted to, instead of having to trust to luck to be able to talk or smile, as one has to do. One would arrange to have a dull fit for dull people and a nice fit for nice ones. But fate generally puts it all wrong!

Examinations on the very first day I come here have rather depressed me, I'm afraid—but there are enough nice people on the spot to make things quite amusing—and, if one tries one's best to enjoy oneself one succeeds sometimes, although, perhaps, you wouldn't say so!

The great disadvantage of my rooms is that they're just opposite the chapel and one is made unhappy on Sundays by the noise of people singing hymns. I suppose it's very nice for the people, who are really happy when they're in Church, but I'm afraid it rather gets on my nerves—they do make such an awful noise—

You must come and visit me some time when they're not singing hymns: perhaps you'll like the rooms better if you don't hear them over the way.

I wish you would write to me sometimes: it would be awfully nice of you.

Yours ever,
Aldous Huxley

TO JELLY D'ARANYI

Oxford Union Society
7 June 1914

Dear Jelly,
You're not a very good correspondent—nor am I—but two wrongs don't make a right.

---

[5] Jelly D'Aranyi (1893–1966). Hungarian born violinist.

However it would be nice to know how, when and where you were. Oxford's very hot and stuffy—typical summer Oxford, without the best part. When all my friends are dead I shall become a hermit and live in a cave—and perhaps you will come occasionally and feed me with buns through the bars of my gate. It would be a charming life!

Yours,
Aldous

TO JELLY D'ARANYI

Sunday
ca 26 April 1915

All good Englishmen write letters on Sunday. So I'll go on. I see an account of your concert in this morning's *Observer*. It must have been jolly and I'd have liked to have heard it.

Do you see that poor Bob Gibson[6] is missing? I'm afraid it looks very bad, though, of course, it's possible he's a prisoner.

Kitchener's armies seem to have begun moving—so that now I shall have a lot more friends out at the front—which I don't like. Friends matter more than anything, when one is young.

I've been twenty-four hours writing this—Sunday night now and I'm almost as tired as I was last night—so good-bye—and do write. And, by the way, isn't your birthday about now?

A.L.H.

TO JELLY D'ARANYI

Cherwell
[Late 1915]

Dear Jelly,
Thank you ever so much for your delightful letter. Actually, I had just started writing to you the day before it arrived, but something had interrupted me in the middle and I'd forgotten to go on.

You ought to see Balliol now. It's too curious. There are only about 60 undergraduates up, and the whole of the Front Quad is filled with soldiers: there are 250 of them there, sleeping four or five in a room—and a lot in my old room. I'm only hoping they won't smash my pic-

---

[6] Bob Gibson was a don at Oxford.

tures and spoil my books—still, if they do, one will just have not to mind.

There was a man at Balliol last term, who belonged to an *ächt Judenfamilie* and was called Reuben Bussweiler. This term he has come up with the name Robin Boswell—rather a clever change, I think!

I'm afraid I have never read *War and Peace*. I suppose I ought to. What I have read quite lately is Turgenev's *Une niche de gentilhommes*, which is a very fine novel, and is, besides,—unlike most of the books of Russian novelists—reasonably short. Tolstoy's books have never less than 700 pages, and Dostoevski is the same!

Most of my time now is spent in reading the most dreadful stuff for my work—Anglo-Saxon, the language of my ancestors a thousand years ago. You have no idea how extremely difficult it is, and most of it is fearfully dull after one has translated it and found the sense—all good books of sermons and moral remarks. But occasionally there is good poetry, very sad and strange stuff, all about disappointment and sorrow.

I am not surprised at your not liking *Oliver Twist*. I remember when I read it about ten or twelve years ago (I was only about so big [small dot] then!)—it depressed me frightfully.

Well, to bed, to bed. The abominable clock on the mantel-piece has ticked away into Wednesday morning, and it was Tuesday night when I started. One day older! How very unpleasant. I do most desperately want to be always young. The only advantage of age, as far as I can see, is that one's ideas begin to settle down: one's mind becomes tidy instead of one great changing muddle as it is when one's young. But I don't think it makes it worth while being old.

> *Au revoir,*
> *Aldous*

Thank you again for your letter: it was sweet of you to write—and I should love another one!

TO LADY OTTOLINE MORRELL

27 Westbourne Square, W.
ca 15 December 1915

Dear Lady Ottoline,
I fear I snow you under with superfluous correspondence—but here is the manifesto of the new [*Palatine*] *Review*. Its exquisite pomposity

delights me—and the abnegation of the sense of humour and proportion implied in the issuing of it gives one a splendidly business-like
feeling—for it is clear that no one ever succeeded, who always preserved intact his humour and his sense of proportion!

Yours sincerely,
Aldous Huxley

TO LADY OTTOLINE MORRELL

27 Westbourne Square, W.
16 December 1915

Dear Lady Ottoline,
I have long deplored the absence of a sliding scale in Collinses,[7] by the
adjustment of which one might exactly express the degree of enjoyment
experienced—rather after the manner of the grace after meat, graduated from "O Lord, for these thy least mercies—," to "O Bountiful Je-
hovah!" Such an arrangement would be a great simplification, and I
should be able to tell you exactly and in a moment how enormously I
enjoyed my stay at Garsington.

I spent last night, till an early hour of this morning, at Ka Cox's[8]
hebdomadal Conciliabule trying to explain to Duncan Grant what the
MacQueen luncheon party was like—but found that the almost supernatural horrors of the Palazzo del Padre Eterno defied adequate description.

Yours very sincerely,
Aldous Huxley

TO LADY OTTOLINE MORRELL

27 Westbourne Square, W.
19 December 1915

Dear Lady Ottoline,
I went to see [D. H.] Lawrence on Friday. One can't help being very
much impressed by him. There is something almost alarming about his

[7] According to the *Oxford English Dictionary*, a Collins is "a letter of thanks for entertainment or hospitality, sent by a departed guest; a 'bread-and-butter' letter."
[8] Ka[therine] Cox (1887–1938). A friend of Virginia Woolf's since 1911. Her married name
was Katherine Arnold-Forster. A *hebdomadal Conciliabule* is a weekly meeting of plot-
hatchers.

sincerity and seriousness, something that makes one feel oneself to be the most shameful dilettante, persifleur, waster and all the rest. Not but what I think he's wrong. All that he condemns as mere dilettantism and literary flippancy—and the force of his sincerity carries one temporarily with him—all this is something much more than an excrementitious by-product of real life. It all comes back again to the question we were talking about the other day—the enrichment of emotion by intellect. And so too with Lawrence: I'm inclined to think that he would find a life unenriched by the subtler amenities of intellect rather sterile. But I think there's a lot in his theory of the world being in a destructive, autumnal period. What seems to me questionable is, Are you going to hustle on the Spring by going to Florida to immure yourself with one Armenian, one German wife, and, problematically, one or two other young people? It may be possible that some Pentecostal gift of inspiration may descend, and I suppose it's worth risking failure for that possibility.

If, as seems probable, I go and visit my Texan brother next year,[9] I shall certainly join his colony for a bit. I think it might be very good to lead the monastic life for a little.

Meanwhile, thank you very much for B. Russell's syllabus. I should have liked to go—but see that dates are impossible. They begin just as I go back to Oxford—so I fear they are out of the question.

Yours sincerely,
Aldous Huxley

TO LADY OTTOLINE MORRELL

27 Westbourne Square, W.
Christmas Day 1915

Dear Lady Ottoline,
Many thanks for your kind invitation. I fear that just after Christmas is impossible—But—I should like nothing better than to come some time rather later in January—I have got some reading to do in Bodleian, for which I shall be coming up to Oxford before term, so that if I might come to Garsington just before settling down among the phantoms of the seventeenth century it would be most delightful. May I suggest exact dates later? I live in a distressing vagueness about such things.

---

[9] Julian Huxley had been teaching biology at the Rice Institute in Houston.

I was looking through Hans Andersen's fairy stories the other day and found myself quite irresistibly reminded of Garsington by the tale of the Tinderbox—in which the three dogs with eyes like saucers, like mill wheels and like the Round Tower of Copenhagen reminded me— I must apologize—of the ascending scale of spectacles used by the inhabitants of Garsington—Duncan Grant's saucers, your mill wheels and Mademoiselle Balthus's round Towers of Copenhagen. The dogs were very nice dogs, if that in any way palliates the insult!

I went again to see Lawrence the other day, whom I like more and more. I find, curiously, enough Mrs. L. is a Richthofen, and a relation, therefore, of a man I knew very well and liked, who was up at Oxford as a Rhodes scholar before the war—and who is now, I believe, killed.

I was rather embarrassed by Lawrence and his wife suddenly starting a fierce argument about their children, during which each accused the other of selfishness and obstinacy and a good many other things. It was all rather odd!

Yours very sincerely,
Aldous Huxley

TO JELLY D'ARANYI

Oxford
6 May 1916

My dear Jelly,

It is ages and ages since I have heard anything about you—or, I fear, since I have written. But I am always very busy working, for my finals, which come off at the end of this term. But now about you—how are you, and where? and is life proceeding as happily as is to be hoped?— But I am afraid, sometimes one rather despairs about things with this vampire of a war draining the life and soul out of the world.

Julian speaks of possibly coming home—but I hope he won't—for, I don't think he'd do much good here either to himself or anyone else. I shall go, I think, to see him this year or next in America, if he's still there. It will be nice to meet him once more—Quite as a stranger: for not only will he have changed, but I myself am so different from what I was two years ago. This is the period of one's life, I think, when one passes most rapidly from stage to stage of one's development. In many ways, I think, Julian is like me, but in certain points very different.

I have been seeing Lady Ottoline Morell a good many times lately. I like her so enormously. I feel in her house more completely "at home" in a more congenial atmosphere than almost anywhere else.

Forgive a dull letter—but I am rather tired. You can return good for evil by writing me an interesting one. I hope I shall see you soon: tell me where you are going to be this summer.

Good bye.

Yours affectionately,
Aldous

TO JELLY D'ARANYI

Grand Hotel
Swanage
Dorset
[Spring 1916?]

My dear Jelly,
Me voilà—popular watering-place and rather vulgar little town—but lovely country: I remember it fifteen years ago. Think of that, and consider that one must be pretty ancient to remember things as they were 15 years ago—I don't remember very much, I admit,—but still. We motored down and the country was lovely—though very few leaves yet on the trees—a late spring—but the swallows and nightingales must be just arriving, last week and next. Should you ever come to Oxford in the summer—which I hope may be some time soon—I will take you to the place, where the nightingales sing more beautifully than anywhere else in the world—"*Tandaradei Singt der nachtigall*" (do you spell it so?)—though why Heine ever supposed it said, *Tandaradei*—I can't imagine. It doesn't say anything so stupid. But when one hears it on a starry June night, with the smell of hay in the air, one tumbles for a moment—plop!—into the *Ewigkeit*. The *Ewigkeit*, you know, is always just around the corner—and one quite often gets a glimpse of it.

I'm going back to Oxford on Friday, I think. I should so much like to see you before I go. Should I find you on Thursday or Friday afternoon? I come back to town on Wednesday and my family stay on here.

Au revoir,
Aldous

TO LADY OTTOLINE MORRELL

Stocks Cottage
Tring
Herts
25 April 1916

Dear Lady Ottoline,
I am sending back the *Chartreuse De Parme*—with many thanks. I don't think I know anything at all like it. Its restraint of manner is unique. There is no romantic devilling of the incidents, no high-lights, no cooking of the evidence by the author. The facts just move with their own impetus and weight: mixing metaphors, they are self-luminous, shining from within, not lit by the writer. At first—so used is one to the method of laying it on thick and to illumination from without—one hardly notices the movements of the soul that are going on: but as one gets accustomed to the Stendhalesque method, things begin to get their real value and one is tremendously moved by what to the untrained eye would have appeared insignificant—if not have escaped attention. The whole business of the vow, for instance—how it would all have been run to death by another man—emotions torn to rags over it—dreadful dialogues about it—as it is, it is mentioned as little as possible, but the effect of the last references to it, when once one has become sensitized to the Stendhal manner, is enormous.

The country is jolly—but infernally cold. Incredible seems the memory that a fortnight ago we were bathing—rashly perhaps—but nevertheless bathing and basking in sunlight. I only pray that some warmth may percolate through on us before Easter, when we go away from here.

Do you know H. J. Massingham—son of the "Nation"? I have been having a correspondence with him about some poems of mine he wants to publish in the second number of "Form," and I am going to see him on Easter Tuesday: I so much wonder what he is like.

My respects to the Pugs—and the rest of the household.
Yours very sincerely,
Aldous Huxley

TO GILBERT MURRAY[1]

The Manor House
Garsington, Oxford
May 1916

Dear Professor Murray,
I must apologize for my impertinence in troubling you. But it occurred to me that you might perhaps know of some official or semi-official post for which I could usefully apply. Office work entailing long hours of eye-strain would be impossible for me: but you might know, I thought, of some post requiring moderate intelligence and not too long continued hours at a stretch. Such as working up facts for propaganda. This demand is, I fear, very brazen and I must beg you to take no trouble: but if you should know of some such post in which I could make myself useful, I should be very grateful if you would tell me to whom I ought to make application. I am at present engaged in outdoor work on the farm, but there is no element of permanency in it to keep me from doing anything else.

Please remember me to Lady Mary. I hope I may find an opportunity to come into Oxford and see her one day.

Yours sincerely,
Aldous Huxley

TO GILBERT MURRAY

The Manor House
Garsington, Oxford
15 May 1916

Dear Professor Murray,
Many thanks for your letter. About my sight:—I can do reading about 5 hours a day: and writing with a typewriter is very little trouble indeed. What would be hard for me is looking up references and turning from one thing to another: the constant alteration of focus being painful.

As to languages: I know French well and am in a condition of having forgotten a moderate knowledge of German, which I dare say I could kick up fairly soon.

Yours sincerely,
Aldous Huxley

---

[1] Gilbert Murray (1866–1957). British classicist and author, supporter of Liberal party.

TO ROBERT NICHOLS[2]

[late May 1916]

It is proposed, my dear Bob, to make a Palatine Anthology—a sort of supplement to the P[alatine] R[eview]—during the summer. It is to include my sonnets, works of Earp,[3] Childe, Graves, possibly Sassoon, perhaps Eliot, Fredegond Shove, and maybe others—and it should be good. So will you send some things along—enough to fill five or six pages. We will advertise the thing and plant review copies copiously and it should, I think, be a success.

How is Devon? Placid, I presume. And your life should be pleasingly vegetal. I sit in the heat—sweating ink with the din of typewriters and the sound of hideous commercial voices loud in my ears. *Quelle saleté, quelle saloperie! Je mène une vie . . . , une vie cul-de-jatte, obscènement hémorrhoidale.*

Farewell and let me have some poems. It should be good I think and an advertisement at least.

Yours,
Aldous H.

TO JELLY D'ARANYI

Oxford Union Society
June 1916

My dear Jelly,
What a long time since I have written—and since you have for the matter of that! This term is nearly at an end, I'm glad to say, because it was getting rather boring. It will be very nice seeing you again.

I saw Mrs Morrell the other day, and she enquired most affectionately after you—but there were some horrid Belgians at tea, when I was there, who talked incessantly about themselves so that I did not get much chance to talk with Mrs. M, which was a pity, as she is so charming.

I have just been reading some poems of Mallarmé, which you ought to read, if you haven't done so, because they are extremely good, though very hard to understand—in fact the later ones are impossible—but the

---

[2] Robert Nichols (1893–1944). English war poet and playwright.
[3] Thomas Wade Earp (1893–1958). Editor and art critic, who, according to J. R. R. Tolkein, was the original "twerp."

earlier ones are quite wonderful—And, his prose works are interesting—about the relations of literature and music.

Silly letter! I've got nothing to say, except take care of yourself, Jelly.

Good bye,
Aldous

TO LADY OTTOLINE MORRELL

Repton
Derby
12 July 1916

Dear Lady Ottoline,
I am so sorry—for my own sake rather than for yours—that I couldn't get over on Sunday. I should so much have liked to see you and Brett[4] and Carrington.[5] But failure of cycle-power—my poor Rosinante being a little indisposed—combined with other causes prevented me coming.

Meanwhile, I am here, a pedagogue undertaking the instruction, mental and moral, of small boys—*ætat* 12–14½. I appear to have taken the place of an incredibly inefficient old parson, whom the boys hated and ragged, and who has contrived to rob them of all the knowledge they can ever have possessed. If I contrive to teach them anything at all it will be a solid gain. The boys are nice and well-behaved—so I find at any rate after one day of them. The masters are an inimitable group of old Calibans. The headmaster a hearty parson—with a sister to look after him, with whom I had tea on arrival together with several of the local ladies—all definitely low-comedy in type—red-nosed spinsters who bridled and mopped and mowed and asked one "whether London was full."

I live in quite pleasant rooms and so far quite like it, tho' one has fits of loneliness when not working.

Yours,
Aldous Huxley
My love to the children and I trust that Socrates' MYSTERIOUS ITCH has subsided.

---

[4] Dorothy Brett (1883–1977). British painter who emigrated to New Mexico in 1924 with the D. H. Lawrences.
[5] Dora Carrington (1893–1932). British artist who, despondent over Lytton Strachey's death, committed suicide two months later.

TO JELLY D'ARANYI

My dear Jelly,
Ever so many thanks for your letter, which I ought to have answered before: but I have really been rather busy. First, I have been doing my final exams, which thank Goodness have now got through very decently with a first. And next I have temporarily become a schoolmaster! I'm here at Repton School, teaching till the end of term. I have boys of about fourteen and a half to fifteen and a half to deal with. I like the boys, but the work is dull—elementary Latin and English history, with of course nothing of my own stuff—English literature—to teach at all. I don't think I shall become a schoolmaster unless I can help it.

I have been making friends lately with another acquaintance of yours besides Manning—that is Guillaume Ormond. I used to go and listen to him play Bach in between my exams, which was very refreshing to the wearied spirit. I liked Manning from what little I saw of him. I hear he has been turned out of the cadet battalion for some trifling offense against a discipline. Poor man, he was raging against the discipline when I saw him. It is of course very hard for a man with that mental capacity to obey the fools who happened to be above him. So that now he won't ever be able to become an officer—or at least, so I imagine:—which will be perfectly awful for him.

Already quite a number of friends have been killed in our offensive and I fear many more will go before it's over. What I feel about it is that the one thing one must not do is to look back. Certainly one way that people survive after they are dead is in the society to which they belong and particularly in their friends. To look back is a kind of betrayal of the life entrusted to one: one must go forward. The best way of remembering them is not by dwelling on the past but the future.

I'm glad you liked my thing on the "Old Home"; I have been writing a lot these last months, and much better than anything I've done before. I am bringing out a book in the autumn.

When shall I see you again, dear Jelly? Shall you by any chance be staying with or near the Hardcastles again? We are going down to Prior's Field this August. When I go away from here on August 1, I shall go to stay with Ottoline Morrell for a day or two at Garsington and shall probably go on through London to Prior's Field. If you are in London about the 4th or 5th of August, may I come and see you?

Unfortunately, I have not got your letter with me here, so have forgotten the number of your address; so I send to Hortense. Do write if you have time. Letters are pleasant here, as I am rather lonely and gloomy at times, not knowing anyone here. *Au revoir.*

Yours affectionately,
Aldous

TO LADY OTTOLINE MORRELL

Repton
Derby
13 July 1916

Dear Lady Ottoline,
Our letters crossed. I wish all the more I could have come last Sunday. May I come and stay on August 1st for a day or two? It would be delightful if I could. This place bores me very much. If I could just talk to the boys without going through their vile work, it would be quite pleasant. But the work is too tedious—and the teaching of it is made more difficult by the hideous shortcomings of my predecessor, who has left the boys with no inkling of what they are supposed to be in the process of becoming. The really trying thing is the prospect of exams, which I shall have to set and correct—a horrible affair.

Oh these old masters! They speak with pride of having been here forty years: there is one who has a disease of going to sleep on all occasions, and another who is a dipsomaniac, and another who is indubitably possessed by the devil, and another whose sole knowledge of the classics consists in the fifteenth book of the *Iliad,* nothing other than which will he teach—is in fact incapable of teaching anything but it: he has been here since the Crimean War. Give my love to Julian [Lady Ottoline's daughter] and Lalage.[6]

Yours,
Aldous Huxley

---

[6] Bertha "Lalage" Penrose. Julian Morrell's cousin.

TO LADY OTTOLINE MORRELL

Repton
Derby
27 July 1916
Thursday

Dear Lady Ottoline,
I hope, by the Grace of God and the mediation of the LNW, Midland, and GW Railways, to reach Oxford about 2.20 on Tuesday. I shall deposit my impediments at Balliol and seek out my Rosinante. If he is well I shall ride out upon him and so hope to get to Garsington at any rate by tea time. However, I cannot guarantee that I have looked up the trains correctly, so do not be over-alarmed if I do not appear punctually.

I cannot describe to you how much I am in demand among the scholastics. No less than six Headmasters have implored me to consider their claims for next term. I went to see David of Rugby last Tuesday. He may offer me a job, which—tho' I should prefer other things—has the merit of being fairly well paid. I think I shall take it if he offers it—but really can't quite decide about it. What chiefly alarms David about me is that I should not be able to see well enough to supervise his boys. I rather think Rugby is traditionally ill-behaved and violent. This place—on the contrary—is traditionally polite—quite extraordinarily so. It saves so much trouble for everyone concerned.

I am in the midst of exams—too awful. I enclose a very good specimen of Futurist prose, after the manner of your Miss Dodge book—intended, I believe, to be a translation of Caesar. Those last words—"The Sequani—kept on being the same"—are grand; so profoundly metaphysical.

About my schools—they published the list on the day I was last over at Garsington: they had the wit to give me a first. In the list published in the Sunday papers there was the most wonderful version of my name: viz "ALDORES HUXLEY"—which is most gloriously Spanish.
Au Revoir Tuesday.

Yours very sincerely,
Aldous Huxley

TO LADY OTTOLINE MORRELL

Prior's Field
Godalming
ca 17 August 1916

Dear Lady Ottoline,
I suppose you saw that curious joke which *The Nation* thought fit to play on me by signing my verses with my father's name. My corrected proofs must have reached them too late for any alteration to be made. I did not think they'd put them into last week's issue and the first I heard of it was a letter from A. C. Benson[7] to my father congratulating him—not without the assistance of a quotation from Coleridge—upon his verses in *The Nation*! Altogether rather a pleasantry.

I went—Bing boy–like—to town for a day last week and saw Delpia and Morton at the Ambassadors'. By the way, talking of Revues, I hear that the Prime Minister's life-saving adventure with Lucy at Garsington has appeared in a Sunday paper and is mentioned in "Some" at the Vaudeville—tho' I gather there have been no specifications of time or place.

I have just heard from my brother, who is hesitating whether or not he should go to Berne with this American Peace Conference, organized by Starr Jordan.[8] Lowes Dickinson[9] is to be one of the English representatives. If he does not go with these people, he wants to come and do some scientific war-work here—bacteriology or what not. He asks my opinion. It is hard to know what to give him. I think this peace thing sounds fairly efficient and useful: it proposes to hold a meeting of belligerents and neutrals in Berne, where a campaign is apparently to be designed for making simultaneous propaganda in all the countries. It sounds all right. Do you know anything about it, and would you advise me to advise him to attach himself to it? He seems very doubtful and applies to both my father and myself for advice. My father is of course against it. To me it seems quite good and efficient as an organisation. You may know if it is worth joining. I have no more plans for the autumn as yet. The fact, however, does not perturb me.

I have finished *Les Liaisons Dangereuses*, which is superb, and have just begun *Lettres Persanes*, which promises well. Also am reading, with difficulty and a literal translation, *The Inferno* and am descending with

---

[7] A. C. Benson (1862–1925). Poet, essayist, academic, he wrote the lyrics to "Land of Hope and Glory."
[8] David Starr Jordan (1851–1931). American peace activist and educator.
[9] Goldsworthy Lowes Dickinson (1862–1932). Cambridge political activist.

tumultuous excitement into Hell's eighth circle. Also the poems of E. A. Poe, so that life, tho' quiet, is not *monotonous.*

I trust the Garsington Chronicle goes well—also yourself and my co-editrix and the family.

Yours ever,
Aldous H.

TO LADY OTTOLINE MORRELL

Prior's Field
Godalming
ca 24 August 1916

Dear Lady Ottoline,
I feel that, like Eliot, one should have a quotation handy from the Restoration Dramatists to express succinctly one's appreciation of the pleasures of Garsington. Or perhaps one might write a poem in seven books just called "The Pleasures of Garsington" in the manner of Somerville or Akenside, out of which suitable quotations could always be drawn.

Thus, Book IV line 217, we find:—"Upon the greensward high adventurous souls / Engage in conversation and in bowls."

Or again Book III line 76.

Or who are these that lie with dewy hair
Beneath the Pleiades and the circling Bear?
Whom Juno's Bird with loud percussive cry
Calls from their beds the profluent wave to try.

I need not multiply citations. You see how valuable such a work would be to your guests.

At any rate, with or without quotations, the pleasures of Garsington are, to me, singularly intense: and I look forward enormously to renewing my acquaintance with them so soon.

I don't think Clive Bell[1] looked up his trains very successfully: at any rate, I went without change to Guildford and I could see no sign of the train going to Southampton—unless by some underhand, slip-carriage way. The journey was trying: the carriage crowded, heated and fetid—to such a degree that two small girls spent the whole of

[1] Clive Bell (1881–1964). British art critic and brother-in-law of Virginia Woolf.

the time in running alternately in quick succession to the window and being sick out of it. I shouldn't have thought anybody could have been sick so frequently.

I return to London on Monday. House-hunting with my family will doubtless be the chief sport. I will suggest Brett's admirable plan of taking bicycles.

Yours ever,
Aldous Huxley

TO OTTOLINE MORRELL

27 Westbourne Square, West
31 August 1916

Dear Lady Ottoline,

Is any time more convenient than any other time? . . . I fear this is like a sentence out of Miss Stein . . . but what I mean is, would it be all right if I came and began to function in my new capacity in about ten days or so? I think it is quite likely that I may have another occupation of a very curious nature to fill my un-manually employed hours. At any rate, what has happened so far is this; a friend of mine wrote yesterday to say that an old lady of his acquaintance, Irish, but the widow of a French nobleman, requires a "discreet literary man" (here you instantly recognize me) to assist her in the compilation of certain Memoirs. Would I undertake the job? I have replied Yes. Most of the material, moreover, is a kind which the lady would not care to put into the hands of an ordinary journalist; the literary man must be discreet. . . . So that I am a little hoping . . . in the teeth, I fear, of an almost inevitable disillusionment . . . hoping that it may prove to be some strangely scabrous chronicle of life under the Second Empire . . . for a knowledge of French is imperative . . . that I am being asked to compile. If so, a copy will have to be kept in the Garsington Chronicle's archives. Still, whatever it is, I think it should be fairly interesting and also to some degree profitable.

But it is all still in the air; possibly the old lady, whose name has not yet been divulged, will not consider me sufficiently discreet or sufficiently literary. We shall see.

London is entirely filled with the Indian population of Oxford. These strange children with devils' faces are omnipresent. They come up on padded feet and pluck one familiarly by the sleeve in omnibuses, in public lavatories, in restaurants—you cannot escape them. I lunched with one to-day in an Indian restaurant. He showered with terrible prodigality dish after dish upon me, till I became surfeited with rice and pulse and those pungent sauces, which so highly season the meat . . . amorphous chunks of it: I horribly suspect that the elaborateness of the flavoured dressing conceals the fact that the meat is made up of gobbets of the baser parts of the more unclean animals. But enough of a sombre subject.

I wonder if you have seen Thomas Earp; it is impossible ever to get a reply out of him. Should you set eyes on him pray galvanize him a little. I fear he is terribly depressed about his re-examination; I don't know whether he has yet undergone it.

My book is coming out, says Blackwell, next week.[2] I am sick of the sight of it. With the exception of about four things in it I never want to look at any of the stuff again . . . nor much want anyone else to look at it. Still, it is the way of disposing of great heaps of manuscript. Fire is the only other solution, but publication is a little more flattering to the conceit.

I met Suhrawardi[3] to-day, who told me of an odd adventure he'd had last night. He was sitting in the Café Royal and happened to be discussing Lawrences's *Amores*[4] . . . unfavourably . . . with a friend. He had the book with him. Suddenly Gertler,[5] who with another man and a woman, was at the next table, interposed in the conversation, upholding Lawrence, I gather. Finally the young woman asked Suhrawardi to lend her the book, and no sooner was it in her hands than they all swept out of the place and disappeared, in a taxi, into the night. . . . Curious. Are you or anyone of interest likely to be in town this next week or so?

Yours ever,
Aldous Huxley

---

[2] *The Burning Wheel*, 1916.
[3] Hasan Shahid Suhrawardy (1890–1965). Bengali poet and critic, who, like Huxley, published poems in *Oxford Poetry 1915*. Not to be confused with Huseyn Shaheed Suhrawarty, fifth prime minister of Pakistan.
[4] DHL's book of poetry, *Amores*, appeared in 1916.
[5] Mark Gertler (1891–1939). English painter.

TO LADY OTTOLINE MORRELL

Garsington
2 October 1916

Dear Lady Ottoline,
We hit on the word the other day . . . the word that justly describes the present widowed state of the cosmos of Garsington . . . "crumbling." Everything crumbles. Footsteps echo hollowly; it is like walking through the deserted palaces of Nineveh. Maria [Nys], one of the latest landmarks of a disappearing civilization, has gone today. Philip[6] and Julian and Mademoiselle[7] and I are the last of the Mohicans. And not only does Garsington but also the whole world crumble. For the last three days special couriers seem to have arrived almost hourly to announce to me the engagement of almost every friend I ever had, of all the women I ever fell in love with. And in the public print I am horrified to see the number of MARRIAGES in London has increased, during the last year, by 35% . . . from forty thousand to fifty-eight. I feel a sudden wave of sympathy with the learn'd Bishop Ingram . . . we do indeed want a CLEANER LONDON.

Everything, however, is a little made up for by the dazzling beauty of my new breeches. I feel like the young Rostov, when he arrived in Moscow wearing riding-breeches of a brilliant blue . . . positively *couleur de fesse de singe* . . . and of a cut hitherto absolutely unheard of in the Russian capital. My breeches, though not of quite such a beautiful tint—I should describe them as *couleur de ventre de dogue*—arouse almost the same awed astonishment in the minds of the beholders. I have been asked by Earp and the Bishop, in their official capacities of President and Secretary of the Co-op, to tell you that they and the Society at large would be immensely honoured if you would become its Senior Treasurer . . . a post, let me hasten to add, that carries no duties and no responsibilities of any kind.

Earp had fled to London, carrying with him all the proofs of the *Palatine* quite uncorrected, which is a nuisance of him. But the Bishop has returned to Oxford and there is a threat of Willie Macqueen, whom everyone had supposed to be lost to the world.

On Sunday we experienced a Muscovite invasion in the shape of Anrep.[8] I was completely fascinated by his boots, which were of the kind

---

[6] Philip Morrell (1870–1943). Liberal MP and Lady Ottoline's husband.
[7] Juliette Baillot, later Mrs. Julian Huxley. At the time she was Julian Morrell's governess.
[8] Boris Anrep (1883–1969). Russian artist active in England, known mainly for his mosaics.

you never believed could exist off the stage . . . huge black Cossack boots, full of wrinkles. He was very cheerful and at times amusing, though he would talk all tea-time about the benefits caused by war to the characters of participants in it. He was very gallant with Maria and insisted on lifting her over all the stiles we came to. After some hours he vanished as abruptly as he had come, leaving on one the impression of boots, a loud and persistent voice and a great round face of the kind you would expect to see behind a glass of German beer. We marched round the estate with him; everywhere there is a Lawrencian atmosphere of fecundity. There is a vast new flock of sheep, all expectant mothers; most of the cows are in the same condition; the sow is quite aggressively gravid; at any moment there may be more pugs to populate the Olympus of Garsington's pugolaters. I could wish my brain were in the same condition.

I hope you will find some alleviation of the horrors of Harrogate. At the worst there might be some comfort in the thought that you were gaining bodily strength through spiritual mortification. The municipalities of modern spas ought to furnish their pump-rooms with a few Beaux Nashes for the entertainment of invalids.

Yours ever,
Aldous Huxley

TO LADY OTTOLINE MORRELL

Garsington
5 October 1916

Dear Lady Ottoline,
(I had started saying dearest Ottoline—but it seemed *peu respectueux*!) I hope that your self-mortification is not breaking your spirit too much. I imagine that you lie in bed dreaming ineffable things about roast beef and dumplings as assiduous nurses come hour by hour to tighten your belt by another hole. How long does it go on for before the first nut makes its appearance?

Your absence plunges us in a studious melancholy. Mademoiselle and I spend the evenings in discussing the problems of philosophy and of the sexes—notably with reference to Earp—and in reading. I write, somewhat languidly: but more contemplate writing than embark into the action of it. I am thinking of doing an article on poetical satire for

[J. C.] Squire,[9] but it's hard having none of my notes: and one needs Quotations.

I saw [Robert] Graves in Oxford and liked him. I couldn't quite make out what he was after—poetry, I suppose, and still more poetry. He has enthusiasm enough to take him a long way.

My tutor held out no hopes of my being able to get a job in Oxford—tho' he said he and Raleigh and Nicoll Smith, the three most important nobs in the English school, were all in my favour—the reason being (it really is hardly credible!) that they have decided that they want no more *Young* men as tutors. I presume this is because of the women who throng the school. My tutor, who was elected only some three years ago, told me that one of the causes of his having been preferred to other people was his age—he is a little barrel of a man of fifty-odd. Looking at the thing purely impartially, it seems a little dangerous to exclude youth completely from teaching does it not? To comfort me my tutor added that if I waited he felt sure there would be a warm welcome for me at Oxford—in 1937 at the earliest! America seems the only prospect—I don't like the idea of it for long. *Mais nous verrons.*

I had tea with Fredegond yesterday and a quite entertaining talk afterwards. She seems to be more forthcoming *chez elle* than in company.

Sunlight, but frost and an East wind, which yesterday brought down the big tree by the boathouse, roots and all, with a large quantity of the bank and the boathouse steps, to boot—a horrid mess, which the "Young Gentlemen" are engaged in clearing up.

I am reading Havelock Ellis on sex and discover (as one always finds one is suffering from all the diseases when one reads a medical book) that I have within me the seeds of every known sexual aberration!—happily undeveloped!

Yours very affectionately,
Aldous

I forgot to tell you how much I enjoyed reading your memoirs. I should like to see the rest if I might.

---

[9] J. C. Squire (1884–1958). British poet and editor of the *London Mercury*.

TO LADY OTTOLINE MORRELL

Garsington
7 and 8 October 1916

Dear Lady Ottoline,
Events, outwardly, are mostly meteorological; great winds blow: the barometer rises and falls like the Adam's-apple in the throat of an Indian poet: there is a lot of boisterous sunshine—very jolly.

I am reading Conrad's *Chance*—an admirable work, tho' like all Conrad's work it leaves you with almost no idea of what it's all about. It is all exactly like a dream:—tremendously important and true things are said—but one forgets them all and is only conscious of the continuous stream of it all, a single impression, blurred and dim yet very intense, almost nightmarish. One gets the feeling sometimes in actual life: it came on me once, I remember, at a meeting of some literary society where I was to speak. I had to stop and explain as best I could that I felt I was going mad, that all the ordinary criteria of reality had ceased to exist and that everyone had become mere phantasms. It was indescribably alarming. Conrad's presentation of life is just the same. It's like being under the influence of a drug.

Still no news of my baroness: nor of Maria. I am positively beginning to believe that the baroness was some very queer dream. The more I reflect over her the more fantastic she seems, utterly improbable.

Sunday. I've just had a very nice letter from Eliot, whom I asked to contribute to the *Palatine*: poor man, he is terribly overworked—fourteen hours a day—and yet a while, till Xmas at any rate, he says he can't do anything.

A communication also from Maria, who sounds depressed in her inability to find a roof to cover her head.

I'm just going into Oxford to lunch with some very nice people called Petersen, who live on Boar's Hill. The eldest daughter is a great friend of mine—a clever and amusing creature, whose greatest gift is an amazing light-hearted irresponsibility which entirely cuts her free from the trammels of quotidian life.

Yours,
Aldous Huxley

TO LADY OTTOLINE MORRELL

Dear Lady Ottoline,

I think we are all behaving quite nicely, though a little saddened by the departure of Philip, who has sought the comparative quiet of Parliament after a hectic period of agricultural sales, from which he would return like a border baron from a foray, laden with ploughs, machines for the propagation of artificial manure, cank-worms for the yeanling flocks and other things even more technical. I have been hewing wood, like Caliban. I find it a very pleasant process, quite annihilating the inconveniences of mental activity. One is like Rimbaud . . .

Je ne parlerai pas, je ne penserai rien,
Mais l'amour infini me montera dans l'âme.[1]

Non cogito, ergo sum felix is the fundamental apophthegm, aphorism or what-not of the rustic philosophy. There is, I feel, a great deal to be said for agri-kultur, judiciously combined with the refinements of the town.

I went into Oxford to-day to see my friend Geoffrey Madan,[2] whom I find quite remarkably spiritually intact after Mesopotamia and a hideous wound. I have urged him to come over when he is in Oxford about a fortnight hence; I think you'd like him. I could wish he moved less in the Geoffrey Young[3] sphere of influence. It is a man I have always instinctively distrusted, I don't quite know why.

I expect my brother will be back in this country fairly soon. What a fool he is to come over. He'll not get back so easily to America.

I was amused by the mélange of abuse and middle-aged patronage to which I was favored by the *Times Literary Supplement*. It would be pleasant to meet the critic in order to tell him one was not such a black-hearted fellow as all that. *War and Peace* is finished; it ought, I think, to be much longer, like the *Encyclopedia Britannica*, so that one could go on reading it for a little of every day the whole of one's life. One

---

[1] "Sensation" (1870).
[2] Geoffrey Madan (1895–1947). English epigrammist and son of Falconer Madan, Bodley Librarian.
[3] Geoffrey Winthrop Young (1876–1958). Elected president of the Climbers' Club in 1913. Huxley's brother Trev edited the *Climbers' Club Journal*, to which in March 1914 AH contributed "A Lunndon Mountaineering Essay."

would die at a hundred and four within a thousand pages of the end. . . . *Au revoir*, I hope, soon.

> *Yours ever,*
> *Aldous Huxley*

TO LADY OTTOLINE MORRELL

> *Garsington*
> *15 October 1916*

Dear Lady Ottoline,
Many thanks for your very nice letter. I hear that your *saison en enfer* is to last nearly a fortnight more, which is sad; for I thought you were returning before that. But I trust you will come back almost grossly hearty and powerful.

Maria is not, after all, returning to her niche by the chimney-corner. I heard from her to-day to the effect that she has flitted to London and is alighting, without any very apparent olive-branch, in the Ark: is looking for a job: is very much excited (I doubt whether the excitement will last after she has found some damnably dull employment); launching, in fact, with a loud splash and all bunting fluttering, into the larger oceans. . . . Garsington a little too quiet, and land-locked, stagnant and its present inhabitants too decidedly flatfishes.

For all which I am rather, personally sorry, as I wish she were coming back here for the time . . . having developed a kind of doggy devotion for that rather absurd and very charming figure.

The march of events is placid though agreeable. I went in to-day (Sunday) to Oxford, where I had luncheon with Lewis Gielgud[4] and Street, another ex-Magdalen man, with also one Bainbridge, a contemporary of Ronnie Knox's at Eton and possessing a great share of his brilliancy of wit. We scintillated pleasantly enough over two bottles of burgundy. I also found old Earp, clothed completely in black, entertaining his guardian . . . an apparently funereal process, for I have never seen him in such clothes before. After infinite efforts and with much abuse heaped by me upon his head we have got all the material for the Palatine into press and have corrected all the proofs; so that it will be out next week . . . quite a good number, I think, though necessarily short, owing to the preposterous price of paper. I hanker very

---

[4] Lewis Gielgud (1894–1953). One of Huxley's oldest friends, older brother of John Gielgud.

much for the Ashby press at Campden; it would be very nice to print oneself, though I've no doubt the actual mechanical process would be worrying and sordid. Still, a hireling might function in the baser processes of production, while one directed the affair from aloft. One would publish by subscription the good, the beautiful, the obscene . . . all in fact that the public would not stand.

I am not writing a book so much as doing notes for one, my historical romance. I tried writing straight ahead, but found everything developed so tremendously as I got things done that it all needed re-casting. I have not sufficient skill to conceive a number of characters and their relations at a single birth; it is only gradually and by hints that I can get the notion of the thing, otherwise than on its barest and vaguest lines. But I confess that the more I try to understand psychology, the more mysterious does it become for me . . . particularly women, who seem to me . . . most of them . . . too utterly inexplicable.

Par exemple. I am bringing in the beautiful Venetia Stanley,[5] who, if we trust Aubrey, was the mistress of a variety of people of the dashing and insolent young courtier type and finally married Sir Kenelm Digby,[6] whom apparently she had loved since a child, and became excessively virtuous as well as an extremely talented wife. It is a sort of Manon Lescaut type, only a nobler stronger and finer character. The thing I cannot fathom in this case . . . and in all the myriad cases one sees of it in actual and contemporaneous life . . . is how a highly intelligent woman, one of the best type, succumbs to the charm of men like the Dorset of Venetia's youth, the common type of arrogance and assurance. One can only gasp with a sickish incredulity when one sees the Bob Nicholses, the Anreps of the world enslaving the Venetias by sheer force of effrontery. The more brazen the address, the more rapid and complete the victory. The characteristics which to me, and I should have thought to all reasonable and decent people, are supremely repellant, are the guarantors of success in relations with women. It is all too too mysterious. I am utterly at a loss to understand it. The psychology of it is totally beyond me. Brass seems to be the essential quality. My horror of the people who possess it is tinged at times with a certain admiring envy. I should like to get temporarily electro-plated with it. To have the address of Bob Nichols, of Charles Munro, of Anrep for a

---

[5] Venetia Stanley (1600–1633). Famous beauty, painted by Van Dyck. Wife of Sir Kenelm Digby.
[6] Sir Kenelm Digby (1603–1665). Catholic scientist, naval commander, diplomatist, he wrote a famous cookbook published as *Sir Kenelm Digby's Closet Opened.*

week would be an amazing experience. One might conceivably begin to understand something of it all, though I doubt if one would ever get to understand the psychology on the woman's side. But perhaps it is merely a question of the psychology of the stags and the does in Magdalen deer-park on an October afternoon. At least, it baffles me.

But this is all a little rambling. Facts, facts.

I am going to see Walter Raleigh on Friday to discuss with him the prospects of my finding a profession. In his letter to me he says that at present an university job is hard to get, as the war enforces stinginess on them all. He says that writing is much more in demand and seems to advise that. I dare say he's right. I wonder whether I had better try and get some reviewing or something of the kind. Raleigh might help me to some and my father is, I think, sufficiently acquainted with the immortal Strachey to exercise a little nepotistic pressure in that direction. What do you think about it? The art of reviewing appears to consist in variations of the formula, "This book is on the one hand good and, on the other hand, at the same time bad."

It might amuse you to see one or two things I have been doing recently, since the things in my book. Soie (not silk, but pug) is, I think, much better. He scratches less but, compensatorily, appears to be more snorious than ever and indulges in much licking and slobbery noises, which I tell Julian are like the sound of Germans eating soup. I have not yet seen his second family.

Mademoiselle is uniformly a well-tempered clavichord, a canary that never has the pip. Julian very active and lively.

I expect my assignations with the baronne will shortly begin. Perhaps I may go up to town for a night before that to see my family and as many of my acquaintance as possible. One gets out of rapport with people's existence so quickly if one doesn't see them personally.

Yours ever,
Aldous H.

TO LADY OTTOLINE MORRELL

27 Westbourne Square, W.
19 October 1916

Dear Lady Ottoline,
I got your note from Maria whom I saw today. We had luncheon together in a small bun-house off Holborn filled with earnest looking

women—all, I am sure, readers at the Museum fleeing from a surfeit of spiritual food to snatch a little baser provender: and I think we must have a little startled them when we began (in that clear bell-like voice of the *Enfant terrible* that one somehow always adopts when discussing in public the tetchier, more scabrous subjects of life) to examine the probability of Maria being seduced by Anrep. I don't think the probability is really so very great. Maria has a good deal of sense—and whatever the irresistibility of Anrep, it does, after all, take two to work a seduction smoothly. The oddest thing is that Anrep has apparently taken a great fancy to me: and all the time he is not warning Maria in a paternal way against the other Russians in the office, he is expounding in eulogies of ALH—all the result of a single meeting. I shall go see him next time I'm in London. I might be able to penetrate his hideous schemes—if indeed he has any.

Maria seems to be very very happy: the only fly in the ointment being your terrors of Anrep and consequent disapproval of her. I think she almost wept over your letter. So far she has no work to do and spends her time being taught Russian by her general.

I went to the Ark but everyone was out. I shall go again when I come up for my Baroness.

I return tomorrow—lunching with Raleigh in Oxford. I hope to get good advice at least from him. I am getting rather gloomy about my prospects. However, all will come out ultimately well in this best of possible worlds.

My brother has just come back from America and is here: it is pleasant to see him again. Good bye.

Yours,
Aldous Huxley

TO LADY OTTOLINE MORRELL

Garsington
26 October 1916

Dear Lady Ottoline,
Please get me out of your head . . . all is really well. Not but what I am looking forward with all eagerness to your return; still, I am in the meanwhile quite happy and very far from being bored with Garsington. I am busy with a good deal of varied writing, quite immersed.

Clive has returned to be a little sunbeam in the house and today arrives the mysteriously impassive Shove,[7] who seems to me to be one of these men as trees walking, though I suppose when one knows him better he quits his rind a little.

I have not yet heard from the baroness, but expect I shall have to go to town sometime next week in order to see her.

I've not heard from Maria since she left the Ark and so don't know where she's gone to. I trust not to share a lodgment with Anrep. The *Palatine*, after much striving, is out, and I expect you'll have got your copy. Oxford rings with the news of a South American beauty who haunts the co-op, an undergraduatess at St. Hugh's. I have not yet seen her, but Earp has come, seen and succumbed. Her fellow undergraduatesses from that highly Anglican seminary . . . a set of cats . . . protest at her being allowed to serve there on the grounds of her being attractive to a certain type of men, of being a Spaniard and altogether too warm blooded for Oxford, in fact of being altogether too pretty. All which makes me more than ever long to see the paragon.

Great hurry and post imminent. Please don't worry about me. I'll write more fully when there's time.

Aldous

TO JULIAN HUXLEY

The Manor House
Garsington, Oxford
ca December 1916

My dear Julian,
You are probably right in what you say about the Y.M.C.A. I am not good in my dealings with such people, and I confess, that if I went it would be with sensations of almost insuperable repugnance. The real difficulties seem to be political. A. The military authorities would probably not permit me to go when they found I had been staying in the house of a pacifist, and all names are submitted for close enquiry by the Military Intelligence Dept.

B. One has to say one is in complete agreement with the policy of the country—which becomes increasingly more difficult as the ends for which we appear to be going on fighting are divulged—that the Rus-

---

[7] Gerald Shove (1887–1947). British economist and husband of Fredegond Shove (1889–1949), English poet.

1917

sians may have Constantinople and the Italians their Mediterranean
empire. And if the policy of the country—*sub consule* George—is to go
on fighting for the mere sake of it, quite indefinitely and without regard for civilization or the lives of the young—then it is a little difficult
to say one is in agreement with it.

I shall see you I expect on Thursday, when I'll stay the night or no
as circumstances require or advise. It will be of interest to see what
Clarke says to me.

ALH

TO JULIAN HUXLEY

The Manor House
Garsington, Oxford
22 January 1917

My dear Julian,

These passport people are the devil—no word from them yet. If I hear
no more I shall come to town next week and see what's up. I'd better
stay at 51 or somewhere, as I suppose the move will be in the midst of
its activity. I'm very busy, writing for Uncle Hump's Poets and reviews
for *Statesman*—hateful work, but fairly interesting—only one feels it a
waste of time. Also somewhat depressed by the departure of Maria
Nys, the only person I have ever cared for passionately, for Italy. Still—
one must say with Donne:

> Dull sublunary lovers love,
> Whose soul is sense, cannot admit
> Absence, since that doth remove
> The cause that elemented it.
> But we, by a love so far refined
> That ourselves know not what it is,
> Inter-assuréd of the mind,
> Care less eyes lips and hands to miss.

But of course that's all nonsense! And one does care a good deal more
than the dull sublunary fellows.

I'll say if and when I come to town next week: I'd better try 51 unless you say to contrary.

An interesting Japanese book to do for the *Statesman*—Noh plays,
symbolic drama of immense subtlety and much of it very jolly.

What news of your going to the Dagoes!

45

How good Wilson is. I don't believe he'll stop worrying now: he won't be happy till he gets it.

Yours,
ALH

TO LADY OTTOLINE MORRELL

6 February 1917

Dearest Ottoline,
I should have liked to come this weekend—with Katherine [Mansfield], but I am going to see my sister at school—staying positively in the lionness's den, tho' no angel sews up their mouths—unhappily, considering the hellish din that seventy or eighty of them assembled at a meal can make.

I think you're right about this bloody work, but it will need a month's notice to get out of it: I shall have to speak to my chief about it.

I've been seeing a lot of people this week—my brother, Mrs. Haldane and Bob Nichols turned up one day. Then, on Thursday, I dined with Eliot in his flat—Mrs. E happily being out we had a very good talk, Eliot in good form all considered and showed me his latest verses—very odd indeed: he is experimenting in a new genre. Philosophical obscenity rather like Laforgue and dimly like a great series of poems which I once planned to be called "Vomic Songs." Eliot's are very good: some in English, some in the most astonishingly erudite French. We proceeded to Omega,[8] where I spent the evening chatting with the Flashing Beauty and trying not to look at the exhibition of copies and translations hanging in hideous gloom upon the walls.

Friday to Mr. Mills[9]—my weekly dose of wine, rounded off by an antique in the shape of Chartreuse made in pre-renaissance times or something of the kind, worth five pounds per glass and deadly at that—proceeding thence to the Sangers[1] round the corner where were Hawtrey[2] and Toti, James and Alix[3]—very queer combination of people.

---

[8] Omega. Artists' workshop in Fitzroy Square, Bloomsbury, started in 1913 by Roger Fry.
[9] Weymer Jay Mills (1881–1938). Wealthy American socialite and author. Attended Mark Twain's seventieth birthday party at Delmonico's in 1905. Huxley later refers to him as the sinister "Viper of Chelsea."
[1] Charles and Dora Sanger. The Sangers were friends of Virginia Woolf.
[2] Ralph Hawtrey (1879–1974). English economist.
[3] James (1879–1974) and Alix Strachey (1892–1973). English Freudians, who, after their marriage in 1920, resided at 41 Gordon Square, Bloomsbury.

I was so immensely impressed by Fredegond's poems: some of them seem to me tremendously good. Do tell old Earp, if you see him to write to me and tell me what he's doing about our anthology.

I heard from Maria at the beginning of the week—rather miserable and ill, tired out by these beastly red cross fêtes and the like, for which she seems to do all the work. I hope she'll stop now and live quietly. Much love to the family.

Yours,
Aldous

TO LADY OTTOLINE MORRELL

27 February 1917

I write from the desk of no less august a personage than Mr. BUTT, who is rarely seen at the office and attends, apparently, to his more important duties at the Palace. Here all is sugar, sugar: one has the impression of being engulfed in the maw of some giant organism in the last stages of diabetes—sugar everywhere.[4]

I examine papers—hundreds of papers describing conferences held between several Offices and the Master Bakers concerning the exact meaning of "outer covering" in the order regarding icing on cakes. So far the keenest brains in the country have not decided whether a *marron glacé* is, or is not, an iced cake: and so on, the strangest enquiries and letters revealing whole worlds of undreamt of activities.

It is amusing in a way.

I found my father in a state of disapproval—mild, but then he is never more than mild—of Garsington, which he thinks is somewhat corruptive of my better self, mistrusts the "cranks" and wants me to get into the "normal current." I sit and look at the fire *sans mot dire* when he talks!

Only for one moment have I not regretted Garsington—and that was when I retired with a cigarette and my Casanova to a HOT BATH of immense proportions and was for half an hour a happy hedonist. Casanova is continually enthralling: the accounts of his transports with his sixty-first mistress are as lively as of the first—and his adventures—! When for a week he makes himself king of a Greek island—terrific.

---

[4] In late February 1917, Huxley began a one-week trial position at the wartime Food Board.

I saw Mrs. Hump[5] an instant today: she departs for France tomorrow in order to write up the war in a new series of articles.

I met Alix S[trachey]-Florence on the doorstep of the Ark,[6] where I was searching, in vain, for Carrington. She was sadly red-nosed and wind-pinched which spoilt her statuesque appearance.

My love to Brett and Julian and Mademoiselle (whom, I hope, you have gingered into leap-yearish action towards Earp).

Yours very affectionately,
Aldous

TO LADY OTTOLINE MORRELL

27 Westbourne Square, W.
1 March 1917

Dear Lady Ottoline,

Many thanks for your letter: affairs do indeed go ill. I will try and see Earp on Saturday and remonstrate with him. I always knew he had this theory that any physical passion was revolting: I once had a long argument with him about it, in which I tried to show him that there was some difference between sadism and the love of two people who cared for one another. But he wouldn't admit any distinction! Droll idea! If I could persuade him that there was nothing so very repulsive in the process, I might do some good. It is this ghastly experience with prostitutes which does this mischief. It utterly disgusted and horrified him once.

I met Katherine in a bus yesterday and am going to see her tonight. Dined last night with [Dora] Carrington and went to the Palladium—but it was disappointing. Tich was ill and Beth Tate sang only one song. The other things had changed since we were there—for the worse, on the whole. However, C and I had some very entertaining conversations. She was at her best and very beautiful—however, I am very constant by temperament!

I have been hoping each day that there'd be a letter from Maria—but nothing. It makes me so absurdly miserable.

Your affectionate,
Aldous

---

[5] Mrs. Humphry Ward (1851–1920). Huxley's novelist aunt. She published *Towards the Goal* in 1917, based on her second tour of the Western Front. She wrote, "It is the last day of February and I find myself on a military steamer, bound for a French port, and on my way to the British headquarters in France."

[6] The Ark. Gower Street residence of Dorothy Brett, Carrington, and, briefly, Maria Nys, later Huxley's wife.

TO LADY OTTOLINE MORRELL

16 Bracknell Gardens, N.W.3
ca 9 April 1917

Dearest Ottoline,

I did so genuinely mean it when I told you that my stay at Garsington had been the happiest time in my life. And I think it has also been the period when I have been conscious of the best and most fruitful development of myself. I won't try to thank you and Philip, because I can't do it adequately, can't even begin to do it. When I look back on these last six months I see it as a crowded hour of glorious life and all the rest relegated to comparative namelessness. I have learned so much from you. I gain so much from your inspiration that I feel I shall never be able to compute the full amount of your giving. From Maria I had a great and violent emotional self-discovery: from you something slower, more diffused, yet very great. You have given so much—and I have been able to return you nothing, I fear, unless a very deep devotion counts at all in the balance against all your gifts of inspiration, almost of creation.

I write in a gap between rushes of work—not violent, as I am still a learner. Today they planted me at the desk of a sideman and I have to deal as best I may with his letters and papers—ranging on all subjects from timber to chemicals, electric lamps to wire ropes. Most of them I simply relegate to a sort of dustbin to wait. What I can, I deal with—almost invariably wrong. In course of time, however, I trust I shall do the thing all right.

I lunched with Lewis Gielgud yesterday and there met Marie Beerbohm—for the first time—not without a certain astonishment and an instinctively Victorian shock at the extent of her décolletage which reached—I exaggerate but by the literally basest inch—*jusqu'au nombril* (the decent obscurity of the foreign tongue!).

Dinner with Mr. Mills—where was a mutual reading of sonnets and an *épanchement* over the brandy, when I heard the further details of his life and saw the photograph of "his tragedy," as he wittily styles the lady. His great stunt is to pretend he is enormously old and past all possible thrill or *frisson* of enthusiasm. He can't, however, be much over thirty: but he is charmingly antique towards me and speaks always as tho' there was some *je ne sais quoi* of bloom and dewy freshness which he had lost but which clung to me. In point of fact, I should say he was quite intensely youthful in spirit.

Tell Junie I got her charming letter and intend to reply as soon as I have time.

Our new home is quite nice—tho' I am a little shocked by the post-rococo touches in the mantelpieces and so forth.

I have a most pleasing room, looking on the garden. The only crab is the cold, which on the bleak heights of Hampstead is intense. We have four inches of snow as regular as clockwork each night.

Love to the household and yourself in particular.

Aldous

TO LADY OTTOLINE MORRELL

14 April 1917

Thank you so much for your letter. Julian inundates me with presents—by which I am extremely touched!

I was so glad to hear you had a letter from Maria. I was feeling so anxious—no news having come for a fortnight. I'm so glad she's happy in the villa—tho' jealous at the same time she should be! You understand the feeling when one would like the other person to be as wretched as oneself! No time now.

Aldous

TO LADY OTTOLINE MORRELL

16 Bracknell Gardens, N.W.3
23 April 1917

Dearest Ottoline,

It *was* so nice seeing you and Garsington again. It seemed so long since I had left it. Next time, I trust, will be more propitious in the way of trains. I am absurdly weary tonight—for to say the truth I had very little sleep on Saturday—owing to the excitement of a letter from Maria—and very little last night, and on top of the most hellish day under the new régime, when more papers have come in to be dealt with in one morning than came in all the ten days when the work was being done by someone efficient and experienced and I was looking on only. I only got away at about seven-thirty, leaving a good three hours work still un-looked at.

I heard from Robbie Ross,[7] whose first letter seems to have gone astray, and lunch with him on Friday. Tomorrow a grand lunch of Mills,

---

[7] Robbie Ross. Best known as Oscar Wilde's executor.

Carrington, Earp, me and, perhaps, Lewis Gielgud—what will be the result? Well, goodnight and love to everyone. I enclose the pawn-ticket for Philip's cycle at Oxford station.

Aldous

TO LADY OTTOLINE MORRELL

16 Bracknell Gardens, N.W.3
10 May 1917

Dearest Ottoline,
I will try and get down on Saturday by the late train—no earlier one being possible as I never get my half day on Saturday but on Wednesday, which is a bore for week-end purposes. Still, I enjoyed my Après-Midi d'un Faune yesterday . . . the first time I have seen London in the afternoon for several weeks. It will be interesting to see Massingham[8] and Lees-Smith[9] and I shall have very delicately to try and insinuate to M that it's high time he should publish my thing in the *Nation*.

I dined with Katherine[1] last night in her delightful rabbit hutch in Church Street and we proceeded to the second house at the Chelsea Palace, where there was a perfectly fabulous woman called Florrie[2] singing a quite unbelievably wonderful song, of which the last lines of the refrain were:—

Talk about the West End with its wonderful sights.
But O-o-o-oh! Those Arabian nights!

And the whole of her mountainous body positively shook with the voluptuousness of the conception. Katherine was very delightful and amusing, a little less acting a part than usual.

I hurried on to Ka Cox's after the theatre and found only Dominick and a stranger in the process of departing, so that I had a very pleasant little tête-à-tête conversation with Ka about Things in General and the fallacies of Bloomsburyism in particular.

---

[8] H(enry) W(illiam) Massingham (1860–1924). English journalist and critic, editor of *The Nation*.
[9] H(astings) B(ertrand) Lees-Smith (1878–1941). Labour M.P. and editor of the *Encyclopaedia of the Labour Movement*.
[1] Katherine Mansfield (1882–1923). Mansfield was living in Church Street with Ida Baker at the time.
[2] Florrie Forde (1876–1940). Music hall performer known for her sing-along act.

I have just received this morning a coming-out notice, to the effect that I am to present myself for re-examination at Oxford on the 21st, which I suppose I will have to do, unless I can get the Air Board people to write a letter about me to the military, which they won't do, I should think, considering the short time I've been there.

Au revoir and love to everybody,
Aldous

TO OTTOLINE MORRELL

[ca June 1917]

Dearest Ottoline,

Thank you so much for your letter and its enclosure from M. (in which she tells me she got my amber all right, which is satisfactory) and pardon this dun-colored morsel of paper, which is all I can lay hands on at the moment in the office. I've been going out a good deal this week, so have had no time at all to write. Tuesday was a very amusing and bibulous evening with Mr. Mills; on Wednesday I dined with Carrington; tonight I accompany my relatives to the Drury Lane Mammoth Film: tomorrow Mr. Sanger[3] has invited me to dine and Eddie Marsh[4] on Saturday—while on Sunday I hope to be able to catch the 9.15 and get to Wheatley about 11.25, to stay the night if I may and return most distressingly early on Monday morning. I think I'll be able to manage to come, but don't meet the train or anything of that sort, as I'm not quite certain.

I saw Lady Bonham-Carter[5] on Monday and had a very pleasant talk with her for about half an hour. When I have nothing else to do in the office I translate the *Après-Midi d'un Faune* and have already done about 45 lines: but it's hard work translating passages one doesn't understand. Thank you so very much for the Traherne.

Love to Julian and the rest of the family.

Your affectionate,
A

[3] Charles Percy Sanger (1871–1930). Barrister, mathematician. One of the Cambridge Apostles and friend of the Bloomsburies. He wrote an influential pamphlet on *Wuthering Heights* in 1926.
[4] Edward Marsh (1872–1953). Editor of five anthologies of *Georgian Poetry* from 1912 to 1922.
[5] Violet Bonham-Carter (1887–1969). Politician and diarist.

TO LADY OTTOLINE MORRELL

Room 549
Air Board
Strand
21 June 1917

Dearest Ottoline,

I was so very glad to get your letter with the good news that you were feeling so much better. It is most admirable: *vive* [Dr.] Haydn Brown.

I should like very much to come down this weekend, but am afraid I might carry infection from Julian to my little brother, for whom measles—at under two—is something to be avoided: so that I think I ought to postpone a visit till the weekend after, when, I imagine, Julian should be no longer pestiferous.

What a life! I have been ceaselessly whizzing. On Sunday I assist the Head of the department in sending a lunatic guest to the local asylum. I lunch now frequently with Evan[6] at the Savoy and with Murry at the A.B.C. Evan has become quite a feature in my life now: he is constantly ringing me up, coming to see me, asking me to meals and so forth. I like him, I think, quite a lot, tho' he is the most fearfully spoilt child. Then I whiz round to Mr. Mills, then fly to Putney to stay the night with an unknown admirer of my works. Then I rush to meet yet another unknown figure—the editrix of *Wheels*, Miss Edith Sitwell, who is passionately anxious for me to contribute to her horrible production. These Wheelites take themselves seriously: I never believed it possible!

While I sit in the Isola Bella, naively drinking in the flattery of the ridiculous Sitwell, in dart Carrington and Barbara [Hiles], borrow half-a-crown from me and whirl out again. What a life! Then an evening with Vernon Lee—each trying to get his or her word in edgeways. Then again at Eliot's, where I meet Mrs. E for the first time and perceive that it is almost entirely a sexual nexus between Eliot and her: one sees it in the way he looks at her—she's an incarnate provocation—like a character in Anatole France. What a queer thing it is. This whizzing is a mere mania, a sort of intoxicant, exciting and begetting oblivion. I should like ever so much to come to Garsington for a bit after I shake the work off my feet. Much love,

Your affectionate,
Aldous

[6] Evan Morgan (1893–1949). Became 2nd Viscount Tredegar in 1934.

53

TO DORA CARRINGTON

London
[early July 1917]

My dear Carrington,
What about stepping across to the Isola on Saturday for lunch, if you've nothing better to do. . . .

I go for the weekend to Evan in the country. Next week I'm free—thank God. I go one day to interview the Head Master of Eton—but I'd throw him, or, anyone else, over for Phyllis Boyd or (with a graceful bow in your direction) for you.

The prospects of freedom are most cheering. I am now educating my successor—a little old cylindrical attorney with a mind that is quite phenomenally slow at grasping the facts of official life.

Forgive my melodramatic melancholy on the night of Mills' party—one of those accesses of self-pity that attack the heartiest of us in the small hours.

Yours,
Aldous

TO LADY OTTOLINE MORRELL

16 Bracknell Gardens
Frognal Lane N.W.3
ca 14 July 1917

Dearest Ottoline,
I must apologize for the mistake which amputated my letter—though I don't suppose you missed very much. I do hope your eyes will soon be over their trouble; what a wretched thing this is, just as you were getting better.

I am going to Oxford on Saturday to stay with the Haldanes for a bit: after that I'd like very much, if I might, to come to Garsington.

Evan and I have been having the most comical adventures this weekend. Driven out of London by the horrors of the air-raid we rushed quite at haphazard into the country and found ourselves ultimately at Burnham Beeches, staying in a boarding establishment managed by a small girl of about 19, exactly like Nell Gwynn, who fell so passionately in love with both of us simultaneously—regarding us rather as gods than men—that we had the greatest ado in persuading her to retain her virginity, pointing out that in common decency we really couldn't take it—being mere passers-by and unlikely to have anything to do with her life. But it was a terrible struggle, the history of which is too long and too fantastic to be imparted in full in a letter. Suffice to say that the parting on Monday was *navrant*: and I believe that Evan and I, by our self control, have almost wrecked a young girl's life! It was all very odd.

Love from
Aldous

TO LADY OTTOLINE MORRELL

19 July 1917

Dearest Ottoline,

I suppose that by this time you have come back from the sea-side—where I trust you were benefited by the air and so forth. I am staying here with the Haldanes for another week and then going on to Boar's Hill with Lewis Gielgud, who is back on sick-leave and wants me to come with him when he goes there for a little bracing up after a spell of treatment in London. We remain there till the thirtieth, I think. Then I should like so much to come to Garsington if you can have me.

Meanwhile I'd like to come over one day just to see how you are—perhaps with Lewis when we are on the mountain: at any rate when it is fine again.

I am learning Italian from such an extremely charming and talented creature—one Yvette Chapelain, half French, half Florentine. A romantic temperament and very musical and intelligent, so that I hope to learn Italian quite without tears.

It's pleasant to be out of London—where I finished up my stay by the most prodigious orgy with Evan—a birthday party of at least twenty-five people, all of them ultimately drunk. Altogether very pleasant.

My love to the family. It *will* be nice seeing you all again.

Yours,
Aldous

TO LADY OTTOLINE MORRELL

16 Bracknell Gardens, N.W.3
ca July 1917

I have just seen the Anglo-French company, which appears to consist of one little man with a grey beard, bent on benefiting the English-speaking world by translating French works of importance. I am proceeding with extreme caution and am to see a rough draft of a contract before going further. He offered to lodge me in his house—but saw his daughter and the breadth of her smile alone sufficed to make me decline in haste. The whole scene strangely Conradesque—pregnant with nightmares, and most amusing. But I shall take care not to be done in.

Love from
Aldous

TO LADY OTTOLINE MORRELL

The Old Christopher
Eton College
Windsor
24 September 1917

Dearest Ottoline,
I've been just on a week now in this comical place, recollecting what I knew of it, seeing it under the new magisterial light, struggling with the art of pedagogy, for which I cannot believe that I am very well fitted, reading a great deal . . . for till the essays begin to come in I have a good deal of spare time . . . perched solitary in my high room that looks one way upon the Southern buttresses of the chapel, golden with this autumn sunshine, and on the other side right over the roofs to the castle gigantic on its hill. A very nice room, furnished with local borrowings, almost the best, I think, in this odd old house, once a posting inn, where Pepys once stayed and doubtless misbehaved with the chamber maid. My fellow householder is a thick square parson of the name of [C. O.] Bevan, the soul of goodness and in his way a very good and certainly undisquieting, though unexhilirating companion. He likes his meals regular, and so forth . . . likes his meals altogether quite a good deal. "In these days of virtually no wine," he said to me today (we are reduced to a single glass of port after dinner, though the Burgundy is always there in reserve if it weren't war time) "I find one needs a good deal of tea after a hard day's work." I loved that "virtu-

ally no wine" . . . it is so wonderfully typical of sound upper class feeling about the war.

Another charming thing—we always dress for dinner, sitting tête-à-tête in our black coats, attended by one of our not inconsiderable seraglio of domestics. We talk about the other members of the staff: an endlessly amusing topic: for they are a comic lot of men, as you would have agreed if you had witnessed the masters' meeting, a large hall-full of the queerest looking men, each of them with all his idiosyncrasies brought out and magnified by the exercise, long continued, of absolute autocracy. I am learning now what I didn't know as a boy . . . the different cliques and factions among the ushers, the matrimonial and social sides. It is a real Nightmare Abbey of incongruous characters.

Then we talk about the boys. We discuss the advisability of allowing boys to be prepared for confirmation by scientific or mathematical housemasters . . . better, surely, the classical tutors, against none of whom could a charge of infidelity to the true Anglican principles be brought. Mr. Bevan quotes cases of boys prepared by science men, who had come to him on the eve of confirmation without a notion of what the Eucharist was. "I did my best of course, in the short time at my disposal, to tell them what the most solemn part of the Eucharist—have some more of this plum tart, it is really excellent—the most solemn part of the Eucharist meant at any rate to me personally. But I am afraid— ah, I didn't see we had cream to-night—they went into the service with very little idea of what their religion was." Very little idea, I should say, to judge at any rate from the service in Chapel on Sunday. It is so long since I was there; but it is all just the same, bored critical boys going through the appropriate gestures with the mechanical skill of long habit, the parson intoning through his Eustachian tubes, the slightly grotesque pomp of the entering procession of Sixth form, Head Master, and Vice Provost, the beadle with his silver rod, the Holy Poker . . . all exactly the same, except for a few prayers couched in the most horrible imitation-seventeenth-century language about the War—"protect with Thy Fatherly Goodness and Grace all those in positions of special danger, whether beneath the sea or in the air *etc., etc. ad lib.*" It is all so familiar, yet seeing it again, one has such a shock of amazement: can it really be, in this, the so-called twentieth century?

I find that I am not cut out for a teacher of boys; or rather, I find that all my knowledge, such as it is, is quite of the wrong sort; remote, vague, facts inextricably mixed up with appreciations and opinions; I am setting to work to tabulate and compress.

I have finished Rimbaud's life, and will send it to you with as little delay as possible. It's most irritatingly written, but does a lot, I think, to help one interpret his works. The *Saison en Enfer*, for instance, turns out to be the most exact autobiography, impossible to understand fully till one is *au courant* with the facts of his life and psychology at the moment of writing. What an incredible creature. It is hard to believe that he was really human.

I dashed up to town for a few hours on Saturday and found Evan and his mistress for lunch at the Savoy; much happier I thought. Another engaging trait I have discovered in the lady is a real delight in tormenting the swarms of unfortunate men who swarm after her, racked with the most agonizing pangs of love—she has a wonderful art, keeps them dangling in perpetual pain, in a way which is quite masterly.

How are things at G.? Junie [Julian] I suppose, goes off to school just about now. I do hope she'll enjoy it. Have you heard from Maria lately? I have had no letter for more than a fortnight and am growing a little disquieted. Do come over here while the weather is yet fine, choosing Tue, Thur or Sat, half holidays.

Love to all,
Aldous

TO LADY OTTOLINE MORRELL

The Old Christopher
Eton Cottage
Windsor
4 October 1917

Dearest Ottoline,
How does Garsington flourish? I have heard no news of it for some time. Here things go moderately well, sometimes quite pleasant, sometimes repulsively tedious.

What is Julian's address? I want to write to her. I do hope she enjoys her school. Remind Brett to let Mr. Sturgess know of my existence, if she hasn't already done so; it would be pleasant to see him.

I have been house hunting for Eliot, who wants to find a cottage where he and his wife can spend the next few months clear of raids, yet within quotidian reach of London. Unfortunately, several hundred thousand people have had exactly the same idea, with the result that almost every available inch of accommodation in this neighborhood is taken, the inrush having been prodigious these last days.

I heard from Maria at last, after a long period of silence; very well and happy and about to return to Florence in a few days time, where she will be working at the University, chiefly at German, for which she seems to have conceived a passion at the moment. I foresee that she will be so well educated soon that we shall hardly be able to speak to her at all. How I wish that I could go on with my education instead of imparting what I have got to others, who don't in the least want it. It is absurd to teach when one wants to learn.

One Saturday I will try, if I may, to get over for the night, but shall have to return on Sunday afternoon as I have early school on Monday, which means a shuddering contact with the world at half past seven.

Love to all the household,
Aldous

TO LADY OTTOLINE MORRELL

Eton College
Windsor
8 October 1917

Dearest Ottoline,
If I can manage it, may I come over to Garsington next Saturday night? If it's fine I might cycle over to Beaconsfield and catch the tea-time train to Wheatley. Otherwise I must see what other times there are.

I went to town yesterday and after a number of blank draws, necessitating shivering pilgrimage through an East wind which pierced me through as I had no coat with me, I at last found Eliot, crouching with Bertie Russell over a dying fire. Our conversation consisted of long silences occasionally interrupted by Bertie saying something characteristic, like: "How much good would it do, if one could exterminate the whole human race"; or, "The girls in London don't enjoy being bombed themselves so much as they enjoy having their sweethearts killed." I told him he was a Little Sunbeam in the House; we all felt much happier.

I caught a glimpse, too, of Evan and Marjorie Waterlow, on their way to Oxford; they said they were going to call on you on Sunday. I long to hear what happened and what you thought of the lady.

Rain, rain. I must go and take school. *Au revoir*, I hope, next Saturday.

Love,
A.H.

P.S. Tell Brett I have not heard from Mr. Sturgess and that I can't call on him till I know his address.

TO LADY OTTOLINE MORRELL

Eton Cottage
Windsor
21 October 1917

Dear Ottoline,

If when you come next week, could you bring the woolly waistcoat which I foolishly left in my room the other day at G—or else would you mind sending it? My brother is coming to stay on Wednesday—so that if you came on Thursday you'd see him.

I have just seen the little Burnham Beeches creature. A new complication has arisen—quite unforeseen. She has fallen into the hands this time not of harlots but of Jesuits—which is worse—who have almost bamboozled her into entering a convent. Her confessor has worked on her mind, telling her that she is infinitely wicked to think about love and to inspire desire in men. This combined with the fact that about six men in whom she takes no interest are quarrelling over her, pressing her to marry and generally making her life a burden, has made her contemplate this course. The confessor paints the rosiest picture of life in the convent—its absence of responsibility etc (he, by the way, could undertake the care of her money for the good, presumably, of the church) and so the plot is hatched. I am happy I found it out. I told her what I thought of the priest and of that article of Catholic morality: assured her she wasn't damned: told her that convents weren't so jolly as they sounded—particularly as she admits she isn't a bit religious. I have made her promise to do nothing more till she sees me and Evan (she is still in love with us) in conclave: and I think our joint forces ought to have no difficulty in utterly routing the powers of darkness. I feel that I'd like to start a good old-fashioned persecution against these creatures who go about terrifying unhappy children in this way. However, I think all will be well if Evan and I are very nice to her and pay her a good deal of attention. Anything rather that a new *"Religieuse"* history. I hope you'll come this week.

Love,
Aldous

TO LADY OTTOLINE MORRELL

The Old Christopher
Eton College
Windsor
8 December 1917

Dearest Ottoline,

Much thanks for your letter. I might, perhaps, see you in town next week. I am in all probability going up on Wednesday to be a Young Poet with Eliot, Graves, Sassoon, Nichols, and the Sitwells at Mrs. Colefax's meeting. It is vulgar, but it might be rather funny. *Wheels,* I see, has come out and contains some astonishingly good things by the youngest Sitwell, Sacha, who must be really something of a genius, thereby differing from the rest of his family. Also some quite amusing things by Iris Tree.[7]

The latest scheme is that I should, if I can manage it, go abroad for six months with Evan, who has to go for his lungs, probably to Sicily. Lady Tredegar would stand the trip for both of us; I think she feels that my respectable middle-aged temperament would act as a slight brake to Evan's whirling habits. The chance is too golden to be missed; the trouble is, of course, the passport. They are damnably strict these days about people traveling unless they have the most cogent reasons, and the passport people say that I should need a pretty strong medical certificate. I am going up to town tomorrow to lunch with Lady T., when we shall discuss the ways and means. There is, I think, just the smallest chance of success—though I do not yet flatter myself with any hopes. If it does come off it will only be because the Morgan family can raise more influence and can wangle more efficiently than any one else I have ever known. However, I shan't think the thing practicable till I cross the Italian frontier. It would be really too superb if it really did come off.

My medical examination, incredibly searching, resulted in complete rejection . . . and if I gather truly from the medical people, I shall get a paper from the National Service people discharging me completely, so that, I trust, I shan't be worried any more.

I am thankful that this beastly term is almost at an end; I live in a state of continual exhaustion and really haven't felt in any way well or alive during these last two months except on the occasions I have been away from Eton. Once you get run down, this climate gives you no chance of running up again; it weighs on you like a stifling damp feather bed.

---

[7] Iris Tree (1897–1968). English poet and actress, daughter of Sir Herbert Beerbohm Tree.

I had great fun last week end, when I was in town; saw Augustus John in full war paint as a Major in the Canadian army, just off to the front; next day lunched with Evan at McEvoy's. Evan had cut his hand in a drunken brawl at John's the night before and had almost bled to death in the night, and I found him crouching over the fire in McEvoy's studio looking like a sick bird, while McEvoy[8] himself was spasmodically trying to paint a nude study from a very lovely little model with red hair. He had to give that up finally, and soon we were all crouching like sick birds and we continued so to crouch for hours, talking of this and that, while Evan and the model became increasingly affectionate. McEvoy's son is up at Eton and is, curiously enough, De La Warr's[9] fag.

I was up again on Thursday, Founder's day, taking another tonic of London atmosphere. I had lunch with Evan and Carrington, whom I hadn't seen for months, not since Brett and I bicycled into Oxford this summer to catch her on her walking tour. She was in admirable form and bowled me over with the usual completeness. We all three went whirling round London in a taxi during the afternoon looking for Phyllis Boyd and growing increasingly relieved and affectionate towards each other when we didn't find her. It was all very pleasant, the more so in contrast with the horrible experience of the following day, when there came to stay a clergyman and his wife, father of one of my housemate's pupils, who had come to see their boy confirmed. They really were bloody; I could hardly refrain from being rude and only achieved politeness by total silence. And the amount that man ate . . . all the parsons who come here seem to eat as much and more as my own parsonic companion. All their passions, inhibited in other directions, focus themselves in a great lust for food. It turns my gorge. And as for their political views . . .

Today was the inaugural meeting of the Eton Political Society. William Temple spoke first, followed by the Bishop of Oxford, followed by George Lansbury[1] . . . all very good in their various ways and all very sound in pointing the right direction for future discussions. I had tea first with De La Warr and his mother, who seems like a very nice woman, and old George Lansbury, whom I liked as much as when I first met him. Everyone is very much pleased to hear that there is a

---

[8] Ambrose McEvoy (1878–1927). English portraitist and friend of Augustus John.
[9] Herbrand, 9th Earl of de la Warr (1900–1976). Labour politician.
[1] George Lansbury (1859–1940). Leader of Labour Party, 1932–1935.

chance of your brother coming, and he will doubtless be approached nearer the desired time.

Well, *au revoir*. I will let you know how the Italian plan proceeds; meanwhile perhaps it would be best to keep it slightly dark, or a least dim, for who knows what fishy shifts may not have to be gone to in order to obtain a passport. Meanwhile I am looking forward to coming to you at the end of term, which is the nineteenth or the twentieth. Will that be all right?

I had a happy letter from Maria; the possibility of seeing her again. . . .

Aldous

TO JULIAN HUXLEY

Cherwell
30 January 1918

My dear Julian,
Many thanks for your note about the two men you are suggesting should come and see me. So far no sign, but I shall be prepared when they turn up.

My holidays draw painfully nearly to their close; I return, in fact, tomorrow—three months more of Cobby. I had hoped to do a good deal of writing during my time of freedom—and have done some, but not quite so much as I had rosily anticipated, for I find the pleasures of social life so intoxicating and distracting after a few months of peopled solitude at Eton that it has been hard to find time to do much but whizz around, at least while in London, where one goes about mixing one's people like discordantly flavoured drinks—Eliot for luncheon, Aunt Mary [Ward] for tea, Sitwells and the Icelander [Haraldur Hamar] for dinner and afterwards the ever-increasingly sinister Mr Mills, the Viper of Chelsea. Or else one sticks to one rich vintage all day long—Marie Beerbohm, fine flavoured, but not full-bodied (for she is remarkably willowy) at lunch, tea, dinner and half the night long. A very remarkable character, Marie; tremendous vitality to carry her through the arduous frivolousness of a perpetually whirling life; the marvellous niceness common to all Beerbohms, which keeps her charming and unspoiled through episodes in themselves somewhat sordid; a good mind, rather like Max's in its fantastic cleverness, which you don't discover till you know her well; and then you are startled to discover the very self-conscious analysis and penetration in a person who appears to one at first sight as a butterfly living wholly in the external life of the moment. And then one is somehow always finding oneself in the profoundly exhausting company of Lady Constance Stuart Richardson, the worst dancer in the world but one of the most remarkable athletes, whose strength is as the strength of ten—not, I think, for the same reason as Galahad's, for she is something of a man-eater and has a strangely hungry look in her eyes and is moreover very much of a certain age, a rather pathetic figure, for her real friends and contemporaries, with whom she shot elephants in Africa, buffalo in the Rockies; bears in Tibet, with whom she head-hunted in Borneo and galloped after ostriches in Patagonia, Olympians like Lord Lucas, seem to have died or been killed. She is a lonely anachronism, one of those travelling English sportswomen of a bygone era—lonely, and therefore disinclined to lose hold of anyone she may casually meet, so that one has to take a good deal of pains to avoid her; otherwise one finds oneself sitting up all night listening to her traveller's tales, and eating bread and honey at dawn in a state of complete exhaustion, while Constance gaily starts a new day; for her iron constitution requires no rest. She rarely goes to bed more than three times a week, and then it is in a blanket on a sofa or in a flea-bag on the floor, and she hardly realizes that the normal human being requires eight hours per night to keep his machinery in working order.

I sometimes wish that she had not been a swimming champion and swum, as I believe was the case, from the sinking Titanic to the coast of America, a distance of three hundred and forty miles, arriving in time for an early breakfast before taking the train to Cody Town to see her old friend Buffalo Bill, with his two trusted lieutenants, White Beaver and Reckless Davies. However, she is a curiosity and so, I suppose, worth a sleepless night or two.

Retiring to Garsington after the restless whirl of London, I contrived to do a little writing and reading; and there saw what was perhaps the last of Bertie Russell before he goes to prison; his trial takes place tomorrow; the appeal, which won't, I imagine, do any good except perhaps to change his six months from second to first division. He read us chapters from a new book on socialism, syndicalism and anarchy—marvelously lucid and intellectual, a twentieth-century Godwin. Old Birrell[2] was there the last week end; charming as usual with his conversation of the old school, wit and wonderfully-told anecdotes.

[2] Augustine Birrell (1850–1933). English author and politician.

I am spending a night here before my return to Eton. Naomi and the infant flourish exceedingly. Mrs. Haldane performs the duties of gardener, war-worker, grandmother, farmer and marraine to some thousands of soldiers with her usual fabulous energy.

You say you'd like a book of memoirs. I will send you the first volume of Casanova, which is all about Venice and north Italy of the eighteenth century, a wonderful picture enlivened by the piquancy of countless amours. One volume at a time is enough; the full six might cloy. I will see if I can find something else suitable and convenient to send.

Did you hear from Maria? She told me she had written to you, but I didn't hear whether you had replied.

I sometimes wonder whether the war is going to last three or six years more. Goodbye. I will write again comparatively soon.

Love from
A.L.H.

TO LADY OTTOLINE MORRELL

Eton College
Windsor
11 February 1918

Dearest Ottoline,
I see they have got poor Bertie Russell at last: I remember him making that remark about the American army last time he was at Garsington: I don't suppose his appeal will do him much good—if it doesn't actually do him harm.

I heard from Gertler the other day that you had come up to town and retired again, with headaches—which I was very sorry to hear: I hope they have passed off again now.

Your brother Henry came and spoke here last week: very well, I thought—not so shy as usual. Our political paper proceeds apace. A young poet has been discovered in the shape of Ld. David Cecil,[3] a very charming frail boy of fifteen or so with quite remarkable talent.

My work this term is less beastly on the whole than last: I have a great deal of going over essays with individual boys—which is sometimes quite interesting, tho' it takes up an immense amount of time, so that I have no opportunity for doing anything else—whether writing or jaunting up to town. However, the time goes whizzing past at

[3] Lord David Cecil (1902–1986). English literary scholar and academic.

such a rate that one is hardly conscious of anything more than the rapid flickering of alternate night and day—which is a grand thing in wartime!

I have had many long and happy letters from Maria—which have been very pleasant reading. They have moved into a new house outside the town—an improvement on the old.

I expect Lewis Gielgud next week for a few days' leave: it will be nice seeing him after so long, seven or eight months. Naomi Haldane has had her baby safely, which is a comfort: I hope both will flourish like green bay trees.

I saw the Burnham Beeches child the other day: she has just done what I urged her for the last four months to do—gone to London to take a lodging unknown to husband or Windsor soldier where she can live in peace. When I hear she has settled I shall make a push to find a cinema job for her.

Give my love to Brett: has the SWAN arrived yet? I hope Junie is well: I wrote to her the other day!

Yours affectionately,
Aldous

TO JULIETTE HUXLEY

Eton College
Windsor
27 February 1918

My dear Juliette,

I was very glad to hear from you, glad to know that my letter hadn't reached you:—for I was beginning to think that you must have struck me off your list of correspondents or else that your metropolitan life was so gay that you had forgotten such poor country mice as myself. However, all is well—and so, I hope are you, and enjoying your holiday.

I have told my sister about you, and said that you'd write to her: Margaret H. 16 Bracknell Gardens NW3. So will you? It would be very nice of you, and I think you'll like her—and if she has any sense she'll like you! When I next go to town which is a not infrequent occurrence—I will let you know, and we might have lunch or dinner somewhere. School-mastering is a profession for which I don't think I was specially suited—but still: it might be worse. I only wish I had any real friends among the masters: it's wretched living in a place where there is nobody one can be fond of, nobody even who particularly interests one. I expect I'll be in town in a week or 10 days time, when it would be very nice to see you, dear Juliette—I'll let you know precisely. No more time at present. Have you met any amusing people? Do write and tell me.

Your affectionate,
Aldous

TO LADY OTTOLINE MORRELL

Eton College
Windsor
1 March 1918

Dearest Ottoline,

If you cannot speak, believe me, I have been unable to sleep, eat or move. A touch of influenza, preceded by several days of creeping chill, the while I dragged an aching carcase about its daily duties—now a little ameliorated, thanks to two days in bed and an armoury of nauseous drugs; but it leaves me in a state of almost incredible feebleness, a half sleeping coma, like the condition of a lotus-eater, to break out of which into any action whatsoever requires two or three hours concentration of such will as is left one. Meanwhile, I hope that you're better—as I 'opes to be.

My Sitwell week end was quite a success, a little marred by the failure to come off of a little joke—the showing-off of the fabulous Mr. Mills to astonished eyes—the creature failing us in the last resort. I saw Dorothy Warren[4] for the first time for a good while, and like her so much. She was looking quite surprisingly beautiful. She is apparently moving into rooms in Charlotte Street where she is to sell antique furniture on a commission: quite close, I suppose to Nina Hamnett,[5] who, I hear, has fallen passionately in love with and is nourishing in her scanty attic that horrid little boy Dallas, Wilfred Childe's[6] friend. He was once quite pleasant while up at Oxford, but he went up to London, took to drink and generally debauched himself until he became singularly repulsive. He is utterly penniless and sits about the Royal, waiting for people to stand him meals, so that Nina's infatuation will

---

[4] Dorothy Warren. Niece of Philip Morrell, she ran the Dorothy Warren Gallery in London, from which the police confiscated several D. H. Lawrence paintings in 1929.
[5] Nina Hamnett (1890–1956). English bohemian artist, author of *Laughing Torso*.
[6] Wilfred Childe (1890–1952). Georgian poet, who edited *Oxford Poetry* with Huxley in 1916.

have saved his life for the moment in providing him at least with a roof and food. It has also caused a breach between N. and Marie Beerbohm, as N., who is violently jealous, suspects M.B. of wanting to get Dallas away from her, which I gather is very far from being the actual state of affairs.

It was most pleasant seeing Lewis again. He is immersed and a little overwhelmed by a love affair tremendously romantic and fraught with the most hideous difficulties and dangers—in Paris. By the way, you might tell Brett, that he sees a good deal of her brother and Zena[7] and also met the Ranee[8] when she was out there. He seems to lead quite a pleasant life in Paris, except for the violence of his work.

This letter crept into another day: I find myself a little less groggy and somnolent but tormented by a horrible rheumatism, or whatever it may be, which runs from my heart to my left shoulder and is, unless I keep it well fed with aspirin, almost unbearably painful at moments.

Is it a fact that, as I hear from Mademoiselle this morning, poor Gertler has been called up? I trust he can wriggle clear.

About a possible week end; the trouble is—which I had forgotten when I saw you the other day—that I can't get away from here now till at least two, whereas last term I could manage earlier and so catch a rather good Saturdays only train to Oxford. All this probably means that I couldn't get to Garsington before six or so and should still have to start back on Sunday afternoon, which makes it all rather a restless rush. I think perhaps I had better postpone it till the holidays begin, which is only a month from now on April 3rd. But if I see the possibility of more favourable conditions between then and now, I'll let you know.

Love to Brett.

> Yours,
> *Aldous*

---

[7] Zena Dare Brett (1887–1975). English actress. Wife of Dorothy's brother, Hon. Maurice Brett.
[8] Sylvia Brooke, Ranee of Sarawak (1885–1971). Brett's sister.

TO JULIETTE HUXLEY

Eton College
Windsor
7 March 1918

My dear Juliette,
I think I am pretty safe in saying that I can come up this Saturday—most of my diseases, influenza and intercostal rheumatism, having been mastered now, leaving no more than a slight weariness of the spirit behind which a jaunt to town will do good to.

We may as well see the Nevinson[9] pictures all the same, unless you can think of anything better. Let us say then 4:00 at the Leicester Galleries. (I say 4:00 and not 4:15 as my train gets in about a quarter to and I am sufficiently a convalescent to require a taxi, so that I shall be there pretty soon.)

Au revoir, then
Aldous

TO ROBERT NICHOLS

The Old Christopher
Eton College
Windsor
16 March 1918

My dear Robert,
They tell me that you are in this country. So am I—damn it—when in the spirit I am wholly elsewhere. But the flesh sticks regrettably here, and the Flesh as we all know, has the last word in most things, and the first as well. But then, *Pureté, pureté . . . par l'esprit on va a Dieu. Déchirante infortune!* [Rimbaud, "*Une saison en enfer*"]

You may, however, be thankful for at least one thing, viz., that you are not a schoolmaster. All work is bad enough, but this is worse than most owing to the human contact in it, which vampires the life out of one. Office work one can do with half one's brain, almost in one's sleep, though the physical strain is awful. This demands all one's energy. The one diversion is that these comic boys have founded a revolutionary political society and produced a paper which contains, by the way, the most stinging review of your productions in *Georgian Poetry* by a most brilliant and wonderful boy of fifteen, or just sixteen, one David Cecil,

[9] C. R. W. Nevinson (1889–1946). English painter.

son of Lord Salisbury, who writes himself admirably well and is a supremely good conversationalist. So fascinating that one is only thankful one is not paederastically inclined: no, positively not in the least, outgrown with my last tail coat.

Tell me your movements, when there is a chance of seeing your *mufle de vieux satyr* again, whether in London or in divine Oxford or—why not?—here, where I can offer you some sort of meal complete with comic parson, at almost any time of the day. My scholastic duties conclude on the third of April, God be praised.

Au revoir,
Aldous

TO LADY OTTOLINE MORRELL

Eton College
Windsor
19 March 1918

Dearest Ottoline,

It was very nice to get your letter. What good news about Gertler: I saw Monty Shearman the other day, who was on the whole reassuring; but this is the definite and final repulse of the powers of darkness.

I had another good weekend at the Sitwells the Saturday before last, and saw a variety of people—Mademoiselle, a little depressed at the thought of the midlands of Scotland in March, as well one might be, Helen Dudley,[1] Waley,[2] Guevara:[3] then an admirable music hall with the Sitwell family, followed by a visit to Monty, rather spoiled for me by the viscous presence of Hutch,[4] and so back up to Chelsea. The next day Osbert and I went to lunch with a fabulous little man called Atkinson,[5] a vorticist painter—better than some, so far as I could judge; but then I can't judge!—a man of about forty-five, of incredible energy. He earns his living by teaching music all day, and is an expert on Scriabin; one half of the night he devotes to vortex-painting, the other half to writing poetry, rather like Sachy Sitwell's, some, I thought, quite good. Add to this a German wife, sister of a di-

---

[1] Helen Dudley. American. Part of the literary set around Harriet Monroe. Bertrand Russell once proposed to her but later retracted the offer.
[2] Arthur Waley (1889–1966). Bloomsbury orientalist and translator from the Chinese.
[3] Alvaro "Chile" Guevara (1894–1951). Chilean painter.
[4] St. John Hutchinson (1884–1942). Prominent barrister and husband of Mary Hutchinson. Monty is Montague Shearman.
[5] Lawrence Atkinson (1873–1931).

rector of Krupp's, together with rich memories of *Kunst-leben* in the forests of Bavaria. All very strange. Atkinson and I got on wonderfully well, drinking champagne at lunch and talking about the *zeitgeist* and the great currents of thought of this age—quite meaningless, but extremely impressive. We parted full of mutual good will and promises to renew our acquaintance, which will be worth doing, I think, as he is a most amusing creature. Curiously enough he had seen me the afternoon before at Nevinson's picture show—how dismal it is—and wondered who I was; odd that I should have come to see him the next day.

Here things go as usual; spring creeps slowly on. At the moment I am up to the neck in an examination paper set to boys at private schools in history: an immense pile which steadily grows the more papers I correct. A most dismal task, but I shall be paid a little money for doing it, which is something—indeed it seems now almost the only thing that matters: how to get more money! I find that as I become poorer I become more extravagant—for extravagance gives one such a pleasant sense of being rich. However, one drifts along somehow quite happily.

May I come to Garsington sometime about the tenth of April? I want to spend some days in town and see my people before they go off for a holiday about the middle of the month. If you see Earp tell him, the old pig, to answer my letter.

Walter Raleigh came down here the other day to read a paper to our essay society; very pleasant, but as much obsessed by the war as ever, if not more so. He seems to be perpetually poring over the unspeakableness of Germany, concentrating on it, thinking about it—an awful state of affairs, since it is obvious that nothing can come out of such wholly negative and sterile ideas.

Our *Eton Review* has appeared and is now completely sold out: there is not another copy to be got and another hundred will probably have to be printed. Two articles were censored by the authorities!

Love to the household.

Yours affectionately,
Aldous

TO JELLY D'ARANYI

Eton College
24 May 1918

My dear Jelly,

Why is it such ages and ages since we have seen or heard of one another? I can't imagine, unless it is my congenital incapacity for writing letters and the fact that I am not often in London—and when I am it's generally for only a day or two. I saw Adila[6] and her husband in the street a month or two back when I was staying a night in town with the Sitwells: that's the last I have seen of your family. And you—why it must be much more than a year since we met. It is as though we had quarreled, which indeed I hope we haven't: for I should be very sorry to have lost your friendship.

How are you? Well, I hope, and happy as much as anyone can be happy in these days. I am engaged in rapidly becoming a typical schoolmaster. Not that the work is as bad as it might be: at least one has a certain amount of leisure and fairly long holidays. Meanwhile one writes a little—moderately well. And that is almost all.

I heard from Julian the other day. He seems to be quite happy in Italy—having had an exciting fortnight's leave in Florence and Rome. How pleasant it would be to be there with him.

What an insipid letter this is. It hardly deserves to be answered. Still, I hope you will answer it: it is meant to provoke reprisals on your part. I hope I may see you again some day soon.

Yours,
Aldous

TO JELLY D'ARANYI

Eton College
6 June 1918

My dear Jelly,

It was nice to see the impossible writing again. There are so many questions to answer, so many, too, to ask, that a letter, I fear, will prove quite inadequate. I was sorry I couldn't come last Friday, but it's almost impossible to get up to Town for anything which goes on at all late, for the trains are so atrociously bad now. But I do get up for the weekend sometimes and hope to be in town this next Sunday, the 9th. Would

---

[6] Adila d'Aranyi Fachiri (1886–1962). Violinist sister of Jelly d'Aranyi.

you by any chance be in if I called in the afternoon? If not it's possible I may be coming up next Wednesday, which is a whole holiday and gives me an opportunity of getting away.

Do I write, you ask? A certain amount, and I have another horrid little book coming out within a month or two. Have I friends at Eton? It depends what you call "friends." Do I hear any good music? Not much.

What then, you may well ask, does my life consist in? Wasting time, for the most part, and wondering what is going to happen in the horrible uncertainty of the future.

And what about you? I expect to hear all that when I see you, I hope, either on Sunday or on Wednesday: let me know which is possible for you.

> *Yours,*
> *Aldous*

TO LADY OTTOLINE MORRELL

Eton College
Windsor
7 June 1918

Dearest Ottoline,
I *was* glad to get your letter this morning. I'm afraid that this weekend—that is tomorrow—is impossible: I am already booked up to the eyes with things to do then. But, the 15th or 22nd or 30th—I don't quite know which—I'd love to come.

I was in town yesterday, where I had gone to see Gollancz,[7] the man who was at Repton and responsible for the school paper and all the political enthusiasm there, and who has now been defeated by the reactionaries, the paper suppressed, the teaching of civics stopped and himself sacked—it is depressing: the forces of evil win every time! However, I didn't see him after all, as he'd been called up to be medically examined and left me in the lurch. However, I saw Fredegond up for the day from Kent, where she is, apparently living in a colony of lunatics—not very good for her, I should think. Also Alix, very statuesque, and Marie Beerbohm, very dazzling, and Henry Mond, very worthy. No more. *Au Revoir.*

> *Aldous*

I'll let you know about dates.

---

[7] Victor Gollancz (1893–1967). British publisher.

1918

TO LADY OTTOLINE MORRELL

Prior's Field
Godalming
31 July 1918

Dearest Ottoline,
Safely in the country after a slightly distracted week in London, where the hecticness and frivolity of social life tends to get on my nerves—tho' I love it while it goes on. However, I am, I find, fundamentally too earnest and too bourgeois in outlook to be able to plunge into it wholeheartedly: it seems such an expense of spirit in a waste of pure folly and not worth while for more than a very little time. Here all is very quiet and lovely—a vast overgrown garden, sunshine, and the smell of flowers. The trees which I remember being planted have now grown twenty-five feet high—a fact which fills me with the profoundest melancholy.

May I come to you about the 18th or 19th of the month? I am going to stay with the Nichols family first, which will be amusing.

I had an amusing evening with Tancred B.[8] and Marie the other day. Poor T. seems to be very much *épris*, but gets small encouragement, I gather. How unnecessarily these things complicate life!

Au revoir: I look forward so much to seeing you all. Love to Junie.
Yours affectionately,
Aldous

TO DORA CARRINGTON

Eton College
Windsor
6 October 1918

My dear Carrington,
It is an age—but literally at least a year—since I have seen or more than heard, dimly and at second hand, of you. I do trust this is not to be the eternally normal state of affairs. Are our courses to be parabolas—perpetually asymptotic? Let the answer, I beg you, be the same as that which his loyal soldiers returned to . . . , one famous day at review, in his quivering castrato the question: "Are we Down-hearted?"

Do you flourish? Are you ever in the Metrollopis? Should you ever like to come and look at a medieval institution and have lunch with a real parson?

8 Tancred Borenius (1885–1948). Finnish art historian.

For me, life jogs along at its usual pace, and that is about all. This letter is meant to provoke reprisals.

Affectionately,
Aldous

Constanza Fasola's family owned properties in Forte dei Marmi as well as in Florence, and, after her stay in Garsington, the Fasolas hosted Maria and her sisters during the war. Costanza nicknamed her close friend "Coccola" (berry), and Aldous later took up the name, calling her "Cocola." In the summer of 1917, Costanza and Maria had the villa at Forte to themselves, swimming and sailing together. Maria commented in a letter to Lady Ottoline that she and Costanza lived in Forte "as if no one but us two exist." Eventually the Huxleys would live in each of the Fasola properties, in Forte and in Florence on Via Santa Margherita Montici. In April 1919, after accepting a job at The Athenaeum *as an editorial assistant to John Middleton Murry, Aldous is finally in a position to marry. That month he ends their long separation by visiting Maria at her family's home in Belgium, where they become formally engaged. In May he moves into 18 Hampstead Hill Gardens, London. The wedding takes place in Belgium on 10 July 1919.*

TO COSTANZA FASOLA

The Old Christopher
Eton College
Windsor
21 October 1918

My dear Costanza,

I hope you are not one of those who intensely object to receiving a typewritten letter; but really you must excuse me, for I find the process of writing with those barbarous and dirty instruments, pen and ink, insupportably unpleasant, and since the ingenuity of civilized man has provided me with a machine with which I can write twice as fast, ten times as legibly and with a quarter of the fatigue, you must really allow me to use it.

I ought to have written before—a fact of which my conscience was reminded when I got your letter today—to thank you very much for your story—which, by the way, I have forwarded to Bâle, as you directed. I liked it a lot. It is slight, of course, but very well done and well thought out and executed. I should certainly go on writing if I were you—on a larger scale and with a greater number and variety of characters; for that is the real problem of story-writing—the invention of numerous characters, the sustaining of their parts when they have been invented and the fitting of them into one another. It is a process which demands a great deal of hard concentrated thought. Go on, and please send me anything else you do.

Did you like my story, which I sent Maria recently? I expect you found it a little too cynical for your taste; for it is very bitter.

I have never read the Goncourt memoirs of which you speak. It is one of the books I look forward to reading at the first opportunity. I can believe that Edmond is apt to put the people he meets too much into classes, to make types instead of investigating individuals. There is a good deal of it in all the novels of his I have read, *Renée Mauperin*, *La Faustin* and so forth. The best of these is *Les Frères Zemganno*, which is really delightful. *Renée Mauperin* begins very well, but ends, to my mind at least, poorly. I think you would like his character of Renée herself, who is far from being the Female Type which you complain of in his memoirs. *La Faustin*, which some people admire a great deal, I don't find very good. There is in it a good deal of the rather heavy brutal sensual atmosphere which you dislike in him. Not that I dislike the book for that reason; I don't mind that sort of thing; indeed, it rather arouses my somewhat gross mind!

I was much interested by your account of the Heller incident, of which I had only been able to gather the barest outline from Maria's hints. What strange people the Nys family must be; I look forward to meeting them with somewhat mixed feelings; in fact, I should rather like to escape meeting them altogether; if only one could love and live in the void, unhampered and untouched by all this deplorable medley of circumstance. . . .

I wish I could see any immediate prospect of being able to get out to Italy. The obstacles are almost insuperable and the only chance seems to be to learn Italian as quickly as possible in the hope of getting some kind of job—for without some specific business there, the authorities will not let one go to any foreign country. I am contriving to learn a little Italian in some of my leisure moments. I plod away at the grammar and read Silvio Pellico—at least when his piety doesn't make me feel sick—and d'Annunzio's *Forse che si, forse che no*, which seems to me very beautiful, so far as I can judge an almost unknown language, and imbued with a kind of Renaissance spirit. His is a world where there is no morality, no society—only individuals giving expression to their individualities in the most intense manner possible, whether through art or crime or passion—what matter, so long as the individuality is fully and intensely expressed.

When I was in Germany, I was too blind to read, with the result that though I learnt to speak the language quite well I never read a word of it; to this day I can hardly make out the German alphabet. The consequence of that was that when I came back to England and ceased to talk German I forgot the whole thing, so that now I am almost as though I had never learnt it. However, I expect I should be able to pick it up pretty easily, particularly if I began to read it. It is one of the things I intend to do, when I have leisure—if that blessed day ever arrives: to devote long periods to thoroughly mastering the various languages I have just *entamé* without going any further—Latin, Greek, German.

Good bye, dear Costanza. Write to me again. I enjoy your letters very much. And go on writing stories and let me see them when you have written them.

Yours affectionately,
Aldous

TO MARIA NYS HUXLEY

The Old Christopher
Eton College
Windsor
5 November 1918

My beloved, I had so counted on getting a letter this morning, but there was nothing on my plate at breakfast except a line from Francis Rodd[9] from Egypt, asking why I hadn't written to him—which as a matter of fact I have. Poor Francis, I am afraid his letter merely irritated me, for it wasn't what I had been hoping or expecting to get. It's such a long time since I heard from you—more than a week, but it seems months and months. I get so anxious when I don't hear, fearing that you are ill, or that perhaps you have suddenly taken a dislike to me and are not going to write any more. It is an incredible relief and happiness when

---

[9] Francis Rodd, Lord Rennell of Rodd (1895–1978). President of the Royal Geographic Society, 1945–1948.

the letter comes at last; I am so hoping for one to come this evening or by the first post to-morrow. Now that the time of our meeting again does begin to approach—though the exact moment and the way it is to be brought about are still horribly obscure—I feel the need of you more than ever and am fast losing all the patience I ever had. This limited unreal life in an unsympathetic atmosphere becomes infinitely unsatisfactory. I want to have you with me so much, always. Meanwhile you must write to me often; that is at least something.

The days go galloping along at their usual pace, leaving very little time to turn round and think. However, I have forcibly snatched some time in the last day or two to read and also to write a little; for that purpose I spent Sunday here: there is literally nothing else to do during an Eton Sunday but read and write—unless one goes to chapel, which I decline to do more than once a day, or takes a walk in the afternoon dressed in a tail coat and top hat, which again I decline to do, as I don't possess a top hat and no human power will persuade me to buy one. So I spent the time in finishing *Madame Bovary* and starting an extremely interesting new book by a man called McDowall called *Realism*, which is about realism in art and philosophy. My admiration for *Madame Bovary* is very great. I must get hold of the *Education Sentimentale* and *Bouvard et Pécuchet* as soon as possible and also the *Correspondance*. What is so splendid about *Madame Bovary* is its wonderful impersonality; Flaubert's own opinion never appears for a moment. I don't think he was at all a born psychologist, like Tolstoy who could quite easily and naturally get inside somebody else, could be a peasant or a grand duke or a cow and absolutely feel their thoughts and sensations: Flaubert, I think, found it much more difficult and it was only by pure mental concentration, that he got inside his creations as much as he did. I always begin wondering, after reading a good novel, what is the best method of setting forth your material. What I tried to do in my 'Happily Ever After' was to get the effect as far as possible through conversation and with the minimum of description, whether of outward objects or of internal states and processes. What I certainly succeeded in doing in that story was getting a very great degree of concentration—a quality which I admire in art and like to find there, though I wouldn't for a moment claim that concentration was a necessary or even a wholly desirable quality in the novel or short story, which may often get its effect by a long-drawn cumulative series of touches. But certainly, every now and then it is a good thing to concentrate the thing. What I want to do is to find some method of getting rid of the infinitely boring description, internal and external, which one finds in novels. The slushy stream of bad psychology which is poured forth by most writers in their descriptions of people's sensations and emotions is appalling; and worse, if possible, are those masses of details about external things which are supposed to create the atmosphere in which the characters move. These, I feel, must be cut down to the lowest possible limit; the description of mental processes should be limited as far as possible to a sort of comment on the conversation—something to show the real tendencies going on in the person's mind while he is talking, perhaps in a totally different strain. Elaborate accounts of sensation should, I think, be avoided; they are largely conventionalized and as a matter of fact people's sensations are rarely very strong. Those great fluxes of beautiful words in D'Annunzio are exciting in themselves, but I doubt whether they really describe anything much; they bombinate in the void. Then about the external details:—I find myself really at a complete loss to know what to do about them. How much should one tell about a character's life? Should one pour forth everything like Balzac or, even more like Zola? Or should one confine oneself, to those few almost too significant details, as in Maupassant—they irritate me so much sometimes; they are so slick and clever and right, too much so. I believe the cinema method is rather a good one to give a series of short scenes, each of which would be a slice of life, with very little explanation in between. But I really can't make up my mind; one can only discover the best methods by experiment, and I will have to write a great deal more till I begin to theorise. I have been getting on a bit with my modern poem, written about fifty lines of it, and thought out and actually begun the introduction to it, which is going to be a kind of biography of the young man about whom the poem is supposed to be—a youth killed in the war. I shall make use of the biography to put in several opinions about poetry, especially the particular poem I am writing; this will at least give the critics something to quote in their reviews, which will therefore be a little less stupid than if they were given no hint as to what to say and had to try and find an opinion of their own.

But why aren't you here to talk about all these things? What conversations we will have—*à n'en plus finir!* If you had lived with my parson as long as I have, you would know how wonderful it is to be with someone who understands what one says and can appreciate one's point of view. To be permanently with someone who could do that seems almost a paradise, and when that somebody happens to be you—well, it will be entirely paradise!

The news continues to be encouraging. To-day I have received two large parcels containing a number of Julian's books and some oddments of clothing—but no word of explanation. I suppose it means that he has gone hastily off into Austria, where his post as Intelligence Officer with a knowledge of German would naturally take him; I shall be glad to hear from him. It must certainly be immensely interesting on the Italian front now.

Good bye, my very dear beloved Maria. I shall be miserable unless I hear from, you to-morrow, for this evening's post has brought nothing, as I hoped it would.

I love you so much, my darling.

Aldous

TO COSTANZA FASOLA

Eton College
Windsor
16 November 1918

My dear Costanza,
Thank you very much for your two letters and the translation of *My Italy*, which seems to me, as far as I can understand or appreciate it, very good.

I don't know why you should have written your second letter apologizing for the criticisms contained in your first. I liked the criticisms, but not the apology! You are right, I think, about the sonnets. As a whole they are not good—the story is obscure and the psychology of it not well worked out—but there are good bits every now and then. My short story is, as you say, rather crowded: it is an experiment in concentration. It could quite well have been made into a long novel, but I like to see what it looks like shortened and compressed like that.

I don't think I shall ever be able to read *I Promessi Sposi*: a romantic work written under the influence of Walter Scott . . . it sounds difficult! The only romantic books I find readable are de Musset's stories, George Sand (but one laughs a good deal, and V. de L'Isle Adam—who himself made the singularly intelligent remark, "*Il y a les romantiques et il y'a les imbéciles*"—most of them, I find, belong to the latter category! D'Annunzio I am finding too rhetorical: it is a wonderful rhetoric, but like *all* rhetoric purely verbal: but marvellous phrases and endless sonorous sentences. I remember seeing a picture of him early in the war when he was making those speeches which did so much to bring Italy in—a photo of him speaking, with a huge mouth wide open in shouting. It was a symbol of his art and of rhetoric in general—the gaping shouting mouth, uttering words that have no meaning but which intoxicate the hearers, numb their intellect—excite their worst passions into activity.

I told Maria what has happened to your ms: it is too silly: to keep it six weeks and then return it. I am writing to the Censor to ask about it. Meanwhile I will keep it.

Write to me again, please. I enjoy your letters—except when they apologize for criticism: if people read what I write I want them to say why they like or dislike it, not to apologize if they don't like. I shall consider it an unfriendly act if you don't criticize!

I am in a great hurry, so good-bye.

Your affectionate,
Aldous

TO LADY OTTOLINE MORRELL

The Old Christopher
Eton College
Windsor
25 November 1918

Dearest Ottoline,

Here is *Bouvard and Pécuchet* with many thanks: I enjoyed it very much. I wish I could have stopped over Sunday into the day of peace: we could have suitably celebrated it. The outbursts in London sounded somewhat repulsive: I hear that one fireman was killed in Trafalgar Square while attempting to put out the bonfire and three policemen were thrown into the river: The most ardent patriot of all being of course, Henry Mond![1]

I was in Oxford yesterday, staying with the Petersens.[2] I saw Raleigh, who holds out no immediate hope for a job, but says he'll think of me if

---

[1] Henry Mond (1898–1949). Son of Alfred Mond, first Lord Melchett. Henry Mond lived in a ménage-à-trois with the artist Gwen Wilson and Gilbert Canaan before marrying Gwen in 1920.
[2] The Petersen family lived at Boars Hill, south of Oxford. The daughter, Frances, was a day student at Oxford from 1915, and Huxley was an occasional vistor. In a letter of 5 December 1917, Huxley asked Frances to tell him more of the character and personal appearance of Flora Forster, the Oxford student poet whose "Ducklington" so impressed him when it appeared in *Oxford Poetry* that he immediately wrote her a passionate letter and received a pleasant reply. Despite Frances's positive report, he soon lost interest in her.

he hears of anything turning up anywhere. Earp too I saw and found very charming—much upset by the death of his Indian friend.

I am making a determined effort to get to Paris for the Xmas holidays. Maria is leaving Naples today and the family will be in Paris for some time before they go back to Belgium. It will be an extraordinary and unbelievable thing to see her again. After two years it seems scarcely credible that she has a real physical existence or that one would ever see her again. I want to get married as soon as may be and start some kind of decent and reasonable life: I only hope that these damned material difficulties don't make it impossible. However, I am keeping the manufacture of castles in Spain severely in check and propose to indulge in no plan making till things are a little less obscure than they are at present.

I hope I shall see you again before long. I enjoyed my glimpse of you the other day very much.

Yours affectionately,
Aldous

TO LADY OTTOLINE MORRELL

The Old Christopher
Eton College
Windsor
3 December 1918

Dearest Ottoline,
I hope you are recovering from your cold and your depression. It is certainly very curious how everybody has become extremely depressed at the arrival of peace. One could regard the war as a nightmare and unreal; but with peace one must look at facts as though they were real—and they are extremely unpleasant.

The prospects of Paris begin to grow a little dim, as it seems that after all M. won't be leaving Naples yet awhile. I should think they will be safely back in Belgium before Easter, and as traveling is likely to be more possible then, it looks as though I should have to postpone my trip abroad till then: I have no burning desire to go to Paris this winter if she is not going to be there.

The main problem before me is contained in that very pertinent song from the Belle of New York—When we are married what will you do? This money . . . I hope we may be able to raise a little from our respective families, enough to live on at any rate for a little in some cheap country like Italy: for I very much want to have a year or so with no other occupation but writing: it would be pleasant and, I think, more profitable. I come more and more to feel that Domesticity tempered by Intelligence is the right formula for a satisfactory existence—like limited monarchy. One needs an atmosphere of sympathy to live in—a permanent atmosphere: changes of air may be bracing, but one wants a good spiritual climate for every day. Loneliness is really impossible. I am really very confident that it will turn out a success; there seems to be every reason why it should.

I exchanged a few words with your nephew this morning and will try to get hold of him again. One has to exercise great tact, for many housemasters are frightfully jealous of anyone else having anything to do with their boys except in a purely official capacity. The boy's soul is supposed to be the tutor's exclusive property, and anything that might be considered a trespass on tutorial preserves is bitterly resented. As a boy here, one didn't realize the hideous passions which seethe in the pedagogic mind; it is only now that I begin to perceive its working. Poor boy, how devastating the home influence must be. Eton is often reproached as being a conservative reactionary place, but it is a hotbed of revolution, a place of progress and liberty compared with many of the happy homes from which the boys are drawn.

I am reading a most curious and amusing book, which I'm sure, if you haven't read it, you would like:—the autobiography of B. R. Haydon, Keats's artist friend. What an ironic tragic figure, a man who passionately believed in his own genius, sacrificed everything for art, laboured like a Hercules, suffered for his ideals—and produced nothing but pictures of unequalled horror. The book is a wonderful revelation of character and full of things, consciously or unconsciously amusing. He knew everybody; the scene with Lamb and the man whose bumps he felt comes from Haydon's life; and there are very good things about Keats and Wordsworth:—Wordsworth looking at a statue group of Cupid and Psyche kissing and turning, after long contemplation, to Haydon with a look of indescribable malignity in his eyes saying simply and with emphasis: "The devils!" I think Gertler ought to read it; he would enjoy this carefully analyzed development of a bad artist,— but one who took as much interest in his art and looked at it as intellectually as even Gertler himself.

I hope very much, if I don't go to Paris—which seems to me rather probable—I shall see you sometime this holidays. Haste.

Yours affectionately,
Aldous

TO THE HON. DOROTHY BRETT

The Old Christopher
Eton College
Windsor
4 December 1918

My dear Brett,

Here are some scribblings of the culminating scene of *Leda*. I can't see it quite. The swan must, I feel, have its wings out, or it will look like a goose. Besides wings are so lovely. Those Ingres pictures of ladies from behind are so lusciously good—and his odalisque is marvellous.

How do you think of doing it? Great haste.

Aldous

Huxley attached four of his own competent sketches depicting the rape of Leda, accompanied by various captions. Apparently the artist Dorothy Brett had agreed to furnish illustrations for his forthcoming volume of poetry, Leda. *See his letter to her of 17 January 1919, in which he thanks her for two completed drawings regarding the Leda myth.*

TO LADY OTTOLINE MORRELL

16 Bracknell Gardens
Frognal Lane, N.W.3
ca Xmas 1918

Dearest Ottoline,

Thank you for the play: I'm glad it amused you. Quite a pleasant time with my redoubtable aunt. George Trevelyan was there—a sadder and a wiser man, I thought, after his Italian experiences—less inclined to preach and to magnify the virtue of the Italians.

I have had two letters from Maria following close on one another, sent from her grandmother's: she's pretty well, I think, but rather depressed by everything. Her father seems somewhat aged and broken by his troubles: I gather his manufactory was destroyed in the last offensive. The grandmother's house appears to be intact. I think she'd like it very much if you wrote to her: her address is: Grand Place 19, St. Trond, Belgium.

About Saturday: my family have made several arrangements which I can't very well get out of but I want to go to Oxford to see the Haldanes and the Petersens some time later on in the holidays. Might I come over for a night then? I should like to very much if I may. I wish I could tell you the difference it makes to my existence having a spiritual home like Garsington. I feel I'm very bad at expressing gratitude: but it's very much there, dear Ottoline.

Goodbye for the present,
Aldous

TO THE HON. DOROTHY BRETT

16 Bracknell Gardens
17 January 1919

My dear Brett,
I would have written before to thank you at more length for the second Leda drawing, had I not been daily expecting you in London: for you said when you last wrote that you were coming early in January, while Katherine was definitely certain that you were coming on the 6th. However, you are not here: so I imagine you are still in Scotland. I am sending this by Julian with a copy of Leda, Part I, for you to read and select the indecent passages from for your illustration. Send it me back, please; for I have no other copy; to the Old Christopher, Eton, whither I return next Wed.

Meanwhile, thanks very much for the blue drawing. It is very lovely—the figures particularly: though I'm not sure that the tree isn't almost better in the first version. I long to see your drawing of the actual swan scene. Other possible things to illustrate are the Jupiter bedroom and the Venus boudoir—in the description of which, you will see, I have carefully mentioned the fact that the bed-curtains hung in Cézanne folds. Thus there are the little glimpses of the world, seen from Jupiter's god's-eye view: the Chinese scene, or the people asleep in the shade of the dromedaries might be jolly.

But we must discuss this at more length. I think you had better come to Eton one day and lunch with me and the parson. You could also see your bank Manager at Windsor! Do come if you can: or if you feel it would be immodest to visit a bachelor establishment, I will come up one Saturday to London. I trust you flourish.

Ever yours,
Aldous

TO OTTLINE MORRELL

Eton College
Windsor
22 January 1919

Dearest Ottoline,
You have probably heard by this time that brother Julian and Mademoiselle are engaged. It makes me laugh rather, but I expect it will do very well: What a clean sweep the Huxley family has made of Garsington—all but Brett; and who will sweep her? She will require a 40 horse power vacuum cleaner.

Just arrived here: rather a relief, in a way, after the tearing restlessness of London. Quiet and regularity—I find them indispensable to doing work.

I went last night to the ballet—*Sylphides*: it really showed up the badness of the dancing: Massine was frightful, Tchernicheva, lovely when she stands still or merely postures, was frightful when she moved and audibly creaked at every motion. Lopokova was the only good dancer, and Diaghileff is giving her the sack because he can get Lydia Kyasht at half the wages:—it really is a bit disgusting.

Maria's despairing letter seems to have been no more than the product of a passing mood: for she has been quite cheerful in all communication I have had since then—which is a relief; for I couldn't bear the thought of her being so depressed.

I hope I shall see you someday soon. Let me learn when you are in London. I hear that Brett has got a studio in town and is in the highest spirits—threatening us all with a big dose of Lily Elsie (which reminds me that our parlor maid here is called Lily Tunnell and our housemaid Louisa Frippance: *c'est un peu fort!*)
Much love from Aldous

TO JULIETTE HUXLEY

Eton College
Windsor
22 January 1919

My dear Juliette,
This is all very pleasing and good. The Huxley family has done well out of Garsington, it seems to me. No more; for it is impossible to say

much about these affairs[3] without relapsing into the keepsake style, which, as you know, is abhorrent to anyone possessing my literary principles.

I am glad you liked *Leda*—tho' I fear your critical faculty may have been a little warped by your personal feelings! For you seem hardly conscious of the profound and painful irony which is the thread on which all its beauty is strung. You must read it again later. It is certainly very good!—but perhaps not so good as your feelings.

Yours,
Aldous

TO JULIAN HUXLEY

Eton College
Windsor
16 February 1919

My dear J,

Will you dispose of Elton and tell him politely that I think that fellowship thing is a wash-out.

I am getting the usher Blakiston here to talk to his cousin, the Master of Trinity about possible openings there to replace poor Tiddy.[4] Meanwhile I trust you will keep your ears pricked for any murmurs on the subject of English teaching.

I am glad Mrs. H. is all right: I didn't write as I heard from Lewis [Gielgud], who had just seen her and heard her views, that she was clearly much mollified, converted by Aunt Sophie's emphatic approval: Aunt S is so completely a M.B.E. that her judgment would obviously carry more weight than mine.

I go up to town on Wednesday and hope to see a man at the F.O. [Foreign Office] to whom Aunt Mary has commended me (or at least I trust she has remembered to do so).

Isn't Squire a queer cove. I don't know that I really like him: in fact I'm pretty sure I don't—tho' why, it's hard to say.

---

[3] Huxley here apparently refers to the two brothers' meeting their future wives at Garsington. He then says he wishes to avoid lapsing into the smooth, pretty sentiments of the keepsake volume. On the same day he wrote to Julian, "Your news [of his engagement] is very good." He went on to say that "the right things to say on this kind of occasion" make him uncomfortable, but "you may consider them very much said."

[4] R. J. E. Tiddy. Huxley's tutor until 1915, he was a lecturer in Classics and English Literature.

Lunched with Mrs. Cornish yesterday, who, without making any of her really startling remarks, was in quite good form. I heard another story of her: at the beginning of the war her son Hubert came down to Eton to argue retrenchment and reform, and after having given his mother a three hour lecture on household economies, Mrs. C, who had been listening attentively, said: "Yes, Hubert, we will certainly decrease the parrot's food," and left the room. What an enchanting figure.

Yours,
A.L.H

TO JULIAN HUXLEY

24 February 1919

My dear J,
I am going to Garsington next weekend—1st–3rd—and as Saturday is a Whole Holiday I hope to be able to get away fairly early and, if possible, to come thro' Oxford on my way. Will you be there? Let me know speedily as I want to settle definitely.

I heard from [Pierre] Legouis—professor of English at the Sorbonne—about vacancies for an English reader. There is one for next November: several candidates (but I probably have the best qualifications) and salary—2000fr per annum=£80, not very sumptuous! It would be possible only if one had something else. I suppose you've heard no more about Oxford possibilities? If I come up on Saturday I want to enquire and see people.

Ever yours,
A.L.H

Let me know at once if you'll be there and I'll tell you what train I'll come by.

TO JULIAN HUXLEY

Eton College
Windsor
6 March 1919

My dear J,
It certainly looks like Oxford for next term: for marriage seems out of the question (father can give me at the outside £100) unless something in the nature of a miracle of unexpectedness happens between now and April.

Curious you should mention a book on XIX French literature, as I have been planning one to do this summer. As for a man in that series. Of English writers of that time I think I'd say I like Borrow[5] best; but I could cope with anyone if I were given time and were not asked to admire him too much. Of Frenchmen, Stendhal or Sainte-Beuve I would like to do—particularly Stendhal who is a really *great* novelist and not sufficiently recognized. Or Flaubert, who is tremendous. Or even Zola.

But let us talk of that later.

I think I can get up for your wedding all right. I don't have to invigilate in trials, so it will be fairly easy if you have it on the 29th.

Can you meet me next Wednesday, 12th, in town before you go to Hindhead? Do: we can talk and arrange. I go to Ernest Clarke[6] at 11:30 and to lunch with Naomi at the Rendezvous at 1:30. Could you meet me 1917 Club at 12:30? Do if you can manage it, and let me have a p.c. to say so.

Saw Richmond[7] of the *Times Literary Supplement* today. Benevolent, but uncertain (I asked him about a literary correspondentship in Paris) as he doesn't know if he won't be turned out by Northcliffe in the course of the next few months.

Ever yours,
A.L.H

TO THE EDITOR, NEW STATESMAN

8 March 1919

Sir,

Mr. Sickert says that Rops[8] is a bad artist; "H. M." tells us that he is ithyphallic and obscene; it is all a matter of taste. But grant he is both, it makes no difference to the question of principle raised by the action of the Post Office. It is not to be suffered that officials should have the power of life and death over anything that attempts to be a serious work of art. If it is bad and indecent, time and public opinion will relegate it to the oblivion it deserves; there is no need that anonymous postmen should interfere.

---

[5] George Borrow (1803–1881). English travel writer and linguist.
[6] Ernest Clarke. English eye surgeon.
[7] Bruce Richmond, editor of *TLS*, 1903–1937.
[8] Félicien Rops (1833–1898). Belgian artist and engraver, associated with Baudelaire.

"H. M." likes Correggio, in spite of his voluptuousness; the Duke of Orleans did not, and, acting on principles identical with those of "H. M." in the case of Rops, he cut great holes in Correggio's "Leda." His confessor had assured him that the picture was ithyphallic and obscene.

Talking about "Leda," I would like also to point out that Michelangelo's version of the same theme is now reposing in the vaults of the National Gallery ("indecent art," to quote H. M., "hidden away in the private rooms of public galleries"), while Lord Leighton's "The Bath," which might be objected to on the best possible grounds, both by "H. M." and by Mr. Sickert, occupies a place of honour on the walls of the British Room.

Yours, etc.

TO LADY OTTOLINE MORRELL

16 Bracknell Gardens, N.W.3
12 June 1919

Dearest Ottoline,

I expect to be at Oxford over next weekend and it would be nice if I could come out and see you on Saturday or Sunday.

I've had a busy time furnishing and my rooms begin to look habitable, which is a satisfaction. I expect to go into them in four or five days time. Brett tells me you are going to have your tonsils out: I hope it will do you good. Stupid of nature to allow these poisonous objects to grow like fungi in one's anatomy and make one ill.

I saw you in the distance at the first night of the Boutique. I was up aloft, watching everyone going and coming in the theatre between the shows. Clive [Bell] doing the round of the boxes was a superb spectacle. One could almost hear his voice across the whole breadth of the building. And Lytton drinking lemonade in the foyer: and Roger [Fry], perspiringly radiant: and Hutch[inson], very man about town, with Nina [Hamnett] looking very gamine. It was almost as good as the boutique itself—which really was stupendous, wasn't it.

I have been staying with my Aunt Mary [Mrs. Humphry Ward], insisting that she shall read [Georges] Duhamel and Marcel Proust for the good of her soul. She is quite ready and tolerant—which is good considering her age and career.

Yours affectionately,
Aldous

TO LADY OTTOLINE MORRELL

16 Bracknell Gardens, N.W.3
14 June 1919

Dearest Ottoline,

This is to wish you many happy returns of whatever the day might be. Above all I hope they'll be happy: I wish it were in my power to guarantee that they should be. Meanwhile I trust that Haydn Brown is doing you good—perhaps there would be a chance of seeing you when you come up.

Last weekend was very pleasant. I wish I could have got on more easily with Sassoon: I felt with him something of the same difficulty I felt with Graves—the sense of being out of control and not knowing how to get into it, which is most baffling. I am afraid I'm rather bad at approaching people—the result of a habit, I think of laziness and arrogance.

I had a most Russian day: A lunch with Carrington and Alix at Isola Bella where appeared Anrep and two poets, his compatriots—one of whom, the most appalling animal, fastened onto me like a leech; and as he lives in London I fear I shall have trouble with him: he is, Anrep tells me, a sexual maniac whose hobby is collecting the basest prostitutes he can find. The other was very nice and also, I fancy, a real poet in his own country—one Goumilov:[9] literary editor of *Apollon*. I saw him again at dinner with Anrep, Lytton, and once again Carrington and was very much alarmed to hear from him that he had procured my book and was settling down to read it with a dictionary! I finished the day by going to Boris Godounov: Quite good, though not a dazzling performance.

Much love,
Aldous

TO LADY OTTOLINE MORRELL

18 Hampstead Hill Gardens, N.W.3
3 October 1919

Dearest Ottoline,

I was glad to hear that you were safely back and that your knee was at least moderately well. What a nuisance knees are: when they're In,

[9] Nikolay Gumilyov (1886–1921). Russian poet executed by the Cheka.

they give welcome to rheumatism and when they're Out they're agonizing.

I hope, all being well (at present one rather doubts all is ever going to be well again), to go to Oxford for a few days on the 22nd for the All Soul's Fellowship exam. It would be very nice if you could have Maria to stay during that time and if I might come out from Oxford at intervals. I have no hope about the All Soul's—but it's worth going in on the offest of off chances.

Have you seen Julian and Juliette since their return to Oxford? Julian is much better, physically at any rate and in some ways mentally. Still rather gloomy though and self-absorbed, so that poor little Juliette is rather an oppressed nationality and, I gather, not very happy—poor child. What a bad business it is. I hope they will get through this term successfully.

Sullivan[1] and I are wondering when, if ever, Murry is going to return. No news of him: he was supposed to come back yesterday. I imagine he'll have to fly if he wants to get over: but if he's wise, he'll remain on the Riviera. I have been seeing a lot of funny old Sullivan of late—and liking him very much: he's a most interesting and remarkable creature. We discuss life with great gusto.

The prospects of a general strike and possible revolution are hardly gay. The men and women in the street (to judge, at least, from the specimens of them in our pension) take it all very lightheartedly. They would be less cheerful about it if the weather had been bad. The *Nation* people are gloomy. Old Massingham took it into his head to go for his holiday last Friday—started for South Wales—and has never been heard of since, Nevinson père[2] got on to my bus two days ago and talked, among other things, of Philip, whose absence from public life he lamented, saying he was one of the few people of any use. It was a very nice unsolicited testimonial.

Well, goodbye and I hope we shall see you all soon. I am *very* happy and very busy. I hope you are the first and not too much the second.

Yours affectionately,
Aldous

---

[1] J. W. N. Sullivan (1886–1937). Huxley's fellow assistant editor under John Middleton Murry at *Athenaeum*. Model for Charles May in D. H. Lawrence's *Lady Chatterley's Lover*.
[2] H(enry) W. Nevinson (1856–1941). Journalist and author, contributed to *The Nation*.

TO J. C. SQUIRE

18 Hampstead Hill Gardens, N.W.3
Monday
ca December 1919

Dear Squire,

Thank you for the letter. Yes, I shall be glad to take on the job. I'll write up some casual notes and show them you to see if they're the kind of thing wanted. I'd like, too, to go over catalogues with you and discuss the thing more in detail.

That Frenchman I spoke to you of slipped softly and silently back to France immediately after our meeting: so I couldn't get him to come to see you.

I will let you have the article on Irish folk tales by the end of the week. I've been having suppressed flu with slight fever and stomach upset, so that I have been feeling less than human these last days.

Yours,
Aldous Huxley

TO H. L. MENCKEN

18 Hampstead Hill Gardens, N.W.3
10 January 1920

Dear Sir,

May I be allowed, as a humble fellow critic, to express my great admiration for *Prejudices*, which I had the pleasure of reviewing recently for *The Athenaeum*.

I only wish we had a few more people in this country capable of producing anything as good and, at need, as destructive in the way of criticism.

Some day I hope I may have the opportunity of thanking you in person for the pleasure I have derived from your book.

Yours truly,
Aldous L. Huxley

TO CLEMENT SHORTER

18 Hampstead Hill Gardens, N.W.3
4 February 1920

Dear Mr. Shorter,
The enclosed card must be my excuse for writing to you. It would be a real privilege if I might come and see you one day. I do a good deal of literary work, chiefly for the *Athenaeum*, but also for the *New States-man, Nation* and other papers; and I should like very much to ask you if there is any possibility of an opening on your paper [*The Sphere*].

I must apologize for troubling you in this way.

Yours truly,
Aldous Huxley

TO H. L. MENCKEN

18 Hampstead Hill Gardens, N.W.3
13 February 1920

Dear Mr. Mencken,
I was very happy to get your letter and the books which followed it have just arrived. I look forward to some very pleasant hours in read-ing them. As a reprisal I venture to enclose a little volume of my own which has just come out, in the hope that it may amuse you. I believe there is to be an American edition with Doran, but my publishers are still in negotiation.

I have no control over the *Athenaeum*, but I am sure the editor, Middleton Murry, would be only too glad to give hospitality to any ar-ticle of yours on the American literary situation. Things are pretty bad here, but I fancy they have not come to quite such a pass as with you. I very much hope that when you come to England, whether in the spring or later on, you will let me know: I would arrange for the local menagerie to show its paces.

Thank you again for the books. I look forward to the autumn and your new *Prejudices*.

Yours sincerely,
Aldous Huxley

TO DOUGLAS GOLDRING

18 Hampstead Hill Gardens, N.W.3
2 March 1920

Dear Goldring,

Dell wrote to me today about the question of my being transferred from committee to Council of *Clarté*[3] going into the rarity of my attendance at meetings. This has, indeed, been shameful—partly because I have been away and partly because I am infernally busy trying to make enough money to live on by writing and have almost no time to spare. I think on the whole you had better transfer me to the Upper House, as I don't see I am likely to have any more time to spare in the immediate future. If you're ever at York Buildings on Mondays or Thursdays do look in at 10 Adelphi Terrace (Athenaeum) about lunch time, and we could lunch together. Phone me in the course of the morning of any Monday or Thursday, Gerrard 4035.

Yours,
Aldous Huxley

TO LADY OTTOLINE MORRELL

18 Hampstead Hill Gardens, N.W.3
4 March 1920

Dearest Ottoline,

I'd be most grateful, in case our little wooden hut scheme doesn't work for lack of the wherewithal, if you'd make enquiries of folk in the neighborhood about the possibility of a cottage. I'm getting rather alarmed about it, as something must be found soon. Tomorrow I go for a little hunt. I hope the hut may be feasible: but don't know about the possibility of raising the necessary four hundred.

It was very delightful seeing you yesterday. One's real friends are few enough to make their coming something of a feast-day:

Like stones of worth, they thinly placed are,
Or captain jewels in a carcanet![4]

Goodbye and much love from us both.

Yours affectionately,
Aldous

---

[3] *Clarté.* Henri Barbusse's movement, especially from 1919–1921, for international peace and social reform. Goldring was the English secretary of the movement. Robert Edward Dell (1865–1940) was a socialist journalist and chief English spokesman for *Clarté.*
[4] Shakespeare, Sonnet 52.

18, HAMPSTEAD HILL Gdns,

N.W. 3.

2.iii.20

Dear Golding,

Dell wrote to me today about
the question of my being
Transferred from committee to
Council of Clarté owing to
the rarity of my attendance at
meetings. This has, indeed, been
shameful — partly because
I have been away & partly
because I am 'infernally
busy trying to make enough
money to live on by
writing & have almost no

A 1920 letter in Huxley's hand.

time to spare. I think on
the whole you had better
transfer me to the Upper
House, as I don't see I am
likely to have any more time
to spare in the immediate
future. If you're ever at
York Buildings on Mondays
or Thursdays do look in
at 10 Adelphi Terrace (Athenaeum)
about lunch time, & we wd
lunch together. Phone in the
course of the morning of any
Monday or Thur, Gerrard
4035.

Yours
Aldous Huxley.

TO H. L. MENCKEN

18 Hampstead Hill Gardens, N.W.3
12 April 1920

My dear Mr. Mencken,
Thank you very much for your letter and the things you say of *Limbo*. I am glad it gave you amusement. My publishers have already sold an edition of a thousand copies to Doran, so I suppose it will shortly make its appearance on your side of the Atlantic.

I enclose, on the chance that you might find one or other suitable for *The Smart Set*, a play (farcical) and a story. The play is about to be published in a quarterly, of which I am one of the editors, called *Coterie*. But as it only has a circulation of at most 400 copies, of which not more than ten can find their way to the USA, I venture to think it won't matter much. The same applies to the story which is to come out in another quarterly, by name *Art and Letters*, which is almost indistinguishable in every way from *Coterie*. I have some more stories simmering on the hob but which I should like to send you when they are thoroughly cooked and finished.

Yours very sincerely,
Aldous Huxley

TO DOUGLAS GOLDRING

18 Hampstead Hill Gardens, N.W.3
30 April 1920

Dear Goldring,
I have done such a stupid thing. I meant to come to you tonight, but starting to do some work after dinner I've just woken up to the fact that it's almost 10:00 and too late, I fear, to sally forth. Please tell your wife how sorry I am. My wife would have come if it wasn't for the fact that she has just had a son and is still in bed. I hope you have a good time in Brussels.

Yours,
Aldous Huxley

TO E. S. P. HAYNES[5]

18 Hampstead Hill Gardens, N.W.3
ca 1920

Dear Ted,

Thank you for your very jolly letter and all the pleasant things you say about my "Fool's Paradise." You will find "mormal" in the prologue to the *Canterbury Tales*: it was the cook, if I remember, who, besides being an expert at making "blancmanger," had a mormal on his shin—some kind of ulcer or carbuncle. "Bejauna" is feminine of "bejaunus" from *bec jaune=blanc bec*=fresher.

By the way, I went into Chatto's today and arranged for them to send the "Leda" to you at the N.W. The other they have already sent: so I suppose it's at the N.W. office. I was pleased to learn that Henderson of the Bomb Shop[6] was so amused by it that he ordered 100 copies on the spot.

One day next week would be very pleasant for dinner. May I let you know nearer the time? Thank you again.

Yours,
Aldous

TO H. L. MENCKEN

18 Hampstead Hill Gardens, London N.W.3
26 May 1920

Dear Mr. Mencken,

Many thanks for your letter. It certainly astonishes me that even the Purity League should take offense at my poor pink pyjamas. But you know the mentality of the smuthounds—I bless you for the gift of that enchanting word—better than I. We are, at the moment, doing quite well here; for we have the Guitry company of French players in London doing Sasha Guitry's plays, so that it is actually possible to hear *cocuage* discussed upon the stage in a proper comic spirit. And our audiences really enjoy it just because it's 'so French'; though they wouldn't of course tolerate anything of the same character in English, nor would the Lord Chamberlain suffer it to see the footlights.

---

[5] E. S. P. (Ted) Haynes. A well-known lawyer and writer, he was married to Huxley's cousin Ria.
[6] Henderson was the proprietor of this socialist bookshop at 66 Charing Cross Road.

I think the best solution will be simply to omit the offending passage. It is simply a touch of romantic picturesqueness, the removal of which will make no material difference to the sense or spirit of the thing. If any other emasculations require to be made I rely on you to perform the operation.

I met here recently one Mr. Smith of the *Century Magazine* who told me he knew you; and, further that Mr. [George Jean] Nathan proposes to come over here this summer. I should be very happy to meet him if he does.

Yours sincerely,
Aldous Huxley

TO MARGUERITE BENNETT[7]

The Chelsea Book Club
65 Cheyne Walk, S.W.
26 June 1920

Dear Mrs. Bennett,
You may perhaps have heard of this little book shop and picture gallery on the river in Chelsea, where I am now acting as manager. Among our other activities we hold periodical lectures. I wondered, if it's not being too importunate, whether you would do us the honour, sometime in the autumn, of giving a recital of French poems here. We should, I think, be able to raise a fairly intelligent audience for you among the customers and club members who come to our shop for French books in which we largely specialize. Dates are vague at present; but I should suggest sometime in October. In any case, that can be arranged later.

Yours sincerely,
Aldous Huxley

TO MARGUERITE BENNETT

1917 Club
4 Gerrard Street, W.1
16, Bracknell Gdns, N.W.3
late June 1920

Dear Mrs. Bennett,
My editor has condemned me to go and hear a lecture by Saintsbury on Wednesday afternoon. I am afraid there is no getting out of it, as

---

[7] Marguerite Bennett. Arnold Bennett's first wife.

something must be written about it and there is nobody else to go. I am very much disappointed, for this will prevent my coming to hear you at the Anglo French society. If there is any means of escaping from Saintsbury, I shall come to Scala House. Otherwise I fear I must wait till your next recitation, which is on Wednesday fortnight, is it not?

I must apologize for saying I could come and then not coming. Saintsbury was sprung on me only today.

Yours sincerely,
Aldous Huxley

TO JULIAN HUXLEY

18, Hampstead Hill Gardens, N.W.3
ca October 1920

My dear Julian,
Yes let us have tea if possible on Wednesday. Say where and when. I shall probably be at the *Vogue* office that day—Holborn 308, address, 2 Breams Buildings, Chancery Lane—and could meet you pretty well anywhere in town. Very, very busy: but moderately well, tho' my doctor tells me that if I go on at this rate I shall probably have bad eyes and resultant nerve troubles in middle age. Hence aspirations to leave the whole bloody building next Spring, settle in Italy where one can live for 20,000 lire (=£250) and see if I can't make money by calmly writing what I want to write. We shall see. *Au revoir* Wed: let me know what you'd like to arrange for that afternoon.

Yours,
A.L.H.

TO H. L. MENCKEN

36 Regent Square, London, W.C.1
16 March 1921

Dear Mencken,
The arrival of your letter today brought violently to the surface a remorse that has been festering in my mind for months past. For I have owed you a letter for I hardly know how long, and what is more, a letter of thanks for the second series of *Prejudices*, which were a real pleasure to me. The first essay, on Contemporary Letters in America, was really admirable—and I have been meaning ever since before

Christmas to write and tell you so, but have not succeeded; partly because I have been horribly busy earning my livelihood, which is no excuse at all, partly because I have been lazy, which is more adequate as a justification.

I wish I had a new book to send you in revenge; but I have had neither the time nor the energy to do anything but the quotidian journalism—reviews, literary articles, dramatic criticism and the most fantastic hack-work (happily well paid) for an American fungoid growth which has established itself over here recently, called *House and Garden*. However, I am not sorry that these last months have been so intolerable, for they have brought the whole thing to a head, reduced the journalism business to the absurd. And I am now engaged in burning my boats preparatory to starting in a week's time for Italy, where money looks four times as plentiful as it does here and where, even though the principal industry of the country is the manufacture of paper money, it is still possible to live fairly cheaply. There I shall spend the next few months writing to amuse myself and seeing if I can make the process pay. If so, good; if not, then back here to journalism. My wife has gone before me to prepare my way and on Easter morning I shall enter the City of Florence in triumph, resurrected from this tomb of darkness. My address there will be 1 Via Margherita Montici, Florence—or at least, that will always find me.

You speak of Lawrence. Rumor assigns a pleasing reason for his writing so badly now. It is said that he was psycho-analysed last year and that with the scotching of his numerous complexes and resultant sanity—for he used to be a bit of a sexual maniac—he has entirely lost the power of writing novels and is only at home when he is pouring forth little lucubrations about baa lambs and daffodils. He is living in Sicily at present, where I shall not go and visit him; for he and his Prussian wife, *geboren* Von Richthoven [sic], are the most formidable couple I have ever known—or were, at any rate, before the psychoanalysis, since when, of course, it is possible they have become as tame as Anglicans. Am I right in supposing that his book, *Women in Love*, written about four years ago, has been published by subscription or privately or something of the sort in America? If so you should read it. It contains some quite incredibly grotesque things, including some stupendous chapters about an old friend of mine, Lady Ottoline Morrell, who is represented as attempting to murder Lawrence with a lapis lazuli paperweight and only failing to do so because the nimble L. takes cover under a volume of Thucydides which he happens at the moment to be reading. It's all just like Ouida. What an odd thing it is in a man who has done such exceedingly good things!

There is not much history here. The perishing of the *Athenaeum* as an independent paper and its incorporation with the *Nation* is the most significant and most melancholy literary event.

What other news? Mr. Clutton-Brock is now known to write his sermon-leaders in the *Times Literary Supplement* by means of automatic writing; he sits still and his pen disgorges the excrements from his brain at the rate of 1800 words an hour. Result: vast salary for Brock and ever increasing popularity and esteem. I can think of nothing else very epoch making.

I will write again from Italy and possibly send something which you might like to print in *The Smart Set*. Meanwhile, farewell. I suppose there is no prospect of your visiting These Shores during the course of the summer?

Yours sincerely,
Aldous Huxley

TO EDWARD MARSH

36 Regent Square, W.C.1
21 March 1921

Dear Eddie,
I shall be most happy to write in your book. I shall see you probably at tomorrow's first night at the Queen's or whenever "Nightie Night" (good lord!) is going to be done. The easiest thing for me would be to return with you then to Gray's Inn, which is also on the way home, and write *in situ*.

Otherwise sometime on Wednesday—as I leave Thursday morning.

I'm happy to be off: journalism was becoming altogether too much. I only hope I shall be able to make enough money by other writing to be able to escape from it forever.

Yours,
Aldous Huxley

1921

TO DOROTHY RICHARDSON[8]

Castel Montici
Via Santa Margherita a Montici
Florence
ca March 1921

Dear Miss Richardson,
Whenever I wrote from the offices of *Vogue* to your address in Queen's Terrace, the letters were punctually returned on the score that you were unknown. (Dull postmen! They argued themselves unknown by that.) So I gave it up. And now comes your letter about the dripping taps. Let me make one more effort and try to thank you for the advice it contains. I have moved house luckily about six times since that was written and am at this moment engaged in moving once more—to Italy this time, where the water comes out of a well, so that there is no danger of it dripping unless it starts falling upwards. Should you ever pass through Florence, won't you call and have a look at the well?

Yours sincerely,
Aldous Huxley

TO JULIAN HUXLEY

Villa Minucci
4 Via Santa Margherita Montici
Florence
12 April 1921

How are you? We flourish here settled in the wing of a pleasant villa a little higher up the road than the Fasolas. We have three large rooms of which one is so vast—30 ft. long—that we divide it into 2 and use it as a sleep or sit room. Florence seethes with people one knows—embarrassingly. One has to take care to avoid too many social entanglements. Ottoline and Julian are here for the time on their way thro'—O. extenuated with neuralgia, which puts her out of action all day until the evening—poor woman.

---

[8] Dorothy Richardson (1873–1957). Pioneer of stream-of-consciousness technique in her novel sequence *Pilgrimage*. She had written Huxley in response to his comic essay "Water Music," first published in *Athenaeum*, 20 August 1920. In a letter dated 4 January 1938, Huxley declined an offer from Richard Church to comment on her work, adding, however, "Of Miss Richardson's work I know only two or three volumes at most—enough, however, to make me think her work very interesting and technically significant."

I do a certain amount of work in the mornings, eat and sleep a good deal, read as little as possible, very rarely go sightseeing, occasionally visit the natives.

Florence is splendid when one is outside it. As a town it is rather a disappointment. There is practically no exciting architecture. I pant for the intelligent nobility of baroque. This late medieval stuff, such as the Palazzo Vecellio, is just boring, like the Oxford Colleges. However, there are some good pictures. Matthew grows enormously. I hope Francis does the same.

Love,
Aldous

TO NAOMI MITCHISON

ca 1 August 1921

My dear Naomi,

Your letter provokes a tardy reprisal. But the writing of letters is one of the things I am not very good at. You knew it already perhaps? My excuses are better than usual: I am busy half the day and I am idle during the other half. Obviously there is no available time in which to write letters. I am busy with a comic novel which I am pledged to finish in seven days' time—and which I shall not finish for another fifteen or twenty days. It is to be published in the Autumn I hope. Meanwhile I am grieved to hear of your unsuccess with your literary products. Your error is to write about Vercingetorix when you might write about me. What the public likes is not ancient Gaul but modern Gall (a ripe *paronomassia*). Gossip over 2,000 years old is apt to lose its spice. You should push on if not to modern times at least as far as the Renaissance. I have discovered the most superb historical character whose biography I propose to write some day—Paganini, the violinist: one of the real comics. He is the sort of man one should write historical novels about.

Why don't you come and spend a summer on this coast? It's perfect for children, it's not too hot if you lead a sensible life and go to sleep after lunch; it's extremely beautiful, a combination of sea, wooded plain and mountains and the present exchange is cheap. We calculate to be able to live in comfort on £300 a year here. The worst is however that haven't got £300 a year—and I hesitate whether it is best to remain in Italy and risk not making the £300 out of the novel, stories or occasional journalism or whether it is wiser to come back to England to a certain £700 or £800 a year (on which one could live at about the same degree of comfort) to regular work and to fatigue. It's a problem. What a monstrous thing it is to have no money of one's own. In any case Maria and I will be returning in Oct.; perhaps for good, certainly for a month or two in order to find a new flat in which to put our furniture. You don't know of a convenient place of four or five rooms I suppose: not more than £100 a year? No—it isn't likely. We shall see you then I hope.

TO RUSSELL GREEN

29 Viale Morin
Forte dei Marmi
(Lucca)
5 September 1921

My dear Russell,
Compelled to return rather precipitately to England to arrange about finding a new flat—the term during which I could keep my furniture in the old having been, for one reason and another rather curtailed—I send out a tentative appeal to you and to Tommy, if he is there. Quite likely there will be accommodation at father's house; but if by chance there should not be, could you suffer the presence of self and better half in one of the rooms at Regent Square from about the 17th or 18th of this month for a few days? I should be full of gratitude if it could be arranged.

By the way, it occurs to me that it might be of interest to you to know that we propose to fill a flat with furniture and let it. As Regent Square is a transient glory, it occurred to me that you and Mrs. R. might care to take the flat and pay a small rent for furniture over and above the flat rent. Or if you don't want it yourself, I'd be glad if you'd let me know if any one of your acquaintance would like the arrangement.

All this business is a great vexation of spirit.

In any case, I hope to see you soon and, let us hope, the good Thomas quite soon. As the post has suddenly become three times as slow as it has ever been before, will you answer about the possibilities of Regent Square to my father's address: 16 Bracknell Gardens, Hampstead, N.W.3.

It will be pleasing to hear six months arrears of contemporary history. Flourish.

A.L.H.

By the way, I believe I left a tie pin in my room when I departed; you might ask Mrs. S. if it's still existent.

TO LADY OTTOLINE MORRELL

155 Westbourne Terrace, W.2
3 December 1921

Dearest Ottoline,

Your letter bewildered me. I cannot understand how anyone could suppose that this little marionette performance of mine was the picture of a real *milieu:*—it so obviously isn't. You might as justifiably accuse Shaw of turning Garsington into Heartbreak House or Peacock of prophesying it in Nightmare Abbey and Gryll Grange. I have made use of the country house convention because it provides a simple device for getting together a fantastic symposium. My error, I admit, was to use some of Garsington's architectural details. I ought to have laid the scene in China—nobody could have had any doubt then that it was a marionette show.

For, after all, the characters are nothing but marionettes with voices, designed to express ideas and the parody of ideas. A caricature of myself in extreme youth is the only approach to a real person; the others are puppets—marionette of a superstitious woman with a passion for horse-racing, marionette of a book-loving antiquary, marionette of a garrulous cynic, marionette of an artist resembling Lord Byron and painting like Caravaggio, marionette of a serious young lady and of a frivolous ditto, marionette of Mr. Clement K. Shorter (a real figure, I grant you) and marionette of a deaf woman. (I admit that Brett is deaf; but you will observe that the only individual characteristic attributed to this person is not one of Brett's and that the physical peculiarities mentioned are shared by all deaf people.) They have about as much reality as Dr. Opimian and Lord Curryfin in *Gryll Grange*, and rather less than the Captain and Mazzini Dunn in *Heartbreak House*. I shall be grateful if you will tell me anyone of whom these marionettes are supposed to be portraits. I may say that other people have told me that they are portraits—of people I scarcely know and who have never been near Garsington. So you see why I am bewildered by your letter.

If I had set out to describe Garsington—which I have neither the desire nor, for that matter, the capacity to do; for I am not a realist and don't take much interest in the problem of portraying real living people—the picture would have been, as you surely must see, a little less mechanically simple than *Crome Yellow*. As it is, the thing is merely a little comedy of ideas, where the personages are just voices—*et praeterea nihil*. They are puppets, devoid of all emotions, devoid indeed of most of the attributes of living humanity. They are just alive enough to talk—that is all. My mistake, I repeat, was to have borrowed the stage setting from Garsington. I am sorry; but it never for a moment occurred to me that anyone would have so little imagination—or perhaps so much—as to read into a comedy of ideas a portrait of the life of the place in which it is laid. Ask yourself honestly, has it any resemblance? As for treating your friends with contempt—well, what is one to say? The only contempt I have shown consists in not writing about them; but about a series of perfectly fantastic marionettes with generalized qualities and a capacity for talking.

Next time I write a puppet-comedy of ideas I shall lay the scene a thousand miles away from England. That will, I hope make impossible misunderstandings such as this. For it is absurd—and at the same time distressing and painful to a degree—that a long and cherished friendship should run the risk of being broken because the scene for a comedy of puppets has been laid in surroundings partly recognizable as real. I did not imagine when I was writing that people could argue from the reality of the place to the reality of the people; and they must indeed see portraits in trees and hear them in the wind who find real persons in a collection of marionettes, not only unlike anybody of my acquaintance, but also deliberately and studiedly, unlike any whole and complete human being.

This incident is to me another proof of something I said in the book: we are all parallel straight lines destined to meet only at infinity. Real understanding is an impossibility. I write something which seems to me immediately and obviously comprehensible for what it is. You, running on your parallel, read into it meanings I never so much as dreamt of. Others, on their parallels, find other meanings and contemptuous portraits of people unknown to you.

What is one to do or say? I really don't know except that I am always
                    Yours very affectionately,
                            Aldous

TO H. L. MENCKEN

155 Westbourne Terrace
5 February 1922

Dear Mencken:
I left word with my publishers to send you a copy of this little book when it came out: but on making enquiries about various matters at

their office recently, I find it wasn't done. So I hasten to remedy this defect of courtesy, with the hope that the thing may amuse you a little.

I am back in this decaying Metrollopis, functioning chiefly on the great Mr. Condé Nast's publication which, though not inordinately high, the Crow[9] pays adequately—which no literary journal does.

When I have hoarded a few pence, I shall flit off once more to some cheap Dago State for rest and refreshment. But meanwhile I am pretty well fixed here.

And you—is there any prospect of your early arrival? I have been seeing an acquaintance of yours in H. B. Liveright, who has been here astonishing the natives and whom I liked very much.

Yours sincerely,
Aldous Huxley

TO JULIAN HUXLEY

Vogue, Rolls House
Breams Buildings, E.C.4
7 June 1922

My dear J,
I have aroused in the *Vanity Fair* man a certain enthusiasm for popular science, and he would like to consider an article or two from you. I should think one on Heredity and perhaps one slightly Wellsian forecast of the possible achievements of biology in the future (pointing out how much more interesting is control of life than control of machinery) would be a good beginning. But really what you like, so long as it is pretty light and bright—as it will be next to photographs of Lopokova and the Dolly Sisters.

The ideal length is 1750 words and the pay—American rights only—about one pound (can't find symbol) per hundred words. Mr. Crowninshield has no objection to *réchauffé* English articles, provided they are up-to-date and not too heavy or technical.

Yours in haste,
ALH

---

[9] Frank Crowinshield (1872–1947). Editor of *Vanity Fair*, owned by Condé Nast (1873–1942).

TO EDWARD MARSH

155 Westbourne Terrace, W.2
19 June 1922

Dear Eddie,
It is very kind of you to invite me to contribute to *Georgian Poetry*, and I hope you will not think me rude or ungrateful if I say, no. The fact is that I write very little verse nowadays and what I do write I like to print only in my own books or in *Wheels*, which has become, after all the years, a habit.

Yours,
Aldous Huxley

TO H. L. MENCKEN

Schloss Hellbrunn bei Salzburg
13 August 1922

I hear from various sources that you are now or shortly will be in England, and Saxton, of Doran and Company, tells me you frequent Dicke's Hotel. I wish I were there to see you but I am taking a beer cure in Salzburg and listening to Mozart, going on to Italy for a few weeks tomorrow. Do let me know there:

Villa Tacchella
Forte dei Marmi
(Lucca)

How long you will be in Europe and if there will be any hope of seeing you.

Yours,
Aldous Huxley

TO JOHN MAYNARD KEYNES

Vogue
Rolls House
Breams Buildings
London E.C. 4
9 October 1922

Dear Maynard,
I met Clive the other night and asked him to deliver a message to you. He probably has not done so. At any rate, it was this:

Mr. Condé Nast, being a great admirer of your works and having the economic reconstruction of Europe greatly at heart, is most desirous of securing an article on the subject from you, to appear in *Vanity Fair*. Would you be prepared to write one? About 2000 words or more if you wanted more space. And at what rate?

Will you let me know here; and I will communicate with Nast or the amiable editor of *Vanity Fair*, Mr. Crowninshield, so that if necessary they can write to you direct about it. You will probably be nominated for the Hall of Fame; but you mustn't mind that.

I had never made use of the permission you so kindly gave, months ago, to have the Duncan and Vanessa paintings in your room photographed. The plan for having an article on mural paintings fell through at that time. But we may revive it again; in which case I will let you know when the photographer would come and take the pictures.

Yours,
Aldous Huxley

TO MARY HUTCHINSON

Vogue
Holborn 308
4 December 1922

May I keep you to your promise, dear Mary, next Thursday?

There is a choice of music: the Magic Flute at the Old Vic; or else the Philharmonic at the Q[ueen]'s Hall with a programme, choral, instrumental of Brahms, Delius, and finally—to produce the ultimate *frisson* of mingled *volupté* and horror—Scriabine's "Prometheus."

Will you come? Ring me up tomorrow morning about 11:30 and say—as I so much hope dear Mary—yes.

How much I enjoyed last Friday: I always used, in the past, to be so terribly shy and nervous of you. Why? I hardly know—unless it was your air of impenetrable serenity that disquieted me. What are you really like? I am able now to be curious as well as frightened.

Aldous

TO MARY HUTCHINSON

155 Westbourne Terrrace, W.2
Fall 1922

My dear Mary,
The last post has gone. But remembering that you like receiving letters—even, I venture to hope, from tired business men—I am writing to say how much I shall enjoy coming to dine with you tomorrow.

All I ask—since I have given up the Hungarian Quartet to pass an evening with you, is that you should one day give up an evening to come with me to a Quartet. May we take that as a settled principle? It only remains to fix a good programme and a convenient day.

Aldous

TO MARY HUTCHINSON

Brussels
Tuesday

Your old gentlemen, dear Mary, were content I hope last Thursday? My evening was less agreeable than theirs. A dullish concert, relieved by a flash of Delius—followed by a literary *conversazione* at Miss Royde-Smith's. Such is life in the Great West. But I shall ring you up on my return—Thursday morning I think—to find out if the old gentlemen are dining with you on Friday or Saturday. At this distance from the metropolis I don't know if there are any good concerts on those days. But if there aren't, does it really matter?

As for the goodness of the food in this country—well, all I can say is that I wish we could get anything like it when we dine, as I so much hope we shall, on Friday, or Saturday, or Monday, Tuesday, Wednesday, Thursday . . .

Yours,
Aldous

TO MARY HUTCHINSON

In the Train
20 December 1922

Mary,
When shall I see you again? May it be soon? Boxing Night, you say, was vacant. Is it still?

My head turns a little when I think of you—still as enigmatic as ever, still somehow a little alarming in your serenity.

The drunk man sitting next to me—the one in the pink paper hat—is singing a sentimental song

—My arms embrace an emp-er-ty space
—You brought the sunshine to our ally
—That's why I'm jealous of you.

—Curious fragments.

He is gone now and so am I, Mary.

A.

TO MARY HUTCHINSON

155 Westbourne Terrace, W.2
Late December 1922

A la cruelle qui exige
Que l'on respecte ses appas
Va, savon nu et callipyge
Dire que je n'obéis pas.

En Souvenir de la nuit de
Noel et pour demander
Quand je vous reverrai

Si je suis impatient, comme l'est sur le Sèvres
Un berger que sa nymphe anime d'un regard,
C'est, Mary, qu'une main s'est portée à
Mes lèvres—
Inespérée—et non (dites, non!) par hasard.

[To the cruel one who demands
That one respect her charms
Go, soap naked and round-bottomed
Say that I will not obey.

In remembrance of Christmas night
And to ask when I will see you again.

If I am impatient, like the shepherd of the Sèvres,
Whose nymph revives him with one look,
It's because, Mary, your hand unexpectedly found my lips
And not, say not, by chance.]

TO MARY HUTCHINSON

Mrs. Hutchinson
River House
Upper Mall Hammersmith
Telegram
28 December 1922

Have risen early to beg you forgive a stupidity that was rather offensive and to request an opportunity not to repeat it.

Aldous

TO H. L. MENCKEN

The Athenaeum
Pall Mall, S.W.1
December 1922

Dear Mencken,
I enclose a little fictional machine which you might find usable in *The Smart Set.*

How goes life in the Great West? Here we are made daily conscious of a steady increase in imbecility. The Press and now the Wireless Telephone are doing wonders in the way of spreading darkness, vulgarity, fifteenth-rateness, folly, mental idleness, cant, confusion, waste of energy: one can see the results at once. The gulf between the populace and those engaged in any intelligent occupation of whatever kind steadily widens. In twenty years time a man of science or a serious artist will need an interpreter in order to talk to a cinema proprietor or a member of his audience. However, perhaps it's all for the best: who knows. In any case, the Consolations of Philosophy will never fail us here in England so long as the Upper House retains its present 2/3 majority of titled brewers and distillers.

The seasonable benedictions.

Yours,
Aldous Huxley

PS
I shall be moving house sometime in January to 44 Princes Gardens, S.W.; but the address of this conventicle of Bishops and academicians will always find me.

TO MARY HUTCHINSON

5 January 1923

I feel like a man who has had malaria and who suddenly, after a long respite, recognizes the old symptoms and knows that in a few hours he will be shivering and raving with fever. But for my sort of fever there is no specifical quinine. Only, perhaps, work. But, damn it all, I don't want to work: I want to play—not a game but a new sort of music, a Mozartian relationship! Dear Mary; some time, I am not entirely without hope, there may be altered circumstances and, for me, a happier conjunction of stars. And then I shall have so much tenderness to give you—all you deserve. Why did I never take the trouble to find out before that you were what you are—so decent, so tremendously nice (there don't seem to be any but these idiotic words, but what I mean is so serious and important) as well as all the rest?

Will you forgive me, Mary, for having been such a dull bore last night? In the circumstances—incipient malaria, you know!—it's difficult to shine.

I am sending the Aubreys so that I shall in any case have an excuse for seeing you when I come to fetch them again after you've finished them. But I shall want to see you long before that. Goodbye. I kiss your hands because I am not allowed to kiss your mouth.

A.

TO HUMBERT WOLFE[1]

44 Princes Gardens, S.W. 7
15 January 1923

Dear Wolfe,
I hesitate very much to pester you—for I know how hateful it is to be pestered. But bitter constraint and sad occasion have brought me to it: so that I hope you'll forgive me.

Some three weeks ago I put in an application to the Labour Ministry for a permit for my child's German nurse (who was here in England for six months last year and is now on a holiday in Germany and to come back). After promising that the permit would be ready

---

[1] Humbert Wolfe (1886–1940). Poet and civil servant, known for his epigram, "You cannot hope to bribe or twist thank God! The British journalist. / But, seeing what the man will do unbribed, there's no occasion to."

by today, I find that nothing has been done at all and that consequently it may be weeks before we get her back. I should be enormously grateful if you could in some way cause the wheels of God to grind less slowly—for the nurse's absence is putting a great strain on my wife.

The nurse, who was my nurse when I was a child, was with my family for fifteen years and has been with me, in England, Italy and Belgium, for the last eighteen months or more. When she came last year to England we had no dealings at all with the Labour Ministry; but this time the Home Office has pushed us on to your department.

I hope we shall someday work in our long postponed luncheon. I have just moved into the flat lately occupied by Miss Royde Smith. Perhaps we shall see you when you come to her parties, which now take place on a lower floor.

With every possible apology,

Yours,
Aldous Huxley

TO MARY HUTCHINSON

44 *Princes Gardens, S.W.*7
16 January 1923

Dearest Mary,
Next Saturday at midnight they are doing a little play of mine called "Happy Families" at the Cave of Harmony.[2] Could you and Jack come to dinner here and proceed at leisure to the club afterwards? I hope so very much. Or perhaps if you can't dine, could you meet us here or there or at the Tower after dinner? The season of concerts is about to begin again. Will you come with me one evening if I can find something really suitable to you—an evening of Mozart, for instance, just to indicate how two people might know one another, lightly and profoundly—might, if only . . .

Could you ring up Kensington 6551 before 11:00 tomorrow, Wednesday, morning and tell Maria if you can come.

Goodbye,
Aldous

---

[2] London cabaret run by Elsa Lanchester.

TO MARY HUTCHINSON

27 February 1923
Monday
Midnight

Reopening after fifty millenniums—or were they in fact no more than fifty days?—the tomb in which a certain little Eros, cruelly massacred while still (worse luck) an innocent, lies buried, I came this evening upon the Canopic Vase, shaped in the form of a woman singularly graceful and slender, containing one of my own hearts—embalmed, but still despite the coolness of the receptacle, still palpitating. Ah, Mary, these Egyptian explorations, these secret treasures, these serpents of the old Nile (how more than ever alluring tonight!), these poor captive Romans . . .

Brief Lives, Mary, brief as Aubrey's[3]—and yonder all before us lie. . . . And talking of Egypt:

Nous ne serons jamais une seule momie
Sous l'antique désert et les palmiers heureux?

A sole mummy, non: mais
Sous les palmiers, même sous
Les chènes, ne serons nous pas—
Peut-être et j'ose espérer—ne
Serons nous jamais un seul
être vivant, une seule âme, un
Seul corps?

[We will never be a single mummy
Under the ancient desert and happy palms?]
A single mummy, no: but
Under the palms, even under
The oaks, may we not—
I dare to hope—
May we not be one living being,
One soul, one body?
            —S. Mallarmé (1842–1898), "Tristesse d'été"]
                              A

---

[3] John Aubrey (1626–1697). Author of biographical notes not published in a definitive edition until the 1898 *Brief Lives*, ed. Andrew Clark.

TO MARY HUTCHINSON

ca March 1923

Masks, Mary? You were so right about the masks. The Catholic Church which knows so much more about the soul (pardon the expression) than all the upstart psychologists, always arranged that confessionals should be dark: when the face is hidden, the heart reveals itself. Masks? Darkness?

And what about Cambridge? There are charming lines in Laforgue: you remember?

> *"Si tu savais, maman Nature,*
> *Comme je m'aime en tes ennuis,*
> *Tu m'enverrais une enfant pure,*
> *Chaste aux 'Et puis?'"*

> [If you only knew, Mama Nature,
> How I love myself in the troubles you give me,
> You would send me a pure girl,
> Chaste compared to all those "what nexts?"
>
> —Jules Laforgue (1860–1887),
> "Complainte-placet de Faust fils"]

Mais cette fois-ci je n'ai le moindre désire de m'aimer. [But this time I haven't the least desire to love myself.] There are others besides myself. And as for this *enfant pure*—no, no.

Dear Mary, are you ever in London towards the middle of the day? Could you, would you, then, lunch with me next Tuesday or Wednesday?

Aldous

TO MARY HUTCHINSON

44 Princes Gardens, S.W.7
dated 2 March 1923
sent 2 April 1923

It would delight me very much, dear Mary, if you would dine with me on Friday or Saturday night and go to what is perhaps the only good play written in this country for several centuries—"At Mrs. Beam's"— which I saw when it was first done several years ago by the Stage Society and which I should like very much to see again, particularly in your company.

Could you, would you come? Please do.

Did you have a pleasant Easter holiday? I spent this afternoon on the Heath, my sole outing (except for an afternoon at the Club reading Sir Richard Burton's notes to the *Arabian Nights* and his essay on pederasty: but that I count as study and self-education, not holiday).

Goodbye. I shall be so happy if you can come.

Aldous

TO MARY HUTCHINSON

44 Princes Gardens, S.W.7
5 April 1923

Alas, dear Mary, I shall be gone by the time you return. Otherwise *Mrs. Beam* might have entertained as well next week as this. Your retreat sounds charming. Retreat—advance? *Mais on ne me permet pas d'en faire—les avances.*

This town has become too insupportable. I am leaving earlier than I intended.

Au revoir,
A.L.H.

TO MARY HUTCHINSON

65 Victoria Road
Kensington, W.
18 July 1923

The misery of dashed anticipations: the cold unhappy anger of the disappointed against the raiser and the destroyer of charming hopes: and then the delight of renewed hope, the profound gratitude.

—Dearest Mary, I wish I could flatter myself that this recital of the morning's feeling will be of interest to you. Perhaps a little? Will you tell me tomorrow?

TO MARY HUTCHINSON

65 Victoria Road
26 July 1923

Not my heart's blood Mary; but by a charming and symbolic accident the nearest ink happened to be red—the nearest paper pink.

How much I enjoyed seeing you again—how very much! And now you're going away, and then I'm going away . . . melancholy, melancholy. And yet it might be so gay and delightful—just a meeting—all the enchantments—and then away again with hardly a footprint to show.

Dear Mary, I wish I could see you again, before I go. Would there be any hope of seeing you tomorrow evening—on your way back, perhaps? Or on your way out even? I shall be working and only longing by that time to be called from labour. Or in the country—how delightful it would be to see you for a moment there! Say yes, or at least something like it, please.

A

TO MARY HUTCHINSON

65 Victoria Road
27 July 1923

"No answer today." But confess, Mary, that there might have been an answer—or very nearly an answer—on that balcony, with that moon busily uniting, like Lord Haldane, a "Pathway to Reality" across the water. It is my misfortune never to be there at the same time with you and the Pathway. I always have to go away, miserably—to write letters in red ink, which you receive the next day (centuries later), when they seem in your morning eyes curiously ludicrous and inapposite. It is my misfortune a little, as well, no doubt, as my fault. For it is my fault

Se Dentro del tuo cor morte e peitate
Porti in un tempo, e che 'l mio basso ingegno
Non sappia, ardendo, trarne altro che morte.

[If within your heart you bear at the one time death and pity, and my miserable wit does not know, though burning, how to draw anything from you but death.—Michelangelo Buonarroti, *Rime* 151]

My *basso ingegno* has drawn of late altogether too much death out of love. I don't want to suffer at all any more, at any rate for a long time.

I want to laugh and exchange delightful sentiments, ideas, and kisses. And meanwhile you are always no more that the rustle of a skirt disappearing round the corner: you are a perfume in a corridor and the discreet closing of a door. And one evening conceivably—I flatter myself perhaps unduly—you might feel that it was time, today, for an answer. But I would be a long way off: and by the time I arrived you would be feeling something entirely different and it would be the same rustle, the same evanescence of perfume, and the same closing of a door. And I should feel the same desire to curse, to cry, to laugh and to struggle as I feel now. Shall I see you again before I go? You needn't answer. But on the other hand you might. *Chi sa?*

I was charmed by your article. How many characters have you hung up in your wardrobes? What fun it is dressing up as somebody else. There is a lot in the book I have just been writing about that. And that reminds me that I must go on with writing my revision of it. Damn. Goodbye, Mary. Will there be any answer? You must promise to come and stay with us in Florence. There are so many pathways in the Italian landscape.

Aldous

TO T. S. ELIOT

15 Via S. Margherita a Montici
Florence
19 January 1924

Dear Tom,
I am enclosing an article on Breughel, which I think would do much better for the *Criterion* than the other I sent you; this last, on rereading, seems to me too long and rambling. Breughel is more to the point and briefer.

London, to judge by your letter, can be no gayer than it was. I hear that its literary amenities are to be increased by a new magazine, edited by Mr. Edgell Rickword.[4] To me, the prospect is only mildly exciting.

In haste, yours,
ALH

---

[4] John Edgell Rickword (1898–1982). Leftist editor of the *Calendar of Modern Letters* from March 1925 until 1927.

1924

TO MARY HUTCHINSON

8 March 1924

Another Beauty for you. Can it be a portrait of Lalla [Vandervelde⁵]? Montie [Shearman]⁶ would know, perhaps. We fled from Castile where the cold was indescribable—sleet driven by a 70 m.p.h. gale all the way from Madrid to Burgos. And as for the temperature at the Escorial— Siberian. What a strange masochist Philip II must have been! Such frightful mortifications of the flesh; when he'd only but to go 2 or 3 hundred miles to find sugar cane and cotton growing, Here the Spanish cold has given way to a familiar English autumn weather. Dark but lovely.

Love,
Aldous

TO ORLO WILLIAMS⁷

15 Via S. Margherita a Montici
Florence
14 May 1924

Dear Orlo Williams,
I have to thank you very much for a very long, pleasant and interesting letter. The news about your illness is distressing: but I hope the inflation you report will be permanent and the horror definitively averted. I only marvel that you should pass your convalescence at Hastings, when the whole Italian peninsula lies open, complete with the best bathing, excellent mountains and, if required, exceedingly powerful aperient waters. Personally I never mean to live for any length of time, if I can help it, in England again. The horrors of the eight months winter are too much to be borne. True, we have had a relatively very bad winter here: but the worst of it was over so soon and the intermediate spells were so brilliant, that it hardly mattered it all.

We live outside the town—you probably know the little church of S. Margherita at the end of the ridge on which the *Torre del Gallo* stands: our house is next to it—consequently contrive to see almost nobody which is most essential, considering the society of Florence. I do a lot of work—got a volume of short stories done this winter, which is to be published in a few weeks time and am at work now on a long and

---

⁵ Lalla Speyer Vandervelde. Author of *Monarchs and Millionaires* (1925) and wife of Belgian socialist politician Emile Vandervelde.
⁶ Montague Shearman (1885–1932). Barrister and art collector.
⁷ Orlo Williams (1883–1967). Author and reviewer.

difficult book. I think you will like some of the short stories: they are tolerably good, I think. We have had J. W. N. Sullivan staying with us for the last four months—very good and stimulating company, which I miss very much now that he is gone.

Reggie Turner I do occasionally see and much like. The other great Florentine attraction is Norman Douglas, incredibly mellow and jolly: one of those very tough knots whose characters are not essentially affected by their actions but remain, in spite of the toughness of them, extremely pleasant and even admirable.

I saw a very kindly reference of yours to *On the Margin* in an Italian review (I stupidly forget the name) this autumn. Thank you, indeed. As for Italian books worth reading—I asked for a list from Carlo Placi the other day—who suggested practically nothing. Ojetti's *Cose viste* he thought the best thing that had appeared of late. *Chi sa?*

I read a so-called futurist novel the other day, called *Un Ventre di Donna*—not at all futurist in the main, but a rather good personal narrative by a woman who had undergone a serious operation on her ovaries. As an account of illness it's good.

If ever you come this way, do let me know. There is always a dish of spaghetti and some wine on tap and often a spare room. Please remember me to your wife.

Yours,
Aldous Huxley

TO SYDNEY WATERLOW[8]

Villa Fasola
Forte dei Marmi
(Lucca)
8 July 1924

Dear Waterlow,
May I thank you for your admirable article on Rimbaud in last week's *New Statesman*. It seemed to me about as good as it could be. I only wish there could have been more of it.

---

[8] Sydney Waterlow (1878–1944). Served as British Minister in Bangkok, 1926–1928. Virginia Woolf wrote in 1929, " . . . he would like to go back to Bangkok and be important in the East forever" (*Diary*, vol. 3, 224). Huxley apparently did not go to Bangkok, since on 4 March 1926 he writes to Julian about having stayed with the Guillemards at Government House and of his plans to leave for Java on 5 March, thence back to Singapore and then on to Borneo, Southern Philippines, Manila, then to board a liner for San Francisco on 7 April. Waterlow was a cousin of Katherine Mansfield.

I have not seen Rickwood's book. If he has made many mistranslations like the one you point out—which is sufficiently gross and glaring—it must be rather unsatisfactory, if only because the man can't know what Rimbaud's poetry is about. So far as I'm aware the decent life and criticism of this fabulous creature still remains to be written. Those dismal affairs of Paterne Berrichon[9] are very depressing. Claudel's introduction is all right; but a bit too Catholic. Those reminiscences by his sister of the last illness were very moving and somehow rather frightful. Is it recorded anywhere that he talked with anyone on subjects other than financial in the second part of his life?

Here, at the edge of the Mediterranean, with the Carrara Mountains at the back, I don't envy you London; nor look forward very much to going there in August—which I shall have to do. The only compensation will be seeing a few people.

Yours sincerely,
Aldous Huxley

TO MARY HUTCHINSON

23 September 1924

Dearest Mary,
Maria tells me that I had a most depressing effect on you the other evening. How can I counteract it? By telling you how much I enjoyed Sunday evening? And how I wished that our Last Ride Together might have continued and continued forever, through the rain? But I know, alas, only too well, by experience, how little such an assurance, coming from me, is calculated to raise your spirits. If I knew that it would, I think I should find the ascetic life still more hopelessly difficult to lead than I do now. What successful lover would desire to quit the world for the Thebaid? But I have not been successful. Still, I am yours hopefully and in all circumstances very affectionately,

Aldous

P.S. If only you'd come to Italy . . .

---

[9] Paterne Berrichon (1855–1922). French man of letters, editor of Rimbaud.

TO T. S. ELIOT

15 Via S. Margherita a Montici
Florence
19 December 1924

Dear Tom,

I have been dreadfully busy all the autumn, doing a book of essays and what not—all vaguely suggested by travel—for the spring. Hence I've not been able to do the thing on journalism which I hoped to do. But I am enclosing a rather rambling disquisition about a great many things and nothing in particular, which you might care to print in the *Criterion* in its place.

How are you both? I should like to hear of you, and whether you're still intending, sooner or later, to come southwards. There is a passage in Boswell, where Dr. Johnson talks about climate. "Sir, no man is made happy by a climate,"[1] or words to that effect. But Dr. J. is quite wrong. If one's temperament is not too sociable, one can easily dispense with society on condition that one has sunshine and the country.

I have had no news from the literary world—except rumors, both from Murry and from [J. W. N.]Sullivan, of some sort of bust up on the *Adelphi*. But in spite of it, I contrive to keep my head and remain calm! Who, by the way, is a very good new critic of novels who writes in the *New Statesman* under the name of John Franklin? Is there a Mr. Franklin?[2] Or does the name—surprisingly unfamiliar; for I thought I'd heard of everyone who ever wrote an article in the weekly papers—conceal some old friend? I fancy it can't. For there aren't many old friends who could write with such sense and such judgment.

Do let me hear how you do. Maria joins in sending you both our best wishes for the festive etc.

Yours,
Aldous Huxley

---

[1] Boswell, 9 May 1772. Johnson said, "What is climate to happiness? . . . What proportion does climate bear to the complex system of human life? You may advise me to go live at Bologna to eat sausages. The sausages there are the best in the world; they lose much by being carried."
[2] Franklin was, in fact, Sydney Waterlow.

TO CARLO LINATI[3]

15 Via S. Margherita a Montici
Firenze
22 January 1925

Dear Signor Linati,

Please excuse me for not having written before to thank you for sending me a copy of the *Corriere* with your excellent article. The fact is I have been dreadfully busy these last ten days, finishing off some work which had to get done in a hurry, so that I had no time to write. Now, I am happy to say, the work is done and I have a little leisure.

I liked your article very much. It seems to me that you have made all the main points that are to be made about my books. The first, of course, are very young and, in a sophisticated way, jejune. But they are improving, I hope, in sense and ripeness. I will send you a copy of my new novel [*Those Barren Leaves*], which is just on the point of coming out, when I have one. I think it is the best thing I have done so far.

Have you read E. M. Forster's *A Passage to India*? If not, do so quickly. It is a masterly book, which you certainly ought to write an article on in the *Corriere*. It is the best study of the relation of the English to the Indians that I know: all the hopelessness of the situation, the impossibility—with the best will in the world—of achieving anything is exquisitely and undidactically set forth. And then the writing is beautiful. Forster is one of our most interesting novelists at present. The book, if you want to get a review copy, is published by Edward Arnold.

I hope if you're ever in Florence you will let us know. It is possible that we may be in the north of Italy some time this early spring—for I have a great longing to see again all those miraculous towns on the Via Emilia from Bologna to Parma and then Mantua and Verona and Brescia—in fact *all*, if it were only possible. In which case I should try to take in Milan, which I don't know at all well—in fact, except for the Brera[4] and the cathedral, practically not at all. If we do come that way, I will certainly give myself the pleasure of making your acquaintance.

Yours very sincerely,
Aldous Huxley

---

[3] Carlo Linati (1878–1949). Italian writer associated with Milan's newspaper *Corriere della sera* and translator of Joyce, Lawrence, and Yeats.
[4] Brera Art Gallery, Milan. One of Italy's most important art galleries, with works by Raphael, Mantegna, and Caravaggio.

TO T. S. ELIOT

15 Via S. Margherita a Montici
Florence
30 January 1925

Dear Tom,

Thank you for your letter and the return of Breughel. There were, of course, three considerable Breughels: but it is only the elder who counts. The second Peter, who imitated his father's style as closely as he could, spent most of his life copying Peter I's pictures. When he wasn't copying, he was very coarse and dull. Still, one must be grateful to him for having left versions of pictures by his father otherwise unknown. The other, Velvet Breughel,[5] painted in a more modern style than his father and did those very laborious landscapes and animal studies which (I don't quite know why—unless it was because of their great realism) were so popular during the 17th and 18th centuries. He used to conspire with Rubens sometimes, putting backgrounds to his figures. There are some very amusing joint-productions of theirs at the Hague—"Adam and Eve in the Garden of Eden," stupendously painted nudes by Rubens and very pre-Raphaelite parrots, snakes, and what-not in the background by Velvet Breughel. But he was really a great bore and worth nothing. It's only the father who is really good.

I'm afraid the *Criterion* never arrived. A certain percentage of one's correspondence always falls irretrievably into the great gulfs of incompetence and dishonesty which surround the Italian postal system. I am sorry for this, as I'd have much liked to see it. Meanwhile I hope you have received a copy of my book which I told the publishers to send you.

I have just been reading, in a French translation, the life of Mrs. Barclay[6]—of *The Rosary*. Have you ever read it? If not, do. It is really most extraordinary and raises fearful problems. For Mrs. B. was obviously an amazing woman—all the stigmata of greatness, and an enchanting character too. A real messiah, but of the servant's hall; the Shakespeare of the mentally defective. But genuinely a messiah and a literary genius—that's the point. You ought to go into the question. It's difficult, obscure and fascinating.

---

[5] Jan Breughel the Elder, aka Breughel de Velours (1568–1625). Brother of Peter Breughel II.
[6] Florence Barclay (1862–1921). British writer of popular fiction. *The Rosary* was the best-selling novel of 1910.

Do you know old Miss Paget—Vernon Lee?[7] She is one of the few bright spots in the moral and intellectual night of Florence. A really astonishing person. Such wit and learning I have never heard displayed so gracefully in conversation before. She is a sort of female Dr. Johnson— and would really be worth recording, I think. Much better in talk than in writing: but still, some of her critical lucubrations are very interesting, I think. Have you ever thought of getting hold of her for the *Criterion*?

Ever yours,
ALH

TO MARY HUTCHINSON

15 Via S. Margherita a Montici
Florence
12 February 1925

My dear Mary,
The drawings of M. Cocteau were very welcome—less for the sake of their author, I confess, than for that of their giver. The volume confirmed me in my previous opinions, viz: that you are charming and that Cocteau is an accomplished drawing room entertainer. I, who frequent no drawing rooms—only libraries and occasionally bedrooms—acknowledge his talent for charades, *bouts rimés* and pencil games without, however, taking very much interest in it. Life, it seems to me, is not so long that one can afford to spend any of it in playing Heads, Bodies and Tails and Dumb Crambo. There are other and more interesting occupations—such as those, for example, of the younger Gordianus, described by Gibbon: "Twenty-two acknowledged concubines and a library of 62,000 volumes attested the variety of his inclinations, and from the productions which he left behind him it appears that the former as well as the latter were designed for use rather that for ostentation!" Much better than drawing room games, I think? It is a succinct description of the Life of Reason, a boiling down of all Professor Santayana into one sentence. And still more interesting than the Life of Reason are the numerous possible lives on the further side of reason. So that, all things considered, I cannot see that one can be expected to take much interest in Monsieur Cocteau. All the same I am delighted to have received the book. For I am very glad to think that you are still sufficiently interested in my salvation—even across the in-

---

[7] Vernon Lee, pseudonym of Violet Paget (1836–1935). English novelist and essayist on Italy. In his Hearst newspaper essay "Good Conversation" (October 1931), Huxley referred to her as a "good writer and superb conversationalist."

tervening gulfs of space—to desire to convert me to Cocteauism. I have no desire in return to convert you to anything: for I hope that you will be always just as you are—only, perhaps, a little more indulgent to your humble soupirant . . .

And there the letter ought, very neatly, to have ended. But having various other things to talk about, I shall, against all rules of elegance and wit, continue it.

First a question. (Not that I have much hope of it being answered: for Maria tells me that you are a hopeless correspondent and have left I forget how many of her letters, sent to every possible address from Hammersmith to Jack's chambers, without reply. Still, one never can tell; I ask in a mood of pious hope.) Who is the lady to whom, according to one of my spies in the Foreign Office, Gertler was about to be married—and from whom, blenching at the last moment, he eloped, with Walter Taylor![8] Anyone we know? Or have new planets swum into his ken? And meanwhile is he painting better that he was six months ago? I hope so. It was dreary soulless sort of stuff then—mere surface and luscious paint and nothing whatever underneath: all sacrificed to his lust for a skin of juicy velvet.

Your brother Jim[9] has led us to a lovely place, south of Rome, where, I hope, we shall get a very nice little house. Are you coming there this summer as you seemed to think you might when we saw you last? Ideal place—sea, mountain, wine like the best burgundy, not too hot but guaranteed fine weather, view of Vesuvius and the dome of St. Peter's, Roman remains, the Pontine marshes in the middle distance with herds of buffalo and genuine cowboys on horseback and armed to the teeth, the house standing in its own park-like grounds, modern conveniences, usual office. Bath, h&c., fourteen yards from the sea etc etc. I really think you ought to come. It would be great fun and the place is really marvelous. Let your English house at an enormous rent and come whizzing out in the car. Do.

Meanwhile, dearest Mary, you must write. You have no excuse. If you don't we shall know it is because you are grown too proud, with too much conquest, to honour us with your attention. Write then, or I shall play Diogenes to your Alexander.

Yours,
Aldous

---

[8] Gertler's patron.
[9] James Strachey Barnes (1890–1955). Mary's brother, author of *Fascism* (1931) and *Io amo l'Italia* (1939).

TO SYDNEY SCHIFF

15 Via S. Margherita a Montici
Florence
May 1925

Dear Schiff,
Your letter of a few days since has given me a great deal of pleasure. Your praise, the praise of Stephen Hudson,[1] is worth having. And you give it so generously. Too generously, indeed; for the book, I feel, doesn't deserve so much. It seems to me all right so far as it goes; but there's something unripe about it, jejune. I confess to the fearful ambition of writing, some day, a Good Book. It is presumptuous and perhaps even silly. The question is really this: can one add a cubit to one's moral stature? All that can be said is that it's more feasible than adding cubits to one's physical stature. But how obscure, how fearfully difficult everything is!

Those were charming words of Stella Benson. I have never met her. She lives somewhere remote, doesn't she? A different hemisphere? Or is that merely a false deduction from the books?

Do you never pass this way? We are a bit provincial here, I know; but there are compensations. The sun atones for much. We shall be here in any case, I think, till the beginning of July. If you are anywhere in the neighbourhood between now and then, do let us know. It would be most delightful to see you. As for England, I shall be there some time or other between July and October. At present I can't exactly say when. I shall come and knock at your door when I arrive.

Sullivan was to have come to stay with us again this year, as he did last. But, poor wretch, he seems to have been ill and further concerned about his little daughter's illness; and we are still waiting for him to turn up. I hope he will, finally; for he is the best of companions.

Our best wishes to your wife and you. The object you remember at the perambulator stage has grown into a large boy. Five years old a few days since; when I cease taking that fact for granted, I find it hard to believe.

Ever yours,
Aldous Huxley

---

[1] Stephen Hudson was novelist Schiff's pen name.

TO MARY HUTCHINSON

15 Via S. Margherita a Montici
Florence
9 May 1925

Dearest Mary,
If I had a pen, I would write with that. But I haven't. Moreover, I have almost forgotten the art of writing with that barbarous implement; and the use of it exhausts me. So you must put up with the machine. But it's unsuitable, I admit. This dreadful clarity—it isn't really suitable for intimate letters. Any more than electric light—though some, I admit, disagree with me on this matter—is suitable for love. One of the charms of letters is that it should be very difficult to read them. You feel, when the writing's illegible, that you're nearer the real, inscrutable person. Moreover, from the writer's point of view the machine is unsatisfactory; for he feels that he ought to be as lucid as his script; he is ashamed to clothe an obscurity or a hint in glaring printed letters. Here am I, for example, writing legibly, but feeling totally obscure. I set down coherent sentences; but what I feel like inside, is:

qwertyuiopasdfghjklzxcvbnm,=;964^£_'(=?61/4lkjhgfd_v///

Perhaps you know the feeling. It is that sense of internal obscurity—black as the inside of a cow, isn't that the phrase?—that has kept me from answering your last letter of I don't know how long since. A charming letter, a long time and a correspondingly vast ingratitude on my part. But not ingratitude really; an inability, rather, to reply with any degree of brightness from out of my obscurity. Not that I can reply much more lucidly now; for I still feel as obscure as ever. Not that it's entirely unpleasant to be in the dark. There is something even rather exciting about putting out all the lights. And my word, what a lot go out as soon as you begin traveling beyond the fringes of this snug civilization of ours! Even Tunisia—a few hours from Europe—they begin to go out, the seemingly fixed immortal lights. You arrive and see that all our adjectives have no meaning there. And they seem such good adjectives: just, cruel, progressive, barbarous, intelligent, civilized, amusing, good—all quite inapplicable. And obviously even emptier of meaning—our meaning—in other remoter places. It's obvious, of course; and one had known it theoretically, for ever. But one forgets theories; the practical experimental knowledge always comes as a shock. The lights go out with a click. I'm inclined to believe, now, that it's only by establishing, experimentally, a really total darkness that one can subsequently make a light that will show up everything in its real and proper colours—a natural daylight, not a disguising and partial artificial light. Imaginative people can doubtless do the whole business at home, in their own heads. But I am not imaginative; so that I feel that I should have to do it by traveling. The secret, I fancy, must be something in the nature of a realization that the part has an autonomous and valid existence and is not less, but equal to the whole; that everything is relative and dependant for significance on everything else and that yet, precisely for this reason, there is something fixed and absolute. In any case, whatever it may be, the secret must definitely be illogical, non-rational. Of that, I think, there cannot be a moment's doubt. And it must be apprehended immediately, as a sensation in the pit of the stomach; a theoretical knowledge of it would be of no value. My chief objection to the polished and graceful life of civilization is that it is so absurdly narrow; to live it—play it, perhaps would be better—one must accept implicitly so many limiting assumptions. Personally, I have lived so long and so exclusively in a private literary-intellectual world, that I am case-hardened and find the greatest difficulty in getting out, into contact with other forms of existence—forms of existence in many respects much more satisfactory than mine. But enough. I grow tedious. And besides, all this is really too explicit. My final opinion remains qertlkjhzxcvo754-=¾ ^ ½=???? Particularly ???? Not forgetting my penultimate opinion which is about you and cannot, I feel, without a certain incongruity and even impropriety be baldly typed. I am not an amateur of arc lamps—at the most a discreetly shaded light, on the floor; or correspondingly a scribbled unreadable postscript which, for lack of a pen, I cannot write. Only confining myself to reproaching you, dearest Mary, for your failure to accompany Jack or, what would be better still (for I am not insisting on conjugal inseparability, far from it) to come to Italy and to us unaccompanied. Farewell, meanwhile, and flourish.

Aldous

TO ROBERT NICHOLS

The train, near Chicago
13 May 1925

A day's march nearer home, my dear Robert, and not such an uncomfortable one as I had feared. Indeed, the journey has been admirably good. Given the privacy of these compartments and their comforts, one wouldn't mind going on for days!

The Grand Canyon was quite up to specifications and only man was vile. (But then, poor devil, he can hardly fail to be when he is as closely concentrated as he necessarily must be round the point where the railway touches the canyon.) One trundles in motor buses along the brink of the chasm. Or if one has more time or, being a woman, likes the shape of one's haunches in breeches, one mounts a mule and goes off with a movie cowboy down into the gulf. The breeches, I must say, added something to the charms of the scene.

How delightful it was to see you again, my dear Bob, after all these years—and how still more delightful to think that you will soon be returning to civilization. Hollywood is altogether too antipodean to be lived in; it gives you no chance of escape. Italy seems to me clearly indicated. And after all it's in the grand poetic tradition. Every good English poet, with the exception of Shakespeare, has been to Italy for a more or less lengthy period. It is an indispensable phase in the poetic life—also in these days of high taxation and high prices, and of the purely prosaic life!

I hope Don Juan [Nichols's satiric poem] prospers. I liked what I've heard of him very much. He ought to be a bit of a monument by the time he's done. He should flourish, I am sure, in an Italian scene.

Farewell, dear Robert. If I don't thank you in set terms for having made my day in Joy City so truly joyful, it isn't because I am not grateful—I am, exceedingly—but because I don't want to write you the usual Collins. Take thanks as richly implied, if not actually uttered. Both our loves to both of you.

Yours,
Aldous

TO RUSSELL GREEN

15 Via S. Margherita a Montici
Florence
8 June 1925

My dear Russell,
Just seen Thomas Wade [Earp], who gave me your address, to which I have taken the liberty of sending a letter to Chaman Lall,[2] whose

---

[2] Chaman Lall. An early editor of *Coterie*, later an Indian M.P. who hosted Huxley on his Indian tour.

whereabouts Tommy says you know. Will you be very kind and send it on to him? I am hoping to go to India this autumn and had been wondering for some time how I should get into touch with our friend. I'm delighted to hear that he is in Europe, and want very much to get hold of him. Give him my love if you see him.

From Tommy I had tolerably good accounts of you, for which I am heartily glad. I hope we may meet sometime when I am in England, which will be, D.V. and W.P., towards the middle of July. You shall tell me about life in London. Though cordially thankful to be out of that hideous combination of Sodom, Gomorrah, Babylon and modern Aden, I am still curious about its life. Prepare your most curious (in the book seller's catalogue sense of the word) anecdotes against the time of my arrival.

In the meantime farewell and flourish.

> *Yours,*
> *Aldous Huxley*

TO ROBERT NICHOLS

> *15 via S. Margherita a Montici*
> *Florence*
> *14 June 1925*

My dear Robert,

Many thanks for your letter of May 14. I will certainly read Keyserling. I had seen it appreciatively mentioned, meant to read and then forgotten. I perceive that I have been addressing all my letters to "Glen Avenue" (abbreviated "Ave.") instead of Glen Airy. I hope they reached you.

It is most kind of you to think of my theatrical friend. A most able young man who knows the business inside out and is a real creator as well as a very skilful stage technician. The things he has done in Belgium are most remarkable—the more so as he is only 23 or 24 now.

But Brussels is a one horse town and there are no opportunities. He has got into touch recently with one or two American theatre people and I hope something may eventuate. The movies sound pretty bloody. Couldn't you stir up a pogrom?

I heard from Phil [Nichols] that you were coming to Europe in the autumn. I'm sorry you should have chosen this particular time, as I think (finances permitting), that we shall just be leaving for Asia when you arrive. India in any case. Then, perhaps, Australia, Pacific islands, and America. In which case, if you're back on the Coast, we might hope to see you in your hemisphere.

Meanwhile we leave this house on July 1. Address till further notice: The Athenaeum, SW1.

Yours,
Aldous Huxley

TO JULIAN HUXLEY

Tuesday
1925

My dear J,
All congratulations on King's College. It is splendid—and I hope it means money as well as honour and glory. It also means London instead of Oxford—which is a slight improvement of environment.

As for Thursday: we are having tea with Gertler in his studio 13 Rundale Crescent, Hampstead. So come and pick us up there at about 6:00, and we will go and have an early dinner somewhere. It will be delightful.

With regards to next week—I must have written my suggestion badly. What I meant was: could we come on Monday or Tuesday for a couple of nights or so. Now I find that Tuesday will definitely be the better date (21st). So may we come then, say till Thursday or possibly Friday morning? We will expect your answer on Thursday at Gertler's.

Love from both of us,
Aldous

TO MARY HUTCHINSON

The Athenaeum
Pall Mall, S.W.1
22 July 1925

Not very much work done, as I expected. Some of your scent, Mary, still clings about me; and when I move I suddenly catch little whiffs of it— and there's an end for the moment of any pursuit of the *mot juste*. And I sit, reflecting—not without jealously, dear Mary—that Clive is with you: that perhaps he is profiting by tenderness and fires and meltings which not he evoked and which by right are mine—mine: and I am cursing myself that I didn't take the key you offered and—*quel goujat!*—I so ungallantly neglected to take. Too late now, I'm afraid. But tomorrow—

if, perhaps, I can fix something for the afternoon (it depends on all sorts of things) if—will you? I shall telephone in the morning if it's a possibility. Good night—but not *too* good, Mary.

A.

TO MARY HUTCHINSON

Reims
ca August 1925

Proust has followed us everywhere. In Holland it was Swann's Ver-Meers. And now, in this devastated area (devastated morally, it seems, as well as materially) who should I see but Andrée and Albertine. The physiological contemporaries of Dr. Cottard fairly imposed themselves on the mind. Ah, what we authors are responsible for. With love,

Aldous and Maria

TO MARY HUTCHINSON

You remember Sainte Beuve's article on the effects in actual life of Balzac's novels. All the best people turned into Rastignacs, Princesses de Cadignans, Madame Marneffes. And Dostoevsky is responsible for half the suicides of young men that take place in Western Europe. And as for Proust—how dreadfully he has complicated love and made it conscious. And as for Sodom and Gomorrah, why even in Reims they have read him. As for Paris and London—the statistics, I imagine, would be very impressive. Even my own small efforts seem to have their influence—to judge at any rate from the letters I receive from young American girls. The poor creatures seem not to notice that my principles are really those of St. Augustine. Notwithstanding, I am always your

A.

TO MARY HUTCHINSON

19 Grand Place
St. Trond
Belgium
ca August 1925

Immersed fathoms deep in work, rain and Maria's relations to the third and fourth generation, I push up a little periscope and look back over a week that seems half a lifetime to last Sunday and Dover. Is it possible that there was ever such a day, Mary, and such a place? Here, at the heart of the patriarchal system, it is hard to believe it. I doubt if I shall fully believe again till Paris. Will you persuade me there that it really was true?

The atmosphere here is impregnated with the misery and horror of old age. The patriarchs preside, a little deader every day—life and interest in things slowly ebbing: the immediate, trivial environment assuming an ever greater, more exclusive significance—the house, meals, servants—all the rest of the universe ignored. And all because the testes and ovaries are not making their internal secretion into the blood. The whole cosmos is changed in consequence for them.

The misery of it. But perhaps when one reaches that point one doesn't find it miserable: that is the only, rather feeble, comfort. Meanwhile . . . . meanwhile India, books, Paris. Desperately even. All knowledge, desperately, while it's possible to acquire it—while there are still internal secretions. Not to mention the eternal.

Finished my Crébillon essay, I am now frantically re-writing a long short story against time. How are you? Enjoying Wittering? I hope so; but also hope you're not enjoying it as much as when you were there last. *A bientôt*, darling Mary.

A.

TO MARY HUTCHINSON

19 Grand Place
St. Trond
Belgium
12 August 1925

You expressed a desire, dearest Mary to see Crébillon.[3] Here he is. I hope the essay will sufficiently whet your curiosity in its subject to make you turn to the originals. *La Nuit et le Moment, Le Hasard au Coin du Feu* have amusing and profound things in them. A little monotonous, perhaps, as wholes—but justified by the excellence of their

---

[3] Huxley's introduction to Crébillon fils (1707–1777) appeared in Eric Sutton's translation of *La nuit et le moment* (*The Opportunities of a Night*) 1925. In her letter to Mary, Maria refers to the pink pajamas that she must hide from the profane eyes of her old-fashioned grandmother, adding, "Sometimes I go and look at them with an unbearable longing to kiss you." The Hotel Bergère promised to be comfortable, modern and "fairly luscious. . . . It will have two rooms—one with a *very large bed* for you—near each other—could not bear to have you at the end of a beastly and public passage."

parts. We could do with a few such *contes dialogués*—a little variegated, as regards to subject matter and characters—about our contemporaries, ourselves. Why shouldn't Polly Flinders [Mary Hutchinson's pen name] undertake the job—from the lady's point of view?

I haven't yet thanked you for your letter and the pleasure it gave me. To know that you think of me there, at Wittering, in the night. I remember with precision certain statues, certain Parian whitenesses, certain expressions almost of agony, certain excruciated laughter, certain gestures like the desperately ecstatic gestures of dancers poised on the brink of miraculous possession by the god. I remember and I look forward. In the mean time, however, I am as deeply immersed as ever.

About Paris: yes, the 24th by all means. The *Hotel Quai Voltaire* seemed dubious of its capacity to harbour us; but we have secured rooms definitely in another—I forget the name, but will get Maria to write the details. We are due to arrive at about 5:30 or 6:00 in the afternoon of the 24th. When does your train get in?

Well, I must plunge again. Goodbye, Mary—these are bubbles from the depths.

A.

P.S. The name of the hotel is:—

    Hôtel Bergère

    Rue Bergère

Which is in Montmartre. It is said to be comfortable. If we don't like it, we can move out after a night. Meet there unless we meet previously at the station—which may be possible, if you indicate the time your train arrives.

TO MARY HUTCHINSON

ca 20 August 1925

Isn't this a charming piece of paper? It belonged to a biologist of the fourth generation here and was found in the attic with a botanical specimen and a green sun-shade, which have been given me—what a token of esteem!—to take to the Indies. Does human dignity mean anything? I wonder. And if it does, does it mean children—or French letters? Opinions must surely remain divided.

Meanwhile, if human pleasure means anything, it means among other things letters from Mary and the prospect of seeing Mary—on Tuesday, alas, instead of Monday—but in any case soon. It means also—what? Shall we discuss what it means in Paris? And will you say the things you refuse to say in your letter, the words you won't use? Unspoken, they reverberate in me too.

Terribly busy still; the daily round of work is broken once a week by an injection of anti-typhoid serum, which produces a lump like a pigeon's egg in the middle of the back and a temperature of 102 for ten or twelve hours.[4] Not agreeable; but better, I suppose, than typhoid. During my last bout of fever I thought of the beginning of an erotic poem:

> Under the golden-fruited vine
> Androgyne with androgyne
> Languidly toys, and each by turns
> With various fires perversely burns.[5]

Cetera desunt: but I leave to your imagination 3000 lines describing all the possible amatory permutations and combinations of two hermaphrodites.

We'll meet your train on Tuesday. If we miss in the crowd, go straight to Hotel Bergère.

A bientôt, darling Mary,
A

TO MARY HUTCHINSON

SS Genova
Off the Italian Coast
15 September 1925

So many things have kept me from writing, Mary. First the attempt to write a story—a vain attempt, for I found myself in a season of spiritual drought. Then, in answer to imperious commands from New York, the concoction of a long article about Tunisia. And finally on the top of everything, the final preparations and enervations. Writing professionally, I find it horribly difficult to write *en amateur—en amant*, should I say, Mary? The pen repugns us, the sight of paper induces a sort of disgust. Enormous inhibitions have to be overcome before I can

---

[4] Maria, in a letter to Mary dated 17 August 1925, complains of "painful, hot, and lumpy" injections in preparation for their trip to India.
[5] In a story published in *The Smart Set*, April 1923, Huxley's protagonist in "Over the Telephone," Walter Traill, struggles with the same opening lines of an incomplete poem, but he gets only as far as "Languidly sports," thinking he should perhaps say, "Languidly toys."

bring myself to write a letter. And the letter when written is too stupid to be worth reading. So I've waited for a moment of leisure—relative even now; for I have worked even today and the prospect of that damned story looms before me. This is the fruit, written in bed on the first night of our voyage.

In bed—and there are three beds in the cabin: one is unoccupied. Nature abhors a vacuum. The void is eloquent with regrets, desires, recollections. On our next journey, Mary, you must accompany us. I will write a play—three hundred nights at twenty pounds a night—and invite you on the strength of it—to the West Indies, Peru, Samoa: it shall be somewhat tropical, in any case. Deep calls to deep—Temperature to Temperature. I have always found it so. Will you come? Yes. All that remains to be done is to write the play. Give me a subject—I am so bad at inventing dramas myself. Maria, when I apply to her, is fertile in suggestions—but they are always so naively obscene that they would only do for the répertoire of secret theatres in Montevideo. Perhaps you could think of something chaster, Mary. I am sure you could; you are less innocent.

We left Genoa this morning. So far, the voyage has been most agreeable. Sea flat, sky blue, cabin comfortable as cabins go, food incredibly copious and pretty good—only man, as usual is vile. And not without exceptions. Among unspeakable Anglo-Indians, male and female, some tolerably pleasant. Perhaps too, we may discover more—both good and evil. So far our acquaintance is limited. The Doctor is in tremendous form and knows all the addresses in Aden and Bombay where one can see ladies emulating Europa and Pasiphae—but with donkeys and St. Bernard dogs. Not my taste, really. I have never believed in being *too* kind to animals. Have you? Yes, I remember a *faible* you expressed for swans. I grant you, they have a charm. But quadrupeds—no. Not quadrupeds.

In Florence saw our friend Luigino Franchetti, who marries triumphantly a week hence. Both he and his fiancée in a most extraordinary state of exhaustion owing to the enforced chastity of betrothal—chastity, if reluctant, being so much more tiring than excess, so fatal to the health. I think they'd both die if the marriage were put off for another month. I tried to get news of Jim, but nobody seemed to know any, except that he has now taken to performing miracles. Rather an alarming development, I feel. His specialty, according to Luigino's fiancée's mother, is miraculously stopping ships at sea—I hope he won't take it into his head to stop ours. Jim permitting, we get to Naples tomorrow morning and spend the inside of a day there.

I have thought of you, Mary, with each of your delicious cigars—thought, with how much affection, that you are a darling, charming and sweet, and with what precise desire and recollections that you are beautiful and voluptuous. I shall still remember even when the cigars are finished, that your body is round and slender like a white serpent's and that when your hair is tied in a little pig tail it is a *détournement de mineure*—of how deliciously perverse a minor! I shall remember, too, the charming expression of gaiety and malice which you had when I came out of the bathroom and saw you there, sitting on the bed, at Fontainebleau. I shall remember—but I shall remember everything. Ah, decidedly, I shall have to write that play, so that we can sail in splendor to Callao or Tahiti. Quickly, quickly think of a plot.

I hope you will have got the copy of my book which I sent the other day, by the time you get this letter: Looking at it, with tolerable impartiality after all these months, during which I had forgotten all about it, it seemed to me not bad at all. Readable, at any rate. I hope you will find it so.

Yours,
A

TO MARY HUTCHINSON

Srinagar
Kashmir
25 October 1925

Your letter, Mary, was altogether charming and reminded me—albeit superfluously, for I think of it constantly without need of such *memento vivere*'s—of what Shakespeare calls, marvelously (let us add our floral tribute)

"The stealth of our most mutual entertainment."[6]

How mutual it was, Mary! At least I inferred as much—scientifically, on good behaviourist grounds and without resort to either my or your introspection; which however confirmed the observed facts, I think. I am only slightly melancholy when I think of other entertainments a hemisphere away, where the other half of the mutuality is not (let us be purists at least in grammar) I. These green-eyed monsters—never, however docile they seem, completely tame.

[6] *Measure for Measure*, I. ii. 143.

My wit is always of the staircase kind and, for no particular reason, I thought the other day of a quatrain I ought to have invented and presented months ago. Or perhaps it should have arrived on your birthday, so as to justify its title "Birthday Honours." Here it is:

Fount of all honour and preferment's path!
You make my titles daily to increase:
Your Garter's Knight, Companion of your Bath,
And now Commander of your Golden Fleece.

And luckily, in this case, the fleece is golden. The compliment is not for brown beauties.

Here we are, still among the Himalayas, and shall remain for a week or two more—not because Kashmir is really very lovely: it isn't—being paradisiacal only in relation to the Punjab in summer, which is hell, not to Europe; (I have seen better picture postcards in poor Tom's favorite Switzerland; how is Tom,[7] by the way?) but because it is quiet and I must work for a bit, and cheap, which is important in any place where one proposes to stay for long. In the intervals of labour I study the comedy of life in an absolute 17th century monarchy—which is what these native states still are—with Mr. A as its *Roi Soleil*.[8] It is curious to see in a place like this how circumstances create types. I had thought the courtier extinct. But here he flourishes and prospers by the same technique which was employed by the officers of King Canute. And the intrigues! We have been friendly with an under secretary of state and so know a good deal about them. Minings and counter-minings, prodigious treacheries, monstrous panderings and prostitutions. And not on the part of the blackamoors only. For instance, the present prime minister [G. E. C. Wakefield] is an Englishman who owes his position to a flashing and facile daughter, who captivated Mr. A while he was heir apparent, got her father appointed his private secretary and state secretary. Later the English Resident [Sir John Barry Wood] interfered, had the man ejected from his state secretaryship and advised the daughter to go back to England, as the scandal had become too open. But when the old Maharaja died, a month ago, the Resident was away on tour in the mountains and Mr. A, without waiting to consult him, which would have been the correct procedure, appointed his secretary Prime Minister; so that he is now all-powerful and, the Resident is in a ticklish position and can't turn him out. Meanwhile the daughter returned from England and was married a

[7] T. S. Eliot, a friend of both.
[8] Sir Hari Singh became Maharaja (ruling prince) upon the death in 1925 of Sir Patrap Singh.

week ago—handsome pearl necklace from Mr. A—with great pomp of orange blossom and virginal white flowers. The Resident made a graceful speech at the reception and the Prime Minister's only rival (another Englishman), the Finance Minister, whom he has overthrown by his machinations, seconded the congratulations. Delicious farce! Meanwhile all who like grow immensely rich at the expense of the state and the unfortunate Kashmiris wallow in the most abject poverty.

We went the other day to the Central Asian Caravanserai, where all the traders who come down from Turkestan to India stop on their way through. It takes them six weeks to walk from Yarkhand in Chinese Turkestan and they can only do the journey, in either direction, once in a year—when the snows have melted and after the rivers, swollen by the summer's melting, have subsided. This is their season. The place was full of queer yellow Tartars, with their wares—furs, Chinese silks, carpets, hand-made cotton, jade—which they exchange in India for cotton piece goods, otter skins and silver for re-sale, next year, when they go back again over the passes, in their own country. Their medium of exchange is pre-Revolution 10-rouble pieces. Some of them are said to be immensely rich. We bought two carpets, two fur coats and 12 yards of material for something under six pounds. Not excessive. And there is something so fantastic and romantic about these creatures walking down through hundreds of miles of diabolical mountains to sell their goods.

What news in the literary world? I read Bunny's[9] book before leaving and thought it worse rather than better. But Mortimer,[1] I suppose, will duly find it a masterpiece. I read nothing but a little Shakespeare, a textbook of elementary algebra, the history of India and miscellaneous items out of the EDW–EVA volume of the *Encyclopaedia Britannica*. Write again, Mary. M sends her love.

Aldous

TO MARY HUTCHINSON

Srinagar
Kashmir
2 November 1925

I was touched by the predetermined valentine which you found in your archives, Mary. Oh, my prophetic soul! And what a funny little piece

---

[9] David Garnett (1892–1981). English novelist. The novel in question is probably *The Sailor's Return* (1925).
[1] Raymond Mortimer (1895–1980). British writer associated with the Bloomsbury circle.

of fossilized life to have dug up. A fossil belonging, I should say, to the Miocene or Pleistocene period—to a period when a part, or perhaps even the bulk of my spiritual flora and fauna were the same as they are now. You never knew me at all in my tertiary and secondary periods, in the days when my soul was inhabited by the mental equivalents of giant lizards, when the air of my mind was full of the wheelings of toothed birds and the growth of monstrous cryptograms and fungi fledged my yet uncultivated spirit. (I have fears that my oratory may have got the better of my geology; but never mind.) No, you only knew me from Oligocene times onwards. This fossil of Etonian days is, geologically speaking, very recent. How few traces one possesses—or at any rate I personally possess—of those remote times. Now you quote it to me, I remember writing that letter. But the memory was deeply buried. I should never have dug it out unassisted. St. Valentine's Day 1918; and to-day, unless my hagiography is faulty, to-day is All Soul's Day. It would be All Bodies' too in the calendar of any reasonable church; for how absurdly arbitrary it is to separate them.

I was delighted, too, by all the news that came in the other letter you wrote. Your conversation with Lytton about masculine and feminine beauty—that must have been delightfully like Lucian's (or pseudo-Lucian's) dialogue on the same subject. There, if you remember, he makes the Greek—an ancestor of Lytton's (but collateral, I take it, since *ex hypothesi* he wouldn't have begotten any children)—go into raptures about the statue of Venus in the temple—but seen from behind. The unrefined Egyptian had praised its forward-looking aspect; but the Greek reserved his ecstasies for what Lucian called *ta paidika meré*, "the boyish parts." I can sympathize with him, up to a point. But I fear I shall never be what Sir Richard Burton[2] called the Chinese—"omnifutuent."

And what grand news about the Todd![3] I always suspected the dildo's existence. But I was never lucky enough to see it. As a Literary Man, I am charmed you should use this fine old English word. The classical reference is in Donne—"your bed-staves, dildoes and your velvet glass."[4] What the velvet glass was, I have never been able to discover. The greatest scholars to whom I have put the question have confessed themselves as ignorant as I. The New English Dictionary is

[2] Sir Richard Burton (1821–1890). British scholar-explorer who published an unexpurgated version of *Arabian Nights*.
[3] Dorothy Todd. Editor of British *Vogue*, 1922–1926. Huxley wrote for *Vogue* and other Condé Nast papers in the 1920s.
[4] Donne, "Elegie II, 'The Anagram.'"

silent. So too is Grierson, the editor of Donne and a man whose notes on other obscure points are always illuminating. Glasses of course are obvious; every school boy knows that large test-tubes, filled with hot water and corked, are largely employed by ladies in Miss Todd's position. But velvet glass? How can glass be velvet? Or velvet, glass? Does it mean glass covered with velvet? And if so why? Would there be something, perhaps, in the long pile of a choice Venetian velvet? I leave the problem to your ingenuity and your imagination. As for bed staves—those are familiar. I remember encountering somewhere, in late 17th or earlyish 18th century literature—it may even have been Fielding; but I am a sadly desultory reader and can't remember—a delightful locution, viz: "In the twinkling of a bed staff."[5] Which proves (a) that bed staves were in common use at the time and that the users didn't really know how to use them. For a bed staff could only be said to twinkle if it were used with great rapidity. And in these matters, surely, one should hasten slowly. In this part of the world they have a proverb which says: *Takht balli balli; rann galli galli*. Which means literally : Hill slowly slowly; woman sweetly sweetly. In other words: Mountains must be climbed gradually and women loved without haste. These rude mountaineers have anticipated all the wisdom of Marie Stopes.[6] *Rann galli galli*—her advice to newly married couples is merely that.

Our life runs on its usual course—quiet reading and writing, tempered with periodic sociabilities. These last are interesting, not because the people concerned are remarkable, but for precisely the opposite reason—because they are so very very ordinary. They make one realize how excessively odd and remote is the society of high brows and immoralists which we generally frequent. These folk, as Tommy would say, whether Indian or European, are mostly just nice upper-middle class folk, with all the ideas or absence of ideas, and prejudices of their class. One moves among them like a Martian. The Indians are distinguished by a certain childishness, which is particularly engaging. They have adopted all the English ideas about what constitutes a 'good time'; but they are sporting, bibulously social, game-loving in an entirely infantile way. We went out for a picnic with a party of them yesterday and they spent the whole day playing cricket with stones and bits of wood, improvising see-saws, putting the weight, seeing who could throw stones the farthest, hiding from one another, running

[5] Thomas Shadwell, *The Virtuoso*, 1676.
[6] Marie Carmichael Stopes (1880–1958). Early advocate of birth control and sex education.

races and playing practical jokes. It was the world of the preparatory school; charming, touching, but quite below good and evil.

We know most of the high officials by this time and they take us round to see the sights appertaining to their departments, such as the gaol, where there is a gruesome row of little cages full of condemned murderers; the lunatic asylum, with more cages, in which stark naked madmen sit howling like wolves or gibbering; the fortress, made of mud and falling to pieces, the technical institute, where the taste of several hundred budding artisans is irreparably ruined by the teachings of the worst European conventions; the museum, full of moth-eaten stuffed birds and Kashmir shawls. The tit-bits yet in store for us are the silk factory, the leper asylum and the electric power station. Some of these officials are charming. There is a fat old doctor, or Chief Medical Officer, who tells us about the extraordinary number of stones he has extracted from the bladders of the local poor; there is the Assistant Governor, who has lived on the frontier of Turkestan, where the people are of the purest and most unmixed Aryan stock, look like Greek statues, talk a dialect of Sanskrit, are so barbarous that they do not know the use of pottery and live in a country so poor that for three months of the year they have nothing to eat but mulberries. The father of the Assistant Governor was a great traveler, who spent forty years exploring the Himalayas and wrote an account of all his voyages in verse. His son is also literary and means some day to write novels; but so far, he tells us, he has got no further than the titles, about which he corresponds lengthily with his learned friends. Then there is the Minister of Agriculture, who has a romantic history. Born a Hindu, he was married as a child to a wife he never saw. He went to England for his education, fell in love and was loved, but could not marry; returned home and lives a bachelor, though his wife is still alive. A nice creature. Our friend the Superintendent of Customs and Excise was perhaps less fortunate; for not having contracted a child marriage, he was able to wed his English inamorata, a very vulgar, lively little woman, whom we find it difficult to avoid. But she's an odd type and interesting to study; for she's one of those people full of frightful talent, gifted, but appallingly so, a genius of the servant's hall. She sings, but what songs! With a good voice, but used to express what sentiments! And now she has begun to paint, incredibly competently in a vulgar way. I have no doubt that she could write novels, if she tried, like Marie Corelli's.[7]

---

[7] Marie Corelli (1855–1924). British writer of popular romantic novels.

Wrapped in herself completely, she is totally ignorant—absolutely unaware of the existence of anything good or decent. One wonders whether a woman of that kind—and I have met others like her—would have been able to profit by a proper education, or whether the bad taste is inherent and absolute, whether she would have gone on singing "Roses in Picardy" even if she had heard "Che farò senz' Eurydice?"[8] These servant's hall Shakespeares, of whom Mrs. Barclay of "The Rosary"[9] was the most extraordinary (you should read her life, by the way; she was undoubtedly a genius of the first order, but born among the lower stages of the human Hierarchy), have a great fascination for me. The problems they raise are so many and so odd.

The weather grows daily colder. The valley is full of gigantic plane trees, which are turning scarlet, and poplar avenues, which have gone yellow. The snow is coming lower and lower down the mountains. It will be a relief to get down to the plains, I think. We leave in ten days or a fortnight—none too soon—and shall do the round of Rajputana. We have already collected an introduction to one Maharajah. I hope it will be useful. Mr. A., unfortunately, has gone down to his winter capital and we had no chance of seeing him. Our only royal lion has been a Kapurthala prince, the son of an Indian father and a Spanish chorus girl, educated in France and exceedingly polished. Next to him our best bag has been the English Resident, a wicked old man, who was Political Secretary to the Government of India until two or three years ago, when he was turned out, it is said, for corruption, and relegated to this second-class residency. A sinister and rather amusing old dog with an extraordinary wife, very aristocratic and dotty, with a very pale powdered face, a dim manner, as though she drank or took drugs, queer shabby clothes and a small army of pug dogs and parrots.

In the intervals of all this giddy sociability, I work, read and meditate, not to mention eat and sleep, enormously. The even tenor of my life was disturbed the other night by a colossal hornet, the size of a small monoplane, which crept up my trousers and stung me on the leg. About half an hour later I came out in immense white blisters from head to heel, felt shivery as though I were on the point of having influenza and was finally very sick. However, the effects wore off gradually in the course of the night and I had only a swollen leg, next morning, to remind me of the incident. I enclose a photograph of myself looking like a mixture of the Prince of Wales and the Kronprinz doing

[8] Famous aria from Gluck's *Orfeo*.
[9] Best-selling novelist (1881–1927).

a tropical tour—incredibly raffish. I discover entirely new traits in my character when I contemplate it. Also a charming one of Maria in the fur coat we bought from the Tartar traders, and which looks like the coat Ivan the Terrible must have worn. Write again, Mary.

Aldous

TO SYDNEY SCHIFF

Srinagar, Kashmir
(as from Race View Golf Road, Lahore)
11 November 1925

Dear Schiff,
I have owed you—for how long I am ashamed to think—my thanks for your letter about India. What with travelling, packing up, seeing things and people, and working in the intervals, I have been very neglectful of my correspondence. I have doubts whether I shall be able to follow your friend's advice in its entirety, as we shall probably not be going into southern India at all, so that we shan't see Madura and the other fine places in those parts. The distances are really portentous here. From Bombay to Lahore is just about the same as from London to Rome. And from Lahore this place is distant two hundred miles by train and two hundred more by motor. Where there are through trains and comfortable carriages one doesn't mind these journeys. But in the south, I am assured, the railways are frightful; you creep along for days and days in hideous discomfort. However, I hope that we may make up for missing the South and Ceylon by going to Burma and the Dutch Indies. They are said to be almost more lovely.

This place is rather a disappointment. One has seen the same thing before in Europe. It is Switzerland and the Italian lakes on a larger and coarser scale, with a flat plain, among the mountains, resembling a slice of France—all poplar avenues and cornland. The palaces and gardens of the Moguls are very inferior to anything of the kind in Europe. The local art is mostly abominable—they have practically forgotten how to make shawls. But the real fun, of course, is found in the people. Kashmir is a small and very corrupt despotism; there are courtiers and intriguers; plots and counterminings; Judas-like betrayals, monstrous prostitution and pandering. The English, I may add, appear to play the game quite as successfully as their darker brothers. The present prime minister is an English adventurer whose chief claims to Mr. A's favour (Mr. A has now come to the throne) consist in an oily compliance to every caprice of the despot and the possession of a pretty daughter. We pick up scraps of gossip from acquaintances, Indian and English. It is an Arabian Night's Entertainment.

Still more fascinating, of course, is the study of the relations existing between the English and the educated Indians, particularly when such relations have been complicated by a mixed marriage. The cruelties, the humiliations, the pompous make-believes, the snobberies. . . . Proust should have lived here for a few years. I look on with a horrified amusement at this farce which is always potentially a tragedy and which is obviously destined to work up, within a few years, to some unheard-of and appalling dénouement. One day, I think, you ought to persuade your wife to come and have a look at it all. It would amuse you both.

Maria joins with me in sending kindest regards to your wife and yourself.

Yours,
Aldous Huxley

TO MARY HUTCHINSON

Race View, Golf Road, Lahore
11 November 1925

We got back to Lahore last night and found your telegram, Mary, awaiting us. How unhappy I am that any complaints of ours should have made you send it! For I forget the complaints and whatever blank mail days were their cause and remember only the charming, tender, amusing, letters. Today, alas, I can only thank you for them once again with brevity, for the mail leaves at four and we are already at lunch time! It is fun to be back again in India after Kashmir. It is hot here and the light is strong and yellow, the people are duskier, more numerous and wear gaudier clothes than up there among the mountains, where the height undoes the effect of the latitude and creates a sort of Switzerland under the Tropic of Cancer. We spent the morning in the museum, looking at a collection of ravishing Indo-Persian pictures, painted during the days of the great Moghuls, and later, exquisite battle and hunting scenes; courageous emperors cutting the trunks off infuriated elephants, portraits of great men smoking hookahs—which the erudite spell "huppahs." And finally, from the early 1800's onwards, amazing portraits of Europeans—Lytton's father seen in terms of Oriental despotism! But the most charming things were the scenes of domestic life.

Ladies at their toilet—smoking the hookah while slaves adjust their slippers. Or reclining on the roofs of their houses looking at the clouds—their favorite occupation, apparently; for there were dozens of pictures showing them amusing themselves in this innocent way. And there were also less innocent pleasures. . . . We saw plenty of love scenes between magnificent nabobs—smoking the hookah while they dally—and languishing beauties with gazelle's eyes and bosoms astonishingly globy. And then several pictures labeled with such titles as "The Timid Bride," showing reluctant beauties being led up to Pashas squatting on carpets and smoking, inevitably, their hookahs. You would have enjoyed them.

One of our friends here was telling us last night about the Nizam of Hyderabad, who, besides being the richest and most avaricious man in India is also one of the most copiously married, having (at any rate when our friend visited him a few years ago) no less than 285 concubines: there are probably more now, as his subjects present him with superfluous daughters and sisters on his birthday. The ladies, it appears, live in a huge barrack with numbered rooms and are known only by their numbers. Our friend struck up an acquaintance with the superintendent of the Zenana and got him to explain the whole system. Their names and numbers are registered in a huge ledger, in which are recorded their ages, height, details of personal appearance. At the end is a column headed "remarks," where the Nizam records his opinion about their more intimate charms. Twice a month, there is a general inspection and march past of the beauties and the Nizam ticks off in the ledger the number of those he fancies. He takes a list of the numbers and each evening telephones to the superintendent to say which of the ladies is to be "exalted" that night. The lady is apprised of the fact by a symbol; a special shawl is brought into her room and spread on the bed. No word is spoken: but the lady knows that the moment of "exaltation" has come. If the Nizam changes his mind at the last moment, the shawl is snatched away and replaced elsewhere. Children are born, on the average, at the rate of two a week. On these auspicious days all the government offices are closed. Hyderabad is the paradise of civil servants.

This same friend gave us a very good description of how he saw the special train containing the Maharajah of Petrala's concubines draw up at a station for the beauties to be fed. There were several hundreds. Pleasing to think that this biblical mode of life still goes on. But I fear we shan't have any chance to observe it. M had tea the other day with a lady of 27 who has 8 children (the eldest of whom is 14½) and looks 20 in spite of it. I was not allowed in, of course. But in any case, the language is a terrible barrier.

Goodbye. Write often. *Je me souviens, je me souviens des heures et des entretiens. Qui sont le meilleur de mes biens—Dansons la gigue.*[1]

A

TO MARY HUTCHINSON

Race View, Golf Road, Lahore
30 November 1925

A letter came today, Mary, and a cutting from *The Nation*. Thank you for both. We have devoured and ruminated them with infinite pleasure. And so Wittering is to go—and my first visit there—how momentous, Mary, and how often, how voluptuously remembered—is to be my last. Shall I be invited to the new house?

Here we are plunged in a whirl of social life—of the most fantastic character. Dinner parties with titled Indian barristers of fabulous wealth and whose wives wear brooches consisting of blue enamel disks on the face of which two enormous diamonds are made to revolve by clockwork in concentric circles and in opposite directions. (They are 8-day brooches and are wound up every Sunday evening.) Interviews with aged politicians who have been in jail and can talk of nothing but themselves. Dinners with distinguished English judges and their wives. Tea parties with Indians who have married English women—and what Englishwomen mostly. They are called L.L.D's in these parts—Land Lady's Daughters. Owing to the fact that their own women are kept shut up in cages, they are perfectly ignorant and incorrigibly domestic, the poor Indians are fairly bowled over by any female in the least skittish, gaudy, or impudent. They go down like ninepins before kittenish vulgarity. Practically all the English wives are blond barmaidish creatures, prancingly vulgar. To the Indians they are the most brilliant and deadly of *femmes fatales*. It is pathetic. And whenever one of their own women emancipates herself and becomes ordinarily civilized, she achieves an incredible success. The debasement of respectable women—I use the expression in its technical sense!—leads to a corresponding exaltation of the courtesans, the best of whom are a kind of

---

[1] Paul Verlaine (1844–1896). Aquarelles: "Streets-I."

Aspasias. In the United Provinces, I am told, they still preserve the tradition of courtly manners from the days of the Great Moguls; and up till a few years ago the boys of good families used to be sent to them every day for several hours in order to learn deportment and courtesy. There is an old Indian judge here who, as a child of 8 or 9, used to be taken daily to the house of the most accomplished dancing girl in Lucknow. I hope that, when we are in those parts, we shall be introduced to some of those courtly beauties. So far we have seen only the prostitutes quarter here—from outside!—driving through at night to look at the painted women sitting at their balconies and windows, or in little rooms on the ground floor, open to the street, and through the doors of which one sees the furniture pertaining to their profession—a bed, nothing more.

We have had some concerts at the houses of friends. Curious music and more interesting than I had thought it would be. The principal instruments are a kind of huge lute and a kind of viola, accompanied by kettle drums which are beaten with the palm and finger tips. The lute, well played, is an extraordinary instrument, full of unexpected tones and the viola is very rich and sweet. The music is all traditional and consists of themes treated to innumerable variations. Harmony has gone no further than the bag-pipe-like droning of the dominant. Many of the melodies are in the pentatonic, black-note scale and are consequently very like Scotch tunes in the same scale. One was very like one of the negro plantation melodies. Some are marvelously romantic in an oriental way—a snake charmer's tune, all in descending semi-tones; a strange howling camel-driver's tune. Altogether, it is all very fashionable and Stravinskyesque. The Sitwells would find it too marvelous. The appearance of the players is superb. They come into the drawing room and sit on the floor. The lute player is an old man with a walrus moustache and long hair, very like Paderewski's with a little crimson plush fez embroidered with gold on top. He looks like a German *en noir*. The kettle drum player is a thin fierce looking savage and the viola-player has a beard and classical features and looks like Jesus Christ, but stupider. When they sing, it is fabulous. They lift up their faces and howl like dogs, producing their voices from somewhere between the adenoids and the nose.

We went to Amritsar the other day, saw the golden Temple of the Sikhs—incredibly hideous, but full of queer pilgrims—the park where General Dyer shot down the unarmed crowd and a number of male prostitutes painted and dressed up as women. These last abound in the

Punjab where the habits of most of the male population are highly classical. And of the women too, I gather, particularly when there are several wives or concubines shut up in the same harem.

Haste. The mail calls. Goodbye and remember me, often.

A

TO MARY HUTCHINSON

Jaipur
9 December 1925

The mail goes to-day, in a few hours, and your letter—the charming one (they are all charming), the one containing the rather cutting cutting about poor old Lalla—has just arrived, with our *chhota hasri* or first breakfast. (One has two breakfasts here; indeed, most meals seem to get duplicated. The amount the English eat in this country is something fabulous. Six meals a day. It's to keep up their prestige and to show their superiority to the blackamoors who only eat one meal, or at the outside two.) So I am quickly writing a few lines on my machine, in bed, while Maria corrects the typographical errors in her letter, which this will accompany. Great haste, as there is only about an hour in which to write, dress, eat another breakfast before setting out on an elephant, lent to us for the occasion by a local nobleman to whom we have had introductions, to visit the ruined city of Amber. Ah, these elephants! We rode on one yesterday, to visit another ruined city inhabited exclusively by monkeys—preferable, I must say, in most respects to the average human inhabitants of ordinary cities. The discomfort of elephant riding down hill is beyond all belief. The grandeur of one's position, the scarlet trappings, the gold ringed-tusks—these are no consolation. Still, we will have to go through with the ordeal yet once more, since we should offend our host if we refused his proffered pachyderm. And I foresee we shall have a lot more elephant riding before we have done with our Rajputana tour; for we have introductions at almost every town to the ruling princes, who keep elephants by the hundred and fairly heap them on their guests. These are the penalties of greatness. In this town, providentially, the ruling prince is still at school and we have introductions only to his nobility. We were particularly thankful about this when we went to see the royal stables yesterday. There, in enormous loose boxes, built of massive masonry, stood rows upon rows of elephants. Fabulous beasts! We saw one of them relieving nature yesterday. It is a spectacle comparable only to that of Niagara or the Mount Everest at sunrise. Grandiose. One comes away full of a sense of awe and impregnated with the Higher Pantheism.

This is a charming town, the best we have seen so far. Built at the beginning of the 18th century, on a rational plan, like New York, with streets 120 feet wide. The houses are all pink and look exactly like the architectural backgrounds in Italian primitives. The people are gaudily dressed and wear jewelry all over them, wherever jewels can cling, including rings on their toes. The staple industry of the place is the manufacture of phallic symbols in marble, which is painted and gilt. Every shop is full of them. That is because this part of the country is backwards and orthodox. Orthodox Hindus—the great majority—worship Shiva under the form of the lingam or phallus and his wife under the aspect of the yoni, a word whose translation I need not append. Lingam and yoni are always represented in company. Sometimes the symbols take the form of two conical sausages lying, loose, in a sort of stone sauce boat. At other times they are indissolubly joined together; a thing in shape very much like a Roman lamp, with significant markings on its upper surface, represents the feminine deity and out of the middle of it projects a little tower, the male. I think we shall have to buy a small specimen for inclusion in the family chapel.

No more, for I must get up. The elephant paws the ground and trumpets. I will write more at length by the next mail. Your letters are exquisite. Write often. I remember you often and in many aspects. That of the *détournement de mineur* is my favourite, I think. Good bye, Mary.

Aldous

TO MARY HUTCHINSON

Taj Mahal Hotel, Bombay
22 December 1925

I write this on the only available paper (M has a praiseworthy habit of pinching anything that may be useful in the hotels where we stay, from *Bromo* and upwards) and in the waiting room of the wayside station where we are spending three midnight hours, waiting for the train to take us to Indore—M sleeps, her head pillowed on her arms on the table, in the attitude of one who sleeps off a debauch. But, alas, we have had nothing but hard boiled eggs and tea. A fearful sobriety reigns. It is only pure fatigue. But I am not tired and have no talent for sleeping except in beds—sometimes *mal à propos*, I think? (But I had every justification surely.) And as I feel I'd like to write, here I am, Mary—writing, *faute de mieux*.

Your last letter was a charming one—as usual. The story of Poppington Park—or whatever its name is—has begun to penetrate into darkest India: but only scrappily. I was charmed to hear more of it— and straight from the horse's mouth, so to speak. What good cases Jack has! Wasn't he in that most amusing one—about the time we left—of the MP who would drink cocktails out of carnal chalices and whose wife objected? I certainly remember some details on the subject. Foolish and excessive M.P.! He stands rebuked by the proverb: "Good wine needs no bush."

We have been spending several days in considerable splendour as State Guests at Udaipur. Richly picturesque, with lakes and marble gazebos on islands and an immense, grandiose and untidy palace, with sacred cows standing on the front steps and elephants wandering about the courtyards and pigeons making messes in the throne room and hundreds of beggars sitting vaguely about. Inside the most unheard-of mixture of mosaics and art-noveau *cache pots*, Persian miniatures and oleographs after the imitators of Poynter, golden thrones and clockwork toys. The last chapter of Forster's book in fact—which is a description of the scenery of the place as well as its prevailing spirit— the spirit of all these places, all India in fact. They've lost their own tradition—grown rather ashamed of it and haven't yet been able to understand ours, whether in art, science or anything else. The result is the most extraordinary mess and absurdity. These oleographs hanging next to the old Persian miniatures are symbolic of it all. At Jodhpur there was, surprisingly, a brass bedstead and a wardrobe in the throne room, with a few sporting prints on the walls. In the treasure house 4 or 5 million pounds worth of jewels, pearls unimaginable, emeralds as big as crocodiles' eggs—(and in one case 200 cigarette cases ordered from Asprey's for presentation to distinguished friends), with a complete set of jewelry in silver and turquoises for the State elephant including four anklets weighing about ten pounds each, two earrings of a stone, a tiara and several bangles for the trunk.

From the artistic point of view it's all rather monotonous. The Mohammedan stuff from the Taj downwards is abominable. The Hindu things, however, are much more interesting; but the tradition is very rigid and when you've seen two or three temples you've seen all. And the sculpture is turned out by mass production—miles of it—all pretty good, but none better than any other, none superlatively good. It's all anonymous, craftman's work.

We go on to Indore, then to Cawnpore to see all India assembled at the yearly Congress—which ought to be very curious.

Let us have more news, quickly. What of the manicure young lady? I cannot but suspect that the worst or best, has happened by now. And the young boy whose downy face you painted—alas, my own chin and cheeks, like a record in a musical box. Middle age creeps on apace. The only remedy is to live much, strongly and multifariously while the thing lasts.

Goodbye,
A

P.S. I am enclosing a letter to that man who wrote the book about Proust—Quint.[2] But I left the book in the train and can't remember his full name or the address of his publishers. Will you be very kind and address the envelope for me. Thank you.

TO MARY HUTCHINSON

Benares
6 January 1926

We are resting and working here at Benares after a most strenuous period of traveling, followed by the All India Congress at Cawnpore. M gave you an account of it last week, no doubt. A strange business, very impressive in certain respects. Not that the speeches were interesting— they were as boring as all political speeches always are, more boring, since half of them were delivered in languages that to us were incomprehensible gibberish. The people were interesting—from Gandhi, half naked, doing the holy man with an adoring young English woman in attendance, handing him his spectacles, adjusting his loincloth etc.—a most unsympathetic looking man with a foxy shopkeeper's face—to the Swaraj party leaders, who exploit Gandhi's holiness and consequent influence over the people, for their own political ends. They are all very high caste, lordly, rich and aristocratic. (This is the country where aristocratic feelings still flourish and the canaille is really treated as canaille.) Some very fine looking, intelligent men among them. And whenever you see a particularly sensitive, powerful or intelligent face, you can be quite sure that the owner of it has been in gaol for at least

[2] Léon Pierre-Quint (1895–1958). Biographer of Proust.

six months for political crimes. Presiding was our friend Mrs. Naidu,[3] one of the few free, well-educated, socially accomplished women in India, and consequently hugely successful even in her matronly age. With an attached daughter, who has read my complete works and knew E. M. Forster when he was in Hyderabad, and refuses to marry; and a younger sister, who lives in Germany and has those earnestly gushing manners of the German artistic intelligentsia. All the other women, even those completely out of purdah, were nonentities, didn't know how to behave, were hopelessly shy. And some of them came to evening parties completely veiled, looking like corpses and never uttering a word. One evening we had an immense dinner party, three and a half hours late, off the floor. At such functions there is always a lot of schoolboyish teasing and joking among the men, like the rudimentary wit you find in boarding house society at home. Even intelligent and aristocratic ones take part in it. That is the stage of social evolution at which they have arrived. There is nothing remotely resembling a salon, no easy and general conversation. Social life is still rudimentary. It is due, I suppose, to the locking up of the women.

This is a disappointing place. All the buildings are exceedingly bare. Aurangzeb pulled down all the good, old ones and the temples built since his day are very poor—though I don't know why they should be, as in other parts of the country late Hindu architecture can be very fine. The spectacle of the people bathing and drinking in the holy and filthy river is curious. One goes out in a boat in the early morning and watches them gambolling about at the water's edge, bathing, saying prayers, cleaning their teeth, rinsing their noses, drinking, washing their clothes and throwing bits of burnt corpses into the water. The corpses are put on neat little bonfires which crackle away in the most cheerful manner. The effect is not in the least gruesome, curiously enough. All round the bonfires people go about their business, children play; nobody seems to worry. That is one of the rather disquieting things about these people. They never do things consistently, as we do. We put on glum faces when we go to church or attend funerals, behave respectfully in the presence of the Great, perform ceremonials in a serious and impressive way. But these people don't. They won't hold the same emotional attitude for more than a short while at a stretch. They alternate hornpipes and funerals with astonishing rapidity; indeed, they perform them simultaneously. They see no need for symbolical

---

[3] Sarojini Naidu (1879–1949). Poet, and first woman to become president of the Indian National Congress.

ceremonies, whether religious or of state, to be performed efficiently and without hitch. Everything is gone through hugger mugger. And kings see nothing incongruous about having cows lying on the front steps and pigeons making making messes in the hall of audience, beggars sitting about and doing their toilet in the court-yards and corridors of the palace, and a bed and chest of drawers in the throne room. Similarly, those who profess to love music don't trouble to listen attentively, but begin to talk in the middle of the performance. And yet I think they really do enjoy the music. It's just that they can't be bothered to be consistently attentive. It's a habit of mind which is very strange to one. One follows their emotionalities with ponderous slowness. The more I stay here, the more profoundly grateful I am that I have no official connection with this fantastic impossible place.

The favourite deity here is Shiva and the town is full of innumerable phallic symbols—the form under which Shiva in generally represented—in consequence. Round the main temples are shops where they sell nothing else but little yoni-lingams for private devotional purposes. I am enclosing a snapshot we took a few weeks ago at the sacred lake of Pushkar. It represents one of these yoni-lingams being adored by an ecstatically gazing cow. The thing like a Roman lamp is the yoni—the upper surface is often *rehaussé* with red lines to give it a certain appearance of realism—and the little pillar is the lingam, which is supposed to be embedded in it. There must be literally millions of these things in India. Rather a sympathetic deity, I think—don't you? I shall purchase a few specimens for distribution to the pious at home.

I had a long letter yesterday from Sydney Schiff—written, I should guess, while slightly under the influence. So extraordinarily flowery was it in its compliments. But perhaps he is just trying to imitate the epistolary style of Marcel Proust, notorious for the length, the flattering sweetness of letters that were all protestation and complimentary formulae. He gives certain news, as that Wyndham Lewis has three books in the hands of the publishers; that the Sitwell menagerie is at Amalfi and that Edith goes about saying that her sister-in-law writes sweet letters to her twice a week. (Do tell us more about the happy pair, or trio—nay quatuor, for I suppose Willy[4] is there, or even quintet, when you count Edith; sextet—I had forgotten Helen.[5] Oh, and Mrs Leverson![6] It's the

[4] W. Somerset Maugham (1874–1965). English writer.
[5] Helen Rootham (1875–1938). Translator of Rimbaud. Edith's governess and later her companion.
[6] Ada Leverson (1862–1933). English novelist, friend of Oscar Wilde and Osbert Sitwell. Known as "Sphinx."

happy septuor I want news of.) Beyond this I have heard nothing of the world at your end of the universe. Only what's in the papers—that after having been frozen, you're now being drowned and blown away. We had a shower of rain yesterday—the first since we left Kashmir—and were rather pleasantly impressed by the sight, sound and smell of it. There are compensations, you see. Benares is so remotely beyond the limits of civilization that we cannot obtain copies of the "News of the World"—hence are entirely without knowledge of the progresses of the Hailey Morris case and Jack's exploits in connection with it. Our last N of the W was of December 6th, when Hailey Morris had been bitten by one of his wolf hounds and was expecting to be tried the following week. Since when the veil has been drawn. At Delhi, I hope, we may secure back numbers. The *causes célèbres* in this part of the world are merely repulsive, not obscene. The chiefly interesting case is one of a man at Simla who, in a fit of temper, kicked a rickshaw coolie to death. Although an Englishman and of high standing, he has, I am glad to say, been committed for trial. But I dare say they'll find means to get him off. Beyond that there is very little of the human touch in our news.

This letter, I calculate, will reach you towards the end of January. From the time it reaches you up till, say, February 8th direct your letters—and I hope they will be *long* and *frequent*, like the loves of the blessed in Mohammed's paradise—as follows—care of Thomas Cook and Sons, Rangoon, Burma. We shall be in Burma, all being well, up to about the first week in March; after February the eighth, therefore, write care of Thos Cook and Sons, Singapore, Straights Settlements. How long we shall be in those parts I don't know. It depends on the nature of the place, the climate and finance. After that, I suppose, America. By the time we return we shall have seen all the world's monsters—and shall be ripe, in consequence, for human society. I hope you will provide it, Mary.

Love,
Aldous

TO SYDNEY SCHIFF

Benares
14 January 1926

Dear Schiff,
I was delighted to get your very friendly letter, which reached me here after traveling I don't know how many thousands of miles—to Kashmir

and back, among other places. We have been living quietly here among the comforts of a very tolerable hotel for the last ten days or so, resting after a very strenuous month of traveling through the Indian states of Rajputana, followed, just after Christmas, by a yet more strenuous four days at Cawnpore, where we attended the All India Congress. Rajputana was interesting as a spectacle, both as regards art and landscape. The finest Hindu temples and palaces in northern India are to be found there. We had introductions and were, consequently, state guests at most of the capitals; so did the trip in relative comfort. If you go to the more out of the way places as an ordinary unprotected tourist, it is not very pleasant, I fancy. As state guests, however, we were treated very well; lodged in comfortable guest houses, given good food and provided with carriages and even motors for taking long distance trips. Remarkably handsome, considering that we weren't officials and were in no position to do anything, whether for good or evil, in return. We only met one of the maharajas in person—Bikaner, a very advanced and European gentlemen, with no more than two or three wives and no concubines. Amiable, but not so romantic as one might have wished. Cawnpore was very curious. An immense concourse—eight or ten thousand people in a huge tent, ourselves among the perhaps five or six Europeans present, sitting in considerable splendour—or rather squatting, for there were no chairs and everyone sat on the ground—among the big wigs. Next to Gandhi, one day—a man to me exceedingly unsympathetic, with a low foxy shopkeeper's face, strange in a saint. He wears only a loincloth, gets up every morning at four to pray and meditate, passes Mondays in silence and starves periodically for a week or so at a time. His asceticism is the secret of his popularity. The Indian masses admire only saints—and saints are rarely very good politicians. Gandhi is attended by a young English woman called Miss Slade,[7] who sits by him, adoringly, like a dog, handing him his spectacles, adjusting his loincloth, feeding him when his meals are brought and so on. He treats her as a dumb waiter. It is part of his mystical stunt to ignore the existence of people—quite the wrong mystical principle, incidentally—and, I was told by Mrs. Naidu, the woman politician and President of this year's Congress, that when she tells him how absurd it is to have these female adorers hanging about him, he professes not to know that they're women at all. The other leaders impressed me much more sympathetically. Whether they'll

[7] Madeleine Slade (1892–1982).

succeed in getting what they want, I wonder and somewhat doubt. The British government has so many trump cards in its hand: power to begin with, then the Hindu-Moslem hatred; then the conflicting interests of native princes and democratic nationalists. It wouldn't surprise me if the English were still sitting here, very tight indeed, fifty years hence. Moreover, the Indians are so appallingly patient, so dreadfully "spiritual" and "other-worldly." People who are so much preoccupied with Higher Things as these poor imbeciles are, won't get much of the Lower. India is enough to convert the most convinced believer in religion and spirituality into an ardent materialist, epicurean and atheist. What these people need is a good supply of Nietzschean missions.

Here at Benares one sees Indian religiosity. Innumerable pilgrims drinking and bathing in the filthy waters of the Ganges and worshiping— but without any sort of joyous or orgiastic ceremonies—the innumerable phallic symbols which fill their shrines and stand about on the ghats. I enclose a snapshot of one of these symbols, taken, not here, but at the sacred lake of Pushkar, near Ajmere. It is a yoni-lingam or bi-sexual symbol, the thing like the Roman lamp being yoni or female half and the little pillar sprouting out of it, the male. The cow, or bull, is generally found standing sentinel and gazing with rapturous eyes at the divine object. It is typical of the Indians that they should regard these cheerful divinities as symbols of the Highest Truths, not of the most human.

I was glad to hear all your news. Let me have more, if you have the time. I am sure a study of Sitwellian affairs would well repay the labor at present. You ought, I feel, to organize a special scientific expedition to Amalfi for the purpose. Good news of Lewis and his books; I shall look forward to seeing them when they appear. Do you see Sullivan ever? I have heard no word since I left, except from H. M. Tomlinson, who told me that he had seen him, in the usual form and beaming, and that he was writing his monumental work on Beethoven at last.

We go on from India to Burma, after a stay in Delhi, during the first or second week of February. Thence to Singapore, for a look at the Islands. I feel there must be more in them than met the eye of Conrad. Care of Thomas Cook and Sons, Singapore will be our address on letters posted in London up to, say, March 5th. After that, who knows, we hope to push on to America; but nothing is certain. Give our best regards to your wife. I hope she keeps well, in spite of the English winter.

Yours,
Aldous Huxley

TO MARY HUTCHINSON

Maiden's Hotel
Delhi
21 January 1926

Your presents, Mary, reached us at Benares a week ago, just after the mail had left. So thanks had to be bottled. They have matured meanwhile. Thus a vintage gratitude I offer. Charming little diary: and the wishes you pencilled in for New Year's day the best that could be pronounced. May there be many engagements with you recorded on those blue pages, and after the engagements there will be, perhaps, certain little hieroglyphs and mysterious symbols like those which Stendhal recorded in his diary or, nearer his heart, on the inner side of his braces—the shorthand and undecipherable record of long drawn pleasures and delicate complicated feelings. Let us hope so.

Meanwhile here we are at Delhi, living in a tent because the hotels are so full that they cannot offer us a room. Rather cold: for by a stroke of what can only be described as genius the English have decided to make the capital of India in a place which for 8 months of the year is unbearable with heat and for the remaining 4 with cold. We are surrounded by politicians and attend debates of the local parliament. Slightly boring so far: but I hope for comic incidents in the future. Still, what a bad business it all is—this politics: particularly here, where it is all so hopeless, such a nightmare. The longer one stays here, the more nightmarish and hopeless the place seems. And one finds oneself feeling very patriotic about Europe. This place where there are no women, no social life, no culture in the sense of socially available culture—only learning and pedantry and technical knowledge—no probing curiosity about the facts of the outside world—this place is not for us. And I find that most of the intelligent Indians one meets are only anxious to get out of the country.

The postman champs at the gate. Mailday succeeds mailday with a vertiginous rapidity and somehow there is never an occasion to write in the intervening space of time. Write often, Mary. I think frequently and with great pleasure of the engagements that will be made in the course of 1926, of the hieroglyphic comments on them that will be written.

Aldous

TO MARY HUTCHINSON

Delhi
28 January 1926

If you were here, Mary—I wish you were—you would agree that Delhi, not Paris, is the place where Proust should have lived. All the prides, snobberies and deceptions, all the humiliations and social agonies, all the masks and courtesies of Paris are here, but magnified, exaggerated and complicated. Everything is on a larger scale. The Dreyfus case is here the eternal black versus white case. The aristocracy is composed of ruling despots with harems—with, on the opposite side, another ruling class, of poor birth, but made insolent by the possession of powers which the jewelled despots have to respect and pay court to—with a feigned courtesy that covers a hatred all the more bitter for being impotent. Round these there circulate crowds of sycophants of all colours. And in opposition to both stand the nationalist and democratic politicians, themselves enormously aristocratic. They have their hangers on, flattering, suffering agonies of humiliation, trying to climb painfully to acquaintance with Pandit Motilal Nehru; just as the other sycophants try to climb into the favours of Maharajas or English officials. The only thing that is lacking is the intellectual element. There is no culture in Delhi; the comedy of artistic snobberies and intellectual pretensions is unknown. It is a pity. We circulate among the comedians, fascinated. We enjoy the advantage of being able to penetrate almost everywhere—among the politicians, owing to our connections in the Indian camp; among the officials owing to the colour of our skins, the faint reverberations even here in imperial Delhi of my literary name and the fact that Maria is one of the very few presentable women in India; and, for the last reason especially, even among the princes. One could spend a long time botanizing here. The only trouble is that however long one spent, one could never discover more than a very little about the blackamoors. All their domesticity is a closed book, into which one is lucky if one gets the briefest occasional glimpse. In any case, however, we cannot stay long. Time presses and on Sunday night we leave for Calcutta, shall spend a day or two there and proceed to Burma—the beginning of the real tropics, luxuriant vegetation and all. After that to Singapore which is, I gather, the genuine article—the palm house at Kew, with half guinea orchids blossoming on every bush. Did you, I wonder, get a little package we sent some time in the first week of December—a Benares scarf and a pair of transparent trousers made of flowered black muslin (to be worn, I hope, only on the days when my little diary records an engagement with you)? I ask, because there seems to be some doubt whether other packages sent at the same time have arrived and so that belated representations may be made to the post office if it hasn't. I have fears that it may somehow have got engulfed in the Christmas rush, may have sunk below the surface of the postal stream, never to reappear. I hope not. The trousers had a certain charm. I think it might be well to get another pair or two made before we leave India.

It is, generally speaking, a most unsatisfactory country to buy things in—first, because there is practically nothing of the slightest interest or beauty to buy and, in the second place, because what there is costs far more than it would cost in Bond Street. This town is famed for its jewellery and its ivory. The jewellery is very sumptuous, but barbaric. One sees princes in the shops buying thousands of pounds worth of huge uncut emeralds and pearls. The ivory is, surprisingly enough, quite good, but we have as yet failed to find any of those exquisitely carved ivory dildoes of which one hears so much. As for brass—it is abominable and the good old stuff is exceedingly rare. We were fortunate in finding one or two quite pretty old morsels at Jaipur. I am hoping we may do better in the way of objects of art in Burma and Singapore, where the Chinese element in the population is so numerous.

M has gone to-night to a party at Viceregal Lodge, from which I am excluded owing to my failure to bring a tail coat with me; so that I am solitary in our tent. (The princes and their suites have occupied all the rooms of the hotel left vacant after the wants of the permanent official residents have been satisfied. We common tourists are left out in the cold.) Outside, not very far away, the jackals are lugubriously howling. A pair of amorous cats make me reflect how fortunate it is that human beings know how to make love in silence. The noise in the streets of a great city at night . . . I wish you were here, Mary. Good night.

Aldous

TO MARY HUTCHINSON

On the Irrawaddy
14 February 1926

St. Valentine's day, dear me! and the anniversary of that first letter, dear Mary, I wrote you how long ago—and from the banks of a very different river. Time, time. We sit still, sucking in the future as the Italians eat macaroni. And then, one day, the macaroni comes to an end and we suck at vacuity. What a lot of *pasta asciutta* we have drawn in since that first Valentine's Day letter! And what still remains! Meanwhile here are my Valentine greetings.

Here we are floating on one of those rivers which ought to have been celebrated in ragtime songs—Way down on the old Irrawaddy: or else by Fragson[8] *tout le long de l'Irrawaddy etcetera.* A noble river. We have been steaming up it for the last 3 days from Mandalay—so far that we are actually out of the tropics again: a league and a half beyond Cancer, more than a quarter of the way to the pole! Our destination is Bhamo, which is almost on the frontiers of China and is the place where the caravans come in from the further east or form up to carry Burmese jade and amber into China. After a peep at it, we shall turn round, slide down again to Mandalay and from there another 200 miles down the river to a place where we shall take the train for Rangoon.

We have steamed through all the sceneries; flat lands like Holland, park-like expanses of greensward dotted with trees—pure Thames; hills like the Rhine and now through dense subtropical forests of teak and tall ferns and innumerable nameless trees, many of them wildly in flower. Every now and then we pass a village. A few wooden houses on stilts. A pagoda, white or gilded. A monastery with high tiers of roofs. Men and women in the same skirts of silk or batik-patterned cotton standing on the shore, smoking immense cheroots which it is only possible to compare to phallic emblems. Naked children swimming, or running in the sun—amphibians. Nobody doing any work—for no self-respecting Burman works. He leaves that to the Indian immigrants, who do everything—even act as policemen in the towns—while the Burman smokes his, or her, symbolical cheroot and looks on, laughing generally. Most sympathetic. But the result is that they're being steadily ousted from their own country.

Their buildings are bad, but marvelously amusing. The great Pagoda at Rangoon is a sort of Sitwell's paradise—all wood-carving, and gilding and looking glasses—the merry-go-round style of architecture. Mandalay is even more gimcrack; palaces entirely made of gilt teak and mirrors—even the trams are like something out of the Wembley Amusement Park. Burma seems to exist in a sort of comic golden

[8] Harry Fragson (1869–1913). British music hall singer and composer, even more famous in France.

age—everything is very jolly, nothing matters but fun. Money, art, work, knowledge—they don't seem to be considered. Cheroots and marionette shows and wearing flowers in one's hair and building more roundabout-like pagodas—the whole duty of man. Meanwhile the Indians and the Chinese get hold of more and more of the cash and land.

Our fellow passengers are dim. A pair of earnest and lesbian ladies of unequal age are the most intellectual. Then there is a soldier, who at least knows the country: and a professional bore who trots out statistics and information about photography: and a spinster from India, traveling alone, timorous and pathetic; and a Scottish family who eat a great deal—their money's worth—and don't speak much. The rest of the ship swarms with Burmans who lie about on the deck smoking and eating fruit and crayfish. I hope we may find some letters when we get back to Rangoon. It is a long time since we have had any news. Our movements have been too confusing for the mail to reach us. An occasional newspaper tells us that the winter is still diabolic, that Sir Basil Thompson[9] has been fired for fumbling, and so on. That is all. I long for more interesting news. No more—except perhaps a little poem about

A young lover from Burma,
Whose mistress had reasons to murmur.
"Your will," she repined,
"Is too weak, and your mind
Should be larger, your character firmer."

Je t'embrasse,
A

TO MARY HUTCHINSON

Rangoon
22 February 1926

After nine days incessant steaming up and down the Irrawaddy—from latitude 16 to latitude 25 and back again—we are again in Rangoon, in a good hotel, praise God! With bath water that is clean, not drawn from the murky river, large rooms instead of oven-like little cabins and

---

[9] Sir Basil Thomson (1866–1939). British colonial administrator, prison governor, head of Scotland Yard, director of intelligence, and mystery writer. He was found guilty of an indecent act in Hyde Park in 1926.

majestic electric punkahs as big as spread eagles. Reclining, all but naked beneath the fan, we have been reading your delicious letter of a month ago, laughing at all the fabulous items of news it contains—Ottoline's crudded blood, Willy Walton's adventures into heterosexuality, Maynard's party and your most shocking adventure in the trousers (which I had the foresight to tell you not to wear except in *my* presence, provocative Mary). And then there is the melancholy description of poor Boris, weeping over Roger's insanely boyish escapade. Not that I personally would have minded much at being deprived of Helen.[1] She is too metallic for my taste; but perhaps, in intimacy, she develops qualities more furry, feathery, and softly pneumatic. And in any case, how can one ever tell what it is that ties one person to another? Mournful, too, is the news of the collapse of l'affaire Ponsonby. I hope some graceful substitute is in sight.

Our steamer coming down from Mandalay was more curiously freighted with humanity that that which took us up to Bhamo. It was like Pembroke College in Dr. Johnson's days—a Nest of Singing Birds. For there were no less than three writers aboard—self (the only one really, of course; but let that pass!), a man who writes adventure stories and plays, called Dale Collins[2] and a Roumanian princess literary, and like all Roumanian princesses, in three languages and bearing the wonderfully improbable name of Princess Savagein.[3] She was Tom's Princess Volupine[4] in youth—rather bitchy, but with ideals; a philosophizing cock teaser. You know the type. Mr. Dale Collins, who is an Australian with the richest cockney accent and looks like a rather unwholesome sort of bank clerk, was bowled completely over. They were together and he fell. I didn't fall, in spite of the promises of pneumatic bliss, but spent some hours examining the most interesting specimen. There will be ample opportunity for continuing the examination; for the Princess—perhaps she is really Prince Carol's friend, Miss Zizi Lambrino;[5] who knows?—is going with us as far as Singapore: five days through seas progressively more and more tropical. One should be able to discover something, I think in these circumstances.

As for the river below Mandalay, that was comparatively uninteresting. The best was above. Below it was too wide, and for the most

[1] Helen Maitland Anrep (1885–1965). Wife of Boris Anrep and companion to Roger Fry.
[2] Dale Collins (1897–1956). Australian novelist.
[3] Henrietta Sava-Goiu. Maria encouraged Aldous to have a shipboard affair with her.
[4] See Eliot's "Burbank with a Baedeker: Bleistein with a Cigar."
[5] Joanna "Zizi" Lambrino (1898–1953). First wife of Carol II of Romania. He divorced her in 1921.

part, banks that were too flat. Also it was uncommonly hot. But some of the Burmese villages, where the steamer stopped, were curious. Everywhere the brightly coloured skirts, the immense phallic cheroots—which taste, when you smoke them, exactly like so much paper or common garden bonfire, not tobacco—and in the background innumerable pagodas with their bells tinkling in the hot wind. Sometimes a crowd of people standing round the performance of jugglers or dancers on a slack rope. And each village with its own peculiar industry. One producing nothing but lacquer work (we are bringing you an amusing lacquer-painted walking stick). Another only drums. Of these, our steamer shipped an enormous cargo—thousands upon thousands of tom toms of every size, going down to Rangoon. Along one long stretch of bank stand the remains of what was once the capital, nine hundred years ago—scores of immense pagodas rising above the trees, which have swallowed up the fifteen thousand lesser shrines that once adorned Pagan. A little lower down, in an arid country of clay hills, are the oil wells, hundreds of little wooden towers and big cylindrical tanks, several of which were on fire, sending their clouds of black smoke across miles of sky. The workmen were on strike and doing a little sabotage. They have some spirit, the Burmese. Perhaps a little too much; it extrinsicates itself a little too frequently in murder. The priests give sanctuary to the criminals in their convents. Sometimes, it appears, they do a bit of murdering themselves.

On Thursday we go to the Straits, where we shall stay in some splendour with the Governor.[6] After that to Java, with perhaps a preliminary diversion in the opposite direction to Siam—it depends on whether the information I have just received about Sydney Waterlow being appointed as British minister at Bangkok is true, whether he is actually there and whether he will put us up. I hope to get the facts at Singapore; here, nobody knows anything. I think it would be amusing to go and see Ambassador Waterlow in Siam; his voice and his moustache among the Siamese would be, I feel, extraordinarily dramatic. We should be in Frisco about the middle of May and in England towards the end of June. So go to Paris in May and receive us in your secret house—it sounds too romantic—when we return. How much I look forward to it, Mary. But don't till then, I entreat, dance too often in your diaphanous pantaloons.

Aldous

[6] Sir Laurence Nunns Guillemard (1862–1951). Governor of Straits Settlement, 1919–1927.

TO MARY HUTCHINSON

Gawet, Java
10 March 1926

How much you would like this island, Mary! Not merely because islands, as the Freudians maintain, are Female Symbols, but because it is so beautiful, so entirely fabulous and fantastic. Indigo mountains streaked with emerald green cultivation, palms in the foreground and immense butterflies as big as aeroplanes and Javanese dressed in batiks and buffaloes with naked copper boys sitting or even lying in hieratic attitudes on their backs. Here and there a volcano, a hotel, a Dutchman, a tree of gardenias, a half guinea orchid. The mornings are fine; but in the afternoon it pours with rain. The atmosphere is like a bronchitis rattle. In the plains one walks in the palm house at Kew; but here, at 3000 feet, it is the conservatory of a private gentleman who cannot afford quite as much coal as the state. It is a place to come back to—for a long time, and, if possible with a motor. One of these winters, Mary, we will all embark for an equatorial Cythera. And there are so many others besides Java and just as marvelous, they say. But they need time: the ships go irregularly and don't make connections. One must be prepared to wait a week in out of the way corners of the spice islands or on the coast of Papua scanning the horizon for a funnel. But decidedly it would be worth doing.

Singapore was also delightful. The island is like an English park—but in the equator. Green slopes, great trees growing here and there, overhead huge clouds, like clouds over the Cotswolds (such a relief after the staring blue of India), but here and there—un-Englishly—a palm, a mass of white orchids looking like little doves sitting in a row on a branch, a tree covered with prickly scarlet fruits or with enormous orange flowers, an emerald and golden bird. And all the time, of course, the soft damp heat.

We stayed with the Governor. Tremendous state—a minor Buckingham Palace. But quite nice people, especially the Governess—if that is the name of the female of the species. It is an immense town, four fifths Chinese, prodigiously prosperous and busy. One doesn't realize what an astonishing affair this British Empire is until one begins to wander about it. These vast towns like Singapore and Rangoon which we have brought into existence in the course of the last 50 years or so are exceedingly astonishing. And then, how curious, coming down by train to Singapore from Penang—hundreds of miles through one continuous rubber plantation, all the world's motor tyres and abdominal belts and French letters and crape soles and whirling sprays, and hot water bottles—all from English trees. And everywhere Englishmen, playing tennis, eating porridge at 8:30 A.M., drinking whiskey at 6:00 in comfortable clubhouses, dressing for dinner even in the jungle and to entertain the local orang-outangs. Most extraordinary. One can't realize it till one sees it—and when one has realized it, one doesn't know what to make of it.

I hope we may find several letters on our return to Singapore. England seems remoter than ever. It is impossible to believe, here, in the existence of north east winds and March coming in like a lion and going out like a lamb and the pussy willows on Palm Sunday—what a charming and absurd substitute for coconuts!—and the first primroses, the snowdrops and the aconites. Quite impossible to believe. Write and reassure me of the real existence of all those phenomena, and tell me how you are and what you are at the moment—whether urban or rural, literary or gay, chaste or abandoned, also that you would like to see me again as much as I would like to see you.

Aldous

TO MARY HUTCHINSON

The Europe Hotel
Singapore
19 March 1926

Here is a little bird that comes from Java. Made of a horn—not one of mine, Mary, I hope! Not the creation of that delicate, gentle, deaf-mute idiot you talked of so longingly in your letter? I trust not. You would long for the Chinese, if you were here—the ladies only, not the men. They are exquisitely elegant—the colour of old ivory and with black eyes, bright and impassive, like the eyes of Marie Laurencin's girls. Their necks are long and slender, like yours. It would be, for you, something of a Narcissus complex. In winter they use dildoes of resin; in summer of rock crystal, curiously carved, or of jade. They wear black silk trousers and all the younger ones have given up squashing their feet. Their hair has the same sheen as their pantaloons and they wear it in a row of gold pins and a pink tropical flower. Civilization oozes out of them at every pore and more copiously than sweat from a Dutch woman. Oh, the Dutch women. . . . Like walking cathedrals, and all pregnant, all the time. A haunting nightmare: let us draw veils.

But now about you, Mary. Tear down the veils again, rip them as you ripped—with a little gesture as impatient as that of Tom when he ripped his pajamas, but an impatience born of sentiments different from his—your flowered nightgown. In my memory you live Adamitically, in only your hair—and that tied up behind, like a schoolgirl. *Détournement de mineure.* It is with a slight effort that I endow you with tailor-mades and shoes. Why aren't you here to comment on this extraordinary world of Dutchmen and tropical flowers and thunderstorms and Government House and volcanoes and jungles and American tourists and enormous butterflies, with eyed wings and veined wings, orange and yellow wings, enamelled metal wings, vast wings of thick black velvet? Why aren't you here to lie naked under the mosquito nets, like a mermaid in an aquarium, through the hot-house afternoons and nights, under the delicious fans, talking, dozing, kissing, reading, getting up every now and then to stand under the nerve-startling, pleasurably agonizing cold shower bath, and returning to the dim twilight of the mosquito net aquarium refreshed—to begin kissing again? You ought to be here. It is preposterous that you aren't. Yet one day I shall make you come.

I hope you will like the bird. I am bowled over by its beauty. Such a felicitous invention. Given a horn, it seems inevitable. And yet it's only the Japanese who have thought of it. Dim people—but much may be forgiven them for their birds. Goodbye, Mary. Love me. Postpone the idiot till my return. I will be your half wit.

Aldous

TO H. L. MENCKEN

Dollar Steamship Line
SS President Cleveland
San Francisco
5 May 1926

Dear H. L. Mencken,
I'm entering the USA by the back door—though I suppose they call it the front in California—from the Orient, where I have been spending some months to satisfy myself empirically that all this rigmarole of Light from the East etc. is genuinely nonsense. Having done so, I am now one my way home—*orientis partibus adventavit Asinus*, as they used to sing in the blasphemous—and passing through your continent. Will there be a hope of seeing you? My wife and I will be spending

some three weeks or so in New York from about mid-May onwards. . . . It will be a great delight if you're visible.

I regaled myself during two or three days of this voyage with your fourth *Prejudices*. Very magnificent. You ought to have some of your best passages recorded for the gramophone—you read so well aloud; there are really Ciceronian thunders. Have it bawled by some sonorous comedian like Hackett or Forbes Robertson into the phonograph and then circulate it to do its missionary work among phonograph owners. The majority of people in our modern world are not educated up to the point of understanding what they read in books. They can understand a thing when it is spoken *viva voce*. E.g. the soldiers in The War, who had to have the army textbooks read out to them, lectured into their brains, instead of reading for themselves. A twelve-inch disk of *Prejudices* would penetrate further than a book.

Yours,
Aldous Huxley

TO MARY HUTCHINSON

ca 10 May 1926

Grand Canyon: We have been in America five days. I have seen its two most remarkable natural phenomena—the canyon and Charlie Chaplin. Both very splendid, especially Charlie, who is, in conversation, like Mark Gertler at his best, but more so and better. The most ravishing man. We walked up and down by the Pacific, all afternoon, in the midst of crowds of exquisitely pretty flappers dressed in bathing costumes so tight that every contour of the Mound of Venus and the Vale of bliss was plainly visible. Very attractive they are—like lovely little animals, but of course quite soulless. Poor Charlie succumbed to one of them, a flapper of sixteen,[7] who took care to get *enceinte* and black-mailed him into marriage. I think he hates her now, which is not to be wondered at, if she is a typical American flapper. Los Angeles and Hollywood quite [illegible]. Such comedy, oddness, vitality, vulgarity: it would be worth spending a month here. One could get with all the serious *mondes*. It's amply worth coming all the way to see.

---

[7] Lita Grey (1908–1995). Chaplin's second wife. They divorced in 1927.

TO MARY HUTCHINSON

Hotel Belmont
New York
21 May 1926

New York—marvelous, but a little too much of a good thing. Even my beard grows faster here than it does in other places and I have to shave twice a day. And then I am grotesquely *famous* here and begin to taste, tho' very faintly, the horrors of life as led by Charlie or the Prince of Wales. People recognize me in restaurants—how? And when I went to cash a cheque at a bank, the Manager said that he recognized my signature because he had an autographed copy of one of my works. It is really terrifying. I am anxious to get back to my own country: for I have been so busy being famous that it has been impossible to write to you, Mary. You have no idea how famous one is in America. It is frightful. I long to be back in my own country: I don't like being a prophet, at all. And there are other reasons, Mary. Shall I see you on the Quay at Plymouth? And do you think I should find a *garçonnière* in London? Cast an eye over the advertisements of small furnished flats—very small, one room would be enough provided it is a bedroom. I look forward to endless delights. Do you too?

And now I have to go out and be famous again for the benefit of all the literary critics in New York. And they have asked me to talk on the radio to an audience of forty-three millions. It is fantastic. But such is life in the Great West. How much I look forward to life in the English East.

Aldous

TO MARY HUTCHINSON

The Athenaeum, Pall Mall
London, S.W.1
Monday, late June

Just heard from Maria that she's coming on the evening of 27th. Sunday. She wants you to write to her to say if that will be a convenient date for you—if you'll be in town etc—complaining that you've been most remiss in correspondence.

In haste, Mary, *et un peu las*, but full of the tenderest affection.

A

TO MARY HUTCHINSON

The Athenaeum,
Pall Mall, S.W.1
7 June 1926

Let's have lunch on Wednesday, Mary. Shall I come and fetch you at Albert Road? And will you show me the studio? [Onslow Mews, S.W.7] I am staying at my father's house. Will you ring up—Hampstead 4456—on Wednesday morning, or drop a word to 16 Bracknell Gardens, N.W.3. What a delight it will be to see you.

Je t'embrasse,
Aldous

TO PERCY WYNDHAM LEWIS[8]

69 Eton Avenue, N.W.3
25 June 1926

Dear Lewis,
If there's no violent hurry for the MS, I'll let you have something by the end of next week. Meanwhile, however, couldn't we arrange a meeting? Perhaps you could lunch with me—and possibly also my wife, who may be here then—on Tuesday, 29th—at the Monico, shall we say? (it is at least central) about 1:15. I do hope you will be able to come. I look forward to seeing you and hearing more about the periodical than Sullivan was able to tell me.

Yours,
Aldous Huxley

TO MARY HUTCHINSON

The Athenaeum,
Pall Mall, S.W.1
June 1926

I enclose a note Maria gave me for you, Mary, and which I had left at home when I saw you.

She wrote to me today to ask whether you know Mme Groult [Nicole Groult, Paris *couturière*] sufficiently well to give a letter of introduction to her for Maria's sister, who has some scheme or other to

---

[8] Percy Wyndham Lewis (1882–1957). British painter and author.

talk to her about—in connection with painted clothes, I think. Don't put yourself out in any way about this; but if it's feasible and no trouble, you'd be very kind if you would write a line.

Heavily occupied with work and various people these last days. Tomorrow too. Perhaps Saturday afternoon at Onslow? In any case I see you Saturday evening. Let me know. I am at my brother's. Such fearful haste. I remember Tuesday.

A

TO L. P. HARTLEY

The Athenaeum
Pall Mall, S.W.1
ca late June 1926

My dear Leslie,
Back this evening from New York, I looked into the *Saturday Review* and saw the very civil things you said about *Two or Three Graces*. Thank you. Are you in London these days? I am, for a while. Let me know if you are and suggest a time when we might meet. I will make counter proposals, if your ideas don't coincide with mine.

You must visit those United States. Marvelous isn't the word.

Yours,
Aldous H.

TO ANITA LOOS[9]

The Athenaeum, Pall Mall
London, S.W.1
5 July 1926

Dear Anita Loos,
I am delighted to hear that you are to be in London at the end of this month. I propose to stay here at any rate until the beginning of August, perhaps till nearly the middle of August, and I look forward immensely to seeing you—that is if indefatigable Lady Colefax will allow you to be seen by anybody but herself! (However, I have hopes that she may by then have retired to the country; lions who reach these shores at an unfashionable season have a fair prospect of freedom.)

---

[9] Anita Loos (1888–1981). American author and screenwriter.

This address always finds me. I give no other, as I move about, staying with different people or passing a night or two now and then at my studio. But I come here almost every day to doze among the Bishops and Presidents of all the Learned Societies who are, ex-officio, members of this sublime institution. Please let me know when you are coming and where you will be staying. We must certainly do something about it.

Yours,
Aldous Huxley

TO ALBERT RUTHERSTON[1]

The Athenaeum
Pall Mall, S.W.1
7 July 1926

Dear Rutherston,
Thank you for your letter of the 3rd. Needless to say I should be delighted to have one of my books adorned by you. But I don't see how it can be managed in the immediate future. The only suitable book would be a volume of selected essays, which Chatto and Windus propose to bring out in a limited edition at Christmas. It is obviously impossible to bring out two limited editions of the same book and as I am bound by contract to Chatto's, I cannot let them down in this matter (nor for that matter would I want to, as they have always been very nice to me). I hope that some more auspicious opportunity may present itself later. I will let you know as soon as there is a prospect of anything. Meanwhile thank you for the honor you have done me in wanting to decorate a book of mine.

Yours,
Aldous Huxley

TO MARY HUTCHINSON

Onslow
Thursday, early July

The place is haunted, Mary, by your invisible but perfumed ghost. I embrace it, unsatisfyingly. May I hope tomorrow to caress something

---

[1] Albert (Rothenstein) Rutherston (1881–1953). English portrait painter and illustrator. William Rothenstein (1872–1945) was his brother. In 1924, Huxley sat for a portrait by William Rothenstein.

more than a disembodied memory? Come after Osbert [Sitwell]'s dinner. I will be waiting—impatiently.

A

TO MARY HUTCHINSON

Onslow
12 July 1926

Mary, I have as pledges, pawned against your return, the following: 1 ring, 1 garter, 4 handkerchiefs, 2 gloves, 1 pair of trousers (diaphanous), 1 coat.

Will you come and have lunch here on Wednesday—a picnic in disorder and perhaps also in bed? Or if you can't do that come after lunch, the earlier the better. I will ring up tomorrow and find out which you can do. *A bientôt*, my charming Mary.

A

TO MARY HUTCHINSON

2 Round Church Road
Cambridge
Monday, late July

The enclosed—is it correct?—is for the goatskin (*Quelle faunesse!*) which you bought for Maria.

And now, sweet Mary, thank you for the charming handkerchief. Will you come and be personally thanked on Thursday afternoon? I shall be back probably by lunch time on that day; but I don't yet exactly know, so I won't suggest meeting at lunch. In any case, I'll ring you up when I get back. But write here and say if you can come to Onslow at about 4:00. Will you come? Yes. I insist on it, Mary.

A

TO MARY HUTCHINSON

Cambridge
21 July 1926

Come then at about 4:00 tomorrow, Thursday, but not for the last time, Mary. I am already so melancholy with the sight of these colleges and waters and green lawns (what an ironically incongruous introduction to the realities of contemporary life!), so full of thoughts of Gray's "little victims" at play, of transience and the stanchless flow of time, that I can't bear the sound of the words "Last Time." Such a knell, such a funereal decisiveness in the sound. Let it be uncertain: let there be at least the possibility of repetitions. But in any case we will dine together. Dearest Mary.

A

TO PERCY WYNDHAM LEWIS

The Athenaeum
Pall Mall, S.W.1
23 July 1926

Dear Lewis,
I enclose an article which I hope will do for the paper. I hear from [Charles] Prentice that you're thinking of calling it *The Enemy*: a good title, I think.

Will you be in town in the middle of next week? Perhaps, if you are, you will lunch with me one day—Wednesday or Thursday, for example.

Yours,
Aldous Huxley

TO MARY HUTCHINSON

In the train between Calais and Brussels
Friday, 6 August 1926

Your letter, sweet Mary, reached me yesterday and was a comfort in the midst of an agony of packing and other last minute activities—activities which seem to have been prolonging themselves, futilely and without the achievement of much, for the last days. I wondered what you were doing, imagined you floating among roses and gambolling children, very ravishing, like a Marie Laurencin heroine. I had not visualized the work—of what? fact, fiction, reflection? In any case, I hope I may see the finished product. What a strange and charming dream we have dreamt in the last weeks. A few brief hours, during which, however, we abolished duration and space, made one another free of paradise and eternity, unchained ecstasies and, touching bodies, moved through one another's minds like divine presences, apocalyptic gods.

Epical and supernatural moments. And between, quiet idylls, exquisite precisely for being so natural and domestic. One lives on so many different planes, and fully, delightfully on each; every human being has as many storeys as the Woolworth Building and shoots effortlessly and imperceptibly in spiritual elevators from floor to floor. (The disaster is when two Woolworths come into contact and their occupants get out at different floors!) Meanwhile, the train carries me along, further and further through time and space. Across gulfs I send you impalpable kisses of melancholy and loving remembrance.

What have I been doing since I last saw you? To begin with, I lunched with Tom, who looked terribly grey-green, drank no less than five gins with his meal, told me he was going to join Vivien[2] in her Paris nursing home to break himself of his addictions of tobacco and alcohol, and was eloquent about Parisian luncheons with resoundingly titled duchesses. In the intervals we had a very pleasant and friendly talk about books. Then I went down into the country to see old Sullivan, who has broken his leg and is wrapped in melancholy and irritation. I found him being wheeled about in a bath-chair by his landlady and her daughter,[3] who is also his concubine, a rather queer silent girl, who was at school with Katherine Mansfield and knew her intimately. The mother on the contrary chattered like a magpie—about philosophy— to the fury of Sullivan, who got more and more annoyed and ruder and ruder. A comedy, but rather a pathetic one, I don't know why. On Bank Holiday walked on the Heath which smelt, through all its hundreds of acres, like a small and stuffy church on a wintry Sunday—human, all too human. In the evening to see Koteliansky,[4] who had Mrs. Dobree[5] with him, curiously attractive in her rather low, canaille way. On Tuesday I lunched with Mr. Beverly Nichols, that plump and rosy-bottomed ex-friend of Tommy's who proposes to write an article about me in the *Sketch*.[6] It will be awful, no doubt; I adopt ostrich tactics towards these things and don't read them. In the evening went to see D. H. Lawrence, who is over in England for a short while, and found him charming, so much quieter than he was—it's the approach of middle age, with success and the removal of the horrors of the war. Even Frieda was calmer,

---

[2] Vivien Eliot, d. 1947. [Tom] Eliot's first wife.
[3] Mimi Bartrick-Baker, later Sullivan's wife; a Queen's College friend of Mansfield.
[4] S. S. Koteliansky (1882–1955). Russian translator and friend of D. H. Lawrence and Katherine Mansfield.
[5] Valentine Dobrée (1894–1974). Painter and friend of Carrington.
[6] Nichols's article was reprinted in *Are They the Same at Home?* (1927), 157–158.

and only occasionally talked about the Womb. On Wednesday had a last look at Colebox,[7] where the only other guest was Madame Bussy;[8] so nice, I think. He [Simon Bussy] unfortunately wasn't there. I so adore his ogreish laugh, his fee-fo-fum amenities and cannibalistic compliments. On Thursday I went to call on Tommy and was met at the door by May, who refused to let me into the flat—the reason being, as Tommy explained later, that they have had to sell all their furniture, owing to the malt kiln being unlet, and that May is ashamed of exposing their nakedness. Still, now one has let it, definitely, don't you know from the end of the month onwards, after which one will be able to give up writing and until one will be able to borrow money for the rent from Stulick. I took him with me to the Eiffel,[9] where I had asked Anita Loos and her husband. Anita is quite enchanting. One would like to keep her as a pet, instead of a Pekingese or a Siamese cat. She is tiny, pretty in a charmingly ugly way, with enormous eyes, and has a drawling little voice in which she brings out very good and fruity comments on the universe. She told me that she hopes shortly to retire, feels that she deserves complete rest, having started work in the movies when she was seven. What she really likes is sewing and whenever she takes a holiday she spends it enthusiastically and indefatigably stitching underclothes—which neither she nor anyone else can wear, when they're made. Her husband [John Emerson] is middle aged and seems nice. A certain factitious charm attached to him, owing to the fact that he had such acute laryngitis and had to communicate by means of gesture of which he is a comic master, and by writing innumerable little notes on a block. Meanwhile I forgot to say that I lunched with Eddy, whose furry body I quite forgot, while talking about Beethoven and Mozart with him; and bought about two hundred weights of gramophone records to take with me to Italy. One final and violent scamper to-day and then off at four o' clock, by astonishingly empty trains and boat. Forgive the typing; I have no ink in my pen and you wouldn't be able to read what I wrote with it, even if I had ink. These French trains—it is like going on something at the Wembley Amusement Park, such bangs and crashes and sickening oscillations. Goodbye, Mary, and remember that you are coming soon to Italy.

Aldous

[7] Lady Sybil Colefax (1874–1950). English society hostess. Virginia Woolf refers to her as Lady Cornflax (Diary, vol 3, 158).
[8] Dorothy Bussy (1866–1960). Sister of Lytton Strachey and wife of French painter Simon Bussy (1870–1954).
[9] Eiffel Tower Restaurant, 1 Percy St.

TO MARY HUTCHINSON

Florence
1 September 1926

Here, dearest Mary, are two Cautionary Pictures, illustrating the Fatal Results of Solitude on Ardent Temperaments.

When absent Mars left Aphrodite chaste,
Her own soft hand the god of war replaced
And amorous Leda, when her love was gone,
Sure she was ravished
While she raped the swan.

We are here for a few days, in Florence, getting our car—or trying to get it; for the whole bureaucracy of Italy is embattled against us and the struggle promises to be long and desperate. In the intervals of the fight we enjoy Florence, which seems more than ever desirable now that we cannot live here. Meanwhile the mountains await us—bracing but all too mountainous—rows and rows of perpendicular Dolomites, just like the Mappin Terraces[1] at the zoo, where the wild goats live, on an enormous scale. The only compensation is that it will probably do us all a lot of good. Indeed, Maria had already begun to hike up and down precipices for two hours every afternoon. Here she could not walk for half an hour on the flat.

Saw Jack in Venice for an hour or two between trains—well, and in good form, though somewhat haunted by Bernerses, Colefaxes, Erlangers, Cunards, and such like, who seem to swarm at Venice like maggots in a cheese.

I have just finished an introduction to B. R. Haydon's autobiography and am meditating novels, writing articles for America in between times, and reading Gide's *Faux Monnayeurs*—the oddest book. You feel that it must have been such a relief to the man to confess at last, openly, that he preferred boys to girls. What a fool!

Maria has cut her hair—successfully this time.

Love,

A

---

[1] Reinforced concrete structures designed by architect John James Joass to replicate a mountain landscape, 1913–1914, Regents Park Zoo, London. "A great improvement on the old style of wild-beast cage," according to a character in Saki's story "The Mappined Life."

TO MARY HUTCHINSON

ca September 1926

Arrived here today to meet my brother Julian and find Trieste the most civilized town of Italy—such shops as exist nowhere else in the country. But nothing else—no art, not even any lovely Italian girls, only heavy Austrian and Jugoslavian types. [Maria's hand: Monstrous large langoustes and delicious! . . . illeg.] Cryptic interruption. After which I can only suggest that, as you have got as far as Belgium, you should now take a slightly longer stride and come to Cortina, which, since we have a house,[2] isn't half bad. Do.

Love,
A.

TO NAOMI ROYDE-SMITH

Savoy Hotel
Florence
21 October 1926

My dear Naomi,
This is to introduce Miss Elsie Werner,[3] who is on her way back to New York from a brief stay in Italy, where she and I have been revising a dramatized version of *Antic Hay*, which she has made—with incredible ingenuity. I am sure you will enjoy making her acquaintance. And perhaps the play will interest you. In any case I am sure you will be able to give her some useful advice about the possibility of placing it in London. Perhaps Milton[4] would like to look at it.

I hope we shall see you soon in Italy.

Yours,
Aldous Huxley

TO MARY HUTCHINSON

Florence
23 October 1926

Even the saints, it seems, enjoyed their simple pleasures every now and then. St. Cecilia's was evidently a genuine temperament. Florence is

---

[2] Villa Ino Colli, where they stayed from September 1926 until February 1927.
[3] Elsie Werner. American screen writer.
[4] Ernest Milton (1890–1974). British actor and Royde-Smith's husband.

marvellously lovely, though haunted, for me, at the moment, by toothaches and dentists. I have just this moment finished revising the dramatization of *Antic Hay* which an American woman has undertaken, and cherish hopes that it may make our fortune. There seem to be managers on the watch for it: and she even received a telegram from a cinema director who seems to want it for the screen. What fun if it comes off.

A.

TO MARY HUTCHINSON

Cortina
12 November 1926

Thank you for your postcard, Mary, of the androgyne. Alas, that one must become a snail in order to know what being a hermaphrodite is really like!

You wrote charming things on the back of this card. The solitude isn't so much a matter of choice as a fact to be accepted, like the possession of ten fingers instead of twelve.

I have sent you a copy of my travel book. I hope and think you may find it entertaining. There are good things in it, I think. And I like the idea of such a book, in principle—a receptacle in which there is a bit of almost everything. I like a sort of Gothic profusion in literature, but expressed in terms of classical elegance.

Reading MacDougall's book on Abnormal Psychology. Very queer and appalling what can happen to one's mind—a dog barking too loud when one is a child or an old gentleman unbuttoning his trousers, and one can be turned into Dr. Jekyll and Mr. Hyde, or a hysteric, or a neurasthenic. The astonishing thing is that any of us are at all sane. Also a life of Chopin—what fun these romantics had! They had so many things to believe in which nobody can believe in now, they could intoxicate themselves with such grand nonsense. Liszt is still better—as a life—than Chopin. Reading aloud Walter Scott's life of Dryden—very pleasant reading and a historical document throwing light on the age in which it was composed as well as that with which it deals.

When are you coming to Cortina, Mary? For it is decided now that you are coming, isn't it? When the snow has fallen. . . . In your breeches you will be almost the hermaphrodite of your postcard—when you take them off too?

A

1926

TO MARY HUTCHINSON

Cortina
14 November 1926

I have been in such a trance-like state of preoccupation with work that time has passed unnoticed and reality has retreated behind the figments of imagination. I have often wanted to write to you, Mary, but the days slipped past and it is hard when one is deeply involved in work to give effect to wishes unconnected with it. Yesterday I actually began a letter—and now today comes your postcard—Bronzino's lovely Venus on one side and you emerging from the written words as deliciously naked and desirable, on the other. A whole fantastic and charming romance on the back of a postcard. How vividly I remember it all: I would be sitting reading—"Educational Psychology" it was generally. Suddenly there would be the discreet knock at the door. I would open, and "Educational Psychology" gave place to more serious things. How incredibly quickly we had no clothes on! It was almost miraculous. And when you had gone, I was perfumed all over with your scent and the taste of it was in my mouth. And the contours of your body were in my fingers, like the notes of a piece of music one has learned by heart. Why don't you come to us here, Mary? We could renew all the pleasures—invent new ones perhaps, if there are any that we have still left untried. And in the intervals we will talk, read, work. The place is not so bad as Maria may have led you to suppose in her last letters, which were written in the course of a week of rain. One day it was icily pelting, the next we breakfasted in pyjamas on the balcony and I spent the whole morning writing in the sun, almost naked. Today we drove up to a little lake in the woods and had a picnic lunch. It was so hot that Baby took off all his clothes and we should have done so too but for the governess and the fact that, if anyone had passed, we should have got penal servitude for *oltraggio al pudore*. And it will be like that most of the winter, even when the snow is on the ground. And even when the snow or rain is falling it isn't *so* bad. The house is warm with central heating. One can draw the blinds and simply remain in bed all day. Why don't you come, Mary? You could do skiing—on scarlet skis, the discovery of which in a shop here has converted Maria into an enthusiastic winter sportswoman—and in the most ravishing of callipygous breeches. *Do.* I insist. If you can't come at Christmas or before, come in January when the children's holidays are over. The skiing is best then. Or bring the whole family at Christmas. Think of it seriously. Nothing would be more enchanting.

I work hard at my new book [*Point Counter Point*], which promises to be very complicated and difficult—perhaps too difficult for me, as the point of it will be to show a piece of life from many different points of view and to display events and objects existing as they do, in many different ways simultaneously—in their everyday practical, their emotional, their artistic, their scientific, their political, their economic, their religious aspects. Thus any human being is a mass of organized molecules, a physiology, a part of the social organism, believes himself to have an immortal soul and to be of cosmical importance, is a patch of colours that can be painted and can look at the world as patches of colours, can feel enormous emotions, can worship gods; every act he performs can be interpreted in terms of physics and chemistry, of psychology, of morality, of economics, his life can be described in the style of the natural history textbook or in that of *Paradise Lost*. And every aspect is equally "true." I want somehow to imply all this, projecting the characters against the extraordinary, complex, and mysterious background of the world, showing things in unusual lights, hinting at modes of existence of which we ordinarily take no cognisance. It remains to be seen whether I can manage it.

In the intervals I read a lot of ponderous books—a portentous but, so far as I have got, very good *Sociologia Generale* by an Italian, Vilfredo Pareto,[5] a book on the *Biology of Death*, a history of Greece, a handbook of geology—with occasional dips into other literary worlds. But the days are too short—particularly when one needs, as I do, 8 hours of sleep. I wish I could reduce them; but it doesn't really do.

Write soon again and tell us all the news. I had heard in an official letter from *Vogue* that "Miss Todd is no longer with us." The reasons were not given. Was she exercising her conjugal rights with the Garland[6] too publicly—or what? The Franchettis have been such a comedy, but are now gone. I shall be curious to find out when we go to Florence, what has happened. Poor Luigino—he will soon be nothing but a mass of horns. And he is so painfully jealous.

Write, then; and meanwhile think about coming and make up your mind in the right way. *Je t'embrasse.*

A

[5] Vilfredo Pareto (1848–1923). Italian sociologist and economist.
[6] Madge Garland (1898–1990). Fashion writer and editor at *Vogue*.

TO J. ST. LOE STRACHEY[7]

Villa Ino Colli
Cortina d'Ampezzo (Belluno), Italy
14 November 1926

Dear Mr. Strachey,

I need hardly tell you how much pleasure your letter, which has been forwarded to me here after some delay, gave me. Praise from such a critic is indeed worth having. Liking the book myself [*Jesting Pilate*], I am very glad to find my predilections confirmed by your judgment.

With regard to what you say about values, I feel that all our difficulties arise from the initial false assumptions that have underlain the philosophy of science since the end of the seventeenth century. Mind, with its emotions, aspirations and purposes, its memories and anticipations, its sense of values is quite insusceptible of mathematical treatment; it was, accordingly, simply omitted by the mathematical physicists of the seventeenth century from their world-picture. Concentrating on the measurable, the mathematically describeable aspect of the world, men of science achieved enormous and unhoped for success—so much, that their heads were turned and they boldly asserted that things existed exclusively in their measurable aspect, that everything was explicable in terms of extension, objective time and mass. So great has been the prestige of science that we have accepted their assertion that the part is the whole and that the measurable aspect of the world is the total reality. But the metaphysical difficulties in the way of accepting the seventeenth-century scientific world-picture are insurmountable. And now, as far as I can make out, the merely scientific experimental difficulties are increasing. With regard to values, you have something like an absolute scale of values existing in the simplest forms of matter; organism exists from the beginning. The value of harmoniousness, proportion, cooperation seems fundamental. It may be that we are conscious of and enunciate in words (mistakenly, no doubt, but with, let us hope, increasing approximation to the truth) the principles according to which the world is organised, principles which hold good for us on our plane and for the electrons on theirs. All this, however, is very nebulous and obscure. One can only feel certain of things nearer at hand—for example, that no good can come of the modern American tendency to claim that persuading weak-minded people to buy things they don't want is as valuable as the disinterested search for truth!

---

[7] John St. Loe Strachey (1860–1927). British journalist, editor of *Spectator*.

We are established among these, at present, very damp and gloomy mountains for the whole winter. Not very pleasant, but the air seems to do our little boy, who has been rather delicate, a great deal of good; so here we are. Which makes it, alas, impossible to accept your very kind invitation. But I think we may be in London next spring, when I shall write and ask if we may come.

Meanwhile, I hope you have completely shaken off the illness which you mentioned in your letter. I look forward to the arrival of your book with great pleasure.

Yours very sincerely,
Aldous Huxley

TO MARY HUTCHINSON

Hotel Bonvecchiati
Venezia
20 December 1926

Having exhorted you in Chinese to live practically, I am now imploring you, sweet Mary (in English this time), to do the opposite. Onslow was unadulterated phantasy, and if you were to take Confucius's advice there would be no more Onslow. Follow Confucius when I am not with you—never be so unpractical as to wear diaphanous trousers; but when I am there, let the wisdom on this little chicken's backside be your guide; live and love fantastically. Perhaps the ideal life ought to contain something of everything, be a compound of opposites—fantasy alternating with practicality, sociability with solitude, sensuality with eremitic chastity, study with dissipation, respectability with disreputableness, altruism with ruthless egotism. Perhaps the wise man or woman would change seats like the cinema, every Monday and Friday. I wonder, or is there no Mrs. Beeton of conduct? Must each invent his own recipes?

Here we are in Venice, doing Christmas shopping and suffering agonies of cold—for Venice is far colder than Cortina, which has sunshine, while the top of the Campanile is lost in the fog, which is dry, while the walks of St. Mark's and the floor of the Piazza are all in an icy sweat. Still, it's very delightful: and the place grows more and more fabulous every time one sees it. They did not take the advice of Confucius here.

We saw Shaw's "St. Joan" the other night, in Italian, well acted, but a pretty bad play, unless I am much mistaken, so hopelessly without passion or poetry. Luckily we were left in peace and could see it through till the end: all the other times we have been to the theatre recently, somebody has tried to assassinate Musso and the performance has been suspended in the middle. I had thought of complaining to Jim about it.

M flourishes greatly in the Cortina atmosphere, puts on weight and flesh, which I hope she won't lose again when she comes down to the Cities of the Plain (Gomorrah was one of them, if you remember) for any length of time. She drives the new car with great dash and has so far touched only 105 kilometers an hour in it; but hopes on better roads to do 120—which will only feel like 50 in the old Citroen; so be reassured.

Goodbye, Mary. I kiss your hands—among the rest.

Aldous

Oh, I had forgotten to wish you Christmas and New Year Felicities: but then every day is Christmas and New Year's day so far as my good wishes for you are concerned.

TO SYBIL COLEFAX

Villa Ino Colli
Cortina d'Ampezzo (Belluno), Italy
31 December 1926

Dear Sibyl,

Thank you so much for your letter and the good wishes, which I return with more than the usual increment on the foreign exchange. With regard to King Edward—I'm afraid I must say no. To begin with, I shall probably not be in England during May—though I hope to be there in March. And in the second place I have a dislike and dread of anything like a public appearance or a public speech amounting to a full blown complex—so that even if I were going to be in England, I should still decline, partly for my own sake and partly because of the blight which my complex would inevitably cast on the whole proceedings. I'm sorry not to be able to be more helpful; but I am sure you will understand.

A.B. has put off his arrival at Cortina, owing, I understand, to domestic difficulties with the baby's nurse. I like to think of the great man in the atmosphere of feeding bottles, diapers and gripe water. I look forward to his coming greatly, for Cortina is a vacuum. It is also, to judge by the reports in the papers, the only place in Europe where it is really hot. There is snow in Lisbon, but none here; and while the rivers in the south of France are covered with ice, here it scarcely freezes even at night. However, the snow will doubtless come all in good time and we shall be bored to extinction with the sight of it before the winter is over. Maria joins with me in sending greetings and best wishes.

Ever yours,
Aldous Huxley

TO J. ST. LOE STRACHEY

Villa Ino Colli
Cortina d'Ampezzo (Belluno), Italy
6 January 1927

Dear Mr. Strachey,
I have been reading the book you were so very kind as to send me with great enjoyment.[8] What a country it is! You approach it, it seems to me, in the right spirit—with gusto; as Dryden approached Chaucer: "Here is God's plenty." Or the devil's plenty. It is a matter of taste. Perhaps I should have put in a little more of the devil than you do. But the real point, in any case, is the plenty, and the fabulous, the supernatural quality of it.

I wish you had seen California. It is pure Rabelais, a chronic kermesse. Materially, the nearest approach to Utopia yet seen on our planet. After twenty-four hours of it, you begin to pine for the slums of Dostoievsky's Saint Petersburg!

And then the great Middle Western plains! Endless, and the sparse towns and villages uglier than anything you have ever seen. No wonder they take to curious religions in those regions. It is the only thing, now that drink has been abolished, that is left them. Talking about curious religions—I notice that you attribute no importance to the Tennessee anti-evolution business. So did I, until recently, when I received a pamphlet from an organization called the Science League of America. One state and quite a number of education boards in individual cities, from Georgia to California, have followed the example of Tennessee. All states are being organized by the Fundamentalists for Federal and State anti-evolution laws. Funds for this purpose are freely forthcoming. Anti-evolution bills are promised in numerous state legislatures during 1927. California and Texas have ordered the elimination of

---

[8] *American Soundings* (1926).

evolutionary doctrines from the textbooks of tax-supported schools and colleges. And so on and so forth. Altogether, it looks as though the movement were no joke. In any case, the Science League of America, which has a most eminent and respectable committee of scientific men, seems to take it very seriously. Their pamphlet is quite blood-curdling.

I wonder if you are not a little too generous to the American universities. They are fine, certainly; and it is an excellent thing that the contemporary rich should salve their guilty consciences by founding colleges as their ancestors did by endowing monasteries. But there is a reverse to the medal. To begin with, the standard of scholastic attainment in a great many of these universities is incredibly low. (If you remember, Mr. Babbitt was a university graduate. And I have met plenty of Americans with resounding degrees, who were fabulously ignorant of the subjects in which they had graduated.) In the second place, one must remember the rather sinister influence exercised on universities by the rich businessmen who endow them and who, in practically all cases, are the trustees and governors of American seats of learning. The persecution of unpopular political opinions is almost universal. Veblen's book on the Higher Learning in America and Upton Sinclair's rather lurid, but (according to so knowledgeable an authority as Dr. Harvey Robinson) very well-documented book, *The Goose Step*, make rather disagreeable reading for anyone who has been brought up in the English love of free speech and fair play.

Thank you once more for your "Soundings." I hope to have the pleasure of discussing the inexhaustible and extraordinary subject of the book personally when I am in London next.

With best wishes for 1927, I am

Yours sincerely,
Aldous Huxley

TO MARY HUTCHINSON

Cortina d' Ampezzo
13 January 1927

You overwhelm us with so many beautiful things, Mary. Not Solomon in all his glory . . . You shouldn't have loaded us with so much, really. But how sweet of you! I look forward to thanking you more adequately in person—quite soon now; for time rushes on, never so deliriously quickly as now; for there is nothing in Cortina to impede its course, it slides down a smooth channel, unruffled, held up by no events. Day succeeds day; I work, read, meditate, slide a little on my skis when there is snow—which there isn't often; for Cortina appears to be the one really warm place in Europe—and time slides past, even faster and without falling, as I do only too frequently. The only thing remotely resembling a happening was the arrival and, this morning, the departure of M's youngest sister and still younger friend of sixteen, having the extraordinary plumpness which often goes with that age—in Shelley's words, 'an orbèd maiden.' Very, very youthful, both of them. A little too much so for my perhaps exclusively adult tastes. Conversation that is only a loud and cheerful chirruping, laughter without cause, a puppyish tumbling about—alas, they don't greatly appeal to me. I've no doubt that they should; but *che vuole?* The house is now calm again and we both heave sighs of relief.

I had such a nice letter the other day from your Mr. Lucas, about my book. And another from St. Loe Strachey, who also sent me a (I must confess) dreadful work of his own called *American Soundings*, which is a Paean in praise of all that is most deplorable in the United States. Also one from a lady in California who says that she changed her mind about committing suicide owing to my essays. Curious, this multiplied existence of a writer in touch with so many people in so many places. My favourite and most faithful correspondent is Miss Dodo Doody of Quebec, who is twenty and writes me long letters about the young men she is or is not engaged to. Very amusing letters, too.

I have discovered in the Italian calendar that my patron saint, whose day is on the tenth of the present month, is called Saint Aldus the Hermit—S. Aldo Eremita. I must look him up in the Hagiology and discover what he did—or what, being a hermit, he didn't do.

Je t'embrasse,
Aldo Eremita

TO MAX BEERBOHM[9]

Villa Ino Colli
Cortina d'Ampezzo (Belluno), Italy
10 February 1927

Dear Beerbohm,
I wonder if there is any likelihood of your being in Rapallo during the early days of March. We hope to be motoring along the Riviera at that

---

[9] Max Beerbohm (1872–1956). English writer and caricaturist.

time and I should like very much to seize the opportunity to pay my respects to Mrs Beerbohm and yourself and to present my wife.

I think with so much pleasure of the last time I walked your quarter deck above the blue sea and have always desired to renew that brief and charming acquaintanceship. But Rapallo has always, till now, obstinately persisted in lying off my line of march.

We are up here among the snows and have been here for some months, for the sake of my little boy's health, which responds, I am happy to say, in a marvellous way to the climate. It will be rather a relief, however, to get away, the more so as the only amenity of Cortina, outside the winter sports, is shortly to depart—in the shape of Arnold Bennett, who has been here with the new Mrs A.B. for some weeks. Extremely good company, as usual, and fully as majestic as any of the surrounding Dolomites.

Please remember me to Mrs Beerbohm.

Yours very sincerely,
Aldous Huxley

TO SYBIL COLEFAX

Chalet des Aroles
Diablerets (Vaud), Switzerland
13 February 1927

Dear Sibyl,

Your note, which arrived today, makes me feel horribly repentant for not having written before to thank you for your first letter and your very angelic kindness in taking so much trouble about my brother-in-law's scarves.

Alas, your very inviting dinner invitation must be refused for lack of aeroplanes. We won't be in London till about March 10, I think. Maria leaves for Italy in two days' time while I remain here to work on my book, which has taken me much more time and trouble than I expected it would. I hope to meet her on the last day of the month somewhere in France, en route for Paris, where we shall stay a few days before moving on to London.

We've had a large and lively house-full here, with D. H. Lawrence and his wife next door in another little chalet across the snow. So that my leisure, in the intervals of work, has been very pleasant. Lawrence is really one of the most astonishing of men, full of such fire and life and indomitable energy, in spite of his bad health, that most other people seem more than half-dead in comparison.

Thank you again for your invitation and forgive me for not having written before. Work and a real neurasthenia, noted in the act of writing outside professional hours, must be my not very adequate excuse. Maria sends her love and so do I. *A bientôt.*

Yours,
Aldous

TO MARY HUTCHINSON

St Valentine's Day 1927

One arrow and two pierced hearts
Are emblems of my Valentine,
The double-piercing dart is mine.
But the two hearts, though lacking darts,
(Yet love appropriate skill imparts)
In amorous ecstasies combine,
Soft androgyne on androgyne
Using hermaphroditic arts.

But not unpierced the piercing arrow.
I know the pain that through the marrow,
Like fire along a powder train,
Creeps anxious down sweet torturing roads,
Till pleasure dazzling explodes.
Come, heart; I suffer till I feel that pain.

TO DR. B. G. BROOKS

19 Grand Place
St. Trond, Belgium
15 May 1927

Dear Brooks,
How good of you to send me your volume of poems! I read them with pleasure but without, I confess, entire comprehension. For my mind is not one of those that easily "gets" an incantation. *Voici le temps de la magie*—alas, I am old-fashioned and only really feel at home with the most unmagical kind of direct statement. My chief criticism—so far as

I can criticize—is that some of the magic is too primate and individual, a record of particular experiences which it is difficult to interpret except in the light of your memory of those experiences—themselves of a tenuous and rarefied order. Another point—there are, for my taste at least, too many epithets. This is made inevitable by your extreme brevity, a part of the magical technique which I, as a non-magician, object to—preferring length and a gradual and easy statement of experiences without this desperate research of *le mot juste* and infinite treasure in a little room, which leads to the undue insistence on adjectives. I wish, for example, that you had expanded your Dostoievsky (which I liked). It would have lost nothing of its point and only gained by its length, becoming more massive and solid. However, this probably seems all nonsense to you and beside the point, like a deaf man's criticism of music.

I am glad to hear you are getting married. Marriage is, after all, the only practical solution to most of the problems of living. Let me wish you all happiness.

We are moving southward in a day or two to spend the summer by the Mediterranean—the only possible sea for those who, like myself, are not so well covered with blubber that they can stand the icy waters of the north. I am very busy with various literary works—a volume of essays on sociological subjects, a long and complicated novel. Verse I find almost unwriteable these days. My only recent effort was a thing called *Arabia Infelix* which appeared in an anthological volume with the ironical title of The Best Poems of 1926. It seemed to me not bad. I will send you a copy, if I find one in Italy or, failing that, can remember who the publisher is. I doubt I shall be in England till the winter— perhaps not till spring. It depends on work. I'll let you know when the moment comes. Best Wishes.

Yours,
Aldous Huxley

Huxley had met Brooks during his Garsington days. The title of Brooks's book Interludes and Incantations, *and its epigraph* "Voici le Temps de la magie" *(from a poem by Guillaume Apollinaire) explain the references in the early part.*

TO MARY HUTCHINSON

Cortina d'Ampezzo
30 May 1927

Here we are at last, dearest Mary, having escaped from Belgium and hurried through France at even more than Maria's ordinary speed. Belgium was at once lugubrious and grotesque. The poor old man fading out painfully and finally dying amidst the rather noble and impressive pomps of Catholic ritual—candle in hand with a monk in a brown habit praying at his side and pronouncing the general absolution. There is something very admirable about the way in which Catholicism turns what, by itself, is a merely physiological and painfully animal process— dying—into something of cosmic significance, a dignified and tragic act of the greatest importance. The ritual sustains the dying man, if he is conscious; and to those who assist at the deathbed it gives a comforting assurance that the mere physiological act is not everything—is in fact nothing when compared to the spiritual drama behind it. Of course, there may be no spiritual drama; the physiological act may be everything. But it is good to act as tho' there were a spiritual drama.

What followed the death was a macabre comedy. Funerals are bad enough at any time; but when one is at the centre of one—and that in a small provincial town in Belgium, with an enormous ramifying family all round—then it becomes the most fantastic of grotesqueries. The prodigal son turned up after years of absence. A great uncle who had just invented a patent substitute for soap and in the intervals of offering condolences tried to persuade us all to push the sales. Cousins who had not been seen for a generation on account of impossible wives or husbands. A whole chapter out of Balzac—and everything done in full evening dress with black cotton gloves at eleven in the morning. And hardly was the funeral over when M's grandmother had a heart attack and very nearly died too. So you can imagine the horror. However, now we are away, thank goodness.

A lovely journey—along the Meuse through Chalons to Troye (which is a charming town). Thence to Dijon and Beaune (what a lovely van der Weyden!) and on to Bourg. After that to the frontier. Then over to Mont Cenis to Turin and from there in one day to Cortina—550 kilometers in 13 hours, a really fabulous feat on M's part. I thought so often of our delightful journey . . . and Avignon and Calais. All so curiously improbable and so charming. Some time we must make another pilgrimage across Europe—each halting place a shrine of the goddess. Meanwhile, however, I shall have to do a lot of work. A book of essays to be finished this summer and then the novel to be got on with. And reading in the intervals, if there are any.

Goodbye, Mary darling. Enjoy yourself, but occasionally find time to remember the absent.

A

TO ALBERT RUTHERSTON

Villa Maietta
Forte dei Marmi (Lucca), Italy
23 June 1927

Dear Rutherston,
I feel extremely guilty—but I find that it is physically impossible for me to get the essays done for our little book this summer. The job I have to do for this autumn is heavier than I thought it would be. Moreover Chattos needs this stuff rather earlier than I expected. So I am up to the eyes—for eight hours a day; more than which I can't manage. I shan't be able to think of anything else till August—which will make appearance in the autumn impossible, I fear. I am really very sorry about this—but I can't help it. I will really try to get your things done before the middle of September. In which case Christmas publication might still be practicable.

We are here by the Mediterranean, with the Carrara mountains at the back. Very lovely: but I am rather too busy to enjoy it fully.

With best wishes and most apologetically, I am

Yours,
Aldous Huxley

TO MARY HUTCHINSON

Villa Maietta
Forte dei Marmi (Lucca), Italy
15 August 1927

I have been so utterly out of the mood of writing letters that I have left your charming birthday greeting, dearest Mary, unanswered for a shamefully long time. First there was the agitation of finishing my book; then, when that was done, a reaction towards complete idleness; followed in its turn by renewed agitation caused by the news that the

MS of the book had not reached the publishers a fortnight after sending. I had to start correcting my duplicate copies and actually rewriting an essay of which I had no duplicate—you can imagine in what frame of mind! And then came the news that the MS had finally arrived. The envelope showed that the packet had remained 14 days in Florence before starting on its journey. A case either of incompetence or of the censorship. If you see Jim, tell him his adopted country is becoming so bloody as to be practically uninhabitable. We are seriously thinking of moving to France. The fascist efforts to civilize Italy result merely in the creation of an interfering police which one would call Prussian if it weren't corrupt and inefficient as well as tyrannous.

Now I am mildly at work on my novel—involving myself in that fictitious world of feelings and thoughts, and consequently resenting the disturbances which come from the real world—disturbances rather numerous at present: for we have had a house full of guests—Sullivan, the Gielguds, M's uncle—and shall have it pretty full for some days yet; not to mention the casual interruption yesterday of Ottoline and Philip driving along in a two seater hung all over with strange luggage, like the White Knight's charger. A curious spectacle which we expect to see more of on their return journey. Philip seems to be less mad, as age creeps on, but more imbecile—the mouth gapes continuously, the eyes and attention wander, there is a kind of involuntary detachment from reality. Add to these American friends of the Gielguds in the neighborhood and friends of the friends with them, and you can realize that my hermitage has been disagreeably violated.

We have been at Forte all the summer, except for a few days when we went to Florence to see D. H. Lawrence, who was very ill with hemorrhages of the lungs, brought on, I am afraid, by sea bathing when he was staying with us a few weeks before. We found him very weak and gentle, but indomitable and full of such obstinacy and energy that, as soon as he recovered any strength, he started getting up, working, walking—with the result that he began coughing up [*this small portion of the letter has been torn off*] . . . himself to be healed afterwards and we now hear that he has been able to leave Florence and is in Austria in the mountains. For which thank goodness.

I have been reading Cardinal Newman recently—very fine as a psychologist. There are analyses of the psychology of thought scattered in the *Apologia* and the *Grammar of Assent* which are really marvelous. And how well he wrote! Also I have tried, yet once more, to get on with Meredith—*Beauchamps's Career* this time. But I doubt I shall be able to struggle through. So empty and so pretentious; so much literature to express so little substance. How did he acquire the reputation he has, or at any rate had? I find it impossible to understand.

On the other hand I have been re-reading *Don Quixote* with extraordinary pleasure. What a book! It couldn't be better.

Otherwise my reading has been mostly rather technical, psychology and philosophy. Interesting, but perhaps a waste of time. Who knows?

[*Small portion of page torn off here*] . . . think of us? I live here the life of a meditative tree and all past activity seems a dream which has no probable prospect of being renewed. But perhaps it will renew itself? I hope so, Mary.

A

TO NAOMI MITCHISON

23 August 1927

My dear Naomi,

I have been hesitating to write for some time; for after all there is no consolation and the best-meant letters are intrusions. And where a child is concerned the horror is so specially unescapable and inexplicable. Child suffering[1] brings the whole thing to a head, summarizes the whole enormous problem. And there is no visible solution. One can't swallow original sin; and equally, I think, one can't swallow mere chance, mere pointlessness, mere mechanism. The only hope is that there may be a paradox, a living and functioning self-contradiction that admits the pointlessness and the wantonness and at the same time admits the point and the purposefulness, which one does feel certain of, at moments, as realities. Not that such a solution is much use to anyone in the throes of personal calamity. One has only one's unassisted, individual self with which to affront the enemy.

We vegetate quietly here. I do a fair amount of work, read a little, bathe, lie in the sun and wonder whether, perhaps, bathing and lying in the sun may not be the best and most meritorious of human activities. Not for very long, however: for the itch to know, to express, soon comes on me again. But it is probably a vice.

Lewis and Mimi [Gielgud] are staying for a few more days. Ottoline Morrell is on the horizon. We have seen a good deal of D. H.

---

[1] The death of young Phil in *Point Counter Point* was probably suggested by the death of Naomi Mitichison's son from meningitis.

Lawrence, who has been very ill—haemorrhage of the lungs—but has at last been able to get away from Florence into the mountains. A wonderful man, who would be great if he had not that streak of fool as well as genius, uncritical babbler as well as intuitive seer. But I like and admire him very much.

Are you likely to be coming this way? We shall be here till December, I think: then shall go to Cortina d'Ampezzo for a month or two, I hope. If you come south let us know.

Goodbye, dear Naomi. Give my love to your mother if you see her.

Yours,
Aldous

TO JULIAN HUXLEY

Florence (as from Villa Maietta)
Forte dei Marmi
8 October 1927

My dear J,
I was so very sorry to hear the bad news about Francis. Let's hope an Alpine winter will send down the glands for good. We shan't be going to Cortina till after Christmas in any case and we haven't yet heard if the house is available. But whatever the arrangements we shall of course be delighted to have him with us. We are expecting to hear any day now about the house and will then be able to make definite arrangements.

We are here for a few days, staying with the Franchettis, while we do various businesses in the town. Florence is fine but very chilly with the usual Apennine wind, and we regret the balminess of Forte, where I sit naked on the beach working and we bathe with regularity.

Germany sounds very pleasant. We have been wanting to tour there for a long time: but the occasion doesn't seem to offer. I write so slowly that I have to be at it continuously if I want to get things done. But we will really make a push to go soon. The Turkestan things sound lovely: they must be like those in Sir Aurel Stein's collection at Delhi, where you see everything from figures that might have come from Pompeii to pure Indian, pure Chinese, and a marvelous mixture of the two styles.

I have just been re-reading Burtt's *Metaphysical Foundations of Modern Science*. What an excellent book! Do you know it? If not, do read it. Also Pascal's *Penseés*, which are really terrific for profundity and clarity. What a prodigious figure! And in honour of the centenary, I have been looking at Bossuet, who is exceedingly fruity and at least twenty times as intelligent and clear headed as all the modernists of the last fifty years put together. *The Variations of the Protestant Churches* is admirable. I have just finished Lotka's *Elements of Physical Biology*, which is fascinating: but I wish I understood the mathematics. When I've done with my present book I think I must really spend a few months on these bloody noughts and crosses and try to understand something about the Frick. It's really too humiliating to gape at an equation as though it were Chinese. If only one had nine lives, never needed sleep and could think every hour and then with other people's minds:—one might begin to understand something about this fantastic universe. Or perhaps one wouldn't—it seems more likely!

Our love to you all. Will let you know more definitely of Cortina plans later on.

Yours,
Aldous

TO LADY OTTOLINE MORRELL

Villa Poneti
Bellosguardo, Firenze
8 October 1927

Dearest Ottoline,
How very kind of you to send us the lovely books. We have embarked on the history, reading it aloud with great enjoyment. It's very sane and decent and sensible and to the point—which is refreshing. I have had no time to do more than glance at poor Katherine's diary—parts of which, however, I read when it came out in *The Adelphi*. A sad book— sad both because of the fate of the writer and because of her intrinsic character.

We are here in Florence, staying with the Franchettis for a few days, while we pack up summer things and take the winter ones out of camphor from the trunks stored in Costanza's house. A melancholy task, symbolic of the transience of things. Florence is icy with north wind: but we left Forte warm, balmy and beautiful as it has never been all summer, so clear and crystalline and brilliantly coloured. I work away and in the intervals read a lot—Pascal in particular: what a man! And Baudelaire: ditto ditto: and Bossuet's *Variations of the Protestant Religion*—a very splendid work; and Burtt's excellent book on *The Metaphysical Foundations of Modern Science*.

We went again to Lucca to see feast of the *Volto Santo*, very fine and impressive with magnificent procession at dusk marching straight out of the fourteenth century. Otherwise we haven't stirred from Forte till now.

A postcard came from Lawrence yesterday to say he was getting on well and expecting to be back in Florence in a couple of weeks. It will be pleasant to see him again. I read his *Mornings in Mexico* the other day: one or two magnificent things in it—but in parts rather unsubstantial.

I suppose you are settling down in London now—to a pleasant and enjoyable winter I hope. Both our loves to you all, and thank you again so very much for the books.

> *Yours,*
> *Aldous*

TO JULIAN HUXLEY

Villa Maietta
Forte dei Marmi (Lucca)
5 December 1927

My dear J,

Your letter arrived this morning. With regard to plans—it seems to me that we had better take the chalet for the whole time and leave the children there. It would be simpler, pleasanter, healthier and probably not more expensive than transferring them to a pension in Feb. What about servants? I doubt if we can bring ours, as a passport in Fascist Italy takes a great effort and at least two months to come by. I suppose they can be got on the spot? At 2000 Fr, if we don't get the price down, for 2½ months the damage would work out at £4 a week each, heating and service perhaps another £1.10 between them or £1.15. Which means overhead expenses of say £6 a week per family plus eating at the rate of say another £4 a week each. Total £10, which is less than what it would cost in a hotel with all the additional advantages. So let's decide for the chalet. Maria has gone to Florence for a few days and returns tomorrow, bringing no less a person than Michael Arlen for lunch. It rains incessantly, but is warm. I work away.

What you say about the disadvantage of week-end boardership needs thinking about. I don't remember it bothering me much—except perhaps my first few terms at Hillside, when I seem to remember tears each time I left P.F. [Prior's Field]. Later I unequivocally liked the change and was stimulated by it. I had in any case intended to have rooms in town, but meant them to be small, while the country should be the main and permanent thing. My friend Wood (who may be prejudiced, as he owns the *Architect and Building News*) answers me that building is cheaper if you want a house with modern comfort and convenience. About £2500 for 10 or 12 rooms with central heating, wash basins in every room etc. which doesn't seem to me bad. And even if you don't get back the price of extras, the difference between buying and selling represents the cost of the comfort you have had and which you wouldn't have had in the ordinary house carefully bought or hired. And after all comfort is worth paying something for. Farewell and love to Juliette.

Yours,
A

TO MARY HUTCHINSON

Villa Maietta
Forte dei Marmi (Lucca), Italy
5 December 1927

I have been owing you a letter for months, dearest Mary. The psychological impossibility of writing letters when I am busy—which I am and have been most monstrously for weeks and shall be for weeks more—is my only excuse; with the Niagara-like rapidity of the passage of time in this perfectly empty and uneventful place, where one day is just like another and life follows an unchanging routine of writing, reading, walking, eating, sleeping. It seems only yesterday that it was summer.

Passent les jours et passent les semaines.
Ni temps passé
Ni les amours reviennent:
Sous le pont Mirabeau coule la Seine.[2]

[The days pass and the weeks pass; neither past time nor love return: under Mirabeau Bridge flows the Seine.]

I shall be very glad when I have got my book off my hands—tho' I wish I had another year to work at it. Mere time so matures and ripens

[2] Guillaume Apollinaire (1880–1914). "Le Pont Mirabeau."

every idea—not in the consciousness entirely tho' to some extent even there; but mainly when one isn't specifically thinking of it—by entwining new experiences and information with old, by relating memories and knowledge to the idea so that it can grow and diversify itself. However, time lacks and I am doing my best to get the thing finished by the end of January. I hope I shall succeed.

What a curious burglary! My poor stick I don't regret as much as I might as I'd already given it up for lost this summer and resigned myself to its absence. But what a tragedy about the Napoleon brandy! That isn't so easily or cheaply replaced.

I have not yet had any time to read the *Polyglots*. I remember liking, and being very much amused by, Gerhardi's[3] first book, *Futility*. But a volume of his short stories were sent to me recently by the publishers—*Pretty Creatures*, which seemed to me about as thin, shoddy, and from an artistic point of view, scandalously unconscientious as stories could well be. He deserved Flaubertian denunciations for those. I see from the dust cover that Arnold Bennett describes him (what a marvellously characteristic Bennettism!) as the "pet of the Intelligentsia." Old A.B. might profitably have a few stylistic hints from Flaubert every now and then.

I haven't read much of late, except stuffy books. A curious and interesting diary of life behind the front as a liason officer and spycatcher during the war, called *Wine Women and War*—worth looking at. That and a terrifically *literary* volume of short stories by old Vernon Lee,[4] which she sent me, and which I fear I can't recommend, (unless you like that late 19th century literariness) are all the contemporary letters I have read of late, except in French, *Sous le Soleil de Satan*, a good theme abominably done—so abominable that I've not finished it: and Kuprine's *La Fosse aux Filles* about life in a brothel, interesting when merely accurate and descriptive, but ghastly the moment it tries to be imaginative. Otherwise recreative reading has been confined to Burton's *Pilgrimage to Meccah*—very superb. What an astonishing man! I've always greatly admired, without envying, that type of adventurer who will put up with any danger or discomfort for the sake of having some fun or satisfying an idle curiosity. Most of us are so terribly soft and bourgeois. Also a life of Lloyd George, very fascinating. And another of Parnell, equally extraordinary. Really, biographies are the

---

[3] William Gerhardi (1895–1977). British novelist and playwright.
[4] Vernon Lee (1856–1935). Pseudonym of Violet Paget, English essayist and novelist, who lived in Italy.

most unlikely reading of all. No novelist would dare to put such eccentric people into fiction as one meets in fact.

Maria has gone to Florence for some days and threatens to return with Reggie Turner,[5] Orioli[6] and Michael Arlen for lunch on Tuesday. It might be quite amusing.

Meanwhile the rain pelts down and the only diversions are the arrivals of the postman, who has brought one of the most extraordinary letters of late—one from a lady denouncing me for destroying her faith and one (much odder) thanking me for saving her from re-entering the Catholic church. One (to judge from his writing) from a lunatic artist, who thinks himself immensely great and unjustly neglected (his name is Mr. Rex Villiers) and would like me to proclaim the fact. One, sadly depressed, from my young Canadian friend, Miss Dodo, who has just returned disillusioned and disgusted from Los Angeles, and several others no less curious. But none from you, Mary. I suppose as punishment for my silence. But now it has been broken, be indulgent and write to say that you forgive it.

Much love from your,
A

TO MARY HUTCHINSON

Florence
1 January 1928

This is to wish you the happiest of New Years, dearest Mary, and to thank you for all your enchanting and really too magnificent gifts. I love my Beppo and Maria's coral serpent is a real work of art. How sweet of you to have sent them! The accompanying little faunesse, whose face is rather like yours, I think, brings all our gratitude.

We leave on the 3rd for Switzerland (Chalet des Aroles, Les Diablerets) and are involved in the usual last-minute work. Florence has been pleasant, with several marvelous days with Lawrence, whom I like and admire more and more, two afternoons with old Vernon [Lee], a most curious New Year party with Americans. But the weather alternates between icy tramontana and warm deliquescing scirocco, both odious.

---

[5] Reggie Turner (1869–1938). Edwardian novelist. As his biographer Stanley Weintraub notes, he was "part of the English expatriate colony in Florence" and was portrayed by Lawrence in *Aaron's Rod* and *Kangaroo*.
[6] Giuseppe Orioli (1884–1942). Italian publisher of *Lady Chatterley's Lover*. Michael Arlen (1895–1956) was the author of *The Green Hat* (1924).

Farewell, Mary, and be happy. More from Switzerland. It's impossible to write seriously now. I hope you got our Piero safely.

Much love,
Aldous

TO MARY HUTCHINSON

Chalet des Aroles,
Les Diablerets (Vaud), Switzerland
10 February 1928

Thank you so much, dearest Mary, for the diary. I hope indeed that the days of 1928 may be virgin, vivacious and beautiful for all of us. Up till now they have been mainly busy. I labour away at my book, which refuses to get finished and which won't appear now till the autumn; so deeply involved in it that I find it difficult to come out sometimes. I shall be very glad when at last it's done.

In the intervals there are winter sports, which I find rather boring this year, I don't quite know why—perhaps because this is really a very unsatisfactory place for skiing. But somehow I feel that even in a perfect place I wouldn't really enjoy it very much. The house has been very full—Julian, excessively energetic, exhausting himself and other people: Juliette, following in his wake: their two children, who hold the world's record for making a noise; our child, who, providentially, holds the world's record for making no noise; his governess, who has become slightly hysterical from what Margot Asquith would call "starvation of the womb"; two cousins of Juliette's, one ugly and sensible, who looked after the children when she was here: and the other pretty, a successful stage dancer, now going on to the cinema, only 20 and tho' fundamentally amazingly innocent, a tremendous cock-teaser, who just doesn't realize what she's doing: and two minutes away across the snow Lawrence and Frieda. He, thank goodness, is getting better than he was and we have daily delightful talks. What an astonishing man! He does take the shine out of most other people. Such insight, such wit, such prodigious vitality in spite of his sickness, such humour.

I have been reading little—glancing at *Le Temps Retrouvé*, which seems to be rather a falling off, tho' interesting in spots; running through Forster's *Aspects of the Novel*, amusing but thin and rather tiresome I thought, so spinsterishly giggly and sniggery and so terribly without guts and testicles—the untesticled quality showing up specially strongly in just those passages in which he expresses himself most decidedly on the side of the gutty books against the gutless, like H. James. Beyond these nothing but a few miscellaneous dippings into Histories of the Popes, descriptions of insects (blood curdling) and other accounts of the habits of animals, among which one might almost classify a biography of St. Francis, so strangely remote and fantastic it seems.

M leaves for Florence next week and I stay here to plod on with my book and hope to meet her en route for Paris in early March. Thence to London where I look forward to seeing you among Lady Harris's stuffed sausages and artificial hams (that sounds like the polite equivalent of the late-Victorian *bustle*). *A bientôt*, then, dearest Mary. Thank you again.

All our loves,
Aldous

TO JULIAN HUXLEY

4 Onslow Mews East
Thursday night
ca April 1928

My dear J,
I got back to find a note from Aunt Ethel to say that the G.B.S[haw]'s had asked us to lunch on Friday next, the 6th. So on the principle that the poor are always with us, I am going to ask you to let me cut our lunch for that day. But I'd like to come in any case afterwards to have a look at the experiment.

Will you be lunching any day next week at the Athenaeum? If so we might arrange to do it on the same day.

I've begun your *Biology and Human Life*, with pleasure and profit. Have you seen the Express's anti–birth control campaign? They are saying that B.C. gives women cancer. Not bad propaganda that!

I hope Juliette wasn't bad. Give her my love.

Yours,
Aldous

TO LADY OTTOLINE MORRELL

3 Onslow Mews East, S.W.7
25 April 1928

Dearest Ottoline,

I was so very glad to have your letter and to learn that you are at last getting over your dreadful illness. What a horrible stroke of bad luck! But I hope that now the tide has turned you will speedily get well again.

Maria is away in Belgium and won't be back till Sunday, when she brings Matthew with her. He will stay a week with us here and then we take him to school. Meanwhile I remain here doing a good deal of work and reading in the intervals.

Much love dear Ottoline; and get well quickly.

Yours,
Aldous

TO MARY HUTCHINSON

3 Onslow Mews East, S.W.7
26 April 1928

Rather a gloomy letter, dearest Mary. Country pleasures sound depressing. Still I rather wish I were out of town. These last days it has been so hot and oppressive that the mere process of keeping alive is tiring and any attempt at work or exercise brings exhaustion. Having written a few lines and corrected some few pages of typescript I feel utterly weary.

Lunched today with Noel Coward, who seems much nicer and more intelligent when he's by himself than when he's being the brilliant young actor-dramatist in front of a crowd of people. He told a good story of Evan and his bride. It appears that E's doctor came to Lois and told her she mustn't be impatient. Evan, he said, was very nervous: but in two or three weeks he ought to be able to rise to the conjugal occasion: but that he mustn't be worried or disturbed while he was rising: above all that he mustn't be troubled by any untoward noise. A very odd story: I suppose E is so out of the habit of ladies that he finds it almost impossible to do anything about them. *Quantum mutatus ab illo* etc!

Lady Harris and Honey came to tea. I rather liked Lady H. A very odd specimen, at any rate. She talked at great length about a mad Italian scientist who has told her in advance all about the weather for the last four years—always correctly—and who can send boxes by wireless telegraphy from Europe to America in 4 hours, and who has also prophesied the present earthquake in the Balkans, adding that it will spread in course of time, inundating most of Italy and Spain with tidal waves and proceeding Westward, where it will destroy Weymouth and San Francisco. Sir Austen Harris believes in him so much that he has sold out all his investments in San Francisco bonds. Honey was very unhappy at school and left after ten days. Also they seem to be going to buy Garsington (Lady H had also just bought a caravan. *Che gente!*).

Am reading *Wilhelm Meister* and confirming my dislike of Goethe. What an odious character! And as for saying he's a great writer—no, it won't do.

I like some of the Yeats poems very much. They have a strange power about them—underneath their superficial literariness and preciosity.

Tomorrow I go to Buckingham Palace to see the pictures and the private apartments. I look forward to an amusing afternoon.

Goodbye, Mary. I hope you're enjoying yourself a little more than you were.

Love from,
Aldous

TO MARY HUTCHINSON

4 Onslow Mews East, S.W.7
ca early May 1928

Dearest Mary,
I gather from Maria that there was some idea of our going down to the country on Sunday. I wish I had known of this sooner, as I have made arrangements to go and say goodbye to relations all that day—which make the project quite impossible, I fear. But we expect you on Friday and, with Jack, on Saturday evening.

A bientôt,
A

TO DR. B. G. BROOKS

Il Canneto
Forte del Marmi (Lucca)
8 July 1928

Dear Brooks,
Thank you for your letter, rather belatedly received here and, I confess, rather belatedly answered, as I am in the midst of an exasperating labour of correcting proofs. Please give my felicitations and best wishes to all concerned, even the young lady—for after all and in spite of everything I think one is to be congratulated on entering the world. As for upbringing—I've given up the problem and taken the path of least resistance. Our little boy has gone to school and, as it happens, is extremely happy. More cannot be demanded, so that's all right, at any rate for the time being.

We have just taken a little house in Paris, or rather at Suresnes, which combines the charms of French provinciality, with the gaiety of the river, the rustic beauties of the Bois and the diversions of Paris at a quarter of an hour's drive from the door. I hope it will be pleasant. We hope to settle in, more or less—and rather less than more—some time this autumn. Perhaps we may see you on your way through to your Burgundian haunts. The address is 3 Rue du Bac, Suresnes (Seine).

Yours,
Aldous Huxley

[The "little boy" is H's son, Matthew. The "young lady" is Brooks's daughter, Jane. "Burgundian haunts" refers to the siting of some of the poems in Burgundy.]

TO MARY HUTCHINSON

Il Canneto
Forte dei Marmi (Lucca)
2 August 1928

How sweet of you, dearest Mary, to remember my birthday and to send me these charming handkerchiefs and those yet more charming photographs. We have often been reduced to the same trick of re-photographing the too exorbitant photograph. Dishonesty in such cases is really the only policy.

Poor Tom [Eliot]—your description called up all the horror. The deliberate dreariness, the voluntarily chosen dismalness and vacuity of his life! dreadful: but I suppose indispensable to his art. But then, I must say, the whole of London seems curiously dismal from here. There was an article in the *Corriere della Sera* yesterday about Lady Ellesmere's ball and the throwing out of uninvited guests including Miss Beaton, with references to Cecil Beaton and the Sitwells being photographed bottom upwards, and David Tennant[7] and the Russian ballet. When I read it I was so overcome by the dismal imbecility of the whole caboodle that I almost burst into tears. However, such is life in the Great West. Here it is vegetative and solar. The sun does most of the living for one; one abandons oneself to its energy. In the intervals I do a little work—hitherto of a rather tiresome sort, correcting proofs, and revising old MSs, but now that's finished, thank heaven—and some reading. I've been collecting material on Pascal—another dreary one, but violently diabolically so, a great genius of dreariness, excitingly dismal. And reading novels by Giovanni Verga, some good, some bad. And the books of an admirable French philosopher, Jules de Gaultier. And the *Journal Intime* of B. Constant. And Shaw's book on socialism—good, but all curiously beside the point as most of Shaw is. The beach is crowded with flashing young Italian aristocrats, like very handsome young chauffeurs, and shapely young women. Pleasant to look at, but rather tedious; the sort of young women who might only exist in bed and naked, and with whom there should be no communication except a physical and nocturnal one. They ought to be trained to hibernate in the intervals of love-making.

Oh, by the way, a sudden and quite irrelevant thought. Do you happen to have any way of finding out about Albert Rutherston? I have sent him 2 batches of MS for a little book which he is to illustrate, but have not received any acknowledgement. That was a month ago and I am growing disquieted. I'd be most grateful if you could turn your antennae towards the Rutherstonian world and discover a) if Albert is alive b) if alive, whether in England c) if alive and in England whether he received my MS and numerous postcards and d) if so, why he doesn't acknowledge them. What a bore the creature is!

Farewell, dearest Mary. It's a pity you will insist on spending your summers in the arctic instead of under a reasonable sky and a proper sun. Love to Jack. I kiss your hands.

A

Did you like Lawrence's book? It's fine, I think. People keep writing indignantly to Maria complaining of it, as tho' she were the author. What

---

[7] Hon. David Pax Tennant (1902–1968). Elder brother of Stephen Tennant, one of the Bright Young Things.

a strange hatred for the truth most human beings have! Or rather not for the truth, because it doesn't exist, but for reality. A loathing and terror. A grown up man like Swift writing "O, Celia, Celia, Celia shits!" and being really dreadfully upset by the fact, torturing himself by thinking of it—it's really extraordinary. And it wouldn't ever have happened if men hadn't first invented a whole mass of lies and set it up as Truth in opposition to reality. A droll world.

TO MARY HUTCHINSON

Il Canneto
Forte dei Marmi (Lucca)
1 September 1928

Dearest Mary,
Thank you for your postcard and all your trouble to find Albert—from whom, however, I have at last had a communication. So Albert's not in heaven and all's right with the world. Life flows on here much as usual under the usual blue sky which has taken on a sort of despairing early-autumnal clarity. The grapes hang almost ripe from the pergolas, the figs have begun to burst with sweetness, the distances are incredibly near and clear and everything is at its climax, too beautiful to last.

We went to the *palio* at Siena—lovely as usual—and have taken one or two astonishing drives through the local mountains. Otherwise haven't stirred. I write a little; read Renan, who is remarkably good outside that dreadful *Vie de Jésus* and the *Decameron*, which I hadn't read for years and had forgotten the rich perfection of. Do you remember the story of the young girl who wanted to sleep out on the veranda to listen to the nightingales and who was found next day by her father, stark naked with her lover, one arm round his neck and her other hand holding John Thomas—and the father calls to the mother saying: "*la tua figlia era così vaga dell' usignuolo che l'ha preso e tienlosi in mano.*" [Come see how enchanted your daughter is by the nightingale, which she has caught and is still holding in her hand.] Too enchanting.

I hope you'll have a pleasant time in Paris. Till when are you going to be there?—because if you were leaving the same time we'd ask you to be very kind and transport Matthew with you to London. Will you let us know on a p.c. what your movements are to be?
Love from us both.
A

TO JULIETTE HUXLEY

Dear Juliette,

Thank you for your letter. I'm glad you liked the book. I think it's certainly the best thing I've done; and in spite of its length it remains quite readable. I've given up press cuttings, so don't see any reviews; but can imagine they're as idiotic as one has a right to expect.

Maria has had to rush off to Belgium today, as her grandmother is very ill and probably dying. Meanwhile, however, the house at Suresnes progresses, and I hope we may be able to inhabit it next week. Have you got the address?

3 Rue du Bac
Suresnes
(Seine)

It will, I hope, be quite nice by the time it's finished. Anyhow, the locality is charming—50 yards from the Seine and three minutes from the Bois de Boulogne, with the open country about ten minutes drive behind and the opera a quarter of an hour in front, across the Bois.

We arrived to find tragedies proceeding here—Jehanne and Moulaert getting divorced in an atmosphere of disaster. They are settling themselves, however, Jehanne resigning herself to the *fait accompli*. When the first agonies are over I think it will all be more satisfactory. The situation had been impossible for a long time. It will be better like this—tho' it's all very deplorable.

What bad luck about the children. I hope poor Francis will get off without his operation. Matthew is back at school and apparently quite happy. We hope to come over to London for his 1/2 –term at the beginning of November when we look forward to seeing you.

Love to you all.

Yours,
A

TO MARY HUTCHINSON

3 Rue du Bac
Suresnes (Seine)
11 November 1928

Will you be very kind and write Boris [Anrep]'s address on the enclosed, dearest Mary. It is an introduction for America which I promised he should have before starting.

A rather dizzy sort of journey on Thursday. But found all well here, the house progressing slowly. I hope you'll persuade Jack to let you come to Paris. Till then fare well. M sends all her love and is writing as soon as she can find a respite from household affairs.

Yours,
A

TO MARY HUTCHINSON

19 Grand Place
St. Trond, Belgium
2 January 1929

Those links, dearest Mary, were precisely, so far as I was concerned, the missing ones—what for months I had been thinking I needed each time I looked at the very dilapidated pair I have been wearing. How exceedingly telepathic of you to have thought of them, and how sweet! Thank you a thousand times.

Christmas here has been slightly wearing—as life always is in the neighborhood of M's mother, who has a genius for getting the maximum of agitation out of the minimum of cause. However Matthew was very happy playing, with an almost frantic intensity, with a small cousin; and I was able to escape periodically from the agitation and do some work. We leave for Paris tomorrow with every prospect of a smart north wind and snow all the way. Not very appetizing weather for a journey by car.

I hope to be coming to England for about a week from Jan 8th, as I have various businesses which must be attended to. I look forward to seeing you then. Meanwhile I must go and pay a farewell call on fourteen aged relations—such are the customs of the country—and so bid you adieu, dearest Mary, with all my love till next week.

Yours,
A

TO LADY OTTOLINE MORRELL

3 Rue du Bac
Suresnes
3 January 1929

Dearest Ottoline,

I hope you have received the little book on Amiel[8] which I sent as a New Year greeting a day or two ago. It has the merit of being small, so won't take up too much room in the new shelves among the new flood of literary tonnage! What a burden books are! I sometimes think one oughtn't to read at all—or else only at libraries like Samuel Butler.

We were both so very glad to get your letter which I'm ashamed, was not answered before. But we've had such a nightmare Christmas—Maria's father, mother, and youngest sister in the house, not to mention Matthew and Jehanne's little girl. So full that I had to move into a hotel, like a hedge-sparrow that's hatched out cuckoos, and have only returned today to the nest. One can easily have too much of family life. . . .

Spain was very delightful, but so terrifically cold at the end of the tour from Madrid onwards. Paris was balmy by comparison. The autumn is the wrong season: one should obviously go in Spring. If you think of touring there do so before the exhibitions close down. Both contain extraordinary collections of art—things it's very difficult or quite impossible to see when they're dispersed in the places where they belong, private collections, monasteries, village churches, etc. We can give you lots of useful information if you think of doing the voyage. And what astonishing things there are to see in a car—little towns on the way from one big place to another, where you can never stop if you go by train. Too extraordinary!

Since returning I've been busy finishing off a volume of short stories, reading the *Paradiso* in the intervals, and the *Odyssey*, both staggering, tho' I don't *like* Dante, whereas Homer is adorable. I've begun a fascinating commentary on the Odyssey in 4 volumes by the French scholar Victor Bérard, the best and most humanely sensible Homer-*forscher* who exists. If you enjoy the *Odyssey* it's worth at least looking into *Les Navigations d' Ulysse*—you'll find it at the London Library.

Have been seeing a good deal of Drieu [la Rochelle] lately, whom I like very much. Also Paul Valéry, very considerably aged, but always very interesting, a first rate mind. But, golly, how dreary most of the French literary men are!

[8] Henri-Frédéric Amiel (1821–1881). Swiss philosopher. Huxley's aunt, Mrs. Humphry Ward, translated his *Journal Intime*.

Valéry's right—he said today when I saw him that an author shouldn't frequent other authors after the age of 24. Once formed, he can only find them uninteresting—as a class, that is to say: tho' of course there are always individual exceptions.

How kind of Philip to offer to send us his book! I'd love to have it. I've always liked such fragments of Greville as I have pecked at here and there out of the enormous mass. It will be delightful to have the marrow of him in one volume, with all the labor of selection performed in advance. We hope to be in London during the second half of January, when it will be delightful to see you both. Maria sends much love and apologizes for not writing—but you will realize that she's been a bit harried and exhausted by the family invasion.

With all my affection and good wishes,

Yours,
Aldous

TO MARY HUTCHINSON

In the Train
15 January 1929

A word, dearest Mary, to bid you goodbye and to apologize for a certain gloominess last Sunday—owing to the fact that for no particular reason I was feeling rather ill and, feeling ill, was feeling more fatigued than the obvious causes of fatigue would otherwise have justified. *Quand même*, it was a very delightful weekend. I hope you thought so too.

Had a dismal journey on the Monday morning and spent a day irritatingly doing small things. Matthew arrived with a very bad cold and was in consequence very melancholy at the thought of going back to school: but when the moment came and we met all the other children on the platform at Waterloo, he recovered all his spirits and we parted quite cheerfully. Beaverbrook I never saw at all, owing to a series of muddles—so that I still have to decide. I so resent the press work these swine put on one with their beastly money. At the same time it's almost a duty to milk them of as much of it as one can. So I remain torn between a desire to send him to the devil and a desire to haggle for the highest price.

Farewell, sweet Mary; why do we live in this filthy climate? Too depressing. The sight of the landscape outside the train windows is really sickeningly dismal. Doesn't the example of Mr. Booth fire you to found a Damnation Army for the propagation of the principles of the Dianic religion? It needs doing.

Yours,
A

TO ARNOLD BENNETT

3 Rue du Bac
Suresnes
19 February 1929

Dear A.B.

I'm so sorry we missed you in Paris. Your letter was forwarded, rather circuitously, to Florence (whither we had gone, very reluctantly in view of the weather) to sell our Italian-registered car. The City of Flowers was 6 inches deep in snow, 15° below zero, every water-pipe frozen, the Arno a solid mass of ice etc. etc. But the cold was nothing to what we met on the Riviera, where a *mistral* or *bise* or what not, was blowing continuously at 70 miles an hour in the midst of the snow and ice. We think ourselves lucky in having escaped—I with a chill on the liver, which leaves me still gloomy and disinclined to do very much, and Maria with a slight influenza. I hope you and Dorothy have got off as lightly.

A rather nice woman of my acquaintance, a Mrs. Haslip, has begged me to call the forthcoming work by the hero of the Francs scandal to your professional attention as a critic. So I enclose the prospectus, with all apologies.

Yours,
Aldous H.

PS have you read André Malraux's *Les Conquérants*? If not, do. It's the most interesting and also—in all it implies, states, takes for granted— a most terrifying book.

TO DONALD FREEMAN

3 Rue du Bac
Suresnes
15 March 1929

Dear Freeman,

Your letter suggesting an article on talkies arrived just as I was finishing the enclosed—which deals with the same theme, though from a rather different angle. Which shows that great minds always think alike.

Perhaps there will be another article to be got out of the same subject on the lines you suggested—the future of the beastly thing, its probable effects etc.

Yours,
Aldous Huxley

TO EUGENE F. SAXTON

3 Rue du Bac
Suresnes (Seine)
7 May 1929

Dear Saxton,

I was delighted to get your letter and have news of the family. All goes well with us here. Matthew is at school in England and happy, also much healthier which is a great comfort. My wife and I have got through the worst winter since the last Ice Age with nothing worse than a liver chill and a touch of influenza between us—which may be regarded as very fortunate. We have now settled into a nice little house, all would be perfect if the climate of Paris were only a little better. I should be happy to sacrifice culture, conversation, the arts and all the other attractions of a capital for sunshine. One of the greatest tragedies in world history was the passing of civilization from warm to cold countries. The only comfort is that (I believe) it's going back again to the Mediterranean in the course of the next generation or two!

I'm sorry you won't be coming over this year. I don't think there's much prospect of our undertaking the opposite journey yet awhile. Matthew's holiday dates make distant travelling rather difficult. I doubt if we shall get further that the Mediterranean this autumn.

By the way, if you have Glenway Westcott's[9] address I'd be so glad of it—for I liked him so much when I saw him, too briefly, at a lunch party at Paul Morand's.[1] It would be pleasant to see him again. Which is not the case with most of the literary men I meet in Paris!

Thank you for your suggestions about the serial. It is quite possible that one of the stories I have in mind to do this summer may work out to 40 or so thousand words. If so, I'd be most happy to submit it to

[9] Glenway Westcott (1901–1987). American author of *The Pilgrim Hawk* (1940).
[1] Paul Morand (1888–1976). French diplomat and novelist. In an interview in the *Chicago Evening Post*, 14 May 1934, Huxley told Samuel Putnam, "I only liked Morand's first book (*Ouvert la nuit*). I have liked the others, progressively, less and less."

Harper's. I can't say anything definite, however, till I see how the thing works out.

Please give all the family our love.

Yours,
Aldous Huxley

P.S. Thank you for the very friendly things you say about the book.

TO MARY HUTCHINSON

Il Canneto
Forte dei Marmi (Lucca)
5 July 1929

What news of you, dearest Mary? The rest has been silence for some time now. I suppose Jack was finally rather relieved at not getting in? As a conscientious MP he would have been bored to death, I imagine, by his duties. And there wouldn't be much point in being an unconscientious one. Jowitt[2] and *"la bella Signora Jowitt"* have been playing star parts in the *Corriere della Sera*. Rather heroic to join a sinking ship, instead of leaving it—for I imagine the Labour Government must sink fairly soon, bombarded as it is from both sides, Tories on the right and the Trade Unions on the left. But then, after all, every party is now a sinking ship; the whole world is a bit leaky. So it doesn't matter much where one goes.

We are installed here in the little house we had last year, among the trees. Very quiet and cool. We had a pleasing 10-days in Rome before coming here, marred by a disquieting fear that it may be almost the last time that Rome, as we know it, will ever be visible by us: for the Fascists, who have an Empire-complex and see themselves as Cato and Augustus and the Mother of the Gracchi; are busily engaged in pulling down all medieval and Renaissance Rome in order to dig up more and yet more antique rubbish heaps. So that in a few years time Rome will be one vast hole with broken pillars and bits of masonry in it, surrounded by hideous garden suburbs and international hotels. *"Si monumentum requiris,"* the Fascists will be able to say, proudly, *"circumspice."*

---

[2] William Jowitt (1885–1957). Although a Liberal M.P., Jowitt accepted Ramsay MacDonald's invitation to serve in a Labour cabinet. He was elected as a Labour M.P. for Preston in the July 1929 election. His wife Lesley (née McIntyre, d. 1970) was a supporter of the arts.

We saw Berners[3] several times—very busy now being the rising young painter. He'll soon be like Alexander, weeping because there's nothing more to conquer.

Forte is quiet so far. The only enlivement has been the presence of DH Lawrence, minus Frieda, on his way from Majorca to Germany. Very ill, but indomitably going on, somehow. He leaves today, abandoning here the most appalling female American admirer, who suddenly swooped down to see him and who has almost driven him mad and would have driven us mad too, if we'd given her a chance.

Have been reading Malinowski's *Sexual Life of Savages*, most interesting and instructive. These Melanesians are so infinitely more rational and civilized, in the majority of their sexual customs than we are. They start what Americans would call their Love-Life at about 6 and continue through infantile promiscuity and adolescent passions to reasonable and on the whole faithful marriage. It's the early start, I'm sure, that's important and the lack of which spoils European life and produces the nervous breakdowns etc. But it appears to be impossible, as the Indians have discovered, to combine childish sexuality with intensive intellectual education. Malinowski's savages are Neolithic men and so not seriously bothered by educational problems. They can afford to spend their childhood and adolescence in idyllic flirtations under the hibiscus bushes. We can't. But, *per contra*, can we afford to spend our childhood and adolescence learning to be, not merely intellectually efficient, but also unhappy, nervously unstable, perverted, mad? It's a nice question.

What do you do this summer and where do you go? Is Barbara still being French-polished? She'll be almost dazzlingly bright before Monsieur Bellaigne has done with her. "The Religious Sense in the Music of Boito . . . "

Farewell dearest, Mary. I kiss your hands

A

[3] Gerald Tyrwhitt-Wilson, Lord Berners (1883–1950). His novel, *Far from the Madding War*, contains a self-portrait: "He composed music, he wrote books, he painted; he did a great many things with a certain facile talent."

TO FLORA STROUSSE[4]

Il Canneto
Forte dei Marmi (Lucca), Italy
13 September 1929

Dear Starky,

Thank you for the account of your English Odyssey. You've seen a lot of good places. Skye and that West Coast of Scotland can be miraculous in good weather—completely immaterial and wholly improbable, magic landscape. But, my God, when it rains: I've spent summers there when it literally never stopped.

I've spent a very quiet summer here *en famille*—bathing, lying in the sun and doing a fair amount of work, occasionally talking to friends of various nationalities, reading histories of Spain, of the Alexandrian empire, of the Inquisition, of decadent Roman society. All very curious. The human being seems to me progressively odder and odder the more I know about his activities. D. H. Lawrence was here with us for a bit early in the summer—ill, but always indomitable and full of an extraordinary vitality. Then we motored round Rome for a bit, nosing about especially in the Etruscan sites. What a charming people they were, those Etruscans, and what a lot our world has to learn from them!—if our world were capable of learning anything but fresh methods of debasing the human individual and exalting the crowd and the machine! Tomorrow we start back for Paris, thence briefly, I hope, to England, and afterwards to Spain to attend a Conference of Societies for Intellectual Cooperation. Golly! Why not sentimental and carnal cooperation? But the conference serves as a sufficient excuse to go and look once more at the Velasquez pictures in Madrid (what an experience!) and to explore, which I've never done before, the Southern Moorish part of the peninsula. It's a most extraordinary country, anyhow. The queerest history of any people in Europe—because it's mainly a history of obstinate denial and destruction, self-destruction as well as destruction of everything else.

Farewell. My address is:—3 Rue du Bac, Suresnes (Seine) France.

Yours,
Aldous Huxley

---

[4] Flora Strousse (b. 1897). Grover Smith notes that some of Mrs. Strousse's published works appeared under the name of Floyd Starkey. Although the Library of Congress catalog lists a few works by Flora Strousse, there are no listings for Floyd Starkey.

TO CHARLES PRENTICE

Cavendish Hotel
Jermyn St., St. James's S.W.1
27 November 1929

Dear Prentice,
Brief Candles will consist of four stories.

1. "The Rest Cure," the story of a woman who goes to Florence for a rest-cure from her bright, active, intelligent, man-of-science of a husband, and gets involved with an Italian of rather low class with disastrous results.

2. "The Claxtons," the story of cranks and their children.

3. "Chawdron," the story of the "spiritual love" of a middle-aged financier for a none-too-virtuous adventuress. The story is told through a conversation, the narrative mingling with and emerging out of a series of reflections on a variety of subjects.

4. (The long story) "After the Fireworks," a story based on an incident recorded by Chateaubriand, who was approached as an oldish man, by a very young female admirer who wanted at all costs (because she liked his books) to become his mistress. Chateaubriand had to keep her at bay almost by force. The letter he wrote to her in expostulation is extant. My hero writes the letter of expostulation but subsequently succumbs to a surprise attack and so embarks on a love-affair which ends quite as badly as he himself had prophesied.

Yours,
Aldous

TO MARY HUTCHINSON

3 Rue du Bac
Suresnes (Seine)
21 December 1929

Dearest Mary,
This is to wish you everything seasonable and unseasonable. I enclose some lines I wrote the other day, which may amuse you at any rate by their subject, which is important, though I don't know that the treatment is entirely satisfactory.

The most lyrically intense passages in Dante's *Paradiso*, which I am just re-reading (with growing astonishment), are perhaps the best expressions of amorous ecstasy: for when you come to the point, you find that the carnal and spiritual are describable in identical terms.

Have been seeing Chile[5] and his young wife recently. Very sympathetic. Also James Joyce, whom I found extraordinarily much pleasanter than *Ulysses* and the *Work in Progress* would lead one to expect—tho' I don't like either of these two books any better in consequence.

From Tom's cousin the Princess I hear that the Eliots, after two moves, have decided that, definitely, they cannot live in a flat and must move back to a house. Is this true? I hope so: it's so abominable when people behave in character.

Love to Barbara and Jack.

I kiss your hands,
A

TO RICHARD THOMA[6]

Hotel Berkeley
7 Avenue Matignon
Paris
26 December 1929

Dear Richard Thoma,
I am here for some days as my house has become too full—what with a son, and niece and various other relatives—to hold me. Can you come and dine with me one of these days? Tomorrow Friday, e.g? Or Sunday? Will you ring me up in the course of the morning tomorrow?

What a bad business about Harry Crosby[7]—so frightfully stupid *entre autres choses.*

Yours,
Aldous Huxley

---

[5] Alvaro "Chile" Guevara (1894–1951). Painter who married heiress Meraud Guiness (1904–1993), also a painter.

[6] Richard Thoma (1874–1957). Poet who also wrote on Alastair Crowley. In a letter to Thoma, dated 16 February 1932, Huxley invites him to visit for a night or two and goes on, " . . . I hope you make it clear in your Gilles de Rais novel that Joan of Arc was really his disciple in sorcery and that she was what the Church condemned her as—a witch. Miss [Margaret] Murray makes the point in her *Witch Cult of Western Europe*, and I'm sure it's sound." Interestingly, Huxley appears to agree with Murray and Crowley, but both their arguments have since been discredited. On 3 February 1930 Crowley was to have given a lecture before the Poetry Society at Oxford on Gilles de Rais.

[7] Harry Crosby (1898–1929). Wealthy American poet; founder of Black Sun Press. Committed dual suicide with a lover on 10 December 1929.

TO ROBERT NICHOLS

3 Rue du Bac
Suresnes

My dear Robert,
So many thanks for the translation of the Turgenyeff essay, which I've not read yet, as I was turned out of the house from Xmas till today by an invasion of in-laws and children, and had to take refuge in a hotel. I'm glad you've not read *Nadja*, which I'm sure you'll enjoy. A most curious and, I think, admirable book by the high priest of *surréalisme*—who of course ceases to write super-realistically when he wants to do something good and produces instead a very beautiful French prose—some of the best now written.

What a pity that we'll miss you when we're in England after January 15. We may be in the Midi later on—but probably near Marseille, not so far east as Villefranche. Still, we'll let you know. Read, while you're there, an entertaining and often pregnant pamphlet—*La mort de la penseé bourgeoise* by Emmanuel Berl. It approaches our gravest problems with the right spirit of irreverence!

I've just heard that the dramatic adaptation of *Point Counter Point* is to be put on by Leon M. Lion this spring. God preserve us! Let's hope it won't be quite so awful on the stage as it was in the typescript I read. I doubt if I shall have the courage to go and see. The ostrich is the wisest of animals! Love from us both to Norah and you.

Yours,
Aldous H.

TO CLIVE BELL

3 Rue du Bac
Suresnes (Seine)
7 January 1930

Dear Clive,
We are doing a slight Box and Cox, I fear. M and I accompanying our infant to England on the 14th and, having stowed him away at school, propose to stay about a week. How unfortunate that you should have chosen just that week to be in Paris! But if you'll be there may we propose ourselves to tea with you on Wednesday afternoon the 15th? It would be most pleasant to see you—and I hope you'll prolong your week in Paris a little so that we may coincide there at more leisure. I don't

know if we shall go South. So far the weather has not been sufficiently filthy to make us long to. But doubtless Providence has its little jokes up its sleeve and I dare say we may flee later on towards at least the illusion of warmth which the Mediterranean provides so brilliantly.

Meanwhile I hope the 15th afternoon may find you at home?

Yours,
Aldous H

TO CLIVE BELL

3 Rue du Bac
Suresnes (Seine)
13 February 1930

My dear Clive,

Thank you for your letter. Yes, it's quite possible even probable that we may be in Italy in May and June. But meanwhile do give us more information about the immediate future.

We may very likely be going South about a week from now—to look for a house somewhere between Hyères and Marseille and also, if he's well enough to receive visitors, to go and see D. H. Lawrence, who's at a sanatorium near Grasse. Please tell me (a) if you are likely to be at Cassis and till when (b) if you are returning to Cassis (c) if you are coming to Paris and when and for how long? We wouldn't want to be in the Midi more than a 14-night—say from 20 February onwards.

Had a curious 3 weeks in London looking at the rehearsals of a play which somebody made out of my novel. A very odd and, tho' rather painful, instructive experience.

Give my love to Raymond and Eddie and with my love my address and a request to remember the same when they're in Paris. M sends greetings. Don't forget to give me details of your program.

Yours ever,
Aldous H

P.S. We're going to Cocteau's Répétition Générale at the Française tomorrow—which ought to be curious. Have you read Berl's Mort de la Pensée Bourgeoise? A most amusing pamphlet.

Campbell Dixon wrote the stage adaptation of Point Counter Point (This Way to Paradise). It was produced by Leon Lion (1879–1947), who also produced Huxley's play The World of Light (1931).

TO IFAN KYRLE FLETCHER[8]

Suresnes, France
23 March 1930

Dear Sir,
I never knew Ronald Firbank well. I used to see him from time to time at the theatre when I was doing dramatic criticism. He often attended First Nights, in spite of an overwhelming shyness which made the presence of other people an agony to him. Sometimes the agony was so great that he would do extraordinary things that made him conspicuous and so increased his self-consciousness. (E.g., he would get up in the middle of an act or start rummaging under his seat.) He must have derived some curious painful pleasure from his embarrassments. The last time I saw him was at Robert Nichols's wedding. We sat with various other people in the Café Royal. As I took my seat at the table opposite him, Firbank gave his usual agonized wriggle of embarrassment and said, "Aldous—always my *torture.*" Which must, I think, have been his spontaneous reaction to most people, at any rate, at first. A little later he was telling me of his intention to go to the West Indies to live among the negroes so as to collect material for a novel about Mayfair.

Yours sincerely,
Aldous Huxley

TO SYDNEY SCHIFF

3 Rue du Bac
Suresnes
28 March 1930

My dear Sydney,
Thank you so much for your letter. We were with poor Lawrence when he died—a very painful thing to see an indomitable spirit finally broken and put out. The disease had made terrible ravages since we last saw him in the summer, and our visits to him—we arrived at Vence about ten days before his death—were sad affairs. I am going slowly to work collecting Lawrence's letters—many of them very remarkable. But not for immediate publication.

We were in London for three weeks for that wretched play [Campbell Dixon's version of *Point Counter Point—This Way to Paradise*],

---

[8] Fletcher was Firbank's biographer.

but I felt so convinced that you'd be gone like swallows to some more rational climate that I didn't even attempt to get into touch with you. I'm very sorry I didn't try and also that the reason for your staying on in England should be such a sad one. Please tell Violet how much I feel for her in these tragic circumstances.

We have just bought a little house in the Midi—between Bandol and Sanary (address:—Cap de la Gorguette. Sanary. Var.), a ridiculous little house exactly like what one imagines to have been the home of Bouvard et Pécuchet, but easily transformable and with a very nicely planted vineyard and fruit garden; sheltered, yet only 200 yards from the sea. We go down there next week for three weeks. During May I think I shall be in England. I wonder where you will be?

That play. . . . It was rather painful: there were many moments when one wished that the operation could have been performed under anaesthetics. Still I learnt a lot from attending the rehearsals—learnt in the first place that actors are incredibly stupid and don't know their business—and am now writing a play of my own, which may or may not be produced, but will be, I think, in any case producible. Yes, Lion was a bit of a disaster. So bottomlessly commonplace. But I suppose one can't expect anything else. Actors being in general what they are, the producing of a play is like the performing of a quartet on instruments made of packing-cases and string. Talking of quartets—I thought the introduction of the music in the last act rather thrilling. If I could have altered the dialogue a bit and if Lion had not been Lion, it would have been, I believe, very impressive. The music itself seemed to me a most extraordinary symbol—producing supernatural effects totally unobtainable in other ways.

I'm sorry you didn't send your letter about *Point Counter Point*— and also glad in a way; for though I don't think I'd have resented your criticism, I know that it would have disturbed me inasmuch as it would have turned my mind back onto the book and distracted me from what I am thinking about at the moment. I find I have a most useful capacity for forgetting and so being able to start with a more or less clean slate each time. Reminders of past work disturb me.

Let me know where you are likely to be in May—or if you'll be in the Midi by any chance round Easter time. Maria joins in sending greetings and best of wishes to you both.

Yours,
Aldous H.

TO MARY HUTCHINSON

3 Rue du Bac
Suresnes (Seine)
1 April 1930

Dearest Mary,

A word to say that we are ordering your room at the Berkeley and that we hope you'll come down to Bandol where, if we can't actually put you up (I don't know what accommodation there'll be) you can stay in a hotel next door. We start on Thursday. Mark and his bride (they are getting married on Thursday) will be coming down there for a honeymoon that will be almost indistinguishable from a silver wedding.

I heard a very good piece of information the other day, which I hope Jack will discreetly broadcast to this effect. Last year Bodkin,[9] the then public prosecutor, came over here to discuss with the French authorities ways and means of stopping the influx of indecent books (including *Ulysses* and *Lady Chatterley*) into England. (The recent onslaught on Lady C here was finally due to his machinations.) A young deputy and barrister called Bergery[1] (a friend of Drieu's[2] whom I met the other day and liked) was told to entertain him. They dined well: and after dinner Bodkin asked Bergery to take him to some place where he could see girls being whipped. Which Bergery refused—saying he was a member of parliament and not a guide for Anglo-American tourists wishing to work off sex-repressions. This is first-hand and vouched for. Some day it will have to be published—for it is the most delicious commentary on the smut hounds and their mentality.

How are you, Mary? I think of our *entretiens* in London with pleasure. I hope you will come to Bandol. Our address there is:—

Les Flots
Cap de la Gorguette
Sanary
(Var)

It's nearer to Bandol than Sanary, however. The big trains probably don't stop at Bandol at this season. One must either change at Marseille and

---

[9] Sir Archibald Bodkin (1862–1957). Director of Public Prosecutions, 1920–1930.
[1] Gaston Bergery (1892–1974). Deputy in the Conseil National from 1928, later served as Vichy's ambassador to Moscow and Ankara.
[2] Pierre Drieu la Rochelle (1893–1945). French novelist and poet. Huxley distanced himself from Drieu after the latter became increasingly sympathetic to fascism.

get into an omnibus train (one hour from Marseille). Or go to Toulon where, if you came, we could meet you. Anyhow there is a bus going every ¼ hour from Toulon to Bandol. Our house is next to the Hotel de la Gorguette. Love from us both.

Yours,
A

TO SYDNEY SCHIFF

The Athenaeum
Pall Mall, S.W.1
6 May 1930

Dear Sydney,

Thank you so much for *The Castle* and for my waistcoat, which I so stupidly forgot. I am enclosing the first 3 acts of the play—rather illegible, I fear, and still not quite "definitive." The last act takes place in the tropical island, begins with a philosophical conversation between the two young men and ends with a Voodoo ceremony which has got to be as thrillingly impressive as the stage can make it.

I so much enjoyed my evening with you both last night and must only apologize for having stayed so late—which was in a sense your fault for not having allowed me to be for a moment bored and so preventing me from realizing the passage of time.

There seemed to be no opportunity last night to talk about your *True Story*, which I read with great pleasure and an admiration of the very subtle way you had made the consciousness of the hero expand through the first half of the book, as he grows up—so that everything grows up including the style, the words, the thoughts. Virginia is a fascinating character and I only regret that your method, which entails looking only through Kurt's eyes, shouldn't have allowed you to get inside her skin and give us her vision of the curious events. But as a piece of observed, strictly "behaviourist" psychology, her character is masterly.

Ever yours,
Aldous H.

TO S. S. KOTELIANSKY

The Athenaeum
Pall Mall, S.W.1
6 May 1930

It may interest you to know that I've just seen a letter sent by Murry to Ottoline on April 30th, saying that he was starting the next day for Vence to see F[rieda]. Well, well! We can only wait for the new developments.
ALH.

TO S. S. KOTELIANSKY

The Athenaeum
Pall Mall, S.W.1
8 May 1930

Dear Kot,
I went into Curtis Brown's today to ask Pollinger whether it was true about the edition of the *Escaped Cock*. I'm relieved to hear that there's no prospect of its being done either here or in America at once. The literary executors will have to decide. Pollinger showed me a long letter from Murry written from Vence about business affairs. The most significant sentence was this: "The best thing would be if I were to be appointed literary executor, which I don't want to be. (!) But if it is necessary . . . etc." So you see where the wind blows! Also there's no will, because M. talks of asking the solicitor at once for letters of administration—with Monty Weekley and, I suppose, himself as executors. But in this matter, of course, L[awrence's] relations will have their say. They can appoint their executor—who might be you, for example?

I wired to Frieda yesterday.

Yours,
A.L.H.

TO MARY HUTCHINSON

Paris
Wednesday morning
Late May 1930

Dearest Mary,
You are always so sweet to me that you make any thanks very inadequate. So I can only say I'm very grateful for all your goodness to me while I was in London and leave it feebly at that.

The sea was incredibly beautiful in the late evening light—like a great expanse of glass, green with its own thickness, and absolutely smooth. And Calais, which I really saw for the first time, thanks to my little spy-glass, was lovely too—the light-house, the two church towers rising above the dunes. So exquisite. It's melancholy how much one misses by seeing badly—but perhaps one's also spared a good many horrors! Only the horrors are probably paid for by the lovelinesses, with a bit to spare on the credit side, perhaps. With my little spy-glass I felt suddenly like a convalescent rediscovering the world after an illness and finding it unbelievably beautiful. However, the repulsiveness of the man sitting next me in the restaurant car soon reminded me that it was something else as well.

I read the *Life of Michelet* in the train. Very peculiar. Among other things, he married by correspondence—a young French governess who wrote to him from Vienna. I'm tempted to explore him more thoroughly. Paris is hot and brilliant. I have a tiresome day of fetching and carrying before me at Suresnes. So farewell, Dearest Mary. Persuade Jack to come South while the sun really shines.

Yours,
A

TO S. S. KOTELIANSKY

La Gorguette
Sanary (Var), France
31 May 1930

Dear Kot,
I'd hoped to see you on Wednesday at Ridgway's—then had to hasten my departure and so missed you. I don't think there's any particular news at the moment. Robinson,[3] whom I saw before leaving, seems to have the situation pretty well in hand (including Frieda in "the situation") and is getting busy about the American tangle. I didn't see Frieda before she left—once I came and she'd gone out with you and the next day she gave me an appointment and forgot about it. So you doubtless know more than I do about any secret history that may have occurred.

Let me hear if there is anything of importance.

Yours,
Aldous Huxley

---

[3] Percy Robinson. Solicitor appointed to defend D. H. Lawrence's interests during the Marlborough Street obscenity trial brought against the owners of the Warren Gallery for exhibiting Lawrence's paintings, thirteen of which were seized by the police on 5 July 1929.

TO G. WILSON KNIGHT[4]

La Gorguette
Sanary
2 June 1930

Dear Mr. Knight,

Thank you for your letter. It is just possible that I may be in London at the time of your production of *Hamlet*—in which case I shall certainly go to see it. Did you see Gielgud's playing of it this winter? Very good, I thought and he has the merit of saying the lines so that one can hear them and as though he believed they meant something—a rare phenomenon among Hamlets.

I have heard once or twice recently Verdi's *Otello* and am amazed each time by its astounding adequacy to the theme. One of the best operas ever written, I think. And have you ever heard his early *Macbeth*? Most curious—a mixture between 1840ish, Italian, barrel-organ arias and amazing passages of the greatest beauty. He adds to the play a scene where refugees are leaving Scotland because of Macbeth's tyranny—quite gratuitous, but of the most poignant beauty; and then suddenly one has "Is this the dagger?" or the sleepwalking scene treated in terms of *O sole mio*! But how I like artists like Verdi who get better and better as they grow older, riper and riper, surer and surer—like Titian, who only really started to paint well at 65 and was at the height of his powers round 80. Verdi's *Falstaff*—and what a marvel that is—was also written, if I'm not mistaken, when the old boy was nearly 80.

I am working on a long complicated novel—rather slowly, as I've not been well; but I hope to get it off my mind fairly soon.

A bientôt it may be: but I don't yet know if I shall be in London for certain when you're *Hamlet* is on.

Yours,
Aldous Huxley

---

[4] G. Wilson Knight (1897–1985). English critic, actor, and professor.

TO FRIEDA LAWRENCE

La Gorguette
Sanary (Var)
6 June 1930

My dear Frieda,
Have you thought of anyone in America to whom letters could be sent for collection and copying? Or shall we ask that they should be sent direct to England? It must be decided soon.

Meanwhile will you give me the addresses of the principal correspondents in the USA. It will be as well to write to them direct before sending a general encyclical to the press.

We're living in a derelict unfurnished house, with ten workmen pulling it to bits and sticking it up again all round us. Rather disturbing. But we must remain on the spot to see that no mistakes are made. How are you? And how is Barbie? Hot I should guess, if the same scirocco as blows here blows also at Vence. But such a scirocco! A full gale for three days—now subsided to a gentle wind, however.

Love from us both.

Yours,
Aldous H.

TO SYDNEY SCHIFF

La Gorguette
Sanary (Var)
19 June 1930

My dear Sydney,
I have scandalously neglected to write, I'm afraid. But what with having been so desperately busy in London and again so busy here—and in what conditions! for the workmen are all round us, pulling the house to pieces about our ears and, generally, failing to put it up again properly, so that we cannot absent ourselves—I have been in no state to write letters. However, here's a momentary lull; so I take the opportunity.

I'm glad those *Candles* amused you. The one or two reviews in English papers I have seen were in the more-in-sorrow-than-in-anger tone. The *mot d'ordre* at the moment is that all literature must be eminently public-schooly with touches of Barrie-esque whimsicality to relieve the gentlemanly tedium. If one's works don't resemble those of Mr. Priestley, then one's damned. Well, well . . .

I have re-modelled the end of my play, omitting the scene on the island altogether—for you and Violet were quite right: it was complete as
it stood—complete, but improvable; for as the woman[5] who runs the
Theater Guild in New York (to whom I showed the play before I left
London) very judiciously pointed out, the third act in its first form was
rather repetitive: you knew too early what the young man's intentions
were. So I have re-written it—keeping however practically all the stuff I
had originally put in, with suitable editions and re-arrangements—so as
to make it dramatically and psychologically a little more dynamic. The
young man starts with the fullest intention of remaining in the highest
of irresponsible spirits, but with each successive conversation his gaiety
becomes more and more dashed, he realizes that he is doing mischief,
not only to the other people, but also to himself—until finally, he de-
cides there's nothing for it but to go away again, back to the next world.
I finished this revised version a few days since and have sent copies to
my agent and Miss Helburn of the New York Guild. I haven't yet had
time to hear Miss H's reaction to the new version. She liked all the rest
of the play, in its original version, very much; and I hope that, if this new
last act makes a better ending, the Guild may perhaps take it on—which
would be a very excellent thing. When I have a clean copy of the new
last act, I'll send it to you to look at.

I've read your two German books with interest. *Steppenwolf* is
good, but not so very good, I think. One could do the same oneself, if
you see what I mean. But *The Castle* is a different story:—it's so exceedingly queer and incalculable in its realistically nightmare-like way,
that it's quite unlike anything. One would need to have a very special
sort of mind to write it; it's something new, something one couldn't do
oneself. I think it's a fascinating book, and strangely significant, whatever the allegorical meaning may be. (And the details are of small importance, really; or rather, you can't specify what the details of the
meaning are, apart from the poetic allegory in which they are incorporated. In a work of art, the truth is always a beauty-truth; and a
beauty-truth is a mystical entity, a two-in-one; the truth is quite insep-
arable from its companion, so that you can only state in the most general terms what its nature is. If you want to know details, you must go
to the original, where it is stated in its own particular terms, whether
literary, plastic or musical.)

[5] Theresa Helburn (1887–1959). Exececutive director of the Theatre Guild. She advised
Huxley on his plays *The World of Light* and *Now More Than Ever.*

I've read nothing lately except historical and philosophical works, so have no literary information to impart. My diversion, and a most hair-raising diversion, has been reading Michelet's *L'Amour*. Have you ever read it? If not, do. It's one of the most extraordinary and appalling works I ever set eyes on. You feel that the whole of its 400 pages were written in a continuous state of erection—erection, moreover, provoked by the most extraordinary stimuli, such as tender broodings on the anatomy of the matrix, or the menstrual flow. The psychology of Michelet has so fascinated me, that I have sent for biographies. The modern one, by Daniel Halévy, is very short and bad; but there is an old one, by Monod, the only man who was permitted to read Michelet's journal (a diary which apparently appalled him by the sincerity of its confessions, and which has never been published). I must get hold of it.

I hope you are settled into your chalet. I shall be happy when we're settled in here: at moments I gloomily doubt whether we shall be for years. Give our loves to Violet and to yourself.

Yours,
A.L.H.

TO S. S. KOTELIANSKY

Cap de la Gorguette
Sanary (Var)
30 June 1930

Dear Kot,
I delayed writing all this time, because I expected to see Frieda and would have liked to talk with her before answering. But now, after all, I haven't seen her. The original arrangement fell through at the last moment; and now Maria is away in Paris, and I must stay here, looking after the workmen, who are altering the house. The nearest I got to Frieda was the Hiltons, who had been staying at Vence and stopped here a few hours on the way home. Their account was pretty reassuring, on the whole. She seems to be acting sensibly.

About the literary executorship: I'd undertake it if it were really necessary. But, quite frankly, I'd rather not, as I have a real dread of distractions from my own affairs, particularly any which involve correspondence; the collecting of the letters already means more correspondence than I like. Moreover, I think that if I were to propose myself to Frieda as an universal literary executor, who should take everything out of her hands, she'd first fly in a rage (which wouldn't matter very much) and then (which would be worse) develop one of those almost insane mistrusts and suspicion-manias, which she gets sometimes. This would make my position difficult, if she consented to the appointment as executor, and quite impossible if (as I think much more likely) she didn't consent. I believe more can be done by remaining on friendly terms and advising in difficult cases than by trying (probably in vain—for she feels all the time that people are trying to do her out of something) to secure an official position of control and thereby becoming (as one inevitably would) one of her worst enemies. Further, I don't see that, for the moment, Frieda can go very far wrong. I gather from the Hiltons that she's got it clearly into her head now that the posthumous things mustn't be published all in a lump; so that the Apocalypse is being reserved till next year—which is all as it should be.

The question of a Complete Edition doesn't yet arise; and when it does, there can be a general discussion about it. In case of any difficult problem cropping up, Robinson has agreed to communicate with Jack Hutchinson, Forster and myself. So that I don't see that anything can go wrong with the literary side of things at present; and the business side has got to be settled by the lawyer, in the case of the American swindlers, and the lawyer and agents in the matter of ordinary publishing arrangements. Any attempt to deprive Frieda of what she feels are her legitimate rights in the matter will only lead, I am sure, to the most violent and troublesome reaction on her part and might drive her into the arms of Murry and others of the same breed.

There seems to be no further news about the MSS from Rosenbach, nor any from the Aga Khan about the pictures—in spite of the old villain having won the Derby! If she doesn't manage to sell one or both, Frieda's position isn't going to be very good, I'm afraid. The Hiltons told me that they'd heard from a friend of theirs in the book-and-MS-collecting world that there was a considerable slump at the moment in Lawrence values. This probably won't last; but for the immediate future this may be rather serious for Frieda and the estate, particularly when taken in conjunction with the American financial stringency. (The book trade is in such a bad way there, that my publisher is about to launch a campaign for selling all his books at a dollar and distributing them through the chain stores—like Boots and Liptons—as well as through the ordinary booksellers. A rather desperate remedy, it seems to me!)

Give my love to Gertler and the Ridgway tea party.

Yours,
Aldous Huxley

TO RICHARD ALDINGTON

La Gorguette
Sanary (Var)
5 July 1930

Dear Mr Aldington,

I must apologize for not having written before to thank you for your pamphlet on D.H.L. Being busy and the frightful distractions of having workmen all round, pulling the house to pieces and putting it, very imperfectly, together again must be my excuses.

I had, as a matter of fact, read the pamphlet when it came out and thought it most excellent. The quotation on the title page[6]—from a letter, I suppose?—was magnificently characteristic. I have met a number of other passages very like it in the letters I have read, addressed to all sorts of people, from Pinker the agent upwards and downwards. There is, for example, a passage in a letter to Pinker, in which he comments on some criticisms made by Arnold Bennett, evidently through Pinker, on the "form" of his novels. It is really magnificent.

I hope you'll let us know when you come down into these parts.

Yours sincerely,
Aldous Huxley

TO NAOMI MITCHISON

ca July 1930

My dear Naomi,

Lewis [Gielgud] tells me of a daughter. This is to wish her all happiness and you too. There would be scope for a grand Ciceronian letter—Corinth on my left hand, something else on my right—but I lack the gift for that sort of thing.

---

[6] *D. H. Lawrence: An Indiscretion* (1927). The epigraph reads, "You tell me I am wrong. Who are you, who is anybody to tell me I am wrong? I am not wrong."

The summer is strange here as all over the world—occasional rain unprecedented for the time of year and when the sun shines, which it does like mad, I must say prodigious winds that never stop blowing either from the west or the east. Which is invigorating but rather annoying. We live picnic fashion without furniture while the workmen add on to and alter the house round us. It ought to be very nice when it's done but it takes the most devilish long time doing and I'm afraid we are in for another six weeks at least of tinkering. When we are installed I hope you will come and see us. It's a lovely part of the world. I've been writing some essays and have now got to begin meditating a novel. What a curious profession it is, this writing business and how lucky it is that the public doesn't wake up to the fact of our peculiar ridiculousness!

Farewell dear Naomi,
Aldous

TO S. S. KOTELIANSKY

Cap de la Gorguette
Sanary (Var)
6 July 1930

Dear Kot,
I enclose the letters from Ada Clarke.[7] Yes, Frieda makes one rather desperate. I will see what can be done to persuade her to give up such control as she has over L[awrence]'s literary remains (remember, it is not an absolute control and that the brother and sisters can veto anything they don't approve of—which makes them quite safe with regard to Murry writing the biography or anything like that). The difficulty will be to find the persuasive argument. I can't go and tell her the truth, which is: "We mistrust your judgment so much and think you are such a fool, that we want you to have nothing more to do with your husband's writings, but to hand over the control to me." The sole result of this would be to make her stick more closely than ever to her rights and to make her less anxious to take advice from anyone. I may be able to persuade her by arguments about business necessity and the like. Anyhow I'll see and let you know.

Yours,
A.L.H.

---

[7] Ada Clarke. Lawrence's sister.

TO MARY HUTCHINSON

Cap de la Gorguette
Sanary (Var)
17 July 1930

How are you, Dearest Mary? How is London? It seems very remote from us here, tho' our icy mistral has been reminding us these last days that the North exists. No news. The workmen hammer and bang away and I have the impression that they will go on hammering and banging almost indefinitely. I do some work and draw and read and don't feel exuberantly well, I don't know why. Cyril Connolly and his young American wife, who are now our neighbors, come over from time to time—he like a highly educated, Eton—and—Balliol street Arab, she a perfect specimen of the hard-boiled young rich American girl. An amusing couple. Roy Campbell, the poet, came from Martigues to see us the other day. I like him very much and unlike most poets he is rather poetical in himself, not the usual unpoetical being dragging round his gift like a great blood-sucking parasite that eats up all vitality and leaves hardly anything to live with. Richard Aldington is in the neighborhood—also Mrs. Edith Wharton!—but I haven't had time to see the one or courage to visit the other. Did you read Tom's translation of *Anabase*? Not very good, it seemed to me: pedantic, affected in spots, in spots ugly. And the original doesn't really seem to me so very remarkable. A few good images—but on the whole rather dull. We are reading *Tom Jones* aloud—which is really very good: such sense, such a tapping of all the nails on the head—knock, knock, knock—only spoiled by those occasional facetiousnesses and mock heroics which were thought necessary and (I suppose) funny in those days. Otherwise have read little but Coulton's *Five Centuries of Religion*, which makes one see that the Middle Ages were quite as awful as any other epoch of history, if not worse!

Farewell, Dearest Mary. Is there any prospect of your coming down into these parts? I hope so.

Yours,
A

TO SEBASTIAN SPROTT[8]

La Gorguette
Sanary (Var)
29 July 1930

Dear Mr. Sprott,
I had heard from Mary that you might be passing this way and am very glad to know that you mean to pay us a visit. We shall be here all August, so far as I know. Our house is between Bandol and Sanary, just off the main road, along which the P.L.M. buses run, next door to the Hotel de la Gorguette, a sign board pointing to which marks the turning from the high road. We are a hundred miles from Nice, so I don't advise you to attempt a visit from there. Toulon is only ten miles away and is connected with Sanary and Bandol by a service of buses leaving directly every half hour. If you come to us directly from Marseille and don't take the P.L.M. bus, you had better go to Bandol station and take the local bus from the Bandol water front to the Gorguette. Sanary station is immensely far from everything. Propose yourself to whatever meal suits you best.

Yours sincerely,
Aldous Huxley

TO G. WILSON KNIGHT

Cap de la Gorguette
Sanary (Var)
3 August 1930

Dear Mr. Wilson Knight,
Thank you so much for your book, which reached me yesterday and of which I have read enough (though little) to be convinced that I shall derive much pleasure and profit from reading it all.

I took your name, I hope, not in vain the other day in a little note, not yet published, on music in the theatre. The occasion was the performance of a rather bad melodramatic play, which had been drawn from a novel of mine. In the last act selections from the slow movement of Beethoven's A minor quartet were played on the stage and produced, I thought, a most astonishing effect—the evocation in the midst of violence and brutality of another world of superhuman serenity. If the

---

[8] W. J. H. Sprott (1897–1971). One of the Cambridge Apostles, he became a professor at the University of Nottingham.

play had been a little better this scene with the music would have been really prodigious. I was irresistibly reminded, when I saw and heard the performance, of what you wrote of Shakespeare's use of music to produce specifically mystical effects—to express the inexpressible. This personal experience made me realize that music provides probably the only way of making anything like a full statement of the mystical case upon the stage. The trouble in most Shakespeare revivals is that the producers choose such wretchedly trivial and vulgar music, expressive of nothing beyond the stupidity of the composer.

Did you see Paul Robeson's Othello? It seemed to me a very extraordinary performance—the really terrifying way in which the black, irrational jungle creature emerged, under Iago's manipulation, from the commanding and heroic general. What an extraordinary resemblance Iago, in his speeches about sex, bears to St. Jerome and the other Christian denouncers of the flesh! He is a real Father of the Church.

Yours very truly,
Aldous Huxley

TO MARY HUTCHINSON

Dalmeney Court, Duke Street
Thursday
ca September 1930

Dearest Mary,
Here I am—I hardly know how, such has been the rush and confusion of suddenly discovering that Matthew went back to school a week before we had supposed and getting him back to England in time. However, it's done and he's back at school. When will there be a chance of seeing you? Can you have lunch with me tomorrow Friday, or,—I was going to suggest dinner but I have this instant been rung up by a hunchbacked French-woman whom we met last year at Barcelona, is here, phoned at random and has caught me—so utterly without reasonable excuses that I have had to invite her to dinner. What a bore! I will ring up in the morning.

Yours,
Aldous H

TO SYBILLE BEDFORD

La Gorguette
Sanary (Var), France
ca September 1930
Saturday

My dear Sibylle,
I forgot to give you this letter. It looks more menacing than interesting I am afraid!

If you want to read something about Greek philosophy which you mentioned the other day as being one of your schemes—you had better begin with the following books in my library: Burnet's *Early Greek Philosophers*—the best and most readable book on the people before Plato: then the two volumes on Greek religion and Greek ethical thought, which contain well-arranged selections: then a few dialogues of Plato, beginning with the *Symposium*, which is a marvel, *Phaedrus* and the *Timaeus*—the latter obscure, but very important. You will find the Burnet and the books of selections together, near the window leading onto the terrace—the Plato on the other side of the room on the bottom shelf, where the book case projects. Goodbye, dear Sibylle, I hope we shall see you at Christmas.

Your affectionate,
Aldous

TO MARY HUTCHINSON

The Athenaeum
Pall Mall, S.W.1.
Tuesday
ca late September 1930

I hope the wedding went off well, Dearest Mary, hats and all, and that Rome is being a success. I am doing a rather wild thing tomorrow—starting off with Sullivan to do a tour of the Great Men of Europe (he is interviewing them for *The Observer*). We go to Berlin, see Einstein, Schroedinger, Heisenberg and I don't know who else and then dash to Paris for the Prince de Broglie and Painlevé. In Paris we hope to arrive on Monday night. I do hope you'll still be there. I've asked Barbara to send a note c/o The Westminster Bank, Place Vendôme saying what hotel you'll go to. We went to the most blood curdling movie the day before she left—*Prison Life in America*—it made you shudder with horror.

Lunched with Min-Chin[9] today—who was most agitated because the invitations for Jim's reception hadn't yet appeared. What a bore the good man is!

Do you enjoy yourselves? Send me a p.c. on spec c/o Thos Cook and Son, Berlin.

Love,
A

Mary's brother, James Strachey Barnes, married Buona Guidotti in Lucca on 25 September 1930.

TO DESMOND MACCARTHY

The Athenaeum
Pall Mall, S.W.1
23 September 1930

Dear Desmond,
I have just read your article about me in *Life and Letters*. I thought it a very good article, *true* and nevertheless most generous—and for that very reason (the generosity of the truthfulness) it depressed me so much that I felt, as I read it, that the best thing I could do would be to retire into a monastery! For, God! How depressing it is to have it brought suddenly home to one from without (however well one knew it before) that one is irrevocably rivetted to one's personality and almost as irrevocably to one's way of life—that one can't say anything different from what one does say, however much one tries—and that, however much one wants to get away, there's no escape. (Or perhaps—which only makes it worse—there is an escape and if one had the courage and the energy to attempt it. . . . But then one never does have the courage or the energy.) Well, well. . . .

Are you in London? If so, it would be very pleasant to see you. Could you lunch with me here one day? Say Friday. Or Monday next week?

Yours,
Aldous Huxley

[9] Probably Humphrey Cotton Minchin. Editor, *The Legion Papers.*

TO THE EDITOR, WEEKEND REVIEW
BROWS HIGH AND LOW

4 October 1930

Sir,

[A. P.] Herbert's article ["Foreheads Villainous Low"] in your last issue is full of spirited rejoinders to quite a number of things I didn't say, as well as to several others which I said only incidentally. Thus, I never said that the present age was without culture or culture snobbery; what I said was that a new anti-culture snobbery had arisen in opposition to the old culture snobbery. Again, Mr. Herbert's testimonials to the class culture of *Punch* contributors are wholly irrelevant. I never suggested that they weren't cultured. Indeed, it is only too obvious that they are. Parts of the paper exhale a wonderfully rich aroma of literariness. For example, the all but serious poems which periodically adorn its pages are almost perfect specimens of that sham-good, "period" literature which can be turned out only by the very well read.

As for the adjective "callipygous," I shall continue to use it until I find an elegant and decorous equivalent in Saxon. No writer can employ words which do not exist or have been exiled from literature. For example, I should never say of anyone that he was steatocephalous, because the word "fathead" exists and is universally accepted; but I speak of the wives of certain African chieftains as steatopygous, because, if I wrote the Saxon equivalent (a favourite word, if I remember rightly, of Squire Western's in *Tom Jones*), my contributions to the newspapers would be refused.

I am, Sir,

Your obedient servant,
Aldous Huxley

TO MARY HUTCHINSON

The Athenaeum
Pall Mall, S.W.1
9 October 1930

Dearest Mary,

I got back last night at about 12:30 after an appalling crossing—fore hatch stove in by a wave, boat at half speed, 3 hours and a bit at sea— and have been very busy all day with odd jobs including taking

Matthew to see the doctor. Tomorrow at 10 I go to the North of England till Sunday.

Maria writes to say that she is angry with you—but what about she doesn't explain—and tells me that I must be angry with you too. Which I duly am! In spite of which, however, I'd love to see you when I get back. May I come to dinner with you on Sunday? Perhaps you'd send a note to the club.

The Great were very interesting in their different ways and the Night Life of Berlin was indescribably awful.

When is Jim's reception? In terrible haste.

Yours,
Aldous

TO MARSHALL DISTON[1]

12 October 1930

I have never engaged in practical politics and so am not really qualified to express a political opinion. It is delightfully easy to be reasonable and equitable on paper—too easy by half.

Having just returned from the Durham mining district, I feel more than usually diffident of expressing a political opinion. All I know is that I shall be enthusiastically on the side of anyone who gets us out of the social and industrial mess, of which the Durham coal-field provides such a terrifying example. Whether any party will or can get us out of that mess is another question.

TO MARY HUTCHINSON

In the Train
23 October 1930

I asked Jehanne to post you a copy of *Amour Terre Inconnue,* which I got in Paris yesterday and didn't have time to take to the P.O. I hope, Dearest Mary, it may be amusing. Had the most awful afternoon, being interviewed by Frédéric Lefèvre. "Une heure avec" was in fact almost 4 hours—and 4 hours with the most crassly vulgar, self-satisfied business-man of letters I have ever met. Third degree methods of inter-

---

[1] Marshall Diston. Treasurer of the London Divisional Council of the Independent Labour Party.

viewing—and the man has a mind whose nuances are about as subtle as the black and white squares on a chess-board. However, he has written the most monstrous flatteries about me—so I suppose I ought to be grateful; tho' in fact I feel rather insulted. He even contrived to bully me into consenting to do a dialogue with him for the radio—in French! I was so feeble after the third hour that I couldn't resist and am now wondering how I can get out of it.

Woke up this morning at Avignon—the sky a sharp pale blue with the hills rather white against it, like the hills in Piero della Francesca background: cypress trees, olives—everything as it should be. You ought to come more often. It can really be done quite cheaply if you take return tickets—nearly 50% saving on the PLM—and travel either by day or with a *couchette*.

I enjoyed England very much this time—even though the whizzing hither and thither was perhaps a little excessive. You were so sweet to me, Dearest Mary. I wish I could thank you enough.

I still think with some astonishment of Little Eyolf—what a *very* odd manifestation. I even wrote some verses about the champagne episode in the train yesterday. I am sending them to Barbara—a Cautionary Tale to one entering life.

Goodbye. Be Happy.

Yours,
Aldous

TO SIMON BLUMENFELD[2]

La Gorguette
Sanary (Var)
4 November 1930

Dear Mr Blumenfeld,
Thank you for your letter. I'm very sorry you had to wait for me that day. I suppose the forwarding of my note via Heinemann's was a slow affair. I read both the letter and the story with much interest. Your friend Sam is very right in what he says about the way in which science (or anything else) can become a religion. I was greatly struck recently by a Russian film "Earth," where there are scenes showing the arrival

---

[2] Simon Blumenfeld (1907–2005). Marxist journalist and author of the novel *Jew Boy* (1935), set in East London, originally published in the United States as *The Iron Garden* (1932). For forty years he wrote a column for *The Stage*, and is listed in the *Guiness Book of Records* as "the world's oldest columnist."

of a motor tractor in a hitherto backward agricultural district! The machine is treated exactly as tho' it were a god—the attitude towards it being half reverential, half wildly ecstatic: people begin to dance before it, like David before the Ark, and its entrance into the village is like a Spanish Easter Day procession, or the end of a revivalist meeting. The thing was particularly striking as, by an unconscious irony, there were scenes of anti-religious propaganda with largeletter captions stating: There is no God. Alas, there is always a tractor or something else to take his place.

The story seems to me good of its kind—but I can quite see why it was rejected by the editors: because they and their readers don't like that kind of story. For it is exceedingly "hard-boiled," as the Americans say. The scene in the hospital with the nurses and the dying man in the background is an obviously true scene: but people don't like truths of that kind. Perhaps they are right, perhaps it is desirable that such things should *not* be true. Anyhow, wishes, being father to thoughts, they believe them untrue: or, if they can't do that, ignore them. They can be made not to ignore them by great literary art, which can "put things across." (That is where the novel comes in—the good novel—in spite of your contempt for it.) Your writing is competent, businesslike and refreshingly without pretentiousness or humbug; but it hasn't got that persuasive, penetrative quality which belongs to consummate literary art. Hence, people who don't like your "hard-boiled" subject matter will be able to resist you—because they won't be snake-charmed into acceptance by your methods of putting things across. Which is unfortunate and depressing—but I think true. I'm afraid you will collect a good number of editor's rejection slips before you've done—in spite of the fact that your stories are intrinsically worth more than a great deal of the stuff currently accepted and printed.

I don't expect to be in England for 3 or 4 months. When I am, I will ask you to renew your very kind invitation to explore the Law and the Prophets (profits also?).

Yours sincerely,
Aldous Huxley

P.S. Am returning the MSS separately in a day or two.

TO G. WILSON KNIGHT

La Gorguette
Sanary
29 November 1930

Dear Mr. Wilson Knight,
Please forgive me for having been so long in writing to you about your book and the *Hibbert* article. I have had a great deal to do of late and it is only within the last few days that I had leisure to settle down to serious reading. I think the book extremely good and that you have really got to the heart of the Shakespearean matter. Things like that judgment of Lee's which you quote are too common. It is hard even to imagine the mentality of a critic and biographer who supposes that a man must be happy because he has achieved success and money—as if those things weren't, for sensitive minds, among the most pregnant causes of the most subtle and irremediable (because externalities without justification) hopeless despair. Those extremes of disgust where sexual matters are concerned were due, I am sure, in part, to a purely physiological idiosyncrasy—(these things undoubtedly play an enormous part in the spiritual development of every man: it is unfortunate that a certain Manichean tradition makes the statement of the fact seem a disparagement and a cynical triviality). "The expense of spirit in a waste of shame" feeling is an intensification of the ordinary "*post coitum triste*" sentiment; and evidently belonged to that unhappily fated class of men in whom a very violent and brief sexual act is followed by an equally violent but much longer reaction. He therefore felt more intensely what everyone has felt at some time or another—even those whose physiology is least subject to violent rhythmical oscillation—that love can never have a satisfying fulfillment on earth and that the only consummation not doomed to end in a waste of shame is the consummation of death. It was physiologically impossible for Shakespeare to think about sexual matters (and therefore, the universe at large) as Blake thought. He *couldn't* accept "Hell" as Blake did. The hell of bodily energy remained hellish for him and his heaven was pure spirituality abstract. There is no way of reconciling these discordant values. Each set remains absolute for minds (and bodies) of a specific type. And that, so far as I can see, is that!

My little article—it is very brief—in which I mention your work will be out in book form next spring: possibly in serial before, but I don't yet know. I'll send you the book when it appears.

Yours,
Aldous Huxley

TO DOUGLAS GOLDRING

La Gorguette
Sanary, Var
18 December 1930

Dear Goldring,

Thank you for your letter. I didn't read *The Fortune* when it came out—but if you send it, will gladly do so now. It sounds a most interesting document; those seamy sides of the war—neither glorious, nor appalling, but painfully revolting, like the Tribunals, or ignobly comic, like the Government Offices filled with Indispensables—have not received the attention they deserve. Your book should be a light on a dark place. If you think it's of use, I'll write something when I've read the book. But I think it mightn't be a bad plan if you yourself did an introduction—"Thirteen years after": your views on the book considered as history and as literature. It would be interesting and you could say a lot in a few pages.

I am sorry you should be feeling dry and barren. It is the most horrible sensation, as I know by occasional experiences—which happily have never been of long duration!

I expect to be here till mid-January: so if you send the book here; within the next 2 or 3 weeks it will be all right.

Yours,
Aldous Huxley

TO LADY OTTOLINE MORRELL

La Gorguette
Sanary (Var)
18 December 1930

Dearest Ottoline,

I was glad to get your letter the other day and to hear your news. This is to wish you in return a very merry Christmas from us both. Under separate cover goes a little thing we found in Toulon the other say—an ornament for a soldier's (or sailor's) shako of, I suppose, Napoleonic date. It amused us and I hope you'll find it pretty. Anyhow, it goes with all our love.

No news here—except that we have made acquaintance with Edith Wharton, rather a formidable lady who lives in a mist of footmen, bibelots, bad good-taste and rich food in a castle overlooking Hyères.

The Connollys go on being bored in the midst of their animals. The only addition to our society is an Anglo-Indian couple—major and wife—superficially the typical Kipling soldier and soldierness, but beneath the surface a very curious and amusing pair. I have been invited to become a member of the *Académie du Var*—which I think is rather distinguished! I shall write it in full letters after my name when I am elected.

I have been reading Andler's enormous 6-volume work on Nietzsche recently. Interesting, but too long—shall never get to the end of it. Also the MS of Lawrence's *Apocalypse*, partly very good, partly rather tiresome in an occultist way. Have you read Wilson Knight's book on Shakespeare—*The Wheel of Fire*? It's good, I think—tho' rather *clerical* in manner. I've not read Bertie's book on Happiness: it sounds interesting—tho' I a little resent the too-too sensible passages I have seen quoted in reviews: to the effect that one should always be looking outwards, always be occupied with work or hobbies. Work and hobbies seem to me fundamentally a getting-out of the problem, a shirking. Work's a drug. The great achievement is to create happiness in the absence of the work-day—when one's soberly oneself and conscious of the fact. Whether this can be done is another question! I doubt it. Bertie's work-drug recipe is the only one that works. But I like to think of people attempting happiness in leisured sobriety.

I read *Cakes and Ale* and confess that I took pleasure in the infinitely malicious description of Hughie Walpole. It needed doing, I think: and Maugham was the man to do it—biliously, with hatred and rather vulgarly.

Love from us both.

> *Yours affectionately,*
> *Aldous*

TO SYDNEY SCHIFF

> Cap de la Gorguette
> Sanary
> 24 December 1930

My dear Sydney,
I was very much pleased to have your friendly letter and to know that *Vulgarity in Literature* had given you pleasure. I have a volume of essays

on various subjects—literary and otherwise—coming out next spring, some of which I think you will like.

I have looked up your question about *Paradise Regained* in Denis Saurat's *La Pensée de Milton*—an excellent book, by the way, particularly in its revised English form (published last year, I think: I have only the French edition here of 1920,): he mentions no French translation, but calls the poem *Le Paradis Reconquis*, which would be the literal translation of *Regained*. I think your idea of *Time Regained* as a title is excellent. I remember, when reviewing the first volume of Moncrieff's translation years ago, protesting against his preposterous title as simply silly. Should you wish to find out more about Milton in French I'm sure Saurat, who is professor at King's College, University of London, would tell you.

How much longer are you proposing to stay in your Chalet? I hope you'll come down some time. We shall probably be going to London about mid-January. Will you be there then?

The play has had no success with producers so far, going to its last act—which I have now completely re-written and greatly improved, I think. I hope now for the best and shall do some active campaigning when I get to London.

We are at last installed in our little house, which only lacks the painting to be quite finished—we are leaving that to the spring. The place is lovely: I hope you'll come and pay us a visit some time. Maria sends her love to you both, as do I, along with all seasonable wishes.

Yours,
Aldous H.

TO SYDNEY SCHIFF

La Gorguette
Sanary (Var)
5 January 1931

My dear Sydney,
I reply at once to your letter with its Proustian enigma. One must be a bit of an Oedipus to solve it and I'm not at all sure of having got the answer right; but here is my attempt for what it is worth. (It leaves out of account the rudimentariness of the whale's body, which seems to me profoundly mysterious; why this very highly organized mammal should be classed along with protozoa living in colonies, I cannot imagine. But either Proust had reasons of his own or else there has been a

misreading of his manuscript.) My feeling is that the sense requires the stressing in the translation of the two antithetical phrases "*vie animale et physique*" and "*dans l'organisation spirituelle.*" Human life is not so much a miraculous perfectioning of animal and physical life as an imperfection in the organization of spiritual life—an imperfection as yet as rudimentary as the communal existence of protozoa in colonies (there is, I believe, a word "polypary" meaning a place where polyps live, on the analogy of "aviary"; but I don't think it's used in English, as *polypier* seems to be used in French; and I believe "colony," which is the current scientific term in English, would render Proust's meaning more comprehensibly) or the body of the whale—an imperfection of such a kind that the body imprisons the spirit in a fortress. This, I believe, is the sense of the passage, which is highly elliptic in the original; such phrases as "an imperfection as rudimentary as the communal life of protozoa" are the telescoping of much longer sentences. For if you think of it strictly grammatically a "rudimentary imperfection" is something which is only just not a perfection. Proust's telescope language pulls out into: "but rather an imperfection in the organization of spiritual life, *a mode of being* as rudimentary as the communal existence etc."

In haste to catch the post and with our love and New Year greetings to you both.

Yours,
Aldous H.

TO MARY HUTCHINSON

Dalmeny Court
Duke Street, Piccadilly, S.W.1
20 March 1931

Dearest Mary,
I got here yesterday and have been up to the ears in rehearsal [*The World of Light*], and am already nearly mad with the infection of Lion's fantastic nervosity. However, he has collected one or two quite good players—an excellent woman, Fabia Drake, and a good man, Aubrey Mather, with (mostly) quite respectable support. I hope the performance may be tolerable in the end—tho' time is brief: it opens on Monday week (with only matinees for a month, then transference to the regular evening bill).

Ring me up in the morning—my phone has been behaving rather oddly and making it difficult for *me* to get on, tho' I remain fairly get-on-able—and let's see if we can arrange something. There is always a box at Lion's present play available (I must in decency go to see it). Would the family feel inclined to dine with me tomorrow and occupy the same in force? The play is said to be funny—but I can't guarantee its funniness.

Maria is in Paris and comes over next week. Ring me up before 12:00, when I must be at the theatre.

Love,
Aldous

TO EDITOR, THE TIMES

31 March 1931

"Decent," in the language of schoolboys, is a valuable portmanteau word. Uprightness and generosity, kindness of heart, justice, thoughtfulness—all these virtues are packed by implication into its two syllables. And along with them go so much modesty, so much unpretentiousness and unportentousness, that the beholder can love without ever being abashed. It is of the essence of "decency" that it does not impose itself, never makes you feel small. Bennett[3] was consummately "decent." I know by personal experience how kind he could be to the literary beginner; how enduring and persevering was this kindness; how unpatronizing his encouragement; how level, as from one craftsman to another, his always sound and patient, painstaking criticism. He was a man on whose friendship you could confidently bank, certain that he would never let you down. His "decency" was solid and durable, not a mere plating of casual amiability. Time and friction simply served to expose other layers of the same sterling material.

A good heart is what we most value in a friend; but a good head is hardly less important. Bennett's was the head of a fine artist, a first-rate critic of books and men. A talk with him was always something to be looked forward to. In his own way he was an admirable talker—admirable in spite of his stammer, to some extent even because of it. For his stammer had imposed upon him a peculiar laconism, entirely his own. He was forced by it to express himself in the fewest possible

[3] Arnold Bennett died 26 March 1931.

words and with the greatest possible directness. Into the midst of other people's loose and rambling conversations he would throw from time to time some concentrated opinion or idea, some piece of compressed information—a bright, hard little pebble of the most admirable and apposite good sense. The effect was always electrifying. His stammer gave to all he said a peculiar quality, at once epigramatic and oracular. He seemed always to be saying the last word on any subject, and saying it in its most succinctly witty form. A statement which on anyone else's lips would have been merely the truth became, when spoken with Bennett's peculiar phrasing, a kind of artistic super-truth—final, decisive, and at the same time profoundly comic. When he said, for example, of Mr. So-and-so, "The man's . . . an ass"; or of a certain lady novelist, "The trouble with her is that she . . ." (a long, long pause) "can't write"—why, then it was somehow absolutely certain that the poor lady couldn't write, and the asininity of So-and-so was beyond all doubt. His praise was as final as his blame. "It's . . . a book," he would say; and immediately you had faith you were sure that it was a book. And when, taking his advice, you read the work in question, you invariably found that he was quite right. Bennett's judgment was singularly sound.

Alas, there will be no more talk about music and painting, no more exchange of information about the latest French books, no more of those brief, judicious, richly humorous oracles about art and life. And with the admirable talker, with the fine and conscientious artist, has gone the friend, one of the kindest, one of the most thoroughly "decent" men I have ever known.

Aldous Huxley

TO J. D. CHAMBERS

Cap de la Gorguette
4 April 1931

Dear Mr. Chambers,
Sebastian Sprott forwarded me the copy of the Lawrence letter you so kindly consented to let me have. Thank you so much for it. It is a very touching and beautiful letter. He thought a great deal about those early Eastwood days towards the end of his life—thought of them, for all that he had suffered during them, as of days in a kind of paradise, but a paradise from which circumstances had for ever shut him out: there

was for him no possibility of return to Eastwood or even to England. He felt it as a great sadness and bitterness.

Give my love to Sebastian when you see him and believe me

Yours sincerely,
Aldous Huxley

TO SYBIL COLEFAX

Cap de la Gorguette
Sanary (Var)
8 April 1931

Dear Sibyl,
Please thank Sir Louis for the very kind invitation to stay with him—which, alas, we can't accept as we have people staying with us whom we can't desert. Would it be possible for you to stay a night with us on your way home? Or alternatively could you and Sir Louis come to lunch with us on Friday, when we have the Noailles coming over from Hyères? It's a long way, I know: but it would be very nice if you could.

Poor A.B. It was all, somehow, particularly sad and depressing. The gloom was enhanced in my case by it all being mixed up in and squeezed in between, interminable rehearsals. I'm glad you liked my little thing. The *Times* official obituary was so dull and stuffy and rather horrid, that I thought it would be a good thing to add an appendix.

Yours,
Aldous H.

TO SYDNEY SCHIFF

La Gorguette
Sanary (Var)
7 May 1931

My dear Sydney,
I ought to have answered your letter—nay, your letters—before; but have felt incapable of letter writing for months and have neglected all my correspondence.

I hope you are better now. Shingles sounds most unpleasant. And how is Violet?

We are tolerably flourishing, I'm happy to say—still in confusion with the house, this time because of the painting, which we put off in order to enjoy a month or two of respite, till the spring. Now we're up to the eyes in distemper—and consequent bad temper. I write away at a novel about the Future—Wells's Utopia realized, and the absolute horror of it, a revolt against it. Amusing, but difficult, as I want to make a comprehensible picture of the psychology based on quite different first principles from ours.

The play was interesting to see produced. Lion did it well and the actors were excellent. Critics on the whole very favourable—at least, all those who matter intellectually, though not those who matter box-officially: for the public remains conspicuous by its absence. Do go to see it if you're in London.

How is *Time Regained* going forward?

Give our best love to Violet.

> *Ever yours,*
> *Aldous H.*

TO LADY OTTOLINE MORRELL

> *La Gorguette*
> *Sanary (Var)*
> *7 May 1931*

Dearest Ottoline,

Forgive me for having delayed so long in returning you Cresswell's[4] letter. I read his book, which I enjoyed and liked him personally when I met him down at your house.

I gather Italy has been very dank—Sanary has only been windy. The painters are in the house—so is my old German nurse! Rather disturbing. I am hard at work on my novel of Utopia. Swarms of literary Germans infest the country-side like locusts. Dorothy Bennett threatens to come and stay with us for 3 weeks. Well, well, well. . . .

Much love from us both. Yours in great haste but very affectionately,

> *Aldous*

---

4 Walter D'Arcy Cresswell (1896–1960). New Zealand poet championed by Lady Ottoline.

TO JULIAN HUXLEY

La Gorguette
Sanary (Var)
17 May 1931

My dear Julian,
You will have had my wire to say that we shall be delighted to join you on your Russian trip—only I think we shall go by land, as we are both bad sailors—and should also like to take the opportunity of seeing places in Germany on the way. Will you tell me in good time what has to be done about passports—whether we try to get them done here, or whether it is best to send them registered to England and have them visaed through the S.C.R. How far does our trip take us?

I am very busy here, sweating away at a novel [*Brave New World*], which I'd like to finish before the end of the summer—but don't know whether I shall succeed. In the intervals have been reading your *Africa*—with great pleasure and profit. Gerald Heard has been staying at Bandol—departed today. We had many good talks about all the odd subjects which he likes.

I'm glad you enjoyed the play [*World of Light*]. The end, of course, is unsatisfactory. I tried very hard to make a better conclusion—rewrote the last act four times—but couldn't manage on within the necessary compass, so had to leave it at an inconclusion, hanging. The critics have been on the whole very nice about it; but the public has remained conspicuous by its absence. I never knew it was possible for a play to make so little money. From the English performances I shant even have fully earned my hundred pounds advance. I hope they'll succeed in selling it to America and Europe. I think it might do better there. Various people I have shown it to in France are very enthusiastic, and I have hopes of getting it done sooner or later here. Moral for would-be successful playwrights: Stick to adultery.

We vaguely think of going to America in the autumn; but nothing is definite yet. Anyhow, I'd like to go there again.

All our loves to you both. I'm glad to hear that Francis is beginning to improve.

Yours,
ALH

TO MARY HUTCHINSON

Cap de la Gorguette
Sanary (Var)
21 June 1931

Dearest Mary,
I am sending separately, with all my love, a copy of my *Cicadas*. I hope you may find some things in it to please you.

We have been living a poisoned existence for the last three weeks—the virus being Dorothy [Bennett]. Thank heaven, she leaves tomorrow for the hotel at Bandol, where unhappily she means to stay at least a month. What a disastrous woman! One has no idea *how* disastrous till she is actually in the house. How poor A.B. put up with her as long as he did I can't imagine. For it's not *merely* a question of cackling and being hysterical and unpunctual: she is also bottomlessly egoistic, insensitive—a thoroughly bad character in a jellied, passive way. *Ma basta.* One mustn't allow her to become an obsession. Poor M has been reduced once or twice to the verge of collapse. Luckily I have my work to retire to: she is less well protected.

How sad that you didn't come! We went for a brief tour of Provence with Eddy [Sackville-West] and Naomi Royde Smith[5] (a comic couple, but very nice and got on well): Stes Maries, Nîmes, Uzès, Pont du Gard, Les Baux, Arles, Aix—Eddy unable, in each tour, to resist buying some bangle or coloured shirt and always passionately keen on the bloodiest bull fights. (All the Roman amphitheatres were full of them.)

Since when I have been working fiendishly hard—and shall have to go on working fiendishly hard. Which I don't much like doing—but I want to get my book about the future finished by the end of the summer. It advances slowly—and the future becomes more and more appalling with every chapter.

I have read nothing much of late. Drieu's new novel—about a drug addict: infinitely depressing and chiefly of interest in the light it throws personally on Drieu. I gather his play has not been much of a financial success. Which is serious for him. Maine de Biran's *Journal Intime* (Vol. II) has given me a lot of pleasure: I find the man very sympathetic and close to me. Gosse's *Life and Letters* is curious and leaves one with a rather nasty feeling about Gosse. He is like one of those birds which sit picking the teeth of crocodiles—living in a busily obsequious symbiosis with literature.

[5] Naomi Royde Smith (188?–1964). Literary editor of the *Westminster Gazette*.

Do write and tell us all your news and the news of London. There's not much here—except that Frieda has gone to America with an Italian *capitano di Bersaglieri*.[6] (Did you read Murry's revolting book on Lawrence, by the way? Vindictive hagiography—a new genre in literature.) It's a slight relief to have these thousands of miles of water and desert between Frieda and oneself—Jack will think so too, I'm sure. What puzzles me is the Capitano. What a hero!

Farewell, Dearest Mary. Why do you insist on living at such a distance—so moistly and boreally?

> *All love.*
> *Yours,*
> *A*

TO FRED URQUHART[7]

> *La Gorguette*
> *Sanary (Var), France*
> *18 August 1931*

Dear Mr. Urquhart,

If you have more than one copy of the MS of your book, you might send it me here. If you have only one, I wouldn't take the risk—however small—of its loss in the post, but would wait till the end of September, when I hope to be in London.

The subject of your novel being what it is, I am afraid, there is no prospect of its being published in England. There are several publishers in Paris who do English books. I don't remember their names at the moment, but could find out without much difficulty.

Since the publication of Proust's *Sodome et Gomorrhe* and André Gide's *Si le grain ne meurt*, the subject of homosexuality has become a more or less completely admitted literary theme in France.

> *Yours very truly,*
> *Aldous Huxley*

---

[6] Angelo Ravagli (1891–1975).
[7] Frederick Burrows Urquhart (1912–1995). Scottish writer.

TO SIR

The Athenaeum,
Pall Mall, S.W.1
25 September 1931

Dear Sir,
I quite agree with those who say that "what is needed in parliament to-day is experience and courage." Only it must be the right sort of experience undergone at the right period of life. The elderly are heavily handicapped in as much as their experience of politics and industry mostly dates from the time when the now decrepit machine was still working, more or less efficiently. Thirty or forty years ago, when our present leaders were at the plastic time of life, certain policies gave to England (or at any rate to one class of Englishmen) immense prosperity. What more natural than that those who were young then should imagine that similar causes must now produce similar results? What, I repeat, more natural—and what more disastrous? For what was good enough for our fathers is quite obviously not good enough for us. Circumstances have changed; the political and industrial system needs to be reconstructed from its foundations. The elderly cannot reasonably be expected to undertake such a job. When it comes to contemporary circumstances, the old are in a very real sense less experienced than the young.

Yours truly,
Aldous Huxley

TO VICTORIA OCAMPO

La Gorguette
Sanary (Var)
10 November 1931

Dear Madame Ocampo,
Thank you for your letter. I should expect to be in the Argentine in January or February next year—unless something happens—between now and then to change our plans. I will write to you at Buenos Ayres nearer the time.

It is very kind of you to offer to introduce us to the country. I am busy at the moment with Lawrence's letters—selecting them for publication. There are wonderful letters among them. His was a most tragic, unhappy existence. Murry, in his *Son of Man*, gives a partial explanation of the unhappiness—but gives it in such horrible terms and is himself such an odious man (treated Lawrence so treacherously during his lifetime and after his death) that one hates to believe even the truth when he offers it.

About people in England—I know very few of the younger ones. Richard Hughes is interesting—but I fancy he is in Morocco. Then there is a curious new man, unknown to me personally, called John Collier, who wrote a book called *His Monkey Wife*, which I think much better because fuller of life, less "classical," than Garnett's *Lady into Fox*.

He has obviously got something in him. You could write to him care of his publisher, Peter Davies. Then there are various Cambridge young men, critics, with Empson at their head—good, but a bit dryly intelligent: *secheresse*. Of the older ones, there are always E. M. Forster, T. S. Eliot, Virginia Woolf: and if you want something good about painting, there's Roger Fry.

I shall probably be seeing some or all of these people when I am in London—which I hope to be from about the 23rd of this month to about the 5th of October—and would prepare the way for you, if you liked.

My London address is—

The Athenaeum Club
Pall Mall, S.W.1

Yours sincerely,
Aldous Huxley

TO FRED URQUHART

The Athenaeum
Pall Mall, S.W.1
10 November 1931

Dear Mr. Urquhart,
I am returning your MS. The book is, of course, unpublishable in this country, of that there is no doubt. I think, however, that, quite apart from its technical unprintableness, you would be well advised not to publish it as it now stands—even if you could find a printer abroad or, privately, here. For it seems to me, frankly, very immature—which is quite natural considering the age at which you wrote it. Literature is an art that has almost no infant prodigies.

You would do better, I believe, to leave the book for a year or two, forget it, then take it out, read it with new eyes and re-write it. For you would certainly feel the need for re-writing. You would see e.g. that Ganymede's language was not right: a lot might be got out of his illiteracy—but it hasn't been got so far. Then, I think you'd find Satan a superfluous stage property; and that the religious discussions were a bit crude; and that the descriptions of theatrical society were not life-like. Nor have you made the Indians preposterous in their splendour and depravity, as they always are in reality. (Patiala's special train full of catamites and concubines is an uproarious joke; so are the Nizams' barracks full of women, etc. etc.) There are other points as well—points which I am sure you will see for yourself in a year or two's time.

Meanwhile I am sure your best plan is to put the book away. All this is not, I fear, very immediately helpful. But I think it may be helpful in the long run.

Yours sincerely,
Aldous Huxley

TO FLORA STROUSSE

The Athenaeum
Pall Mall, S. W. 1
4 December 1931

Dear Starky,
This is to wish you seasonable wishes. May you and I and all of us get through 1932 without too much difficulty—the most optimistic wish that circumstances permit. Meanwhile let's feel as cheerfully bawdy as you were in your last letter as often as we can. It's the only sane attitude in this astounding lunatic asylum of a world. (Queer the way that society is perfectly sane and rational in its details—a hospital or a factory is a model of common-sense—but as a whole, as the thing that engages in wars, imposes tariffs, has relations with other societies, absolutely insane.) Meanwhile London moulders on pleasantly enough. There are plenty of people to exchange literary and scientific conversations with: the libraries are excellent; the clubs very comfortable. But the sun never shines. Which is why I shall get back to the Mediterranean as soon as my child's holidays are over, however few the francs a pound will buy.

Yours,
ALH

TO MRS. CECIL CHESTERTON[8]

La Gorguette
Sanary
31 January 1932

Dear Mrs. Chesterton,
Yes, I will join the council of the Community Theatre with pleasure. Unfortunately I shan't be able to do much active cooperation at present, owing to absence from England. I hope to be over in May, when I will come and see you if I may.

I presume your chief difficulty will be financial—and the next difficulty, literary. For the chronic problems of the theatre seem to be the problems (a) of finding money (b) of finding plays! I do hope you will solve them: where it seems to me that such a theatre as yours is badly needed in England. Our country has the defects of its qualities. English humor and tolerance so easily degenerate into mere indifference and incapacity to take any idea seriously. Your theatre might do much to wake people up to the reality and importance of ideas.

Yours sincerely,
Aldous Huxley

TO MARY HUTCHINSON

The secret, sweet Mary, was a little epigram I made *à propos* of those Help Yourself Honey Girls who figured in our prize winning magazine at Sadler's Wells. Here it is:—

Deep, deep this Flower; and dewily her lip
Invites the Bee with Perfume to explore
A rosy scabbard, where the tongue may sip
The essential Honey of her secret store.

I hope you still enjoy your botanizing.

A bientôt,
A

---

[8] Ada Chesterton (1888–1937). Journalist and founder of the Cecil Houses for homeless women in London. Huxley was a supporter.

TO MARY HUTCHINSON

Cap de la Gorguette
Sanary (Var)
3 February 1932

Dearest Mary,

Thank you for the cutting of Desmond's article about poor Lytton.[9] I saw also Peter Lucas's—all right, but nothing very vivid or clear. But then these commemorative things are somehow extraordinarily difficult to make effective.

Dear Mary, you must be feeling very miserable, and there is no consolation, only sympathy for what it's worth—and that you know you have from us both. How sad, sad, sad it all is; and with such a peculiar pointlessness and meaninglessness, when looked at from without. The only thing is that, I believe, that, experienced from within, even pain and dissolution may seem in some way acceptable.

Here we have had a miracle of fine weather—sunshine without wind, an almost unprecedented phenomenon on this coast. I work very hard at my anthology—do little else. Raymond is staying here, a quiet and pleasant guest. We have seen Mrs. Wharton and the Noailles: nobody else. For the coast is empty. For which one is on the whole thankful.

Our love to you all and to you in particular, Dearest Mary.

Yours,

A

TO LADY OTTOLINE MORRELL

La Gorguette
Sanary (Var)
8 February 1932

Dearest Ottoline,

Please forgive me for not having answered your letter before, I have been so involved in work, that I somehow couldn't sit down to a letter. Poor Juliette was in a state in which she couldn't bear the thought of her old friends knowing anything about the matter.[1] (It was only late this autumn that we were told.) The whole affair is a huge and miserable

---

[9] Lytton Strachey died of cancer in January 1932.
[1] Julian's affair led to his wife's going to stay with friends in Baghdad. A sympathetic Aldous saw her off from the docks at Marseille.

muddle. What will happen I don't know. Anyhow, the immediately important thing is that Juliette should get away from London and try to get calm and well. She is supposed to be going to Baghdad to stay with friends, almost at once. No real decision can be taken till she returns. What a misery!

Poor Lytton—how wretched that was. We saw him just before he got ill, and he seemed so more than usually cheerful and happy and well.

Here all proceeds in the usual way—except that, miracle of miracles, the wind has not blown for a fortnight. The sun shines, the almond blossom is coming out. It's all very lovely. Raymond Mortimer unexpectedly came down with us from Paris, and has been staying—a very pleasant guest.

I am working hard on my anthology-with-comments, which might make rather a nice book, I think. Love from us both.

Your affectionate,
Aldous

TO CLAUDE AVELINE[2]

La Gorguette
Sanary (Var)
17 February 1932

Mon cher Aveline,
De retour d'Angleterre où nous avons passés plus de quatre mois, j'ai trouvé votre livre qui m'aurait attendu depuis—je ne sais quand—Novembre, Décembre? Pardonnez-moi mon silence dû au fait que rien au-dessus d'une letter n'a été re-expédié à mon adresse anglaise—et acceptez mes remerciments tardifs mais non moins sincères du cadeau, ainsi que du plaisir que m'a procuré la lecture du livre.

Il me semble que, des trois récits, le premier est le meilleur—mais tous sont bons. J'aime la manière savamment simple dont vous traitez vos sujets, et j'aime aussi les sujets qui sont des sujets de Barby D'Aurévilly, riches de leur enigme toujours intacte.

J'espère que votre femme a profitée de son séjour en Suisse. Nous avons vu le Dr. Roget l'autre jour et il a tout de suite dit à Maria, "Je crois que vous avez maigrie, Madame"—le croassement ordinaire. Nous en avons beaucoup vu.

---

[2] Claude Aveline (Eugène Avtsine) (1901–1991). Prolific French author.

Merci encore une fois, mon cher Aveline. Faites-nous signe si vous passez de ce côté de la France.

Cordialement vôtre,

Aldous Huxley

[My dear Aveline,

Returning from England, where we spent more than four months, I found your book, which must have been waiting since—I don't know when—November or December? Pardon my silence, due to the fact that nothing other than a letter was sent on to my English address, and accept my late, but nonetheless sincere, thanks for the present and for the pleasure derived from reading your book.

It seems to me that of the three stories, the first is best—but all are good. I like the cleverly simple way you treat your subjects, and I also like those which are the subjects of Barby D'Aurévilly, rich with their enigma still intact.

I hope that your wife profited from her stay in Switzerland. We saw Dr. Roget the other day, and he immediately said to Maria, "I think you look thinner, Madame,"—with the usual croak. We have seen a lot of it.

Thanks again, my dear Aveline. Let us know when you are coming to this part of France.

Cordially yours,]

TO SIBYL COLEFAX

La Gorguette
Sanary (Var)
11 March 1932

Dear Sibyl,

Thank you for your letter, which gave me great pleasure. I am very glad you liked the book. I think it contains certain things that needed saying.

Here life proceeds uneventfully. Edith Wharton and the Charles de Noailles make an occasional diversion, and we have a new neighbour in the shape of Malinowski of Trobriand Island fame, who is staying with an invalid wife and a very valid family of little daughters at Tamaris. Our greatest excitement was going to see an amateur performance of *The World of Light* in French at Marseille. A most astonishing performance—painful at moments though surprisingly good at others.

It would be delightful if you could come to stay: but our possibilities of hospitality are somewhat limited by the arrival of our child with two little friends shortly after Easter; while we expect Maria's sister and then the Mitchisons over the holiday. I shall have to be in London for a bit at the beginning of May—perhaps Maria also—and shall probably accompany Matthew when he returns to school at the end of April. So it really looks, I fear, as though it would be difficult to put you up till later. A visit in late May or June would be most hopeful. Earlier I fear, there is likely to be no cranny in this small house.

Maria sends her love.

Ever yours,
Aldous H.

TO MARY HUTCHINSON

Cap de la Gorguette
Sanary (Var)
19 March 1932

Dearest Mary,

Your letter with the news about Carrington was very distressing. Her death seems to close such a lot of chapters: she was in some queer way, as one now realizes, a symbolical figure, the paradigm of a whole epoch in the life of a whole generation. I hardly ever saw her during these last ten years—but she was none the less representative for me, and her death is none the less the destruction of something important. It was a touchingly heroic act of devotion.

We are just back from a couple of days at Cannes, whither M has gone to get some clothes and I to get a little holiday, as I was tired from having worked in a hurry to get a lecture on my grandfather finished. He was a very remarkable man—I have been greatly impressed by the fact as I re-read his essays. Do you know them? There are some very fine things in them. And he had that heroic, larger-than-life quality which belonged to the really eminent Victorians and which seems to have disappeared so completely in the present age.

Saw H. G. Wells at Cannes, who had not, I gathered, much enjoyed my book. At which, I confess, I was not surprised. The other literary lights of the coast, from Arlen to Maugham, we avoided. Cannes was, of course, extremely lugubrious, dead and empty. *C'est la crise.* M succeeded in buying two charming models from Poiret (who seems to be going bankrupt yet once more) for 700 francs.

I have had to suspend work on my anthology for the Huxley lecture: and now I must write some sort of introduction to Lawrence's letters. Very difficult. It is extremely hard to know how to speak of Lawrence—such a great man and artist, with such strange lacunae and limitations. That miserable little Wells talked of him with such a vulgar disparagement—Wells, if he is a great man, is great in so far as he is a perfect specimen of the Canaille magnified ten thousand times: so bottomlessly vulgar and insensitive, without the smallest power of discrimination either in the moral or the aesthetic sphere: an *âme mal neé* and therefore, in spite of his immense ability, profoundly uninteresting. So I didn't even trouble to argue about Lawrence with him. It would not have been any good. He is as incapable of feeling and appreciating the unique quality of Lawrence as a dog of appreciating music. The difficulty is to render that quality of Lawrence's in a critical introduction, while pointing out the defects of his doctrine.

By the way, has Barbara received a silver framed mirror which we ordered to be sent from an antique shop in Marseille? I ask because we have discovered that the man is a monster of inefficiency and possibly of dishonesty: so if it hasn't arrived we can make even more fuss than we are doing at present about this and other matters.

Much love to you, Dearest Mary, from us both.

Yours,

A

TO EDITH WHARTON

La Gorguette
Sanary (Var)
19 March 1932

Dear Mrs. Wharton,
Your letter gave me a great deal of pleasure. And I am very glad you liked the book [*Brave New World*], in spite of its nightmarishness. I think it contains some things that needed saying—and saying in a more forcible form than that of mere abstract generalization. Fundamentally what is said is the same as what Russell says in the last chapters of *The Scientific Outlook* only, of course, it can be said with more penetrative energy in a novel.

We are just back from a couple of days at Cannes, where we saw H. G. Wells, who had, I am afraid, found the book rather annoying.

I was, as a matter of fact, on the point of writing when your letter came, to apologize for having taken your name in vain—a little article I recently wrote on modern superstition.[3] I cited your admirable Mrs. Manford in *Twilight Sleep* as an example of the contemporary tendency for superstition to be magical rather than religious—to aim at specific acts of power, such as hip-slimming, rather than at a theory of the cosmos. You have got the whole situation beautifully and ruthlessly exemplified in *Twilight Sleep*.

Let me thank you once more for your very generous letter. Your approbation is something I value very highly indeed.

Yours sincerely,
Aldous Huxley

TO LEONARD HUXLEY

La Gorguette
Sanary (Var)
20 April 1932

Dearest Father,
I was glad to get your letter, tho' the news about Julian is not too good. I wrote to him several times in a warning vein—without much effect, to judge by his answers.[4] I gather from his last letter that Juliette has returned and that some sort of definite arrangement is in the process of being made. I feel very sorry for Rosalind[5] in all this: she must have had a very trying emotional and practical burden to support. What a misery it all is!

We have had a very quiet and busy Spring—M at work in the garden and on finishing touches to the house: I on various labours—an anthology with critical and reflective commentaries, which I am compiling; a sort of mixture between A Golden Treasury and a book of essays: then the Huxley Lecture: and then the editing and introducing of the letters of our poor friend D. H. Lawrence, who died two years ago. Occasional glimpses of people in the neighborhood—Edith Wharton at Hyères, who

---

[3] "Hocus Pocus." Huxley's article appeared in the Hearst newspapers, ca 3 May 1932. For Huxley's "putting the case" for the satire on Fordian culture, Wharton wrote, "I was much set up by his recognition of the fact" (*Letters of Edith Wharton*, 547).
[4] Julian Huxley became involved with a young American girl at the time. See Chapter 9 of Juliette Huxley's autobiography, *Leaves of the Tulip Tree*.
[5] Rosalind Bruce Huxley, AH's stepmother.

is a very charming and interesting woman; various French people, such as the Charles de Noailles, who are immensely rich, but rather nice, patrons of the arts, and in whose astonishing modernist house at Hyères one meets most of the French *Jeunes*, alternating with dazzling specimens of the *Faubourg St Germain*—very comic: also a very remarkable woman called Mrs. De Béhague,[6] who lives at Giens.

Matthew is here at the moment with a little friend and the friend's larger brother of 16, who finds himself, I fear, rather isolated, floating between the children and the grown-ups. Matthew is well; but we are still rather distressed by the way in which he so easily gets exhausted and run down, and by the difficulty he seems to have in running up again. The matron at his school tells us that she must always keep him two days longer in bed, when he has a cold, than any other boy—and it's obvious that she's quite right. It looks as tho' he could need very careful and personal health-attention for some time to come. Which makes me rather dubious of the advisability of sending him to a big school like Stowe, for which he is put down—the more so as he simply becomes incapable of taking in anything, the moment he is all run down—is reduced to a kind of mindlessness. It's all a most difficult problem. That he's slowly getting stronger I think is certain. But it *is* slow: and I don't want to compromise the process in any way.

Much love to you all from all of us. We shall be seeing you soon, I expect.

Ever you loving son,
Aldous

TO DOUGLAS GLASS

13 June 1932

Dear Mr. Glass,
Thank you for your letter. It is a thoroughly bad and discreditable business.[7] Imagine giving a man six months for writing down two words that are currently spoken by millions.

---

[6] Martine Marie Pol, Comtesse de Béhague (1870–1939). Wealthy society hostess and art collector. She employed Paul Valéry as her librarian.
[7] In February 1932, Count Potocki of Montalk (1903–1997) was sentenced to six months' imprisonment after his obscenity trial. Huxley, a long-standing opponent of censorship, became an advocate for Potocki. In March 1932 he sent Douglas Glass a contribution to Potocki's defense fund.

As a matter of fact, these monosyllables are not particularly Anglo-Saxon. *Cunt* is, I suppose, from French *con*, from Latin *cunnus*, and whether that is connected with the word meaning *wedge* (shape of the object or *cuniculus*, or borrowed from the rabbit—*coney*) or whether it has nothing to do with either of these words I am not philologist enough to know.

Fuck is, I think, from a very ancient Aryan root which appears in Greek as which in the active beget and intransitively *symfres* to grow and is related to *physis* nature, and is seen in words like physics, metaphysics, physiology. So that, philologically, one might say that Kant's *Critique of Pure Reason* is an essay in "beyond-fucking" or metaphysics. The Latin form of the word is *futuo*: the French, *foutre*. I've no doubt it is to be traced back to Sanskrit.

Well, I am sincerely sorry for your friend and I hope that the monstrousness of his case may be made a reason for reforms of the law.

Yours,
Aldous Huxley

TO LADY OTTOLINE MORRELL

La Gorguette
Sanary (Var)
July 1932

Dearest Ottoline,
I'm so sorry to bother you; but a conundrum has arisen in reference to a point in the Lawrence letters. On Dec 1st 1915 while staying at Garsington Lawrence wrote a kind of essay on the house and garden, beginning: "So vivid a vision everything, so visually poignant, it is like that concentrated moment when a drowning man sees all his past crystallized into one jewel of recollection."

I have the impression that this was not a letter but was written for you while he was in the house. The typescript I have has no name on it, and I can't now remember exactly if it came with your batch of MS. I should be most grateful if you could confirm this—or say no, if it wasn't written for you—on a postcard to A. Frere-Reeves, c/o Heinemann and Co., 99 Great Russell St, W.C. 1.

Just write Yes, if it was—or no, if it wasn't. Frere-Reeves will know what it signifies, as I am writing to him. Please forgive me for bothering you.

I am reading a fascinating book—*Middletown*, which is an exhaustive anthropological study of life in all its aspects in a middle Western town under modern industrial conditions. Do you know it? It came out in 1928—and is very well worth reading, tho' *very* depressing—as any complete and truthful account of most people's existence must be, alas!

Best love from us both, and please forgive my being a nuisance.

Your affectionate,
Aldous

TO TED AND MARION KAUFFER[8]

La Gorguette
Sanary (Var)
26 July 1932

My Dear Ted and Marion,
How sweet of you to have remembered my birthday—(you were the only people in the wide world who did!) I was so pleased and touched by the telegram. We are both looking forward immensely to your arrival and I hope the summer will really behave by the time you come. Up to the present it has given a very half-hearted performance—weather not settled, a good deal of wind. Very tiresome.

I am doing quite a lot of painting now with gouache—a medium I find very agreeable. I hope, Ted, you'll come and make use of my studio, which is now finished. Very nice—over the garage. We will look out for some local nudity to work on.

Best love from us both to both of you.

Yours,
Aldous H.

TO JEHANNE NEVEUX

La Gorguette
Sanary
12 August 1932

Ma chère Jehanne,
Maria m'a dit que vous avez l'intention d'aller en auto jusqu'à Athènes.
Avez-vous pris des informations de l'état des routes dans les Balkans?

---

[8] E. McKnight Kauffer (1890–1954). An important graphic artist best remembered for his posters for London Transport. His wife Marion Dorn (1896–1964) was a fashionable interior designer.

Selon des amies qui ont fait de l'automobilisme en Grèce et ailleurs dans les Balkans, les routes sont complètement mediévales—des lits de torrents où, quelquefois pendant des heures entières, on ne peut pas faire plus que dix kilomètres à l'heure, au grand risque toujours de casser des essieux, défoncer le carter, s'embourber dans la boue etc. D'ailleurs, hors de grands centres les auberges sont affreuses. Julian et Juliette ont trouvés de la vermine de tout espèce en Bulgarie et en Serbie. Votre voyage, je crains, sera une torture—une épreuve d'endurance—plutôt qu'un délassement. Si vous voulez visiter la Grèce, et, en meme temps, fair de l'automobilisme, pourquoi n'allez-vous pas en auto jusqu'à Brindisi tout au fond de l'Italie. (Si vous ne voulez pas aller aussi loin, vous pouvez partir de Venise.) Là vous laissez la voiture, vous prenez ou un bateau ou l'avion jusqu'à Athens—36 heures ou 4 heures, je crois—et d'Athènes vous rayonnez sur les autres points d'intérêt (peu nombreux au fond en Grèce) en auto de louage ou par train, ou même en bateau. Il est facile de tout arranger là bas. Puis vous retournez à Brindisi par avion et vous remontez par autre itinéraire à travers l'Italie. Ainsi vous êtes certains d'avoir des routes praticables, d'hôtels propres, de l'eau plus ou moins potable et une quantité de choses à voir. (Au Balkans vous ne trouverez rien hors d'un peu de couleur locale.) Si vous disposiez de beaucoup de temps, le voyage à travers les Balkans pourrait être curieux. Mais essayer de faire en quelques jours 2000 kilomètres sur des routes du 13ième siecle—ça pourrait être excessivement désagréable. En tout cas, si vous décidez d'aller en auto, prenez des informations exacts sur les pompes à essence, les garages. Sans cela vous pourriez avoir d'embêtements sérieux—surtout en ne parlant pas les langues des pays ou vous traversez.

Love de nous deux,
Aldous

[Dear Jeanne,
Maria tells me that you intend to go by car as far as Athens. Do you have information about the state of the roads in the Balkans? According to friends who have toured by car in Greece and elsewhere in the Balkans, the roads are completely medieval—flooded roadbeds where sometimes for hours at a stretch one can only do 10 km an hour, with real risk of breaking axles, ruining the gear-box, getting stuck in mud, etc. Besides, outside of the big centers, the inns are frightful. Julian and Juliette have found various sorts of vermin in Bulgaria and Serbia. Your trip, I feel, will be torture—a test of endurance—rather than relaxation. If you wish

to visit Greece and at the same time do automobile touring, why not go by car to Brindisi at the bottom of Italy. (If you don't want to go so far, you can leave from Venice.) You leave the car there, you take either a boat or plane to Athens—36 hours or 4 hours, I think, and from Athens you can get to other points of interest, not very many on the whole in Greece) by rental car or train, or even by boat. It's easy to arrange everything over there. Then you return to Brindisi by air and drive up Italy by another itinerary. That way you are certain to have passable roads, clean hotels, more or less potable water and plenty of things to see. (In the Balkans you will find nothing other than a little local colour.) If you had lots of time at your disposal, to see the Balkans could be interesting. But to try to cover 2000 kilometers on 13th-century roads—that would be excessively disagreeable. In any case, if you decide to go by car, make sure to get details about gas stations and garages. Without these, you could run into serious trouble—especially without being able to speak the languages of the countries you cross.]

TO LEON M. LION[9]

La Gorguette
Sanary (Var)
27 August 1932

My dear Leon,
Thank you for your letter. Yes, I am writing a play—but not *Brave New World*, which seems to me more hopelessly difficult owing to the all-but impossibility of giving the *background* its necessary value on the stage (a value which would have to be at least equal to that of the story).

I am writing a politico-economic play more or less about Ivar Kreuger;[1] i.e., a financier with a sincere desire to rationalize the world, but who bites off more than he can chew and is driven into swindling and finally suicide. His daughter falls in love with a young man who has given up his social position to preach communism—and he with her; but he refuses to allow himself to love this incarnation of the luxuries and drives her off with a get-thee-behind-me-Satan gesture, until,

---

[9] Lion was the producer of Huxley's comedy *The World of Light*, staged in London in 1931. He decided not to produce *Now More Than Ever*, the play which Huxley completed in October 1932 and which he discusses above. The play was not produced until 1994 during the first Aldous Huxley Centenary Symposium at Muenster.
[1] Ivar Kreuger, known as the "Swedish Match King," was alleged to have swindled his companies of a fortune before being found dead in a Paris hotel, an apparent suicide.

at the end, the father's sins and suicide make a union possible. Add to this a secretary to the financier—a profound sceptic who riddles both sides with his criticisms and himself enjoys the comfort of a cynical conformity to things as they are. One or two more minor characters, and there you are. I have written an act and a half, and hope to get ahead in the next few weeks. There will be a good deal of talk—but on subjects in which everybody is now interested.

Yours,
Aldous Huxley

TO SEBASTIAN SPROTT

The Athenaeum
Pall Mall, S.W.1
ca September 1932

Dear Sprott,
I have to be in your neighborhood early in October to see D. H. Lawrence's sister, who lives near Nottingham. Will you be in Nottingham then? If so it would be very pleasant to see you.

Yours,
Aldous Huxley

TO CATHERINE CARSWELL

La Gorguette
Sanary (Var)
13 September 1932

Dear Mrs. Carswell,
Thank you for your letter. [Henri] Fluchère is, I think, a quite reliable man: he is a professor at a lycée in Marseille—has been at Cambridge and knows English well, and its literature. A pleasant and quite intelligent chap. He runs a dramatic society in Marseille, and they performed my play, *The World of Light*, in French, before the rank and fashion of the town—a most remarkable business!

Unfortunately I ordered your book rather late in the day and my bookseller, could not provide a copy. I am waiting till I can borrow it off someone, when I get back to London. I wish I'd read it. I see Murry is to bring out another book on Lawrence. Why can't he leave Lawrence's memory alone? Yet another trail of slime.

I have had no news of Frieda recently. I hope the business with George is settling itself amicably and not too expensively. She was cheerfully talking, last time I saw her, of spending £2000 on legal proceedings.

An astonishing phenomenon here has been the vast success of "L'Amant de Lady Chatterley," of which more than 100,000 copies have been sold up to date. That and the "Grammaire de l'Académie Française" have been the two great successes of the year. The French are a curious people!

I hope you are all well. Please remember me to your husband.

Yours very sincerely,
Aldous Huxley

TO MARY HUTCHINSON

3 Rue du Bac
Suresnes (Seine)
17 September 1932

We loved our postcards from Holland, Dearest Mary. It must have been fun: it is really a very astonishing country, I think. We have had a rather crowded summer—always people in the house: which is, *au fond*, a mistake, even if they're nice. At last, however, we're alone—the final guest (a young man, a friend of Raymond's, of surpassing handsomeness, but great dullness, who came to tutor Matthew), having gone today. Thank heaven! We expect, after Matthew's departure next week, to pop across into Italy for a few days for a change of scene.

The Kauffs are in the neighborhood—very happy, I think, and very nice—also relieved to be alone, having had swarms of people in the house, including Mr. and Mrs. Beddington—the double Beddingtons, as we christened them—with whom they had a slight quarrel. We all went over the other day to see the Noailles at Hyères, where they were a great success, the more so as Marion's old Mr. Osborne is Charles de Noailles' oldest friend. We had some rather high-class meetings with Mme. de Béhague and Paul Valéry, whom I like very much—and some rather low-class meetings with the Kislings, whom I like less—he being a rather unpleasant and excessively clever Polish Jew, and she—well, you know her. ... One has got to dig her in the ribs and ask her to sleep with one: it is the only form of conversation she understands (except domestic chat about her children): and if you're not interested either in the children or her *appas*—and her physique fills me with dismay—why, then there's nothing to say.

I am trying to write a play at the moment, and in the intervals do a bit of painting, which I enjoy immensely. It's so nice to practice an art in which all the problems are internal to the art and where one doesn't have to bother about what goes on in the world at large. The painter is in the blissful position of the Jolly Miller upon the River Dee—"I care for nobody, no, not I, and nobody cares for me." How well I understand people who stand from morning till night in front of their easels, daubing away without respite! But the more I paint, the more I resent the laziness of modern painters. Why don't they take the trouble to do those large elaborate compositions that the old men did? It really is an outrage, when one comes to think of it, that a man with the gifts of Derain,[2] for example, should spend all his time turning out those small and absurdly simple compositions. Even if they can't sell them, I do think they ought to turn out an occasional essay in complication comparable to a big El Greco composition, or a Rubens, or a Botticelli. The moderns seem to me to be inexcusably cheating and shirking difficulties: one ought to be severer with them, more insistent in one's demands.

How are you all? Do let me know. We loved seeing Barbara. Love to you all.

Yours,
A

[Probably Col. and Mrs. Claude Beddington. She wrote a memoir, *All That I Have Met* (1929).]

TO J. GLYN ROBERTS[3]

La Gorguette
Sanary (Var)
2 October 1932

Thanks for your letter of the 17th. All good wishes for your project of a weekly paper. The interview will have to wait till I am in England—probably after the New Year.

Yours,
Aldous Huxley

---

[2] André Derain (1880–1954). French painter. One of the original members of the Fauve movement.
[3] Welsh writer (1904–1962).

TO LADY OTTOLINE MORRELL

La Gorguette
Sanary (Var)
13 October 1932

Dearest Ottoline,

I was very glad to get your letter—tho' sorry to hear that the German cure had not been much good. Still, I hope you're bearing up against London all right now. Even here one has had to do a bit of bearing up for the last month. Such rain, such storms and tempests. We went for 5 days to Italy at the end of September—and it was one continuous cloudburst, rising at moments to Niagara-esque dimensions. Driving back at night from Florence to Forte we ran into the most frightful water spout I've ever seen in my life and were held up 2½ hours on a road that had become a raging torrent. We saw Frieda in Florence—looking tired, but reprieved from her operation. She must be back in London now, carrying on this crazy lawsuit against George Lawrence.

I hear the letters are doing well; for which I'm glad: for Frieda will need all the money she can get, particularly if she's going in for luxuries like litigation. She cheerfully contemplates spending £ on her case! I think they make a very remarkable book, don't you—the letters, I mean.

I have just finished a play [*Now More Than Ever*], which Maria is indefatigably typing out preparatory to sending it to London. I hope it will attract a few more people than the last one, which made less money than any play since the Agamemnon of Aeschylus. I think it's quite interesting. In the intervals I do a lot of painting, which I greatly enjoy—tho' it's rather exhausting I find. All the same, what a pleasure! I think the painters have more fun than anyone.

Matthew seems to be happy at his new school—Dartington.[4] We have news of him from Gerald Heard, who goes down there periodically to lecture.

His—Matthew's prowess as a yo-yoist and his "good mixer's" manner have won him apparently a good position in the school! *Tant Mieux.* Much love from us both.

Your affectionate,
Aldous

---

[4] A progressive school in Devon, founded by Leonard and Dorothy Elmhirst.

TO SYDNEY SCHIFF

La Gorguette
Sanary (Var)
13 October 1932

My dear Sydney,

I was very glad to have your letter and to know that you liked my introduction to the Lawrence *Letters*. I think it was time that somebody insisted on Lawrence's predestination to be an artist, and an artist of one special kind. The letters themselves are extraordinary, I think; particularly the earlier ones.

We have had a quiet summer here—enlivened by occasional visitors and, for the last two months, by the presence in the neighbourhood of Ted McKnight Kauffer and Marion Dorn, of whom we are both very fond. They have just gone and the landscape is deserted for the moment: but soon the winter migrants will begin to appear—Edith Wharton, and the Charles de Noailles, and the Aurics, and Mme de Béhague. One day we hope to catch a glimpse of Violet and you flitting past.

I have just finished a play, which I think rather interesting. I hope the opinion may be shared by more people than the handful who went to look at my last play. Have you been at work on anything? If not, why not? I am in process of reading what seems, so far as I have got, a very remarkable book—*The Sleepwalkers* by Hermann Broch, just published by Martin Secker. It has all the qualities one doesn't expect of German novels—subtlety, restraint, composition. If it goes on as well as it begins, it's a first-rate book. Have you read—talking of good books—*Saint-Saturnin* by Jean Schlumberger? One of the most solid and honest French novels of recent years. Very remarkable, I thought.

We expect to be in England after the New Year and look forward to seeing you then, if you are in London.

Maria joins me in sending all manner of good wishes to Violet and yourself.

Yours,
Aldous H.

TO MARY HUTCHINSON

Cap de la Gorguette
Sanary (Var)
14 October 1932

Dearest Mary,

The news of Jack's mother's death was very distressing. One must be thankful for her sake that the end came so quickly. But it must have been very painful and sad for all of you. The terrible thing about dying is that it is the most purely physiological act of a life-time—the act during which the body takes control more completely than at any other time—until there is nothing left but body. Because of this the ritual of the Catholic church is good; for it is dramatically contrived to make the onlookers—and also, so long as any consciousness persists, the dying person—feel that this appalling physiological act has a spiritual significance; that it exists on some other plane than that of the body. That it probably does not exist on any other plane does not matter: the behaving as though it did so exist is pragmatically good. The physiological act is transformed into a part of the rather splendid ritual—and this helps both the dying and those who stand by. I was greatly impressed by this at the death of M's grandfather, who died Catholicly; the scene was lifted to a higher plane of significance. Lawrence's death seemed much more terrible, because it was unbelievably the physiological act. I believe people have made a mistake in abolishing ritual so completely from their lives. Ritual can and, I am sure, ought to be preserved for the enrichment and embellishment of existence, quite regardless of beliefs—just as we preserve good manners, or as we submit ourselves to the conventions of the dance. It is extremely unfortunate that a monopoly of the finest ritual should be held by the Catholics and associated with impossible beliefs—

Ted and Marion have gone—which is sad for us: for their presence in the neighborhood was most stimulating and delightful. The winter migrants have not yet arrived: so the coast is very empty—and incredibly lovely in the crystallizing autumn weather which has now set in after the weeks of rain and storm which made September so unpleasant.

I have just finished a play [*Now More Than Ever*], which M is now typing so that copies may be sent to England. It is on the theme of Kreuger or Hatry—a financier who is ambitious to rationalize industry and is led by his excellent intention into gigantic fraud. I read it to Ted and Marion, and I think they liked it. Let's hope it may make a bit of money.

About Victor R.[5]—I thought him very nice when he was down here. He gets a bit aggressive sometimes through self-consciousness; but one feels that that's somehow just a mistake. What is very sympathetic about him is that he is obviously terrifically keen on his work—which he apparently is very good at, so Gerald Heard, who was here when he turned up, assured me, having heard so from the man under whom he works at Cambridge. All this is greatly in his favour. The only disadvantage I see, from B's point of view, is the family—which I don't know, but which I imagine must be a formidably powerful, closely-knit entity, rather uncomfortable to be a foreign body in. But this is a mere theory: in practice the family may be something quite different. Let's hope so.

I have just been re-reading *War and Peace* and have come to the conclusion that Diana Guinness is exactly like Hélène. Look at Tolstoy's descriptions: they seem to fit like a glove. Or am I mistaken?

I had a description from Schiff of Tom Eliot's farewell party: the guests seem to have consisted exclusively of the *wives* of the rather eminent—such as Mrs. Harold Monro and Mrs. James Stephens. It sounded unspeakably gloomy.

Much love.

Yours,

A

TO SYDNEY SCHIFF

La Gorguette
Sanary (Var)
3 November 1932

I am sending under separate cover a copy of my play. I hope you may find things it to please you: anyhow I'll be most grateful to have your criticisms on it.

The end of *The Sleepwalkers* is better than the beginning—at any rate as an intellectual work, for as a novel I don't quite know where it is. The author is obviously a very intelligent man. I have just read and have been rather struck by a book—you doubtless know it, for it appeared in 29— called *Living*, by Henry Green. A really very good rendering of that, for

---

[5] Nathaniel Meyer Victor Rothschild, 3rd Baron Rothschild (1910–1990). Married Mary's daughter Barbara in 1933. A friend of Guy Burgess and Anthony Blunt, he was rumored to have been the "Fifth Man." In 1986 he wrote a letter to the press stating, "I am not now and never have been a Soviet agent."

us bourgeois, most mysterious phenomenon—the mind of the factory worker.

I haven't read *Snooty Baronet*. It's most kind of you to offer to send it me—I'd be most delighted to have it.

Our love to you both.

> *Yours,*
> *AH*

TO SEBASTIAN SPROTT

> *The Athenaeum*
> *Pall Mall, S.W.1*
> *7 December 1932*

Dear Sebastian,

Could you possibly put me up next Tuesday or Wednesday, 13th or 14th? I want to talk to old Hopkin at Eastwood about one or two things connected with Lawrence, and it would be a great pleasure if I could combine it with a glimpse of you in Nottingham. But of course if it's at all inconvenient don't attempt to bother about it.

> *Yours,*
> *Aldous Huxley*

TO SYDNEY SCHIFF

> *Kingston, Jamaica, B.W.I.*
> *19 February 1933*

My dear Sydney,

I had hoped to see you in London before our departure—but was struck down on arrival by flu, and got up only to board a ship—a monster cruising liner, which we have left here in Jamaica, preparatory to proceeding by banana boat to Guatemala, the next stage in our journey. When we have seen such Maya remains and odd Indians as can be seen there without too much difficulty, we hope to go on to Mexico City, and after that to Yucatan, to do the New Empire Maya sites there. Thence USA.

Our voyage was pleasant; for we called at curious and amusing places—Barbados, Trinidad (a lovely island, and we met some really charming people); La Guayra, the port for Caracas, capital of Venezuela—most picturesque and exceedingly odd in its Spanishness:

Panama, where the mixture of races is even more extraordinary than in the rest of the West Indies—for on top of the usual Negroes, Hindus and Chinese, there are many Japanese, local Indians (Red Men), Arabs, and representatives of all the white races—the whole quietly simmering in the tropical heat: queer and profoundly depressing (as indeed most of these hot countries are, *au fond*,—such a sense of hopelessness).

Tell Wyndham Lewis, if you see him, that he should write a book in the style of *Snooty*—only more so—about a cruising liner. The horror is unimaginable. Hundreds of retired colonels, spinsters and widows with incomes, enriched Lancashire businessmen (including, on our cruise, several bookmakers, who drank nothing but champagne), interspersed incongruously with a few very *bien* people, who keep themselves from the rest (you should have seen the Duchess of Northumberland and her two daughters!) as though they were Brahmins in a crowd of untouchables. And everybody, from morning till night, playing children's games—and in the evening letting themselves be led like sheep by the professional amuser paid by the shipping company into awful jollifications—fancy dress balls, children's parties (where the businessmen and colonels and widows dress up, bloodcurdlingly, as schoolboys and babies), gymkhanas and god knows what else. How depressing our compatriots can be! Oh dear, oh dear. . . .

I wish I could like the feeling of these black places. But I don't. The blackamoors give one *en masse* a sense of hopelessness, though individually and in moments of excitement they are sometimes more cheering—e.g. when we heard them singing topical songs of their own composition at Trinidad.

I hope Violet and you are getting through the winter satisfactorily. It's difficult to believe in it—the winter—here. Hope we may see you later in the year. Maria joins in sending love and all good wishes.

Yours,
Aldous H.

TO MARY HUTCHINSON

Belize, British Honduras

Here, definitely, is the end of the world. Guarded by miles of coral reefs and sand banks, so that it can't be approached except by the smallest ships. And when you get here—a kind of tropical Bosham on a swamp, still showing signs of having been blown to bits—as it was 18 months ago—by a hurricane. However they have a lover's point which is evidently something.

Love from
M and A

TO MARY HUTCHINSON

Palace Hotel
Guatemala
24 March 1933

Have had a delightful time here. Mayan ruins, Spanish churches and altars with Indian primitives, and the most astonishing Indian life in the highlands—huge populations of Mayan stock living up there with all their costumes, and practicing the most amazing mixture of pagan and Catholic religion. They go from the church to the altar in the woods and burn incense impartially in front of Christ and old Maya idols. Most peculiar. We leave on Monday for Mexico—by boat to a small port in Oaxaca state, near which we stay on a coffee plantation: there on mules to the west and train.

Love to all,
A and M

TO LADY OTTOLINE MORRELL

Oaxaca
10 April 1933

A lovely place, and the pre-Columbian ruins here are superb—very different from the Maya things in Guatemala and Honduras, which have a wonderful richness and delicacy; whereas these are more massive and rigid. We came from Guatemala by boat, landed on the Pacific coast of Mexico, stayed for a while on a coffee plantation in the coastal forest, then rode across the mountains (over 11,000 feet) and down into the plains of Oaxaca. We move on to Puebla and Mexico tomorrow. Very strange and sinister country, and dark savage people. Can't share Lawrence's enthusiasm. Rather 50 years of Europe!

Love,
A and M

TO MARY HUTCHINSON

Oaxaca
10 April 1933

Got here from the Pacific Coast, where we landed 12 days ago: stayed on a coffee plantation in the mountains, then we set out on mule back across the Sierra, 11,000 ft high, slept in an Indian house; rode on again with ever sorer bottoms, and at last reached a road and an old Ford; which took us to all but civilization; then another Ford to a train—and here we are at Oaxaca; a lovely place, with marvelous pre-Columbian ruins at Monte Alban.

Love to all,
A and M

TO EUGENE F. SAXTON

Hotel Regis, Avenida Juarez 77
Mexico, D.F.
24 April 1933

My dear Gene,
We changed our plans, because everyone advised us so strongly against the train journey at this season--inches of dust and blistering heat in the desert country. So we are taking the Ward Line boat leaving Vera Cruz on the 27th April and reaching New York on May 2nd. "Siboney," I think, the name of the boat is--or words, to that effect. So sorry to de-range you again. I do hope it hasn't bothered you too much.

Still don't much like this town: but it's exceedingly curious—the life that goes on in it, in different layers, from the Indian upwards—or downwards as the good Stuart Chase would say.

Yours,
Aldous H.

TO RALPH PINKER

S.S. Statendam
25 May 1933

Dear Ralph,
Hope to be in London next week—staying at Dalmeny Court—for a few days, where I expect to be very busy with things connected with my father's death. However, I hope to see you.

Meanwhile, can you prepare for me a copy of the play *Now More Than Ever*? There are several people in New York interested in it, and I want to make some improvements in the first acts—where several defects were pointed out to me by Miss [Theresa] Helburn of the Guild. I would have brought a copy from New York but there was only one in the office and that was engaged.

Yours,
Aldous Huxley

TO RALPH PINKER

Sanary
11 June 1933

My dear Ralph,
Herewith three copies of an article for *New York American*. I will send the *Herald* article fairly soon. Also the revised version of the play, on which I am working at the moment. I think it will be improved.

Various German writers are here—practically all the exiles, from Thomas Mann downwards!—and I have been told by more than one of them that the translation of *Brave New World* was very bad. This seems to me a pity. Particularly as I am tied to Herlitschka [the book's German translator]. Is there any means of escaping and finding someone who will do the job better?

Yours,
A.L.H.

TO J. GLYN ROBERTS

La Gorguette
Sanary (Var)
19 July 1933

Dear Mr. Roberts,
I was away when your book [*I Take This City*] came and have only just looked through it. Its best features are its uncompromisingness and violence. It is good that darts should be thrown and firecrackers let off—good in itself and as an exercise, not, alas, because there is the smallest hope of the darts and crackers having any salutary effect on their victims. About 99.5% of the entire population of the planet are as stupid and philistine (though in different ways) as the great masses of the

English. The important thing, it seems to me, is not to attack the 99.5%—except for exercise—but to try to see that the 0.5% survive, keeps its quality up to the highest possible level and, if possible, dominates the rest. The imbecility of the 99.5% is appalling—but after all, what else can you expect? Swaffer[6] is their prophet—but if it weren't Swaffer it would be someone else very nearly if not quite as Swafferish.

Yours sincerely,
Aldous Huxley

TO ROBERT NICHOLS

La Gorguette
Sanary (Var)
22 August 1933

My dear Robert,
I was very glad to get your letter, though sorry indeed to hear that you have to undergo this beastly operation. What a bore and a burden one's body can be. Your young friend has made no appearance as yet; but she shall be welcome if she does.

I read *Great Circle*—for which much thanks—and though it is very good in its way, written with beautiful taste and an astonishing verbal felicity, it remains somehow curiously unsatisfying, don't you find? In spite of all its intelligence and subtlety, it's insubstantial—not there. (A slightly exasperating feature, for me at least, is that like every American novel now published, it has alcohol as its hero. How boring booze is in literature! Almost as boring, when you aren't screwed yourself, as in life. Booze poisons modern American fiction and distorts all its values—for nobody dares condemn boozing since Prohibition, nobody dares even to find it unaesthetic. A young girl going out and vomiting into the gutter, an old lady tumbling down stairs, men and women stinking like swine in a stye—these are just phenomena to be accepted, on the whole with admiration, not to be condemned in any way. Very wearisome.) I will write what I honestly can in praise of the book—and technically I think it's excellent. But where? In what form? Let me know.

I am busy on a book of travels—which is a book *de omni scibile*. Central America is a peculiarly good place from which to look at everything—politics, art, civilization. It's a sort of laboratory where all the horrors of our world have been tried out on a small scale and under

[6] Hannen Swaffer. Tabloid journalist.

simple conditions: a guinea-pig world, so to speak. Also the most marvellous scenery, archaeological remains, Spanish churches and Indian life. Some of the most interesting places I've ever been to.

Sanary is full of exiled German *littérateurs*, Thomas and Heinrich Mann, selected Hebrews of varying awfulness, such as Feuchtwanger (God help us). A nest of singing birds. One is very sorry for them: but wishes they could go and sing somewhere else! In five years, no doubt, Tom Mosely[7] will have us all chased out of England. What a bloody asylum we live in. Love from us both to both of you.

> *Yours,*
> *Aldous H.*

TO LADY OTTOLINE MORRELL

La Gorguette
Sanary (Var)
31 August 1933

Dearest Ottoline,
I was very glad to get your letter—tho' sorry indeed to hear that Philip hadn't been well. I do hope he's on his feet again now. You say nothing of yourself: so I hope and suppose that you are all right. I heard of you remotely from Lady Colefax (she passed through Sanary—on her way to Austria! All in a fortnight's holiday), who said she'd seen you at the ballet: but that was all.

We had a very interesting journey. Those Central American countries are really extraordinary—such astonishing landscapes and archeological remains and Spanish churches and queer Indians practicing the oddest mixtures of Catholicism and Paganism. We enjoyed it all immensely—and except for occasional bugs in Mexico and the riding on mules, which is hard on the posterior, were quite comfortable. Maria made a number of excellent photos, which we will show you when next we are in London. We finished up in New York, where we were when my father died—very unexpectedly, so far as I was concerned: for I had not known he was ill. His heart gave out suddenly, just as he seemed to be getting over his illness. My poor stepmother was very lost when I saw her afterwards in London: and she is left rather badly off, with the two boys just growing up.

---

[7] Sir Oswald (Tom) Mosley (1896–1980). British politician and leader of the British Union of Fascists from 1932 to 1940. Huxley here misspelled his name.

I have been hard at work, writing a book of travels,—which is really a book about everything, and which I hope may be interesting when it's done. Also painting with great energy in the intervals. Most of my reading has been about Central America, so I haven't "kept up" very much. Have you read a very fine poem on the conquest of Mexico called *Conquistador*, by [Archibald] Macleish—an American? It's really astonishingly good.

I hear that Kot is about to publish all his Lawrence letters—after having told me that he disapproved of all publication in under 25 years of Lawrence's death! I am glad, for they will be interesting. We missed Frieda in America: but I hear occasional rumours of her rampagings. Best love from us both.

Your affectionate,
Aldous

TO MARY HUTCHINSON

Cap de la Gorguette
Sanary (Var)
24 October 1933

Dearest Mary,

I was in Paris only 4 days and am back here again working very hard, as I want at all costs to get my book finished soon: so, alas, shan't see you and Jack next Friday. What a pity it wasn't last Friday! But if it had been you would have found me almost dead with exhaustion, brought on partly by a series of late nights and early risings, but mainly by boredom—the indescribable boredom of listening to professors from every country in Europe discussing *l'avenir de l'esprit européen*: or rather not discussing it—for they never by any chance said anything to the point. One has no idea, until one attends a congress of "intellectual co-operation," how bottomlessly stupid learned men can be. Like dogs. I hadn't meant to speak: but was so enraged by the imbecility that I sat up one night and prepared a full length discourse which I fired off—to the horror and dismay of the professors, who were really pained to hear something that actually meant something. The only relief in the gloom was Julien Benda,[8] whom I liked very much. And macabre comic relief was provided by Keyserling[9]—the most frightful

---

[8] Julian Benda (1867–1956). French philosopher, author of *Le trahison des clercs* (1927).
[9] Hermann Keyserling (1880–1946). German popular philosopher.

monster I have ever seen; but with a fascination of horror. He is an enormous man, Mongolian in type (a Russian by birth), talks every language with perfect fluency and much faster than the natives; has an elaborate system of charlatanesque philosophy with a jargon of hocus pocus words, and is able to relate any phenomenon instantaneously (and at endless length—for he never spoke for less than 40 minutes) with his system. On the last evening, after a huge banquet of farewell— he seized on me and suggested that we should go and have a drink. We went to the Café de Berry and there he settled down in real Russian style, first to beer—then to vodka—then to oysters and a bottle of Chablis—then to brandy and eggs and bacon: ordered the bill, but before the waiter appeared, popped into the lavatory and left me to pay! And all the time had never stopped talking.

We had a quiet summer, mainly spent avoiding German-Jewish authors, who have settled at Sanary like locusts after being exiled, poor wretches, from their appointed place. One is sorry and indignant—and one wishes they had chosen some other seaside resort. Barbara and Victor were too lazy to come and see us and M was too tired, after the strenuous end of Matthew's holidays, to drive over there. So we only communicated at a distance.

Gerald Heard was with us for a bit and now Eddy is here—very nice. We are making alterations in the house—making a dining room downstairs, next to the kitchen, so as to economize labour. *C'est la crise!*—particularly acute now that you have to spend 30F for every £1 you spent in the past. I am anxiously waiting for the collapse of the franc.

I hope you will enjoy Paris. Our love to Jack. I hope we shall see you after Christmas, if we come to England then—Goodbye, Dearest Mary. *Amusez-vous bien.*

Yours,
A

P.S. We are told that Odette's[1] latest conquest is the *tenancier* of the Ste Maxime brothel—*Qui la comble des cadeaux!*

---

[1] Odette Keun (1888–1978). Writer and mistress of H. G. Wells.

TO FORD MADOX FORD

La Gorguette
Sanary, Var
15 November 1933

If it's just a question of preserving the easel till Seabrook's return and if it's still of use to you, it seems best that it should remain *chez vous*. I am supplied with easels and it would only go into a corner and wait till S. comes back.

In any case please don't do anything about it for another fifteen days or so, as we are going away. I hope very much that, on our return, there will be a chance of renewing an acquaintance begun at a PEN Club Dinner—if I remember rightly—renewing it in more congenial surroundings. I will write again, if I may, on our return.

Yours,
Aldous Huxley

TO C. P. BLACKER[2]

La Gorguette
Sanary Var
1 December 1933

Dear Sir,
I hope it will not be troubling you too much to ask your assistance in the following matter. I have been asked by the editor of *Nash's Magazine* to write on the question of eugenics, particularly the sterilization of the unfit. I am tolerably well up in the history of the sterilization movement in other countries and in the evidence in support of sterilization. What I should like to know, however, is this: whether the bill for the legalization of sterilization in England was actually introduced in the House of Commons. And if so, what was (and what is likely to be) its fate. I have been traveling in Central America for many months and fear I may have missed the introduction of the bill—if it was introduced. You will be doing me a great favor if you will let me know very briefly where the question of legislation stands at this moment.

Yours truly,
Aldous Huxley

---

[2] General Secretary, Eugenics Society.

TO MARY HUTCHINSON

18 St. Alban's Place, S.W.1
Sunday
[ca December 1933]

Dearest Mary,

M is going on very well, on the whole: has been given plenty of dope and so has passed a good deal of the first, worse times in a doze.

Friday, I find, is free; so I will get tickets for *Hamlet*—where, by the way, is it being given?

Since seeing you last we have taken—for seven years!—a flat in Albany. Very nice, with central heating, parquet floors and lots of room. A very decisive step!

Best love,
Aldous

TO EDITH WHARTON

La Gorguette
Sanary (Var)
20 December 1933

Dear Mrs. Wharton,

Many thanks for the quotation from La Fontaine. I had read it before, but did not connect it to *Psyche*. On this last mystery I am now able to throw light. The *Invocation* to *La Volupté* is quoted in Larousse Anthology of 17th Century poets—with another fragment from *Psyche*. In the biographical introduction it says that *Les Amours de Psyché et de Cupidon* was a "*joli roman en prose entrecoupé de vers*," published in 1669.[3] So there, thank goodness, we are!

We look forward very much to coming next week. Matthew arrived today, looking very flourishing, I am glad to say.

Yours very sincerely,
Aldous Huxley

---

[3] La Fontaine's longest prose work and only novel, published in 1669.

TO MARY HUTCHINSON

Cap de la Gorguette
Sanary (Var)
25 February 1934

Dearest Mary,

Thank you for your letter. I am glad you saw M. I was rather worried at the thought of her, alone in that place.

I dodder along with my book [*Eyeless in Gaza*], rather exasperated because I can't quite get the formal relations between parts that I'm looking for, but advancing little by little. I am looking for a device to present two epochs of a life simultaneously so as to show their relations with one another—and also their lack of relationship. For when one considers life one is equally struck by both facts—that one has remained the same and become totally different, that the past conditions the present and that it has no influence upon it. And then of course the relationship between past and present are not the same for two individuals who have lived through the same circumstances. Past event A may have influence on a person X at a given time—and no influence, at the same given time, on person Y who has undergone the same experience.

Am reading mainly Vilfredo Pareto's *Sociologia*—2000 pages—slow but sure. A terrifying book—the only purely scientific, unmetaphysical account of human affairs ever undertaken: a vast coherent system of man's behaviour in society. The most depressing book in the world. I read most of it in 1924 and am now going through it once more—and in light of the events which have occurred since the first reading it seems still truer than it did then, and still more depressing. Partly because of the events, which have punctured all the post-war hopes of lands-fit-for-heroes and reconstruction; and partly, doubtless, because one is creeping into middle age and is less easily distracted by one's appetites; which have grown feebler, and one's passions, which seem such a bore—all but the consuming desire for knowledge and understanding. That grows. And if I didn't have to earn a living and if my eyes would stand the strain, I should do nothing, at any rate for some years, but read and in the intervals travel round, poking my nose into things.

The local news is nil: Edith Wharton at Hyères, with parties of old gentlemen staying—Berenson, Lapsley etc.: curious. And the Charles de Noailles—whose ménage seems on the verge of collapse owing to

Marie-Laure being infatuated with a musician called Markiewich. A few dismal German literary gents in the middle distance. The only startling novelty is the opening, announced for March, of a brothel on our peninsula. It will be called *La Case à Papa* and stands on a cliff overlooking the sea. Such is the march of progress. . . .

Yours, Dearest Mary,
A

TO JULIAN HUXLEY

Forte dei Marmi
24 April 1934

My dear J,

We have been wandering in Italy for about a month now; for I was rather tired and wanted a holiday. Had meant to motor down to Sicily—but it rained so hard and so incessantly, that at last we turned back and stayed with Phil Nichols in Rome instead. It still rains—indeed we have had only about a week of really fine weather in all the time we have been here. Which is a great bore.

Italy is a bit depressing, I find. Awful poverty everywhere. And fascist propaganda more ubiquitous and incessant than ever. We arrived on election day and found the whole of Italy plastered with "Duce, si! Duce, si!" *ad infinitum*. In Rome, there were entire walls of palazzi covered with "si, si, si, si," and in the centre big Ben's face, twenty feet high, in plaster. And one finds children's books about the great man in the shops—in the tone of books about Jesus: and there are now vast organized pilgrimages to his (or His) birthplace. A huge attempt is being made to organize an idolatrous worship of him, as of the followers of Alexander, and Caesar, and the Roman emperors. The masses accept—but hypocritically, I think: they are constitutionally incapable of working up the hysterical emotions of the German masses. One has the impression of an enforced piety.

We start back for Sanary tomorrow and hope to be in London some time in May—look forward to seeing you then. I asked Chattos to send you a copy of my book. They have got it and very nicely, I think.

Love to the family.

Yours,
Aldous

TO FORD MADOX FORD

La Gorguette
Sanary (Var)
4 May 1934

Dear Ford,
So sorry not to have answered your letter of April 20th before. We were traveling in Italy without an address and I only got it on my return. The only 'youngs' I know aren't much in London. Perhaps the best place to enquire for them would be at Mrs. Naomi Mitchison's, River Court, Hammersmith Mall. She generally has a number of them in the offing. Write to her *de ma part*. I think she will help you to find what you want.

Italy was very disagreeable. Rain, and the fascism worse than ever. I only hope we shall miss that accursed plague in France.

Please remember me to Mrs. Ford.

Yours,
Aldous Huxley

TO JULIAN HUXLEY

La Gorguette,
Sanary (Var), France
18 May 1934

Dearest J,
Thank you so much for the book, which arrived yesterday. I have only had time to look at the pictures and read a sentence here and there: but appetite is whetted and I look forward to getting down to it in real earnest.

We hope to be coming over in June—will let you know exactly when. The last weeks have been particularly lovely here, as, owing to the torrential rain of the early spring, all the vegetation is astonishingly luxuriant. For the moment we are out of the North African desert zone in a soft, temperate climate. I lie rather fallow at the moment—writing a little at stories and reading with a view to an essay on the history of that queer sexual religion, of which Lawrence was the latest messiah, but which has had so many prophets in the past—from the Gnostics down to Blake, Milton at moments, Coventry Patmore, Fourier, Laurence Oliphant and so many queer fanatics of every race. I think the study of them may be of considerable psychological interest, as showing the ways (oddly limited in number) in which people find it necessary to justify the actions they find pleasurable and exciting.

At this moment appears your letter. Interesting news about the Zoo. I hope it will come off, if only for the value of the financial security. What a bore this money business is! I should so like to write nothing for quite a long time—hoped this year to be able to realize the dream by selling *Brave New World* to the movies: but the creatures decided at the last moment that the film would be unpopular: so very hoped-for £850 for nothing have vanished. Damn them!

Please thank Juliette for the lovely Greco book which Mme Eisenschitz[4] delivered a few days since. It is the best volume of reproductions I have seen. I shall be most interested to see her sculpture.

I go on with my painting—am taking up oils now, which I find more satisfactory than gouache. What a delightful art it is to practice. So much pleasanter than writing.

Love to you both from both of us.

Yours,
Aldous

TO MARY HUTCHINSON

Cap de la Gorguette
Sanary (Var)
19 May 1934

Dearest Mary,
I ought to have written before to thank you for your very welcome letter about Mexique Bay. I am so glad you liked it; for I like it quite well myself and enjoyed giving it its peculiar shape.

Sanary has been very lovely: for the incessant rains of the spring (the rains which made our stay in Italy so very damp and disagreeable) have made this country flourish in an extraordinary way. Such flowers and greenery I never saw here. I have been doing little—lying rather fallow, as I don't seem to be able to get what I want in my projected novel, reading a fair amount, particularly with a view to writing an essay on that religion of sex, of which Lawrence was the latest prophet, whose origins go back to the Gnostics and the Kabala, and whose earlier prophets include Milton, Blake, Coventry Patmore, Fourier, Laurence Oliphant,

---

[4] Claire Bernard (1890–1969). Artist wife of Willy Eisenschitz (1889–1974), Austrian-born painter and illustrator.

besides dozens of minor religious maniacs. In the intervals paint a bit. Raymond has been staying here—very agreeable as a guest—and a charming companion. He is just finishing his monograph on suicide.

We hope to be in London in June. Please thank Jack for his p.c. I hope the package is not a bore: it will be very kind if you will keep it till we arrive.

Read Tom's Heresy book with some irritation. I never knew a writer who spent so much time explaining what he didn't mean to say and then at last saying so little. The way he makes generalizations and then slips away without giving examples is incredible. E.g. the cruelty of modern literature. But there is fifty times as much cruelty in Aretino and Lasca as in all modern novelists put together. And then the serene way he ignores history. Our age may be bad enough: but after reading any well documented book on the ages of faith can one honestly say they were any better? Their horror was rather different, that was all, different, because there were fewer people and less money. Love from us both to both of you.

Your affectionate,
A

TO MARJORIE WORTHINGTON[5]

La Gorguette
Sanary (Var)
10 August 1934

My dear Marjorie,
About old Pareto:—I have the greatest respect for him, feel he's one of the very few people who have approached sociology in a genuinely scientific spirit, without any metaphysical axe to grind, without any violent political prejudices (beyond that conservatism and that disbelief in progress which seems always to come to people who spend a lot of time studying the facts of human activity) and without, above all, any propagandist zeal for any one, all-explanatory hypothesis. This last is what makes most sociology such rubbish—the mania to explain everything in terms of one set of causes—economic, climatic, psychological, religious and so forth. Pareto is prepared to admit that there are a great many causal factors always at work and proceeds always on that as-

---

[5] Marjorie Worthington (1898–1976). American author and wife of writer William Seabrook (1884–1945). She and her husband were friends of the Huxleys in Sanary.

sumption. His book is therefore extraordinarily well balanced. If it were a bit more readable, it would be a great masterpiece. Unfortunately, he repudiated any "didactic purpose" and wrote purely for his own satisfaction and for the Satisfaction of other like-minded people. Which is a pity. Your friend must have had a weary job translating his two thousand thick pages.

I wonder, by the way, if this is the same translation as that about which T. S. Eliot wrote to me this spring. He is a director of Faber and Faber, the English publishers; and there was some question of their taking on the publication of a translation which was being (or had been?) published, I think, by Harcourt, Brace in America. Now, I think, Jonathan Cape is going to do the book, or thinks of doing it—for they are all a bit nervous from the business point of view. For I fear it's not a potential Best Seller. I hope this translation is the same as your friend's; for I should hate to think of his going through those two thousand pages only to discover that the book had been previously done by somebody else.[6]

You seem to be having a grand time in the country, with none of those droughts and dust storms of which we read such appalling accounts in the papers. Here we are having a cool summer—lots of mistral and *vent du large*, which makes bathing rather painful. Your house is full of about a hundred squalid-looking children, camping in the empty rooms. What a pity that good works and charity should always result in such unpleasantness! At the sale of the furniture, I bought two large mirrors and was furious at missing, by some stupid oversight, the most ravishing picture by the old man. The former owner, from whose heirs we had rented the *Villa Les Roseaux*, was an amateur painter, and my studio over the garage had stored in it a lot of his paintings and photographs; but Willie, with his peculiar code of ethics, refused to let me take anything away with me—an interior, in the most charming Douanier Rousseau manner which I don't ever remember to have seen while you were there, and so presume must have been hidden in the cellars. How glad I am we stole those indecent photographs! I regret we didn't go around snooping some of the paintings.

I am glad to hear that your respective works are going well. I tinker away slowly at a novel, trying to get exactly what I want and not succeeding, which is a bore: but in matters of literary composition I am

---

[6] It was the Arthur Livingston translation that Harcourt was publishing in the United States.

a convinced Micawber. Something ultimately always turns up. In the intervals I accumulate notes for a projected history of the religious and philosophical justifications for sexual indulgence invented by people who wanted to have a bit of fun but couldn't bring themselves to have it unless they first believed that the fun was in accord with the dictates of Pure Reason, or God, or the Categorical Imperative, or the Higher Thought. You've no idea what extraordinary things people have thought of to justify the most ordinary acts. And sometimes having invented amazing theologies to justify the fun, they found themselves compelled by the logic of these theologies to pass from ordinary to really very odd acts—as when a clergyman of the Church of England thought it his duty to have a girl in public on the drawing room sofa, because he was acting for God and God had decided to reconcile Himself with the flesh.

Matthew and Sophie are here, both grown very large; and Maria is kept pretty busy dealing with them. The German population has diminished and passing visitors have been scarce—which is, on the whole, all for the best.

Our love to you both,

Yours,
Aldous H.

TO MARY HUTCHINSON

Cap de la Gorguette
Sanary (Var)
18 August 1934

Dearest Mary,
It seems only a day or two ago that I had your sweet birthday wishes—but I suddenly realize that it is nearly three weeks. . . . Time rushes at such a headlong pace.

There is no particular news: I tinker away at a novel and in the intervals do a little painting—enough to make me respect the people who can conceive and carry out a great composition as I have never respected them before. I have been trying to paint a little group of angels from a postcard of an El Greco. Interesting, but staggeringly difficult. And it makes one realize how extraordinarily poor one's memory is. One thinks one knows a picture well: but when it comes to saying just what colours come where, one is completely at sea. I suppose it would be possible to train oneself in the art of remembering such things. As indeed, in so many other arts of the mind. I am more and more struck by the hopelessly primitive and uneducated state of our minds—utterly ignorant of all rational techniques for encouraging such essential states as concentration on the one hand and "decentration"—relaxed quiescence—on the other; having only the crudest methods for establishing self-control, for directing thought and avoiding distraction; content to live nine-tenths of existence automatically—with all but unconscious fixed habits of thought, feeling, taste, sensation. It's a dismal story of wasted talents and unrealized potentialities; and I come more and more firmly to believe that the most important task before human beings is the perfection of a series of psychological techniques for the proper exploitation of the personality. All this famous "planning" in the social and economic sphere will be wasted and useless if we remain barbarously unplanned as individuals—at the mercy of the social forces we shall have created. Individual planning has obviously been done in India by the Yogis—and there is a lot to be got out of the yoga psychology, which I have been looking into recently. But of course it needs systematic investigation, and would clearly have to be modified for our contemporary purposes. The only people who ever went in for scientific psychological planning in the west were the Jesuits; and, so far as I can make out, their system was radically wrong and, tho' successful up to a point, never got any further and finally broke down. Since then we have been content to drivel along with our current educational systems, most of which neglect all the essential things and leave their victims for all intents and purposes quite untrained.

Paul Valéry is in our neighborhood, staying with Mme de Béhague at Giens, and we have had one or two very pleasant meetings. He talked to me the other evening very fascinatingly about the personalities of his youth—Mallarmé, Villiers de l'Isle-Adam, Huysmans and so on. Otherwise we have been without visitors, beyond a few casual passers-by of no particular interest. The season has been bad for the hotel proprietors this year—*la crise*, a cool summer, change of fashion from sea to mountains, doctors warning people against the sun instead of extolling its benefits. How exquisite this coast would be if nobody came to it! It's sad that all the things one believes in on principle—such as democracy, economic equality etc.—should turn out in practice to be so repulsively unpleasant—hot, smelly crowds; banana skins; building estates like skin eruptions on the landscape; loud speakers and gramophones every ten

yards; roads made nightmarish with rushing traffic. I hope your holiday
is being a pleasant one. How is Barbara? I hope all goes as it should.
Our love to you all.

Yours,

A

TO DR. MYRES

La Gorguette
Sanary
30 August 1934

Dear Dr. Myres,
Thank you for the interesting studies on fitness for motor driving, enclosed with your letter of August 1. A point which seems to me worth
considering, in regard to the psychology of motor accidents is this:
that, on many people, the fact of being in control of a fast and powerful machine acts almost as an intoxicant. They feel their personalities
enlarged by the machine, imagine themselves in some sort superhuman.
Just as dogs are loved because men in relation to dogs are god-like, so
cars are loved for their ability to enhance the sense (and indeed the object of reality) of power. Moreover, it has seemed to me, from casual
observation, that many people use the car as an instrument of over-
compensation. They console themselves for normal inferiority by imagining themselves, and as actually being, supermen in a car. There is an
excellent passage in chapter 25 of *Erewhon*, where Butler talks of the
superiority of those rich men who "can tack a special train to their
identity." Cheap cars have brought the possibility of enlarging the ego
within the reach of a quarter of the population.

Yours sincerely,
Aldous Huxley

TO HENRY MILLER

The Athenaeum
Pall Mall, S.W.1
19 December 1934

Dear Mr. Miller,
Excuse me for not having written before about your book [*Tropic of
Cancer*]. I thought it a bit terrifying, but very well done. I still remain,
I confess, unregenerately a partisan of "ideas." If one can afford to

have them—and there is obviously an economic level below which they're an impossible luxury—they can provide what seems to me an indispensable escape from the immediately personal. There are, so far as I'm concerned, only three alternatives: either a kind of nightmarish obsession with the immediate self; or sainthood; or ideas. For some people the preoccupation with self is not so nightmarish as it is to a schizothyme person like myself, a person for whom adjustment to other people and consequently acceptance of the world is difficult. The cyclothyme can adjust and accept so easily that his consciousness of his own self is not intense—he can forget himself in his experience. Whereas the person of the other type of temperament can't forget himself: experience, being hard to assimilate, makes him uncomfortably more and more conscious of himself. Hence, if one is to escape madness, the need of ideas—or, if one can manage it, sainthood.

Thank you again for sending me the book.

Yours,
Aldous Huxley

TO BERTRAND RUSSELL

E2 Albany
W.1
December 1934

Dear Bertie,
I was so sorry we couldn't arrange lunch or dinner tomorrow—but very glad that a meeting could be squeezed into the late afternoon. I have a long-standing engagement to go, in the earlier part of the afternoon, to visit Wormwood Scrubs prison. I hope and think I shall be back by 3:30; but if I'm later than that, I do hope I shall still find you and that you'll be able to stay on till it's time for you to go to dinner.

Have you ever tried the effect of breathing exercises on insomnia? I have found that slow, regular breathing on some such a rhythm as 6 heartbeats in—breath, 3 heart-beats pause, 6 out-breath, 3-pause—rising to 8, 4, 8, 4; 10, 5, 10, 5, or higher still—produces very quieting and steadying effects. It's a Yoga exercise, of course: but none the worse for that. The cosmology may be bad, but the exercise seems to work.

Yours,
Aldous H.

TO SEBASTIAN SPROTT

E2 Albany, Piccadilly, W.1
5 March 1935

Dear Sebastian,

You asked me—was it two years ago?—to stay with you: but the timing fell through, I forget why. Would you renew the invitation—next week if possible. I'd like to see you again, along with that curious Nottingham of yours, and to hear a little about that other England of which we here in London have really no inkling.

Yours,
Aldous Huxley

TO SEBASTIAN SPROTT

E2 Albany, Piccadilly, W.1
8 March 1935

Dear Sebastian,

I'm so sorry to have been such a bore. But there was a difficulty about dates. Now, it seems best that I should come to you either on the weekend 16–18, if it's free (let me know whenever you like): or on Wednesday 20th. It may be that I shall be in Nottingham anyhow on Monday and Tuesday, 18th and 19th, staying with a man I don't know personally, called Quin. I may come to you either before or after, it will suit me very well.

Your,
Aldous

TO SEBASTIAN SPROTT

La Gorguette, Sanary (Var)
9 March 1935

Dear Sebastian,

You are going to think me a feather-brained imbecile, or worse: for I am going to do what I did last time and postpone my visit. Under heavy necessity this time; for the insomnia which has been plaguing me for several months and which I thought I had got the better of, has come back this last week with redoubled violence; and, in despair, I am taking my doctor's advice and making a bolt for another climate—mountains near

Grenoble first of all, then Sanary. I do apologize for this and also, for my own sake, most sincerely regret it: for I should *very* much have liked to see you. It will have to be postponed now till the autumn. Will you invite me again then?

Yours,

Aldous H.

P.S. If you come across any particularly interesting psychological books in the way of your profession, I wish you'd sometimes let me know the titles. I like to "follow in the train," like these Christians at the heels of the saints.

TO MARY HUTCHINSON

Hotel des Grandes Rousses

Huez, Isère

19 March 1935

Dearest Mary,

Thank you a thousand times for the Shakespeare, which arrived after considerable delays, owing to customs officials at Lyons and avalanches blocking the road to this place. I have been reading *Henry IV Part II* and *Measure for Measure*, in the intervals of ploughing through two thick books which I had to read in the way of business—*Patterns of Culture*, which I advise you to read; for it's a most interesting book—and a work called *How to Choose a Mate*, by that curious creature Anthony Ludovici, who is tiresome and full of violent dislike of everybody, but extremely learned. He is passionately keen that we should all take to incest, as the Egyptians did—otherwise we are doomed, according to him, to inevitable degeneracy. And I must say that the latest evidence in the genetical line seems to point in the same direction. All the same, I'm rather glad I didn't have to marry my sister, or even one of my first cousins.

This is a god-forsaken little place, like all god-forsaken little places in the high mountains. The peaks glare down at one from across the valley: the snow fields rise behind the hotel. When the sun is out, the heat is literally tropical and the skin is frizzled off one's face in about a quarter of an hour. When the sun is in, everything is swathed in a white fog of cloud and falling snow. However, I console myself with the thought that it must be good for me, and take enormous walks on snow-shoes, conscientiously, as one might drink the waters at Vichy. I

303

sleep moderately well, tho' not so well as I should like. The only pleasant features in the scene are the birds and plants. These make a most
heroic and touching pretence that it's spring and that the snow isn't
there. The pussy willows are out and wherever a bit of snow has
melted, large plants of hellebore appear in full blossom, and even occasionally a primrose; while the birds hop about the trees pretending
there's something to eat—which there certainly isn't—and breaking periodically into song. It's like a poem by Wordsworth, complete with its
moral. All the same, I shall be glad to climb down to a more humane
landscape.

Give my love to Jack. I hope you'll have fun in Spain. Given reasonable weather, it ought to be delicious.

Yours,
Aldous

TO GILBERT MURRAY

La Gorguette
Sanary (Var)
5 June 1935

Dear Professor Murray,
Henri Barbusse is trying to organize a mammoth Congress in favor of
peace for this year's Armistice Day. As you probably know, he organised another at Amsterdam, three years ago, which was, however,
mainly a left wing affair. But as Peace associated with Communism is
mistrusted by the general European public, he wants this to be representative of every kind of opinion. He can, apparently, count on the
Catholic organizations as well as his own left-wingers in France; has
got a number of eminent scientists, including the Jolyot-Curies and
Langevin, to cooperate; and is trying—a point on which I strongly insisted—to get representatives from the various professional bodies, scientific, medical, technical and so forth. If he can get representatives
from such professional bodies, the Congress would look really impressive, and might possibly affect government opinion—so much more
important, alas, than mere public opinion! So I am writing to ask you
what you think about the matter—whether you consider such a Congress worth the support of the League of Nations Union and whether
you think that your organization could do anything to secure the adherence to the scheme of professional bodies. Barbusse didn't want to
write officially until the ground had been preliminarily sounded. So

would you let me know what you think about the matter. Barbusse is a very nice, earnest, rather boring man, like an old-fashioned clergyman in communist's clothing. But he has an absolute passion for Congresses and really enjoys writing 2000 letters a month. Seeing that this Niagara of industrious goodwill exists, it should be harnessed as effectively as possible to the cause of peace.

Yours very sincerely,
Aldous Huxley

TO VICTORIA OCAMPO

Sanary
18 June 1935

Chère Victoria,
Merci de vos deux letters. Je pense bien que je viendrai en '36—quoique le moi d'aôut soit difficile pour nous à cause des vacances de Matthew. Mais puisqu'il veut apprendre l'espagnol il pourrait peut-être nous accompagner? Mais comme vous le dites, cette question de distance est difficile à résoudre; car si les avions abolissent la distance considerée en termes de temps, malheureusement ils augmentent en termes d'argent!

Je vais mieux maintenant—quoique je travaille beaucoup, n'ayant pas complètement abandonné l'espoir d'achever mon livre avant l'automne. Je prends, entre autre choses, une cure de travail manuel. Vous . . . beaucoup à me voir demi-nu, piochant d'immenses trous dans le jardin. Le travail manuel me reconcilie beaucoup avec ma profession d'intellectuel!

Drieu a passée une nuit chez nous l'autre jour—de bonne humeur et se portant bien.

A contre-coeur—mais on m'a fait le chantage du devoir—je vais à Paris après demain pour assister à un congrès—tous ces Lettons et Esthoniens, ces Uzbegs et Tonaregs, avec lesquels il faut parler dans des langues qu'on ne connaît pas bien sur des sujets (littérature lettone, uzbegue, etc.) qu'on ignore complètement. Les gens s'aimaient beaucoup plus aux temps où ils ne se voyaient jamais. Combien on adorait les japonais au dix-huitième! Cette idée qu'il faut que les peuples n'ont que se connaître pour s'admirer et s'aimer est une erreur immense. Pourtant je vais à Paris pour y parler même.

Je pourrais, si ça vous intéressait, vous envoyer le texte du discours, qui est sur la nature de l'influence des écrivains sur leurs lecteurs et sur

*les limitations de cette influence, pour votre revue. Je demanderai à
Gerald de vous envoyer quelque chose aussi.*

*Je regrette beaucoup que la santé de votre mère soit si mauvaise et
j'espère qu'elle ira mieux avant l'automne, non seulement "for her own
sake," mais afin que nous puissions vous attendre en Europe.*

Love de nous deux.

Vôtre,
Aldous

[Dear Victoria,

Thanks for your two letters. I think I will come in 1936—although the
month of August is difficult for us because of Matthew's vacation. But
since he wants to learn Spanish, he could maybe come with us? And as
you say, the question of distance is difficult to resolve, because if planes
abolish distance considered in terms of time, they add to it in terms of
expense. I am better now, although working a great deal—not having
abandoned the idea of finishing my novel by autumn. I am taking,
among others, a cure of manual labour. You can often see me half-
naked, digging enormous holes in the garden. Manual labour recon-
ciles me greatly to my profession as intellectual.

Drieu La Rochelle spent the night here the other day—in good humour and doing well.

Against my will—but I get blackmailed about duty—I leave for
Paris the day after tomorrow to attend a conference—all these Lat-
vians, Estonians, Uzbecks and Tonaregs—with all of whom one must
discuss in unfamiliar languages—subjects about which one knows
nothing (Latvian and Uzbek literature, etc.) People got along better
during the times when they never saw each other. How much people
liked the Japanese in the 18th century! This idea that people need only
meet each other in order to like and admire each other is an immense
error. However, I am going to Paris and will even speak there.

I could, if you are interested, send you the text of the speech, which
is on the nature of the influence writers have on their readers, and on
the limitations of this influence, for your review [*Sur*]. I will ask Gerald [Heard] to send you something also.

I am sorry that your mother's health is so bad, and I hope that she
will be better before autumn, not only for her sake but so that we can
expect you in Europe.

Love from us both]

TO CLAIRE MYERS SPOTSWOOD OWENS

The Athenaeum
Pall Mall, S.W.1
30 June 1935

Dear Miss Claire Spotswood,
Yes, of course make use of the quotations. The plan of your book[7] sounds interesting—and I think you're probably right to use the allegorico-realistic form. It's easier, that way, to get everything in. The problem, when one's supposed to be telling a straight story, of covering all the ground is really appalling—as I am bitterly realizing at the moment, being involved in a novel in which I am struggling like a bluebottle on fly-paper.

If you have a copy to spare, I'd appreciate one when it comes out. Address till October is La Gorguette,

Sanary (Var), France, after that as at the head of this sheet.

Yours,
Aldous Huxley

TO SEBASTIAN SPROTT

La Gorguette
Sanary (Var)
22 August 1935

Dear Sebastian,
I have a problem in which, it occurs to me, you might help me; so without compunction, though apologetically, I address myself to you. The facts are these. We have a German friend,[8] a young woman of about twenty-three, a quarter Jewish and of liberal opinions, who has been, for obvious reasons, living out of Germany since Hitler came in. Her passport expires in a few months; and, unless she can change her nationality in the interval, she will get into grave difficulties—impossible to travel, impossible to remain in France, risk of being repatriated with consequent concentration camp and maltreatment etc etc. Do you know of any impecunious Englishman who would be prepared, for a small consideration, to give her his nationality by marrying her? The marriage

---

[7] Claire Myers Spotswood Owens (1896–1983). American author of the feminist utopia, *The Unpredictable Adventure: A Comedy of Woman's Independence* (1935), which Huxley endorsed as "a remarkable book." The in-progress novel is *Eyeless in Gaza*.
[8] Sybille von Schönebeck (Bedford).

would be purely formal; the girl would not expect support from the husband and is of course anxious that the husband should not ever attempt to come down on her for more than the original price of the bargain. Later, she would be prepared to pay for a divorce, if it were desired. She will give fifty pounds—which might, at a pinch, be raised to a hundred; but she can't afford more. The solution it seems to me, consists in finding someone combining impecuniosity, honesty and homosexuality—someone who would be glad of the money, wouldn't try to use his position to get more, and wouldn't find himself likely to be let in for bigamy. Auden, I hear, has just married Erica Mann—on communist grounds, I take it. Our friend is not a communist but on the other hand would pay cash. If you could think of anyone among your acquaintance who would do this, I'd be most grateful if you'd let me know. We like the girl and are anxious about her future, which, unless she gets a husband, will be fraught with discomforts and even physical dangers.

I am hoping to make that much postponed visit to you this autumn, if you will have me. My sleeping, thank heaven, goes better. Forgive me for thus troubling you.

Yours,
Aldous H

TO SEBASTIAN SPROTT

La Gorguette
Sanary (Var)
10 September 1935

Dear Sebastian,
I have been away for a week: hence delay in thanking you for your letter. The young man sounds promising. I will let you have a note when I hear from the girl whether she thinks it all right and, if so, what definite and detailed plan she suggests.

It was most kind of you to take this trouble.

Have been reading a certain amount about dreams recently and find myself unable to believe that all dreams are significant, as they all want us to believe. I have a feeling that psychology is getting a bit too *anthropomorphic* and that in reality quite a lot of things in the mind just happen, casually, without any purpose, conscious or unconscious, and that it's unjustifiable to attribute final causes to all mental events. Like invoking providence to account for accidents. The mind, it seems to me, is a roulette board which is very frequently tampered with by a purposeful being, but which sometimes also works at random—with as much randomness as the structure of the instrument will permit.

Yours,
Aldous

TO SEBASTIAN SPROTT

La Gorguette
Sanary (Var)
14 September 1935

Dear Sebastian,

I have talked to our German friend about your candidate and she thinks he sounds all right. So can you find out from him if he would definitely be prepared to do it for ?50 and if so when and where—the last point having a certain importance because of the registrar. For, if I remember rightly, one has got to be a resident at least 3 weeks in a place, unless one has a special license. She would come over almost any time for the event. Put the matter confidentially to the young man—not as a complete certainty: for it's possible that in the interval some anti-Nazi idealist may turn up prepared to do it gratis—which our friend would prefer, considering the state of her finances. When we hear definitely whether and on what terms he is prepared to do the deed, we'll let you know definitely her decision and detailed plans.

Yours,
Aldous

TO SEBASTIAN SPROTT

La Gorguette
Sanary (Var)
30 September 1935

My dear Sebastian,

Thank you so much for taking all this trouble. It is reassuring to know that husbands are in such good supply and at so reasonable a price. I wrote to Naomi Mitchison at the same time as you; and since my last letter to you. She has written announcing the discovery of what sounds a most reliable proposition, guaranteed by a labour M.P., all 18 carat lug-nunc and thoroughly deserving. So that this for the moment is our favourite. I am sorry that we shall probably disappoint Mr. Richardson: but I think the fact that there will be no need for a divorce in the case of Naomi's man is a very strong point in his favour and against R, in spite of the watch presented to his father by the Prince of Wales. But if anything untoward should happen to the present candidate, I shall make another appeal to you—either for Mr. R, or the window-cleaner's brother-in-law. Meanwhile keep the business in cold storage. Thank you again very much.

Yours,
Aldous

TO SYBIL COLEFAX

Leicester as from E2 Albany, W.1
9 November 1935

Dear Sibyl,

I have been greatly troubled these last two days by the thought that I ought not in these tiresome circumstances, to have asked you for an introduction to Euan Wallace.[9] I did it without sufficient reflection, forgetting that, in the name of friendship, I was indirectly involving you in an unpleasant business in which I had no right to involve you. For this I am, dear Sibyl, very sorry indeed.

I rang up Wallace's Secretary and if Wallace cares to see me shall be glad to take the opportunity of doing so.

Staying here with a philosopher-friend who professes at the local university college, I ran into Harold Nicolson, thinly disguised as a National Labourer and weary to the point of nausea with his election campaign. What a life!

Yours,
Aldous

TO CANON DICK SHEPPARD

Leicester as from E2 Albany, W.1
9 November 1935

Dear Sheppard,

Ever since lunching with you the other day, I have been feeling very much ashamed of the glibness with which I talked of the project of organizing the peace movement. When one has been endowed with that

[9] Capt. (David) Euan Wallace (1892–1941). British Conservative cabinet minister during the 1930s. In 1935 he served as undersecretary of State for the Home Department and also as secretary for overseas trade.

enormous thing, the gift of the gab, one is sadly tempted to make use of it for elegantly expressing ideas which one knows as ideas and not by experience. That I should have talked so much to you—the theoretician to the man who knows the business of dealing with people by the process of self-dedication—is frankly comic, and it is only by laughing at myself that I can take the edge off my shame. Thinking, reading, talking and writing have been my opium and alcohol and I'm trying to get off them on to listening and doing. Meanwhile, excuse me. I was very glad indeed to have had the opportunity of meeting you and hope that we shall have an occasion to renew the meeting often and profitably.

Aldous Huxley

TO CANON DICK SHEPPARD

15 November 1935

Dear Sheppard
I hope you got the message I sent your secretary today. Our troubles suddenly cleared themselves up as though by magic, and the menace suspended over the head of our young German friend by the home office was withdrawn. So I didn't want you to put yourself out by coming here on your way from your meeting to St Paul's.

If you're in the neighborhood any day next week except Thursday, do let me know if you're free for lunch and come in either here or at the Athenaeum. It would be a very great pleasure to meet if you would do so.

Gerald Heard and I today saw Smith, who seems a very good man in his quiet way with much more under his city man's disguise than one would expect at a casual inspection.

Yours,
Aldous Huxley

TO CLAIRE MYERS SPOTSWOOD OWENS

The Athenaeum
Pall Mall, S.W.1
27 November 1935

Dear Miss Spotswood,
Please excuse my failure to write and thank you for your book. A combination of much work with not very good health has made me a worse correspondent even than usual.

So far from being offended I was flattered by what you wrote of me in your book—which I thought a most commendable achievement. At the moment I am finding that my own unpredictable adventure is leading me towards some kind of active and so to say religious pacifism.

This address always finds me and if you ever come to London in winter let me know word of your passage.

Once more please forgive me.

Yours,
Aldous Huxley

TO VICTORIA OCAMPO

ca December 1935

Dear Victoria,

Your cable was much delayed on its way here—for the Albany only forwarded it by post, which was very slow owing to Easter. Hence the long delays in answering it. How can I thank you for taking so much trouble on my behalf and arranging for so generous an offer? I wish I could have accepted the invitation and come to the Argentine this August. The circumstances were against it. For some months now, I have been sleeping very badly, which has meant very little work—so that I am frightfully behind-hand. I am making a desperate attempt to finish my book this summer—if this accursed insomnia will allow me—and the preparation of lectures and visit to B.A. would have made this quite impossible. So there was no alternative but to say no.

I have just received, however, an invitation from the PEN Club of Argentina to come as their guest to the PEN Congress of 1936 at B.A. Stupidly enough, no date is given. I am writing to give a provisional acceptance, dependent on dates; and if the thing arranges itself, I shall hope to see you there in Buenos Ayres—though I hope you will be in Europe before that.

How have you been? Better, I hope, than I have; for I have been living for some time in a state of considerable gloom and depression. "*Profondément triste,*" as Drieu would say! I hope you have been *profondément gaie* to make up for it. Sanary is as ever—sun, wind, olives, cypresses; *las muchachas,*[1] installed in their house (*filant un amour un peu moins parfait, il me semble*); German-Jewish exiles in

---

[1] Probably Sybille Bedford and Eva Hermann.

the background; the aristocratic colony at Hyères in full swing and poor Edith Wharton having had a slight attack of apoplexy; at Bandol, Duranty,[2] the Russian correspondent of the N.Y. Times is staying; so is M. Maurice Donnay[3] *de l'Académie Française ainsi que le* Duc de Broglie[4] *de l'Académie et de l'Institut—ce qui est, il me semble, d'un chic imbattable.*

Thank you once more, *et à cet hiver, j'espère.* Maria sends her love as do I.

Yours,
Aldous H.

TO FLORA STROUSSE

The Athenaeum
Pall Mall, S.W.1
27 December 1935

Dear Starky,
This is to wish you a happy new year and to apologize for my endless silence during the present one—a silence for which there is little excuse except that it has been a general one; for I have found it very hard to write any letter for a long time past. It has been a difficult year, on the whole, starting badly with intense insomnia and inability to work properly, going on rather better through the summer—and now, I hope, turning towards something better in preparation for 1936. I am at last getting near the end of my book and am working at the same time on a big project for the organization and crystallization of the peace movement in this country; for I have come to the conviction that nothing can possibly work or get us out of our present state except complete pacifism of the Quaker or Buddhist kind. The implications of this are, of course, fundamentally religious—Christian for those who believe in Christianity; for those who don't (and Christianity has a very bad record on, peace) some simpler conception of an underlying spiritual unity, realized through the practice of meditation. Nothing short of this, it seems to me, offers any chance of permanent success against the menace of war; for it is only by translating the fundamental religious ideas of human

---

[2] Walter Duranty (1892–1957). British-born journalist for the *New York Times*, awarded the Pulitzer Prize in 1932 for his Russian dispatches favorable to Stalin but now largely discredited.
[3] Maurice Donnay (1859–1945). French dramatist, known for his comedies; elected to the Académie Française in 1907.
[4] Louis, 7th duc de Broglie (1892–1987). French physicist and Nobel laureate in 1929.

unity into political terms—and it would be very easy to do so, if the will to do so existed—that we can escape from destruction.

Beyond this little news except that our common friend little C., has turned out to be too much of a bad thing and we have taken our boy away from Dartington and put him in a school in Switzerland where he seems to be learning more in an atmosphere less charged with the erotic adventures of his pastors, masters and mistresses—in all senses of the word.

Such is life in the Great Metropolis at the moment. I hope it is going on satisfactorily in Philadelphia. Heaven help us all!

Yours
Aldous H

TO JULIAN HUXLEY

La Gorguette
Sanary (Var)
1935

My dear J,
I had a rather mysterious letter from Pinker to say that you had been telephoning him about the presentation copies of *Texts and Pretexts* and *Mexique Bay*—to the effect that I had never received them. But so far as I can remember I did receive them—and never recall having said that I didn't. All this is wrapped in mystery.

Here I labour away without advancing—but hope that some time may somehow finish. Expect to be in London in the course of October. We have taken Matthew away from Dartington: he really seemed to be learning nothing under this system. Besides, the atmosphere seemed to be becoming a bit turbid and unsettled, which I'm sure is unsound for growing children. Have put him in a school at Lausanne, which he liked and where I think he will do some serious work—at any rate he is very anxious to work and there are none of the Dartington reasons for not working. Our love to the family.

Yours,
Aldous

Huxley's letter to Norman Haire was prompted by this letter.

Dear Aldous Huxley,

Thanks for your card which reached me this morning. I am delighted that you are willing to write a foreword. I think perhaps you do not realise how much weight your name carries among the more intelligent reading public. You probably have a fair estimate of your importance as a novelist. But you count for far more than would be accounted for on purely artistic grounds. (This sounds like a back-handed compliment, but I don't mean it that way.) Without letting sociological interests swamp you as an artist, you are an artist who is not content unless incidentally does what he can to make this miserable world a little less miserable. There is a very large public which realises this, and if you are able to say that you think my little book is good, lots of people will buy it who otherwise would not.

I don't think I am more noble than the next man, but it really is not primarily for my own benefit that I am asking you to do it. I have never earned enough by any of my writings to make it worth my while giving up the time to writing that I could be spending attending to patients and earning far more. My object in writing this book is not personal gain—I have written it because I think I have more experience of birth control than probably anybody else in the world, certainly than anybody else in Europe; and because I believe that I can write more lucidly and convincingly than most doctors. I want the book to have a good circulation, because I think it should help to remove some of the misery which burdens the majority of human beings. Incidentally I am pressing the publisher to publish it at the lowest possible consistent with the fact that he is dependent on his business for his livelihood. He is only waiting for the foreword to proceed to actual publication, but a foreword from you means so much that we are willing to wait for convenience.

Yours very gratefully,
Norman Haire

1936

TO NORMAN HAIRE[5]

E2 Albany, W.1
14 February 1936

Dear Haire,

I enclose the proofs of your book and the ms of a brief foreword.[6] The book certainly doesn't need it and I feel myself superfluous and a bit irrelevant. But there you are!—the important thing is that there shouldn't be too many involuntary babies.

All good wishes to you (and, to the potential mothers) for the success of the book.

Yours,
Aldous Huxley

TO GILBERT MURRAY

For Intellectual Liberty
110 Heath Street, London, N.W.1
10 March 1936

Dear Professor Murray,

An association is being formed whose name, "For Intellectual Liberty," sufficiently describes its aim. This association will be organized on a national basis, but will work for the defence of culture and the maintenance of peace (the first condition of intellectual liberty) in close collaboration with similar bodies on the continent. Its French prototype, Vigilance, has been in existence for some little time, and societies having the same purpose have been or are being founded in Belgium, Holland, Spain, Switzerland and the Scandinavian countries. All intellectual workers will be invited to join the association, which will collect and disseminate information, issue literature and take such other measures as seem appropriate for the defence of culture, intellectual liberty and peace.

It is proposed that a number of eminent workers in every field of intellectual activity shall be asked to become representatives, within the association, for their respective professions. Those persons will not be asked to commit themselves in advance to any particular line of policy; but when circumstances arise in which it becomes necessary to take

---

[5] Norman Haire (1892–1952). Australian physician and birth-control pioneer. The first sexologist to set up practice in Harley Street.
[6] Huxley wrote the foreword to Haire's *Birth-Control Methods (Contraception, Abortion, Sterilization)* London, 1936.

steps in defence of culture or the liberty of some particular category of intellectual workers, they will be approached with a view to obtaining concerted action. (In most cases, the giving of a signature is all that will be required.)

I am writing in the name of the Executive Committee for Intellectual Liberty to ask whether you will become a member of this panel of representative intellectual workers.

Yours sincerely,
Aldous Huxley

TO THE EDITOR OF THE TIMES

The Athenaeum
Pall Mall, S.W.1
27 April 1936

Sir,

In his letter printed in today's issue of *The Times*, the Bishop of Durham speaks of the legitimacy of "just wars," and he expresses the opinion that such things as "just wars" really exist. It is worthwhile to record the views on this subject of two of the Early Fathers.

How (asks Lactantius) can he be just who injures, hates, despoils, kills? And those who strive to be of advantage to their own country (in war) do all these things.

Tertullian criticizes the view that truth and justice can be obtained by means of war:

Who shall produce these results with the sword and not rather those which are the contrary of gentleness and justice, namely, deceit and harshness and injustice, which are of course the proper business of battles?

Those who support the opinion expressed by the Bishop of Durham make "justice" dependent on the accidents of politics. In the last year of Elizabeth's reign it might have been right for Englishmen to engage in war against Scotsmen; in the first of James's reign it would not have been right. Christians are apparently justified in killing their fellow-men in defense of whatever happens at the moment to be called "their country." To make justice contingent on political accident is surely to deny the very existence of justice. The Bishop is asking us to promote the real to the rank of the ideal and to proclaim that whatever is, is right.

I am, &c,
Aldous Huxley

PS. The archbishop said (a) there was no difference in principle between police and an army (b) "the use of force, of the sword, by the state is the ministry of God for the protection of the people." These dear old bronze age instruments of warfare! It doesn't sound quite so good if you say the use of poison gas and tanks is the ministry of God.

TO CANON DICK SHEPPARD

La Gorguette
Sanary (Var)
6 May 1936

Dear Dick,

I have re-hashed our conversation for *Nash's*—altering freely so as to make our remarks sound a bit cleverer and more coherent than the shorthand transcripts revealed them, but I don't think altering the sense. The only thing I have done is to develop what was only a brief hint in the original—that is, my remark on the economic implications of pacifism. I don't think we can evade the economic issue—indeed, I think we shall gain by making it clear that pacifism logically leads to a complete overhaul of the existing system, but insists that the overhaul shall be undertaken by non-violent means—thus parting company with orthodox communism. I have no second copy of the script, so perhaps you will ask Mealand [editor of *Nash's*] to show it you, so that you may see what I have added in this context and whether you think it is all right.

I had a talk in Paris with an intelligent representative of the left, who insisted strongly on the fact that 100% pacifism was not likely to find any acceptance among the French. I suppose this is due to the fact that they have had no Quaker tradition preparing the ground for the idea.

I hope you're as well as may be.

Yours,
Aldous H.

PS I am suggesting that Gerald should look at the proofs of the conversation—as there won't be time for me to see them. Mealand proposes to put in bits of my original written answers and I want someone to see that he puts them in at points where they make sense. I expect you're too busy, so will appeal to Gerald.

1936

TO NAOMI ROYDE-SMITH

La Gorguette
Sanary (Var)
7 June 1936

Dear Naomi,

I wish I could have painted the picture that you attribute to me in your dreams! In reality I only laboriously daub without much satisfactory result,—for others at any rate or for myself as critic; though for myself as dauber the process is most agreeable.

Your book arrived today and I have just finished reading it. The analysis of the elements that go to produce a theatrical effect seems to me most subtle and illuminating. Apart from being an extremely good dramatic story, the book is a remarkable piece of abstract dramatic criticism. I rather regret that you didn't make it longer and include the experiences of the people on the other side of the curtain—actors, author and producer. It would have been a quite different work—slower and more complicated and less intense: and I hope that one day, out of your knowledge of the subject, you will write such a book. Meanwhile thank you for *this* book which I enjoyed—so much that I thought I'd like the other as well. And thank you too for the way in which you quote what I think I recognize as a remark of mine—about actors putting more into a phrase than the author had been aware that it contained. I will send you my book when it appears. I don't really know what it's like—a curate's egg or perhaps a bit addled even: I have lost all sense of it.

It is intensely cold here—with alternate driving rain and howling wind. Nothing like the golden heat of the time when you were here. When are you coming again? The franc, I hope, will soon collapse and make traveling cheaper; and perhaps for a little while longer the presiding lunatics will give us peace—so do take the occasion when it offers.

Please thank Ernest [Milton] for his cutting about the funeral of the widow Smyth-Pigott at Spaxton. I met a man recently whose aunt was actually an inmate of the Agapemone[7]—but unhappily he had no information to impart.

Maria sends her best love, as do I.

Yours affectionately,
Aldous H.

---

[7] Agapemone. Literally, "the abode of love." Huxley wrote about the self-proclaimed Messiah, Rev. T. H. Smyth-Pigott (d. 1927), in "Justifications." He enjoyed seven "spiritual brides" per week.

TO JULIAN HUXLEY

La Gorguette
Sanary (Var), France
15 June 1936

My dear J,

I have written to the secretary of *For Intellectual Liberty* passing on your criticisms for the committee to consider. I think they are sound and that the name will have to be changed some time: whether it is good policy to change it at once is another question. I think it may be best to wait till we have a reasonable body of members and then, on an occasion, say, of making a push to get new adherents, change it. Meanwhile it remains to be seen what response we get to the appeal for support recently sent out.

After continuous cold and rain, it has begun to be summer here. The political atmosphere remains, however, uncomfortable—the bourgeois frightened of losing their money, the proletarians frightened of reaction from the right. I learned the other day that Bandol has no less than 150-200 members of the *Croix de Feu*. A most disquieting fact. Probably this is an exceptional case—for a village largely peopled by retired rentiers would naturally have a lot of *Croix de Feu* men: but it indicates the extent to which these people have been organizing themselves in the country.

Love from us both to the family.

Yours,
Aldous

TO MRS. KETHEVAN ROBERTS

The Athenaeum
Pall Mall, S.W.1
30 July 1936

Dear Mrs. Roberts,

I am telling my publishers to send you a copy of my book [*Eyeless in Gaza*]. It is rather a curate's egg—good in parts, perhaps. I should like to have kept it by me for another year or two—but couldn't do so. I think a good deal can be done to modify oneself. It's a question of using the proper techniques: meditation, Mental Prayer, whatever one likes to call them. Their effect will be modified to some extent by the nature of the underlying metaphysic, which may regard the substratum of the universe as personal or impersonal. It seems to me (a) truer and (b) more useful to regard the substratum as impersonal. Moreover it would be possible to produce effects without having any metaphysic whatever, but concentrating, as the Pali canon of Buddhism prescribes, solely on the technique. These effects may be good or bad according to the end proposed—the technique is neutral, like so much machinery which one can use for any purpose, bad or good.

I hope you have been well and are not too much depressed. I had a bad time all last year with insomnia and consequent neurasthenia, but have now emerged again, thank goodness. Meanwhile the political nightmare seems to be growing worse and worse. Whether any of us will be alive three years from now becomes increasingly dubious. One can only go on with the old job of imploring people *not* to kill themselves. There are signs through the prevailing lunacy, that they would like to become sane—but the trouble is that they aren't yet prepared to take the necessary steps without which there can be no preservation. They want the end without going to the trouble of using the appropriate means.

All good wishes.

Yours,
Aldous Huxley

TO OLAF STAPLEDON

As from La Gorguette
Sanary (Var)
31 July 1936

Dear Stapledon,
Thank you for your letter. I don't expect to be in England on the date you mention, so fear I can't accept your invitation. Anyhow I am not a speaker and should probably have declined on that score.

I can't see that there can be any question of a "short term policy" in a world where the means of destruction are growing more efficient every week. Technological progress is not arithmetical but geometrical—the acceleration is itself under acceleration. A short term programme postulates a certain stability of conditions; but there is no such stability. And anyhow I can't see that one can morally accept the position of saying: I disapprove of murder; but I must be allowed to go on committing it for another few years.

As for framing a policy that the public will "stand for"—this is surely quite irrelevant. You might as well say that the public won't stand for evacuating a town threatened by a lava stream, therefore it mustn't be asked to evacuate it—there must be a short term policy of staying. Hundred percent pacifism is obviously difficult and disagreeable; but the circumstances are such that it is *necessary*. The question of "standing for" necessity simply doesn't arise. You've got to take it or leave it; and if you leave it, you're done for. The matter is analogous to the situation in a yellow fever district. The public doesn't like having to screen windows and put paraffin on water barrels—won't "stand for it." But if it doesn't do this it gets fever. A short term policy of risking fever for the sake of sparing conservative prejudice seems to me merely lunatic.

> *Yours,*
> *Aldous Huxley*

TO CANON DICK SHEPPARD

La Gorguette
Sanary (Var)
6 August 1936

My dear Dick,
Thank you for your long and interesting letter. Here are some business matters, first of all. The first item, rather unpleasant, in view of Smith's failure to come across, is the printer's bill for the pamphlet, which I enclose. Chatto and Windus presumably have some money in hand from the sales of the thing to date and there would be no harm, I think, in asking them to pay over what they have. This, with Mrs. Elmhirst's contribution, should go a fair way to settling the bill.

Second point. A young man has written to me from Oxford saying that he has conscientious qualms about taking your pledge, as he feels he ought to do Red Cross work in the event of another war and thinks your pledge would prevent him. I presume you have no intention of stopping people from doing their best to repair the damage of war; but it occurred to me that in some future propaganda leaflets, it might be worthwhile to have a specific word on the subject. The young man's name is R. H. Puse, Christ Church, Oxford and perhaps it might be worth dropping him a brief note.

A third point. It occurs to me that a valuable leaflet might be made up of sayings by responsible ministers of the crown: military experts and the like about the horrors and dangers of another war. These might be followed by their remedial prescriptions—always the same: more armaments. Quotation should also be given from the pronouncements of foreign statesmen, showing that the one hope for peace is a well-armed Britain, France, Italy, Germany, Japan, Russia, U.S.A. It is possible to find identical phrases in the mouths of all the politicians and admirals and generals in the world. This identical claim by every country to arm to the teeth for the sake of peace would be an effective *reductio ad absurdum* of the whole armaments racket. The leaflet could end by a brief statement of the pacifist alternative. I think this would be valuable, because it is always good to be able to condemn opponents out of their own mouths. The first part of the collection has been made by a woman called Mrs. Ursula Roberts (whose pen name is Susan Miles), 19 Woburn Square, W.C.1. She sent me a long essay containing some ingenious suggestions for the organization of peace the other day, the first part of which was made up of just such citations as I have been suggesting. In my reply to her, I suggested that she should get in touch with Miss Rayne; but in case she hasn't, I think it would be worthwhile writing her a note. She is an excellent and earnest woman who has already done local peace organization work in her district.

A fourth point. What if anything, are you proposing to do about this *Rassemblement générale pour la paix* at Geneva on the fifth of September? I'm very likely be going as a representative of the intellectual liberty affair with which I'm connected. Had you thought of going or of sending someone? There will, I suppose, be opportunities for making a lot of contacts with representatives of peace movements all over the place.

The Smith business is really becoming too extraordinary. If he's not a crook, he must simply be enjoying a prolonged feeling of power—like a little boy who snatches another's toy and runs off, holding it up out of reach and shouting, "Sucks to you!"

France is in a very uneasy, disquieted state. I hope to goodness they'll pull through without anything serious going wrong. There might so easily, I think, be a bad financial panic resulting in chaos and violent reaction from the Right.

I hope you've been keeping well. My wife joins me in sending all good wishes to you both.

Ever yours,
Aldous

TO CANON DICK SHEPPARD

9 August 1936

My dear Dick,

I have been asked by Dame Adelaide Livingstone, who is organizing the British side of the International Peace Campaign, to go to the Brussels Congress as the delegate of the Peace Pledge Union. I have answered that I accepted in principle, but that I was writing to you and that you would confirm, if you thought it desirable, or saying no, if you thought it undesirable. The history of the matter is this: I was originally approached by the central organization of the IPC as representing the movement For Intellectual Liberty. They asked if I would take part in the commission of science, arts, and letters. I answered that I didn't accept all their four points, one of which is the organization of an armed collective security. They replied that the Quakers and even the conscientious objectors of various countries had accepted, so that there was no doctrinal bar. So I said that I would go. They have communicated with Dame Adelaide Livingstone; and as there are various other delegates from For Intellectual Liberty going to the Congress, she asked if I would go as the Peace Pledge Union member, there being no delegate from it so far appointed. Seeing that hundred-per-centers are going to be present and that there is no preliminary list of belief, I think it would be good to go. What do you think? And would it be advisable to send anyone else?

I have been sent no agenda of the science, arts and letters commission but it's obvious that the points of discussion will be propaganda and the organization of scientific men as a socially responsible body. The point I shall insist on, as PPU delegate, is the importance of effective local organization in groups as a supplement to mere propaganda. To accept propaganda is the equivalent of an emotional conversion at a Billy Sunday revival; to join a group is to show that you mean the conversion to be lasting and effective. I think this is the thing to stress, don't you? The commission will, I hope, be a body for studying the technical progress involved and there won't be much scope for the discussion of general principles, nor much point in such a discussion. Ways and means are the concern there. And I am sure that this particular device of the Peace Pledge Union is an important contribution to the ways and means of business and that it can usefully be applied even by those who are not hundred-per-centers. It is a way of practically demonstrating that pacifism begins at home and must be lived as well as thought.

["\n\n\n\n\n\n\n\n\n\n\n\n\n\n\n\n\n\n\n\n\n\n\n\n\n\n\n\n\n\n\n\n\n\n\n\n\n\n\n\n\n\n\n\n\n\n\n\n\n\n"]

If you have any other suggestions to make I'd be very glad of them. Also, I wish you'd consider the advisability or otherwise of sending another delegate or of coming yourself. At Brussels, the Congress is much nearer than at its original site, Geneva.

I do hope you're better. Meanwhile the European situation isn't exactly calculated to act as a tonic and restorative.

Yours,
Aldous

TO CANON DICK SHEPPARD

La Gorguette
Sanary (Var)
31 August 1936

Dear Dick,

On second thoughts, I expect you are right about the Congress. I was thinking in terms of purely practical arrangements when I envisaged going; but since (a) there isn't a great likelihood of anything practical being done and (b), if there is a chance of usefully cooperating there is nothing to prevent the Peace Pledge Union from getting into contact at any time with other organizations, it is better to stand out on the question of principle. So I shall not attend the Congress.

As it happens this suits me rather well, as a French friend of ours [Jean Coutrot] has just smashed himself up in a motor accident and is in a hospital in the neighborhood, while his wife and child have come to stay with us here. I am glad to have an excuse for staying a day or two longer.

I expect to be in Brussels on Saturday, and will attend the meeting on Sunday. I hope you won't want me to speak. Will you let me know where you will be in Brussels? I expect to be there with my son.

Yours,
Aldous

TO EVA HERMANN

Metropole Hotel
Brussels
1 September 1936

Dearest Eva,

I was sorry not to have had a final glimpse of you before my departure. However, I carried away very charming memories of our last meeting. Did you? I hope so.

Nothing much here. The congress, I understand from those who attended it, was not very satisfactory—badly organized (why can't these people get competent business men to run the business?), wholly undemocratic; heavy censorship (it was out of order to talk about the private manufacturing of armaments or, to criticize any existing government!). In a word, it must have been almost as gloomy as the writers' congress!

We had a little meeting of Pacifists—quite successful, tho' numerically insignificant; and I made the acquaintance of at least one extremely nice and intelligent man.

Today we go on to Holland—in the train.

Love to Sybille. Think of me when the moon shines.

Yours,
Aldous

TO JOHN HOWARD WHITEHOUSE

Mount Royal
London W.1
16 September 1936

Dear Mr. Whitehouse,
Thank you for your letter and the very kind suggestion you make in it. I have thought over the matter most carefully and think that I had better say no to it—for several reasons. First I am incapable of public speaking. Second, I am very often out of the country for long months at a time. Thirdly, I have no experience of committee work, and am very bad at any kind of administration. A president who, when he is not absent, is both dumb and incompetent is not much good; and I think I had much better, for the sake of the cause that we have at heart, stick to what I can do in the way of pamphleteering and correspondence.

I quite agree with what you say about the I.P.C. [International Peace Campaign] effort. They are all so anxious to bomb in the name of the League, that I can't see that one can welcome their activities; however excellent the end envisaged, the means they want to employ are of such a nature that it is impossible that the end should be achieved.

Yours sincerely,
Aldous Huxley

TO THE EDITOR OF THE TIMES

The Athenaeum
Pall Mall, S.W.1
17 September 1936

Sir,

On page eight of your issue of September 17 you print a letter in which, replying to Lord Ponsonby, Mr. Wickham Steed advocates "collective security" by means of armed resistance to aggression. Only by joining "an adequately armed combination of resolutely peace-loving nations" (so runs Mr. Steed's argument) can we hope to preserve "our freedom and free institutions."

On page six of the same issue you print a report of the address delivered by Dr. A. L. Rawlings to the Engineering Section of the British Association. I venture to quote a few sentences from this report. "Fifty tons of bombs" (the total weight dropped by German planes upon London during the whole of the last war) "could now be brought from the other side of the Rhine by a single squadron and dropped in one night. . . . One single raid could paralyze the whole country. He doubted if gas were the most serious menace. Why trouble to gas the whole population when a few well-directed bombs could cut off food and water and paralyze transport? . . . Anti-aircraft guns of great accuracy and range were available, but how could we hit an aeroplane with them? During the air exercises last year 50 searchlights were unable to pick up a single bombing airplane except by an occasional fluke."

Does Mr. Wickham Steed seriously believe that "our freedom and free institutions" would continue to flourish in a country reduced to chaos by air attack? Panic, starvation and disease do not create an atmosphere propitious to democracy and parliamentary debate.

Advocates of "collective security" assert that in the face of an armed League no would-be aggressor would ever dare to break the law. If there are enough planes, tanks, high explosives, thermite, and vesicants, it will never be necessary to use them. Unhappily there is not the smallest reason to believe that this would be the case. The Arabs in Palestine know quite well that they are no match for the British Empire; nevertheless they persist in fighting the British Empire. Luckily for us and for themselves they have no modern equipment.

In a European war, even a war waged by the League against an aggressor, both sides would be armed with planes, tanks, high explosives, thermite and vesicants; and since, in Colonel Lindbergh's words, there is now no such thing as a defensive war, both sides would use these weapons to the limit in attack. When that happens where will our freedom and free institutions be?

Let us avoid vague abstract words such as "force," "arms," "collective security," "international police force," and think exclusively in terms of concrete contemporary reality. The contemporary facts are planes, tanks, high explosives, thermite, and vesicants. Is it conceivable that we can use such instruments and yet retain our freedom and free institutions? And if we persist in threatening to use such instruments, even in the name of the League, is it not certain that one day we shall be compelled to carry out our threats? We are faced with a single alternative; either we radically change the whole system of international relations or else we cling to the existing system and destroy ourselves.

> *I am, Sir, your obedient servant,*
> *Aldous Huxley*

TO GEORGE CATLIN

Mount Royal, W.1
22 September 1936

Dear Catlin,

The address of *Pax* is:—Bernard S. Coldwell (Hon. Sec.), 17 Red Lion Passage, W.C. The name of B. de Ligt's book is: *La Paix Créatrice*, published by Marcel Rivière. 2 vols so far issued, 1934.

The Dutch Thomists who have condemned war because modern weapons make it impossible to achieve the purpose of war[8] are Fr. Stratmann and Prof. J. A. Veraart, the latter of whom has published his views in *Roeping* (presumably a review) May and June 1930.

I wrote to Allan Young explaining why I did not like Cole's proposal. Gerald Heard is going to be present.

I much enjoyed our lunch.

> *Yours,*
> *Aldous Huxley*

PS. The archbishop said (a) There was no difference in principle between police and an army (b) "The use of force, of the sword, by the state is the

---

[8] In a postcard mailed from Sanary ca 1936, with an illegible date, Huxley wrote Catlin: "Thank you for your letter of the 24th. I find it personally impossible to commit myself to politics involving military alliances and the threat of military action, even under the auspices of the League. Yours, Aldous Huxley."

ministry of God for the protection of the people." These dear old bronze age instruments of warfare! It doesn't sound quite so good if you say the use of poison gas and tanks is the ministry of God.

TO CANON DICK SHEPPARD

Mount Royal, W.1
23 September 1936

Your letter reached me very belatedly, for I was a week in Holland after Brussels and was out of range of the post. It was very sweet of you to say those things; but I remember old Arnold Bennett's remark: "Anyone can write snippets. Similarly, anyone can speak snippets, particularly if he speaks from a written snippet!"

I saw Miss Rayne[9] today and have been hearing about recent developments. It seems to me that there is perhaps a certain danger of the PPU [Peace Pledge Union] getting switched onto a single track of activity and becoming too exclusively an organization for saying no in a particular emergency. That it must be this among other things is obvious; but I do feel that its other functions are almost equally important, and that it ought if possible to be at the same time an organization for experimenting with working models of a possible pacifist society. Attempts to produce such working models have already been made by Peter Scott, Hoyland, and others, and I feel that we should try to work in cooperation with them, or at any rate along somewhat similar lines, in places where circumstances allow of it. Ponsonby, I gather, would prefer to keep the whole movement on a political plane; but I think there is a danger, if this is done, of reducing it to a kind of sterility. Is there any reason why it should not proceed simultaneously along several lines at once? If the groups are to keep alive they will have to have some kind of work in which they can take an interest; and it seems to me that here Peter Scott's and Hoyland's experiments suggest the sort of works that they can do.

I hope you're keeping reasonably well. I am over here with my boy, living in this hotel as our flat is occupied by a tenant till the end of the month. Maria comes over next week. I look forward to seeing you soon.

Ever yours,
Aldous

[9] Miss Rayne. Canon Sheppard's secretary at the PPU.

1936

TO L. P. JACKS[1]

Mount Royal
Marble Arch, London W.1
14 October 1936

Dear Dr. Jacks,
I have a sudden awful qualm that I didn't write to you, as I intended last week—or did I? If so, excuse this second note: if not, excuse the oversight that has delayed my answer so long.

I hope very much there will be a chance of seeing you on Monday afternoon. I should like, if you have no objection, to bring along my friend, Gerald Heard, who, as you doubtless know, is an indefatigable worker in the cause of peace and would very much like to have the opportunity of talking with you. I could arrange to meet you anywhere in London—here if it is convenient to you, or anywhere else and at any time in the course of Monday afternoon.

I read the Alexander Hamilton article with very great interest. What an instructive parallel it is! And how did Wilson manage to miss the significance of it?

Have you yet read Russell's new book, *Which Way to Peace?* It is a most admirably lucid argument leading by remorseless logic to the complete pacifist position.

Yours sincerely,
Aldous Huxley

TO LORD PONSONBY[2]

Mount Royal [London]
17 November 1936

Dear Lord Ponsonby,
I have sent your articles and my own to be typed. When they are all ready, a copy will be sent to the various members of the Literature committee and we can have a meeting to discuss additions, changes, commissions, etc. I am finding that it is necessary to write some of the articles at somewhat greater length than I proposed at first. Some material simply can't be sent out in under 1000 words. I don't think this matters much, as it doesn't look as tho' the proposed limits would be exceeded.

[1] Lawrence Pearsall Jacks (1860–1955). English educator, Unitarian minister, and editor of the *Hibbert Journal,* 1902–1948.
[2] Arthur Ponsonby (1871–1946). British politician, writer, and activist.

Ruth Fry[3] wrote an article on non-violence, which I have had to rewrite, as it wasn't very satisfactory. I want to append to it a series of examples of non-violence—in individuals, in groups and even in governments. The first two are easy enough to find; but I can't think of good examples of a pacifist policy pursued by governments. There must be some examples, where morality is not too obviously tinged with self-interest. I'd be most grateful if you could suggest a couple of cases which would illustrate the good results obtained by governments deliberately refraining from violence and adopting conciliation and decency as their weapons.

Yours sincerely,
Aldous Huxley

TO RAYMOND MORTIMER

Mount Royal
Marble Arch, London W.1
29 November 1936

My dear Raymond,
Maria has gone to Paris for some days; she meant to write and tell you, but I don't know whether she did—so I send you this in case she didn't. This means, I fear, another postponement of our visit till she comes back.

I liked your review of Housman very much. What a queer case of the higher sodomy—or was it also lower? And how drearily bad a lot of his stuff is! I can't get very much even out of his good verse.

Ever yours,
Aldous

TO CANON DICK SHEPPARD

La Gorguette
7 December 1936

My dear Dick,
I have been paving hell with my epistolary intentions towards you—paving it for weeks and weeks. I was so very sorry that I didn't see you while you were down in these parts and that Mrs. Sheppard should

---

[3] Ruth Fry (1878–1962). English Quaker and peace activist.

have come to Cannes only to get flu. Also I hear unsatisfactory accounts of your health since your return. I hope, but don't for a moment suppose, that you are looking after your self.

I have at last finished, at least provisionally—for there will doubtless be corrections to make and suggestions to incorporate—the little *Encyclopedia of Pacifism*. It has taken much longer than I thought—partly because of the dilatoriness of certain contributors and partly because I myself work slowly and because there was more than I anticipated to be done. In some ways, however, the delay has been a good thing, as it has led to the collecting of much more material than I first thought of and to a considerable widening of the whole subject. The book in its present form runs to something under 30,000 words and should not exceed a hundred pages—small enough for the pocket. The script has gone to Gerald, who will pass it on to Miss Rayne, who in turn will probably pass it on to you and Ponsonby, either in its present form, or else in galley proof. I think it should turn out to be useful.

I am collecting materials for a book on the means for realizing desirable changes—such as peace, social justice, etc. Reformers ordinarily oversimplify to such an extent; reducing everything to one cause, they think that one reform, or a series of reforms of one type, will remove the cause and lead to the desirable change. Whereas it's obvious that there is multiple causation and must therefore be a multiplicity of means for making the desirable changes. One must discuss education, economics, politics, industrial organizations, religion, philosophies of life. I think it will be worth making one attempt at a synthesis, even though it cannot but be extremely sketchy.

I heard on the wireless, two nights ago, that you had been trying to persuade the Church Assembly to be a little less militaristic—without much success I gather! It looks as though these people are going to get the war they want, I'm afraid. It's as though they were possessed by devils—doing things that they know are fatal, that they know are wrong; doing them in spite of that knowledge and perhaps actually because of it, in some queer way.

I expect to be in London at the beginning of March and look forward to seeing you then. Meanwhile, dear Dick, I send you my love.

Yours,
Aldous

TO FLORA STROUSSE

La Gorguette
Sanary (Var)
11 January 1937

Dear Starky,
How nice of you to send me the book. I have only glanced at it so far; but it looks interesting. I'm glad last year was a good one for you and hope this will also be—in spite of all the efforts of our rulers, who are evidently quite determined to make things as unpleasant as they can for us. I've had a mixed sort of year—doing rather little of the things that really interest me and a good deal of propaganda for peace, work which I believe to be necessary, but which bores me, as I hate having to rehearse what seems the obvious. It's bad enough when one's writing: it's worse when one's speaking—though I've refused to do more than a minimum of that. I was in London all autumn, driven almost crazy by the pointless activity of urban life. I get worse and worse at town life—feel like an inmate in a lunatic asylum when I'm shut up for long in one of those hideous places. What a relief to get to this paradise of quiet though I felt rather guilty in escaping to a life I like so much.

I expect to be over in America some time this spring, to travel round and look at the country, which I don't know at all. Perhaps I shall see you then.

Meanwhile, all good wishes and again my thanks.

Yours,
Aldous Huxley

TO MARY HUTCHINSON

E2 Albany
Piccadilly, W.1
ca 6 April 1937

I have signed the book and it will duly go off tomorrow. Our troubles are all over now, thank heaven, and have been in a sense worthwhile because so many people have behaved so kindly, offering help and money for the good cause of preserving S[ybille Bedford] from being exported to Naziland as she must have been on the expiry of her passport.[4] Also the man [Terry Bedford] has behaved with a really astonishing chivalry

---

[4] See Bedford's memoir *Quicksands*, Chapter 22, for her account of the Huxleys' key role in arranging the marriage of convenience that allowed her to avoid returning to Nazi Germany.

and dignity. By the last day we had mobilized all the forces that could be called up, from the French Embassy to Canon Dick Sheppard. A most extraordinary performance, rather like a novel by Kafka—ending off very suitably last night in Mr. Selfridge's party on the top floor of his shop, where lions roared at every step, including Michael Arlen with an astrakhan collar on his great coat, too beautifully in the part to be quite true.

PART TWO

1937–1963

On 7 April 1937, Aldous Huxley, together with Maria and son Matthew, set sail from Southampton on the SS Normandie *for New York. They are accompanied by Gerald Heard, a well-known BBC personality, author, and fellow Peace Pledge Union activist, dubbed "the cleverest man in the world" by Evelyn Waugh. The Huxleys have no fixed intentions of remaining in America but are keeping their options open—particularly for Matthew's education. They will never again reside permanently in Europe. Shortly before his departure, Huxley tells Sybille Bedford that he hopes to learn more about American experiments in education and industrial management. After a short stay in New York, the Huxleys and Heard motor across the southern United States, and at Frieda Lawrence's invitation they spend the summer at the Lawrence ranch in New Mexico, where Huxley finishes* Ends and Means, *a book about the causes of the wrong functioning of society and possible remedies. Huxley and Heard spend November through January on a lecture tour. Heard breaks his arm in Iowa, and Huxley must carry on the rest of the tour alone. Maria drives to New York state, taking a house at Dairy Cottage, Rhinebeck, where Aldous joins her for Christmas.*

TO JAY HUBBELL[1]

Albemarle Hotel
Charlottesville, Va.
2 May 1937

Dear Professor Hubbell,
You will have received my telegram in answer to yours, saying that I expect to have the pleasure of accepting your very kind invitation for

---

[1] Jay Hubbell (1885–1979). Professor of English at Duke University and first editor of *American Literature.*

337

dinner on Tuesday. I am writing now to explain that we're traveling very light in a car and that I have no evening clothes with me; therefore must make my appearance, in the words of the hymn, "just as I am, without one plea." About speaking—I am a very bad after-dinner speaker; but on the other hand I like conversation and the exchange of ideas—so that if it were possible for us to sit around after dinner and talk, I should much prefer it to getting up and spouting. Also I think we should pass a more profitable and interesting and lively evening—at any rate, I know that I should; for I get much more out of a two-way traffic of ideas than out of a one-way speech—especially if the speech happens to be my own!

Thank you once again for your very kind invitation.

Yours very sincerely,
Aldous Huxley

TO EUGENE F. SAXTON[2]

The Alamo Hotel
Colorado Springs, Colorado
20 May 1937

Dear Gene,
Our address for the summer will be:—c/o Mrs. D. H. Lawrence, Kiowa Ranch, San Cristobal, Taos, New Mexico. The place is extremely beautiful, and we shall have an agreeable little house. Doesn't seem worth while hunting any longer—particularly as it would seem that accommodation is very hard to come by.

About literary plans:—I hope to get down to my sociologico-philosophical book in a few days, when we are back again in Taos. With luck, this may be ready by the end of the summer. But I can't make any definite pronouncements for quite a while. . . . Anyhow, will keep you posted.

I think the offer of $500 for the book is all right and can be accepted.

We've had a most interesting trip—marred only by a heat wave in the deserts of Texas, which were consequently like hell. However, we ultimately reached paradise in the form of an air-conditioned hotel at El Paso. The truth about this country is that nature never intended human beings to inhabit it—but put every obstacle in men's way, heat,

---

[2] Eugene Saxton (d. 1943) was editor-in-chief at Harper and Brothers for many years.

parching drought, arctic winters, floods, gigantic mountains, swamps. The only part where man seems to be really welcome is the middle South—from Maryland to North Carolina. For the rest he seems to be there on sufferance and at the cost, on his part, of enormous efforts, pains and privations.

We are all well—even Maria who has to bear the brunt of the driving: but shall be glad to be settled in. Our love to the family.

Aldous H.

TO EUGENE F. SAXTON

San Cristobal, New Mexico
8 June 1937

Dear Gene,
Thanks for your letter of the fourth.

The point you raise in your third and fourth paragraphs is a rather delicate one which I would like to discuss with you confidentially. For some little time now I had been thinking that Eric Pinker had been getting a bit slack and feeble in the handling of my journalistic business and, on my arrival in New York this April, I was quite frankly not very favourably impressed by him personally. He seems to have lost grip to a considerable extent.[3] Later I went to stay with Seabrook, who talked at some length about the possibilities of journalism here and very strongly advised me to go to his agent, Ann Watkins. Somewhat dazzled, I suppose, by his accounts of the journalistic business, I decided to go and see Ann Watkins, with whom I was in indirect connection, owing to the fact that she was Gerald Heard's agent and that Gerald and I had decided, for the purpose of putting certain ideas across, to give a series of discussions this autumn, under the auspices of Colston Leigh. I had a talk with Ann Watkins on the morning of our departure for the South and, from a stop further down the road, wrote to Eric Pinker, telling him that I wished, at any rate experimentally, to make a change in the journalistic side of my agency business. I heard nothing from Eric till two days ago, when a letter which he had sent to General Delivery, Santa Fe was forwarded very belatedly here. It appears that he had actually driven down to New Orleans in

---

[3] Huxley had good reason to worry about Eric Pinker, who ran the New York office of J. B. Pinker and Sons. In March 1939 Pinker was sentenced to a prison term in Sing Sing for misappropriating his clients' funds.

the hope of catching me, but had missed me there and so written this letter to Santa Fe. Reading his letter, I felt that I had acted rather arbitrarily in leaving him without notice and, not wanting to do anything unfair, I wrote to him that I would go on with him through the autumn to see how things went. Simultaneously I wrote to the same effect to Ann Watkins. The letter went off yesterday. I happened to speak about the matter to Gerald Heard to-day and he told me that while in New York, he had been present while Colston Leigh and another agent had been discussing Pinker and his present position. The upshot of this conversation was this, that Pinker was drinking himself into incapacity and that his financial position was extremely precarious. If this is the case, it would account for the rather desperate note in his letter to me. I shall of course continue to send such journalistic work as I may do to Eric during the autumn months, in the hope that he will be able to handle it effectively, not only for my sake, but also for his. In the meanwhile, however, I should very much like to have your opinion and advice on this subject. I am extremely sorry if Eric is in as bad a way as Leigh said and do not want to do anything to precipitate a crisis. At the same time I'd like to know exactly where things stand.

I'm sorry to bother you with this long letter. Our love to you all.

Yours,
Aldous H.

TO SHERWOOD ANDERSON

San Cristobal, New Mexico
8 June 1937

Dear Mr. Anderson,
Thank you for your very kind letter of May 7, which has caught up with me at last, after much forwarding, in New Mexico. We passed through New Orleans in front of schedule—so your letter had to follow.

It is very kind of you to suggest that we should stop and see you in Virginia. Unfortunately there is no prospect of our being anywhere near Virginia for a number of months. But I hope very much that an opportunity will present itself before very long of accepting your invitation.

Yours very sincerely,
Aldous Huxley

TO S. S. KOTELIANSKY

Dear Kot,

I shall be glad to hear from you the latest developments in poor Sullivan's case. I had a letter from Mrs. Sullivan, just after he came out of hospital—and the account she gave was very depressing, no prospect of amelioration and meanwhile bedsores and worsened general health. I hope he has got over this to some extent.

I'm enclosing a letter for you to forward to Kruse, if you think it all right. I told you that I'd heard from his secretary months ago saying that the matter would be placed before him on his return from abroad—since when nothing. I'm afraid it looks as though we should get nothing. But still, it's worth trying, I think. It has just occurred to me that it might be worthwhile approaching Science News Service here. They have money, know about Sullivan (whom they actually asked to come and be their director) and may be willing either to give him something outright or make some kind of work for him. Anyhow it's worth trying.

We are spending the summer on Lawrence's ranch—very wild and beautiful. Frieda has mellowed with time and is really very nice. Also we find, to our immense relief, that the Italian captain is an extremely honest, simple and decent man. The rumours that they are exploiting Lawrence and her as a commercial proposition are fortunately absolutely unfounded—they emanate from Mabel Luhan and from Brett, who at one moment actually plotted to steal Lawrence's ashes from Frieda. A long, complicated and grotesque story, such as could occur only in a society mainly composed, as that of Taos is, of middle-aged women with nothing to do.

I hope you've been well.

Yours,
Aldous H.

TO A. E. MORGAN[4]

San Cristobal, New Mexico
26 July 1937

Dear Mr. Morgan,
I have just read your little book, *The Long Road,* and feel impelled to tell you how greatly I enjoyed it and how good I thought it was. The passages in which you speak about the necessity of building up active communities was particularly interesting to me, as I have recently been writing precisely on that subject in a book, which I have nearly finished, which discusses the means which must be employed if the ends we all profess to desire are actually to be realized. At present, it is obvious, we employ means which are utterly inappropriate and often downright evil, and which therefore are in the nature of things incapable of realizing the good ends which we profess to be aiming at. Among the indispensable means—which include political, economic, educational, religious and philosophical readjustments—I have placed the creation of just such communities as you write of. The historical precedents are extremely instructive. Benedictism not only preserved cultural and spiritual life through the dark ages; it also re-colonized deserted lands and re-established agriculture after the collapse of the Roman empire. Similarly, the Cistercian revival was both spiritual and practical; for it led to the draining of swamp land, the clearing of forests and the systematic improvement of the breeds of cattle, horses and sheep. The function of the community of devoted individuals is to do the urgently necessary jobs that neither government nor individuals in the ordinary way of business will undertake. In the past these jobs (I am speaking only of practical matters, not of spiritual and cultural activities) were agriculture, care of the poor and sick, education, making of books. Today such jobs are mostly undertaken by government or individuals in the ordinary way of business. The essential jobs which are not performed by these agencies are the jobs of introducing self-government into industry, agriculture and business; the job of distributing the wealth created by industry in an equitable way; the job of creating a small working model of a better future society in which there shall be cooperation, unlimited liability within organic groups, self-government all round to the limits of general social efficiency; and finally the job of practicing and preaching non-violence (in the sense in which Richard

---

[4] First chairman of the Tennessee Valley Authority.

Gregg[5] uses the word) as an essential condition of domestic and international peace.

I have recently been reading R. A. Parker's book on J. H. Noyes and the Oneida Community. What a very strange and profoundly interesting story! And, obviously, what an extraordinary man of genius Noyes was! Whether his sexual arrangements are universally applicable may be doubted; but his psychological insight into human character was really astonishing. There is no doubt that no community can hope to succeed that is not based on the best available psychological knowledge.

My wife joins with me in sending best wishes to Mrs. Morgan and yourself.

Yours very sincerely,
Aldous Huxley

TO ROBERT ALLERTON PARKER

San Cristobal, New Mexico
26 July 1937

Dear Mr. Parker,
I should have written before to thank you for the great pleasure which I have derived from reading your two books. The book on Noyes interested me enormously and convinced me more than ever that there are very important practical lessons to be learned from the Oneida experiment. I hope you will some day be able to make available the further evidence regarding the habits of the Oneida people which you told us that you possessed, but were not yet in a position to publish. There are a lot of things one would like to know: whether, for example, male continence led to a more frequent repetition of the act than was possible under a system of male incontinence; how long the average connection lasted; whether more than one connection was entered into at the same time, or whether the general rule was a succession of connections; how many persons the averagely attractive man or woman had established intimate relations with in the course of his stay in the community. And so on.

As for Father Divine,[6] he is simply hair-raising. The only consolation is that people like his followers are capable, as history shows, of being profoundly influenced by personages less fantastic than Father. St

[5] Richard Gregg (1885–1974). American author of *The Power of Non-violence* (1934), influenced by Gandhi, whose thought also influenced Huxley and Martin Luther King.
[6] Father Divine (George Baker) (1880–1965). Influential African-American preacher.

Peter Claver,[7] for example, had as great an influence over negro slaves as Father has over the oppressed in Harlem; and Claver did not have to call himself God or make use of Father's corybantic techniques. The trouble seems to be that the chances of getting a Claver are considerably smaller than the chances of a Father turning up.

Thank you once more for your very kind gift and for the pleasure which the books have given me. It would have been easy to spoil these fascinating subjects; but you have treated them with such skill, tact and intelligence that one gets everything that is to be got out of them.

> *Yours sincerely,*
> *Aldous Huxley*

TO EVA HERMANN

San Cristobal, New Mexico
1 August 1937

Dearest Eva,

How very sweet of you and Sybille to telegraph on my birthday! Except for one other wire, which combined birthday greetings with a demand for a preface I once rashly promised to write and which therefore cannot count as a purely disinterested manifestation of affection, it was the only birthday good wish that arrived on the day itself. I was greatly touched and pleased.

I am greatly enjoying America, which, I now realize, I simply hadn't seen before this occasion. What an extraordinary, queer, fascinating country! When I have finished the job of work I am busy on at the moment, I hope we shall set out on our explorations again and have a look at some more of it. From New York we went South, through Washington, Virginia, North Carolina—full of lovely places, where we stayed with very nice people—over the mountains of Tennessee, where we saw Morgan, the head of the T.V.A, thence through Alabama and Georgia, northern Florida, to New Orleans which is like a kind of negro Marseille; then through 1000 miles of Texas, mostly desert, into this astonishing country of huge mountains, dry plateaux, Indians, Mexicans and also, alas, of artists—for they abound in Santa Fe and Taos. However, we're far away on a mountain and take great pains to see as few of them as possible. One day you certainly ought to explore this Wild West—also the deep south—it's very well worth doing.

---

[7] St. Peter Claver (1581–1654). Spanish Jesuit missionary at Cartagena, the main slave mart of the New World.

I hope you're having a lovely summer—handsome young men, good bathing, fine weather, romantic moonlight. My love to Sybille. I will write to her soon.

Your affectionate,
Aldous

TO CLIVE BELL

San Cristobal, New Mexico
7 August 1937

My dear Clive,
In a letter just received from England today I hear that your son Julian[8] had been killed in Spain. There is no consolation; but at the risk of intruding I felt that I would like to tell you how deeply we both sympathize with Vanessa and yourself. It's a horrible business and confirms me in my conviction that there's no alternative to pacifism. Meanwhile I hope you're well and that poor Vanessa is not too much overwhelmed. Please give Maria's love, and mine.

Some day you should come and explore this very strange country. We drove right through the South and out across Texas to this Wild West, where we are spending the summers on a mountain, 9000 feet up, overlooking a desert that is completely empty except for an occasional village of Indians or Mexicans, reinforced in the summer by tourists hurrying along the highways in cars. You would find a great deal to astonish, interest and amuse you in the various parts of the country. I had no idea, till this summer, of the depths of its strangeness.

Greetings from an old friend,
Aldous

TO S. S. KOTELIANSKY

San Cristobal, New Mexico
27 August 1937

My dear Kot,
I have had your two letters and another from Mrs. Sullivan. Poor S.— what a horrible, painful business this illness has been. But it's better on the whole, I suppose, that he should have died now than lingered on,

---

[8] Julian Bell (1908–1937). English poet killed while driving an ambulance for the Republican side in the Spanish Civil War.

getting more and more helpless. The only redeeming feature of the whole affair was the equanimity and courage with which Sullivan himself faced his disaster.

About business. I have already sent to Mrs. S. the residue of the fund, which amounted to fifty-five pounds—not 70, owing to the fact that at S's request one payment of 20 pounds was made on one occasion and another of fifteen, to cover doctor's bills, I understood. There has been no news from Kruse and I don't imagine there will be. So we had better rule him out altogether. I think your scheme of getting a certain number of friends to subscribe to provide the boy with proper education is a good one. I will of course join in. I only hope that it may be possible to screw something out of the Civil List. Is there any prospect of Sullivan's books bringing in further royalties? Or did S. always get such an advance that there was no prospect of future sales bringing further revenue? If the advances weren't too large, the royalties should produce some small income. I wrote to the Science News Service editor, but have had no answer. Either the man is exceedingly uncivil; or else he is away on holiday.

I expect to be lecturing the whole of this autumn and shan't be back till after the new year. This being so, I think it will be best if you will organize the creation of the fund for the boy—the more so as, from about the beginning of October onwards, I shall be hurrying about this country without any fixed address, so that it will be rather difficult to correspond with me. My permanent address here, from which letters will always be forwarded, is care of Harper and Brothers, 49 East 33rd Street, New York City.

I hope your heart hasn't been troubling you too much this summer. We are all well, thank heaven; and I have just finished what is, I think, rather an important book discussing the sort of things we shall have to do if we want to make the improvements in the world that we all profess to desire. It covers all the ground from politics to philosophy.

Ever yours,
Aldous H.

TO FLORA STROUSSE

1425½ N. Crescent Heights Blvd.
Hollywood, Calif.
8 November 1937

Dear Starky,
Thank you for your letter and the kind invitation to stay. The latter I can't accept, alas, as I am travelling with Gerald Heard (with whom I am talking in dialogue form) and we are booked to stay with some member of the Bok family, I believe, for one night, after which, if we prolong the stay, with the Quakers at Pendle Hill. But I hope I shall have a chance of seeing you.

We were in New Mexico all Summer, staying in D. H. Lawrence's ranch, 9000 ft. up in the mountains, about 20 miles from Taos. Very lovely; and good for work. I finished a book, which is to come out in a week or so. Since mid-September we have been in California—very agreeable and amusing and fantastic and interesting. A place of virtualities, where absolutely anything might happen. Meanwhile almost everything is happening—movies, astronomy, sweated labour in the fields, philanthropy, scholarship, phony religions, real religions, all stirred together in a vast chaos in the midst of the most astonishing scenery, ranging from giant sequoias and rock peaks to date palms and red hot deserts.

I hope you've been well and happy.

Yours,
Aldous Huxley

TO MARY HUTCHINSON

The Belvedere
Baltimore
8 December 1937

A line, Dearest Mary, to wish you all a merry Christmas—scribbled in the train, so that it may be rather illegible, I fear. I am involved at the moment in that formidable affair, a lecture tour—involved more deeply than I ever intended to be; for Gerald Heard, with whom I had arranged to give a series of discussions, fell in the first snow a fortnight since and broke his arm; so that I have been left to carry on the programme single-handed. Which is a tiresome and boring business—the only compensation being that one makes a certain amount of money, tho' not enough, I find, to make up for the tediousness of the proceeding.

Winter is setting in here—very grim at moments, but with intervals of the most brilliant icy sunshine when the country is incredibly beautiful. It seems all the colder as we came direct from Southern California, where November is like a very propitious English June. That's a part of the world, I must say, that's very well worth getting to know. Fabulously beautiful to begin with—with every kind of landscape from high plateau desert and yet hotter sub-sea-level desert, with date palms, on the one hand to mountains of every shape and kind on the other: naked red-hot mountains like those of Arabia, or great Dolomite-like affairs alternating limestone crags with endless forests in which you come every now and then upon groves of sequoias anything from 2000 to 4000 years old. These big trees are really marvelous—the most impressive natural objects I have ever seen, with a strange character of their own, a kind of aged serenity immensely impressive and moving. Then of course there's the sea coast—barren in the southern part of the state where the land is almost a desert except where irrigated, when it takes on the extravagant fertility of an oasis—green further north, where you can have bits of country like Devonshire, and then the really fabulous spectacle of San Francisco. In the agricultural parts of the state are the orange groves—hundreds of miles of them, alternating with avocado pears, persimmons, walnuts, peaches, cotton and fields of lettuce and artichoke as large as English ducal estates. All strangely extravagant—and against this background a fermenting life that is still in a state of almost complete virtuality: not yet having become anything, still becoming. Los Angeles is a city of a million and a half, spread out over an area as large as London, with one motor car for every 2 people. Going out to dinner, one constantly has to travel thirty miles each way and frequently the house one goes to turns out to be perched on the top of a mountain with terraces and gardens and swimming pools scooped out of the slope and the most spectacular panoramas in every direction. And then the strangest variety of people—the movie world in its own little suburb of Hollywood—less fantastic than it was, owing to higher taxation, but still odd enough: with its fearful Jewish directors, and the actors, and the film writers, who make more money than any other kind of author and are generally speaking not authors at all. Our chief friends in that world were Charlie Chaplin and Anita Loos, both of whom are really very charming. We even had a glimpse of the ordinarily invisible Garbo, whom we met at Anita

Loos's looking infinitely ninetyish and perverse, like an Aubrey Beardsley drawing dressed up, for added perversity, in a very sporty Lesbian tailor-made. Not that she is exclusively a lesb. Rather omnifutuent—her present boyfriend being Stokowski the conductor, who is like Arthur Rubinstein without the qualities of high spirits and amusingness and with Rubinstein's flair for showmanship carried to greater lengths in his music.

Besides the movie people there are many other worlds—a strange man[9] with the finest collection of modern paintings I have ever seen in a private house and who spends all his spare time proving that Bacon was not only Shakespeare, but also a Rosicrucian, a follower of Isis, the incestuous lover of his mother and I don't know what else: then there is an academic world provided by two huge universities, The Institute of Technology, a number of small colleges and the Mount Wilson observatory. Mostly a bit dreary, but with high lights such as Hubble, the astronomer, with whom we spent several evenings, including one at Mount Wilson, looking through the hundred-inch telescope—a really astonishing experience.

Since leaving California (which we did separately—Maria by car, I by train in company with Gerald Heard) most of my contacts have been medical, partly owing to Gerald's accident, partly by mere coincidence; and I have been seeing fascinating and, I believe, very important work in psychology carried out in Chicago and on cancer at Fort Wayne.

This tiresome lecture business goes on through January. I hope that by that time Gerald will be able to stump the country with me. After that I expect we shall be setting out for Europe; unless by some miracle the movie people wished to make use of a comic scenario I wrote while at Hollywood. The only concrete offer I received while there was to adapt the Forsyte Saga: but tho' I might have earned vast sums in the process, the prospect of living for several months with the ghost of poor John Galsworthy was too formidable. I simply couldn't face it!

Our love to the family. I hope that all has been going well with you. How is Jack? and Jeremy?[1] and Barbara? And Victor? And above all yourself, dear Mary?

Your affectionate,
Aldous

---

[9] Walter Arensberg (1878–1954). American collector of modernist art. In 1937, with his wife Louise, he established the Francis Bacon Foundation in Los Angeles.
[1] Jeremy Hutchinson (b. 1915) son of Mary and Jack (St. John) Hutchinson. Now Lord Hutchinson of Lullington, a Liberal-Democrat member of the House of Lords.

TO EVELYN SCOTT[2]

The Willard Hotel
Washington, DC
8 January 1938

Dear Miss Scott,
I think my last book furnishes a sufficiently clear statement to the effect that I am not a believer in the methods and ideology of communism. It has been described in some left wing quarters as a work serving to prepare the minds of its readers to accept fascism—a diagnosis which mildly astonishes me, but which anyhow shows that I can no longer be regarded by the orthodox as being within the fold. What you say of the machinations of communist journalists does not surprise me. I have seen evidence of similar activity in France. It's a curiously squalid business.

Yours sincerely,
Aldous Huxley

TO ELLEN VAN VOLKENBERG

Royal York Hotel
Toronto
25 January 1938

I found your letter of January 15 at the hotel, when I passed through New York City en route for Toronto, last Sunday. I am writing this in the train—hence the scrawl. It will, I fear, be impossible to establish contact in the near future, as I shall be in New York only for a day, every moment of which is taken up with appointments. This being so, I must leave the question of a meeting till a later visit. Meanwhile I should suggest your getting in touch with the War Resisters League whose Secretary is Dr. Jessie Wallace Hughan (I forget her address: but she is in the phone book). They do good work here and have some excellent people on their board. A good booklet on the subject is Richard Gregg's "Training for Peace." Gregg doesn't live in New York, but at South Natick, near Boston—a very remarkable man, incidentally.

Yours sincerely,
Aldous Huxley

---

[2] Evelyn Scott (1893–1963). American novelist best known for *The Wave* (1929).

TO EMMA GOLDMAN

Rhinebeck, N.Y.
28 January 1938

Dear Miss Goldman,
Your letter of January 11th has reached me here in America after some delay. The events of the last few years have made it clear so far as I am concerned, that the libertarian ideal for which you have fought so long is the only satisfactory and even the only *realistic* political creed for anyone who is not a conservative reactionary.

With regard to the S.I.A. [*Solidaridad Internacional Antifascista*], I am enclosing a small contribution to its funds. Being absent from England, I think it best not to become a sponsor of the organisation, in as much as I shall be unable to do anything to help and I don't think it's satisfactory to be just a sleeping partner.

Yours sincerely,
Aldous Huxley

On the strength of an initial acceptance in February of Huxley's film script "Success," the Huxleys decide not to return to England but instead to leave Dairy Cottage and drive, via Frieda Lawrence's ranch, to Hollywood, where they rent a home on North Laurel Avenue. They move to North Linden Drive in Beverly Hills in July. Aldous becomes ill with bronchitis and has recurrent health problems for the rest of the year. With the help of Anita Loos, he secures a contract with MGM in July to write a screenplay, Madame Curie. *Receiving $15,000 for his eight weeks of work on the script, he considers himself "enormously overpaid." In October, Huxley moves back to Hollywood, at 1320 North Crescent Heights Boulevard, and in November he explores the Bates method for improving vision. By December he notices some improvement in his eyesight. In January/February he is at work on the California-set novel* After Many a Summer Dies the Swan, *and from April 1939 to February 1942 the Huxleys reside at 701 Amalfi Drive, Pacific Palisades, across the street from Greta Garbo. In August 1939 he begins work for MGM, initially for $2,500 per week, on the screenplay of* Pride and Prejudice. *It is released in August 1940 with Huxley's name in the credits.* After Many a Summer *is published in October 1939.*

TO J. WILLIAM LLOYD[3]

710 N. Linden Drive
Beverly Hills, California
4 July 1938

Dear Mr. Lloyd,

I have been reading with great interest and pleasure the book *Eneres*, which you so kindly inscribed for me.

I am particularly interested in what you say about cosmic consciousness. As I understand it, you take the same view of the matter as Bucke,[4] who lumped all his recorded phenomena under one head. But I am inclined to believe that this is illegitimate and that there are two fundamentally different experiences which ought not to be called by the same name. Such experiences as Whitman's—what Herman Melville calls "the all-feeling"—are extensions of the ordinary forms of consciousness. Whereas such experiences as "Nirvana" are experiences on an entirely different level of consciousness. Man is not a dual being, but tripartite; classifiable as body, soul, spirit. Whitman's type of "cosmic consciousness" takes place, it seems to me, on the second level—is an extension of the ordinary activities of the "soul." "Nirvana" is not an experience of the "soul" and has no reference to the cosmos as we normally apprehend it. "Cosmic consciousness," is probably a relatively common phenomenon which, as you say, may occur spontaneously. "Spiritual consciousness"—to give a separate name to the other phenomenon—never occurs spontaneously, but only as the result of the systematic weaning of the attention away from the cosmos as we ordinarily know it—a killing of all cravings, in the words of Buddha. The eightfold path describes Right Attention and Right Meditation or ecstasy. Right Attention is directed to the world of the "spirit," and is accompanied by a turning away from ordinary "mental" and "psychic" experiences, even in their most exalted forms. Right Ecstasy occurs on the "Spiritual Plane" and not on the "cosmic plane" apprehended by the "soul." All these words are in the highest degree suspect: but one is forced to use them for lack of better ones, and because the available evidence, it seems to me, indicates that they do actually stand for definite and distinct psychological realities.

[3] J. William Lloyd (1857–1940). *Eneres* was first published in 1929.
[4] Richard M. Bucke (1837–1902). Friend of Walt Whitman and author of *Cosmic Consciousness*.

Once more, let me thank you for your great kindness in sending me your book.

Yours sincerely,
Aldous Huxley

TO T. S. ELIOT

710 N. Linden Dr.
Beverly Hills, Calif.
12 July 1938

My dear Tom,

I have given two friends of ours a letter of introduction to you. They are Edwin Corle,[5] who is a promising young novelist, and his wife, Helen Freeman,[6] the actress. I think you will find them a very pleasant and intelligent couple.

This finds me like stout Cortez, gazing on the Pacific and about, in all human probability (which is not by any means certainty, since the picture industry is strictly sub-human), to prepare the life of Madame Curie for the screen. Which should be rather an interesting job, if only the sub-humans will leave one reasonably in peace—a most unlikely contingency, alas.

I've just been reading a very remarkable book which, if you don't already know it, I venture to recommend, in spite of its 800 pages—Korzybski's[7] *Science and Sanity*, which is by far the best thing on "semantics" and the problem of the relations between words and things, ever produced.

I hope you flourish. We do, I am glad to say—though I still carry about with me the infective aftermath of a mild pneumonia that got me in the spring.

Ever yours affectionately,
Aldous H.

---

[5] Edwin Corle (1906–1956). Novelist and essayist, who wrote about Native American life in the early twentieth century.
[6] Helen Freeman (1886–1960). Played the queen of Spain in Bob Hope's *Monsieur Beaucaire*, 1946.
[7] Alfred Korzybski (1879–1950). Developed a theory of general semantics.

TO JEHANNE NEVEUX

710 N. Linden Drive
Beverly Hills, Calif.
14 July 1938

Chère Jehanne,
Ton télégramme nous a fait du plaisir et en même temps nous a déçus—
déçus parce qu'il se peut que tu ne viennes pas, fait du plaisir à cause
des raisons de cette déception. En attendant, puis-je te demander une
aide? J'ai besoin de documents. D'abord les meilleures notices
nécrologiques sur Mme Curie dans les journaux et les revues littéraires
et scientifiques. Puis la biographie de Pierre Curie que Mme C. a fait
après la mort de son mari. Peut-être aussi quelques bonnes notices
nécrologiques sur Pierre Curie. Il existe des personnes qui font des
recherches de cette espèce professionellement; donc ne t'embête pas à
compulser de vieux dossiers. Fais acheter les vieux numéros de revues,
etc. si possible; fais copier les passages significatifs où l'achat n'est pas
possibles. Je paierai naturellement tous les frais. Ce que je veux surtout
ce sont des reminiscences personelles sur Pierre Curie et Mme C. Le
côté scientifique, on peut très bien l'étudier ici. Si pourtant tes amis sci-
entifiques connaissent un bon livre sur le côté scientifique, tu peux me
l'acheter et l'envoyer pour supplémenter ce que j'ai ici. D'ailleurs, le
côté scientifique occupera, forcément un minimum de place dans le
film. Si tu as le temps, tu pourras aussi faire, ou faire faire, quelques
photos des endroits mentionnés dans le livre de Eve Curie: la rue
L'Homond, ou se trouvait le laboratoire, les diverses rues que Mme
Curie a habitée avant et après son marriage. Pour les photos rien ne
presse; mais j'aimerais avoir les notices nécrologiques etc. sur M. et
Mme C. aussitôt que possible. Envoie-les au fur et à mesure quand tu
les trouve. Rien ne viendra trop tôt et rien trop tard.
Ils ont l'air de vouloir que je commence avant la fin du mois. J'at-
tends le contrat d'un jour à l'autre. Evidemment avec ces imbeciles on
ne sait jamais ce qui se passera. Mais il est bien probable que je devrai
bientôt commencer. C'est pourquoi que je serai content d'avoir ces doc-
uments aussi tôt que possible.
Mère vient d'arriver du Mexique—en bonne santé, mais plus sourde
et plus emphatique que jamais, hélas. Tendresses de nous tous. Af-
fectueusement,

Aldous

PS J'aurais besoin aussi de quelques notes sur Becquerel. Tâche de dé-
couvrir s'il existe un livre—biographie ou mémoire—qui donne une

*impression d'ensemble de la vie scientifique en France au commence-
ment de ce siècle. La vie de Henri Poincaré, peut-être?*

[Dear Jeanne,
Your telegram both pleased and at the same time disappointed us—disappointment because it may be that you can't come, pleasure owing to
the cause of this disappointment [she was about to remarry]. In the
meantime, may I ask a favour? I need some documents. First, the best
obituaries of Mme Curie from the papers and literary and scientific journals. Then the biography of Pierre Curie that Mme C. wrote after the
death of her husband. Maybe also some good obituaries of Pierre Curie.
There are people who do this sort of research professionally: so don't
trouble yourself consulting these old papers. Buy the old numbers of
these journals, etc., if possible; have the relevant passages copied where
purchase is not possible. Naturally I will pay for all the expenses. What
I want above all are personal reminiscences about Pierre and Mme Curie.
The scientific side I can study well enough here. If, however, your scientific friends know of a good book which covers the scientific side, you
could buy it and send it to me as a supplement to what I have here. Besides, the scientific side will naturally take up a minimal amount of the
film. If you get the time, you could also take or have taken some photos
of places mentioned in Eve Curie's book: La rue Lhomond, site of the
lab, the various streets where Mme Curie lived before and after her marriage. There's no rush for the photos; but I would like to have the obituaries on M et Mme Curie as soon as possible. Send them as they come
when you find them. Nothing will arrive too soon or too late.

They seem to want me to start before the end of the month. I am
waiting from one day to the other for the contract. Evidently, with
these imbeciles, one never knows what will happen. But it is very possible that I will have to start soon.

Mère just got back from Mexico—in good health but deafer and
more bombastic than ever, alas.

PS I also need some notes on Becquerel[8]—try to find out if there is a
book—biography or memoir, which gives an overview of the scientific
life in France at the turn of the century. The life of Henri Poincaré,[9]
perhaps?]

---

[8] Henri Becquerel (1852–1908). Shared the 1903 Nobel Prize for Physics with the Curies.
[9] Henri Poincaré (1854–1912). French mathematician, astronomer, and philosopher of science.

1938

TO JEANNE NEVEUX

710 N. Linden Drive
Beverly Hills, Calif.
4 août 1938

Chère Jehanne,
Je te remercie de ta lettre. Nous avons été si attristés par la nouvelle qu'elle apportait. Qu'en dire? Rien—excepte que pour tout ce que nous puissions faire, tu peux compter sur nous. Viens si tu peux ou si cela t'arrange. Mais evidemment, si tu penses que c'est mieux de rester à Paris pour le moment, il faut rester. Mon contrat demande que je travaille sur Mme Curie pendant 8 semaines: il se peut, cependant, qu'on aura besoin de moi pour le travail ultérieur. Pour le moment je n'en sais rien. Si l'occasion se present de gagner beaucoup d'argent dans un délai assez court, je la prendrai—pour avoir ensuite l'assurance de pouvoir vivre pendant quelque temps sans trop me préoccuper de travaux immédiats.

En attendant, merci de t'être occupée des articles, etc. En ce qui concerne les photos je crois qu'il sera plus sage de procéder tranquillement sans invoquer le titre de cinéaste official—d'autant plus que je viens de découvrir ici une bonne source de documents photographiques. Je n'ai aucun besoin de photos de la maison en Bretagne—puisque je n'aurai pas le temps dans un film de 90 minutes de mentionner ses vacances d'après-guerre.

Des vues de la rue autour de la Sorbonne et de l'Ecole de Physique de la rue Lhomond me seront utiles—ainsi que les approches de la maison du Boulevard Kellermann.

Je t'embrasse bien tendrement.

Aldous

[Thank you for your letter. We are so saddened by the news it contains. What to say? Nothing—except that for anything we can do you can count on us. Come if you can. But evidently if you think that it's better to stay in Paris for the time being, you must. My contract states that I have to work on Mme Curie for 8 weeks. It's possible, however, that they might need me for follow-up work. For the moment I am in the dark. If the occasion presents itself whereby I can shortly earn lots of money, in a short time, I will take it—in order to have the security of being able to live for several months without having to worry too much about immediate jobs.

Meanwhile, thanks for taking care of those articles, etc. As for the photos, I think it would be wiser to proceed slowly without having to invoke the name of the official director—especially since I have just discovered a good source of photographic documents here. I will have no need of photos of the house in Brittany—since I won't have the time in a film of 90 minutes to mention the post war vacations.

Views of the streets around the Sorbonne and of the School of Physics, Lhomond Street would be helpful to me, as well as the approaches to the Blvd Kellermann house.]

TO NAOMI MITCHISON

1320 N. Crescent Heights Blvd.
L.A., Calif.
8 October 1938

Dearest Naomi,

I have just got your letter—as despairing as most letters at the moment and as most conversations, for that matter, even here, at this distance. The position during the crisis time was such, it seems to me, that there was nothing Chamberlain could do that was not morally wrong and immediately or potentially disastrous. It is the story of the Sybilline books. The longer a bad job like the post-war international situation is left, the higher the price that has to be paid in order to settle it. In the end the price to be paid is practically infinite and there is noting not-fatal that can any longer be done. I still think that, in the existing circumstances, Chamberlain's choice between evils was the better one. It seems to me better that the five million or more people who would have been killed in a war should have their lives prolonged if only by a short time. It seems to me better (a) because life in itself is valuable and nobody has any right to decree the cutting short of millions of the lives of his fellow men, (b) because it is theoretically possible, albeit psychologically improbable, that Chamberlain may be able to use the time gained to work for a more lasting solution by non-violent means, (c) because even in the lives of people who are no more active than Mr Micawber things do sometimes just "turn up" and the potentialities of accident, even of happy accident, are enormous, (d) because most people, as I have had experience of this, would prefer to be alive under a tyranny to being dead under a democracy in process of being transformed into a tyranny by war or revolution!—these are not very heroic sentiments but, heroic or not, they are commonly held and I believe that people's wishes in a matter so important to them as this should be consulted; for the more heroic spirits tyranny is intolerable; but after all there are always escapes, through suicide, through revolt and through that liberation of the soul which has been preached by Buddhists, Christians and Stoics alike and which can be achieved. It may be of course—and after all practically every philosopher has said so, except during the last two and a half centuries, when people believed in the existence of human progress as an analogue to technological progress—it may be that this kind of Epictetan, Spinozan, Taulerian liberty is the only kind of liberty attainable by human beings. It may be that, given people with ordinary, unsublimated human appetites, one is mad to expect that any decent political régime can be more than transitory.

As a matter of historical fact, the only tolerably decent political régimes that have lasted any great length of time have been theocracies like India and Egypt in which people accepted the philosphical traditions and social habits current in their neighbourhood as though they were of divine origin, and where, in consequence, a crust of custom had formed, guaranteeing a certain amount of reciprocal forbearance and making harsh acts seem equitable, because traditionally sanctioned. As Bertie Russell points out in his new book on Power, any society which indulges in searching criticism of hallowed beliefs and institutions automatically breaks through that crust of decency and prepares the way for the use of naked and entirely cynical power. The political cynicism of the fifteenth and sixteenth centuries followed the criticism of the humanists (the spirit of Erasmus is the head of a process of which Machiavelli and Cesare Borgia are the inevitable tails); the frightfulness of the French Revolution and the Napoleonic wars follow the criticisms of the Encyclopaedists; our own frightfulness follows the termite labours of psychologists, novelists, logisticians and so forth gnawing away the axioms on which nineteenth century life was founded. There has never been a period in history, as far as I know, when a society has succeeded in combining, for any considerable length of time free criticism of traditions with political decency; for political decency has always been bound up with the acceptance of the traditions, and the end of one has always meant the end of the other. It looks as if the same thing were happening now as has happened so often in the past. These considerations make me extremely doubtful of the possibility of achieving anything by means of large-scale political movements. To my mind the most promising economico-social experiments being made at present are experiments along the lines of those conducted by Borsodi and others for the purpose of improving the techniques of subsistence living. Democracy and personal liberty are possible only where a considerable proportion of the population are economically independent, where neither plutocrats nor the state can bring economic pressure to bear on them. True, in a society where the crust of custom has collapsed, neither plutocrats nor above all the state will hesitate to bring naked military pressure to bear; so that even this experiment seems probably foredoomed to failure. Still, it must be tried, if only because it offers some hope of providing little islands of existence for isolated communities of refugees from the general cataclysm. For the rest one must fall back on the cultivation of the art of inner liberty. There is nothing else.

I moulder along quietly here, having been condemned by the doctors to a régime of twelve hours rest per day, owing to the after-effects of a pneumonia last spring, which I haven't yet been able to throw off. In the intervals I work—did what they call a "treatment" of the life of Mme Curie for the film and am now at work on a kind of novel which attempts not only to describe human antics, but also to explain them in terms of a general theory of antics which tells a kind of story and at the same time tries to analyse the assumptions we make every time a story is told; which builds with verbal and anecdotal bricks that are taken to pieces in the process of being laid. An attempt will be made to synthesize on a more acceptable psychological and linguistic-philosophical basis. I have not got very far and it will take a long time, and perhaps in a world like this the effort will be completely wasted. Still, I think the task is intrinsically important and the attempting of it is the only thing I'm qualified to do; so tinker away at it.

Ever yours,
Aldous

TO EUGENE F. SAXTON

1320 N. Crescent Heights Blvd.
L.A. Cal.
21 December 1938

My dear Gene,
This is to wish you all a happy Christmas and New Year, and to thank you, rather belatedly, I fear, for the books you sent me some weeks ago.

Of these I have read *The School for Dictators*, which is full of good things—though I regretted Silone's wholly unnecessary effort to introduce a comic, satirical note by means of his fictional characters. It contributes nothing; on the contrary, it takes away from the value of an acute politico-psychological discussion. Chateaubriand we read aloud and much enjoyed. The man is an awful warning to men of letters—for he is, *in excelsis*, what all of them are potentially and so easily become in practice. Maria read the Balalanoff book and communicated extracts which seemed very interesting; but I have not been able to go through it, as I am doing very little reading at present, owing to the fact that I am taking a treatment for the eyes, which consists in a fundamental re-education of the sight. Some results are already apparent, and I hope that I shall get further with perseverance. Meanwhile I am reading only as a visual exercise, without glasses.

The book advances, slowly; and I begin to see the full scope of the thing, what its structure will have to be and exactly where the stuff I have already written will have to take its place in the whole. It should begin to look like something in a month or two.

Edna Millay was here recently, reading her poems (the most astonishingly accomplished performance!) and we have had some pleasant hours together. She is a very fascinating creature.

All our love and wishes to the family.

> *Ever yours,*
> *Aldous H.*

PS Who should I run into casually, in a shop, the other day but old George Doran—cheerful and well, but piano and somehow shrunken. The last time I saw him was in his glory as [W. R.] Hearst's ambassador in London!

TO ROGER CAILLOIS[1]

> *701 S. Amalfi Drive*
> *Pacific Palisades, California*
> *29 October 1939*

Dear Sir,

Thank you for your letter and the article from the *NRF* [*Nouvelle Revue Française*]. I agree with many of your criticisms of Benda; but my

---

[1] Roger Caillois (1913–1978). French writer and anti-Nazi who lived in Argentina during World War II.

grounds for criticizing Benda's position are not the same as yours. For me, a *clerc* is one engaged in the attempt to "change the focus of consciousness"—to transcend the personal and strictly human point of view for a new one, founded on direct experience (analogous to the non-rational, immediate experience of sense perception) of the reality about which all the founders of religion, all the mystics of East and West, have been talking for the past 3000 years. To talk of professors or artists as *clercs* seems to me absurd: it is also absurd to talk about the political role of the *clerc*—because the moment a mystic touches politics he is utterly destroyed. (Witness Père Joseph, who started as a genuine mystic, who then used his influence with Richelieu in the hope of "doing good" and who did enormous evil and became convinced at the end of his life—with very good reason!—that he was damned.) The strictly human world—the world of politics—is a world, as all the mystics and founders of religion have always insisted, incapable of manifesting good, intrinsically self-destructive, capable only of getting up to a certain point, then inevitably foredoomed (owing to the nature of human passions) to suicidal collapse. The business of the *clerc* is to achieve more-than-personal consciousness—and in doing so, he does his duty by the world. For (as all the mystics and founders of religion have once more insisted) such people are "the salt of the earth," whose presence prevents the body politic from decay and whose absence is somehow fatal to it. The organised church has, of course, nothing to do with these people—merely exploits the prestige which the mystics who happen to be connected with it, lend to it.

With regard to signing a declaration about Hitler—I regret that I cannot do this, as I do not feel that politics (except such politics as are dictated by the need to "make the world safe for mystical experience") are my affair.

> *Yours very sincerely,*
> *Aldous Huxley*

TO NAOMI MITCHISON

701 S. Amalfi Drive
Pacific Palisades, Calif.
4 December 1939

My dear Naomi,
Many thanks for your interesting letter. The book [*After Many a Summer Dies the Swan*] is, of course, a fable, with characters more or less

stylized from near-realism in the case of some to near-symbolism in the case of Obispo, who is quite frankly and openly Mephistopheles. As for the problems of bondage and enlightenment, normality in the characters presented versus abnormality and the other points you mention—here are a few random reflections.

Nobody, of course, has ever been in any doubt about the immense agreeableness of Human Bondage, in Spinoza's phrase. In the classic struggle between the passions and the reason, the flesh-devil-world and God, it is almost invariably the former who win. The point which every philosopher, moralist and religious teacher has always made is that the pleasures of Human Bondage are correlated with more than balancing pains, both for the individuals concerned and for the societies of which they are members. The sort of thing that is happening at present (which is the sort of thing that, with occasional partial and local respites) has been happening for the last several thousand years—only a bit more so—is the sort of thing that happens when human beings live in Bondage. There is a brand of genially humanistic *weltanschauung* which is enormously optimistic about men and women as they are—in the "unregenerate" or "once born" condition, to use the language of religion. This philosophy is summed up by the phrase that Steinbeck is always using in his *Grapes of Wrath*: A man gotta do what he gotta do—the assumption being that, if he lives in accordance with the dictates of his nature, everything will be all right. What Steinbeck fails to see—and this is what vitiates the whole thesis of the book—is that what a man gotta do isn't always just getting drunk, copulating, being kind to the children and occasionally, losing the temper. Some men are different—not interested in that sort of simple pleasure, but in something more rarefied. The optimists who say that a man gotta do what he gotta do forget that there are lots of people who are like Hitler and Stalin, and who feel that what they gotta do is to dominate their fellows by every means, fair and foul, in their power. The present state of the world is a product of the fact that the "once born" think they are right in doing what they gotta do.

As for my characters being abnormal and insane—of course they are, for the good reason that extreme cases can be used to illustrate a general state of things more effectively and briefly than average cases. It would be quite easy to point the same moral, using, nice, ordinary people with a normal family life; but it would take longer to demonstrate the way in which what they imagine to be their sanity, their decency, their idealism are related to the large-scale criminal lunacy which is manifestly dominating the world today. Nice, ordinary people with a normal family life are the pillars of society; but society behaves like a criminal lunatic. The reason, it is to be presumed, is that the nice, ordinary person with a normal family life is not quite so sane as he thinks he is. Which is, of course, what every philosopher and religious teacher has been saying for the last three thousand years. The nice, ordinary people with normal family lives are the Scribes and Pharisees—are the people who build up our social structures, but always build them with bricks of dynamite, so that they invariably end by blowing themselves up. In the case of the abnormals, whom I have assembled in this book, Bondage takes an obvious form; in the case of the nice, ordinary people with family lives it shows itself more subtly. But at bottom it consists in the same fundamental craving for excitement—an excitement obtainable in many forms: through addictions, through organized sentiments, through possessions, through pretensions and lust for power. Bertie Russell remarked long ago that men would rather die than think—and, as war demonstrates—do die rather than think. They would also die rather than give up personal excitement. The nice, ordinary person with a normal family life likes the pleasurable excitements associated with patriotism, for example; therefore inevitably, he gets the personal tribulations and the social catastrophes associated with war. There is no way out of it except some technique for training people to dispense with excitements and personality—in other words, obtain Freedom. Demonstrably, very few people want Freedom. The overwhelming majority prefer Bondage. Consequently, it seems very unlikely that societies at large will ever rise much above their present level, when the best that they can expect is two or three generations of relative quiet, prosperity and "moral progress," followed by a relapse.

The philosophy of Buddhism, which is the most thoroughgoing and consistent of all the religious philosophies is merely an extended utilitarianism. It points out that, if you want something appreciably superior to the human activities of past and present, Bondage must be given up for Freedom. It further points out that, when Freedom has been attained by appropriate exercise of the personality (just as skill in piano playing can be attained by appropriate exercise of the muscles and aesthetic sensibilities) the Free person will be, to a large extent, master of his circumstances and independent of his environment. (It is worth remarking that the term "Progress" in evolution is applied to the gradual achievement of increasing independence from the environment). Having said this, the Buddhist philosophy goes on to state that, as a matter of empirical fact, very few people care for Freedom enough to take the trouble to attain it. (Christianity asserts the same.) Therefore, it says, there seems little likelihood of the world at large becoming appreciably better than it has been. It has, of course, nothing to say against Socialism (whatever that abstraction may mean).

On the contrary, it admits that the problem of "Right Livelihood" is of the utmost importance and welcomes any change in social arrangements calculated to improve the individual's chances of delivering himself from Bondage. Our particular problem is to discover whether such desirable changes in social arrangements can be carried very far in terms of the existing social patterns of urbanism, mass production, indiscriminate technological advances and the general *abrutissement* of human minds through such devices as the radio, press and advertising. To my mind, this seems highly improbable, and I feel that any effective reform is likely to come only along the lines suggested by Borsodi and his fellow decentralists.

We come now to the question of sex. I think I made one of the characters in the book point out that there is no normal sexual behaviour in the sense that there is normal digestion. There are sexual behaviours adapted to different kinds of individual purposes and different kinds of ideals. If the purpose is to achieve Freedom or Enlightenment, the appropriate sexual behaviour will have to be different from what it would be if the purpose were to be a nice, ordinary person with a normal family life, and *a fortiori* different from what it would be, if the purpose were to be an animal, a playboy or a diabolist. You takes your choice and you pays your money—and in many cases the amount you pays is very considerable.

Next is the curious distinction you draw between "economics" and "psychology." I find this hard to understand. Economics don't exist in nature; they are made by men. Therefore they are products of human psychology. To speak of economics as of something outside human beings is like speaking, as the eighteenth-century liberals spoke, as though Kings and Priests were beings apart from the rest of the human race and as if everything would automatically go right when Kings and Priests, or Economics, were removed or altered. The real problem is to discover how and why Kings, Priests and Economics came into existence and with what features of the behaviour of nice, ordinary people with normal family lives they are correlated. Incidentally, it seems difficult to believe that the improvement of the economic lot of the masses, though obviously enormously desirable for a great many rea-

sons, will solve any of the fundamental problems of individual or social behaviour. There are a lot of prosperous people in the world at the
present time; but I have never noticed that there was any necessary cor-
relation between prosperity and virtue, contentment, freedom from
worry (no peasants ever get angina pectoris or coronary thrombosis),
control over circumstances.

Well, so much for discussion. As for news—there is little enough news
here—beyond the, to me, very interesting fact that I am taking a system
of eye training that has already permitted me to give up spectacles for
reading, that has caused and is still causing a regression of the scar tissue
on my eyes (something which several doctors have assured me is "scientifically impossible"). I have hopes that if I go on patiently and long
enough, I shall get back to something like normality. Incidentally, the
training fits in, in a most curious and interesting way, with the whole
Buddhist, Hindu and Mystical-Christian thesis that it is possible, by appropriate methods, to get considerable control over circumstances—that
even physical Bondage can in some measure be overcome.

Gervas[2] was here a few days ago, very nice and curiously matured
since I last saw him. He expects to get off to Kenya as soon as may be,
feeling that there is some hope there of doing valuable work: for in
Kenya, one has a kind of *tabula rasa* to work on—whereas the obsessions
and hallucinations of Europe make effective work extremely difficult.

I've not heard from Lewis for some time and am very sorry to hear
that he's not in a good way. Meanwhile, what course is the nightmare
going to take next? God knows.

Our best love to you.

> *Your affectionate,*
> *Aldous*

TO JULIAN HUXLEY

> *701 S. Amalfi Drive*
> *Pacific Palisades, Cal.*
> *12 December 1939*

My dear J,
Thanks for your letters.

Arrangements made to date are these. A dinner here one night with
Edwin and Grace Hubble, Anita Loos and her brother, who runs one

[2] Gervas Huxley (1894–1971). Huxley's cousin and fellow pupil at Hillside Preparatory
School, he was the husband of the novelist Elspeth Huxley.

of the largest medical insurance groups in the country, Charlie Chaplin if he is not working on his film, possibly Bertie Russell, if he is here.

Then, on Wednesday the twentieth, you are to lunch, or otherwise see Walter Wanger,[3] who will doubtless have such film people with him as might be of use. Here is a word of warning. Don't involve yourself with such people as Goldwyn and Mayer. Goldwyn is just a showman, whose sole interest will be to get himself photographed with you. Mayer is even less satisfactory; for he is one of those big Jewish executives in this place, whose behaviour is directly responsible for the mounting anti-semitism so conspicuous here. He wants to be known as the man with the highest salary in the country; therefore insists on being paid a wage of two million dollars, despite the fact that, owing to income tax, he would have just as much to spend if he accepted much less and gave the difference to his employees.

His attitude towards employees is that of the American Industrialist of the eighteen-nineties. Recently, too, at the height of the Jewish persecutions in Germany, he decided to become a sporting gentleman and purchased fifty-one race horses. To make matters worse, he is the kind of Pecksniff who always associates himself conspicuously with Causes. Recently, when Dr Buchman[4] was here (they call him locally "the Christian Louis B. Mayer") he gave a luncheon for him, made a ridiculous speech and then addressed a monster mass meeting of Groupers on moral rearmament. The sole result of trying to make use of him would be to make your movement stink in a great many nostrils. So I strongly advise you to keep clear. Incidentally, I don't think you will get much out of any of these movie people. Wanger is better than most—but muddled. Capra (whom I could get you in touch with, if you liked, through Ronald Coleman, who is a very decent fellow) is very well meaning, but a bit stupid outside his speciality. His "Mr. Smith" struck me as very pathetic—all the more so as it was one of the few "idealistic" efforts made by the movies. All it amounted to was the sentiment that, if everybody were nice, how nice everybody would be! No smallest effort to explain why everybody wasn't nice, nor how they could be persuaded to be a bit nicer. In general, any kind of popular propaganda through films, articles or radio must be in the nature of things unsatisfactory, for the good reason that such propaganda, in order to be popular, must be enormously simplified and abbreviated—

---

[3] Walter Wanger (1894–1968). Hollywood producer.
[4] Frank Buchman (1878–1961). American evangelist and founder of the Oxford Group, later, Moral Rearmament.

which means that it must falsify the facts, which are invariably very complex. This is the great paradox of all propaganda: that if it is to be swallowed by large numbers, it must be more of less false to facts, therefore more or less mischievous. I don't myself know what the way out of the difficulty is. Another weakness of such media of propaganda as the films, radio, press and so forth is the fact that there are so many films, broadcasts, articles etc, that people become blunted to the stimulation and no longer react to any given piece of propaganda, however ably presented, except as yet another device for giving them a momentary "kick." That is why I have very little hope of any one achieving much by these methods—unless, of course, you are a dictator and can prevent people from seeing, reading or listening to anything except your own outpourings. In which case the effect is achieved rather by the silence regarding what is censored than by what is actually said—by negative propaganda rather than by positive. But this cannot be done under democratic institutions, so that any piece of propaganda made under such institutions is liable to be stultified by the multiplicity of stimulants going on all around.

About Bird[5]—I don't think you need bother about him. He is one of those amiable, extraverted, Babbit-educators who are marvellously good at collecting money from the rich, making speeches to chambers of commerce and rushing about. The Hubbles, to whom we spoke on the phone about your coming, thought it would be best to leave him out altogether.

I will see what can be done about Disney. Meanwhile I hope you realize what distances in this town are. Disney, for example, is about twenty miles from here; Pasadena about thirty-odd; Wanger about seventeen; Universal about twenty. You will probably be about six hours of each day in a car. (Incidentally, I hope Matthew will be here so that he can drive you round; we will hire an extra conveyance, as ours will be needed to get me back and forth to the studio where I am afraid I may have to be working for a good deal of the time. However, it will arrange itself all right in some way, though with considerable expense of time and energy on your part, I am afraid.)

Gerald is here—that is to say, he is fifteen miles off, on top of a hill, without a car!—and we will arrange something with him. I don't imagine he'll want to come to our dinner; but we can probably fix another time.

[5] Remsen Bird. President of Occidental College, 1921–1946. He was the model for Dr. Mulge, the unctuous university president in *After Many a Summer Dies the Swan*.

Miss Black has telephoned, and we are leaving arrangements open, so that you can fix a time when you know more certainly about other appointments.

I wish you could have stopped longer, so that your stay could have been a little more peaceful, less of a crowded hour of glorious life. I suppose there is no hope of persuading you to linger?

Please remember us very kindly to the Evanses. Love from us both.

Your affectionate,
Aldous

TO RAYMOND MORTIMER

701 S. Amalfi Drive
Pacific Palisades
15 December 1939

My dear Raymond,
Your letter to Maria came today and gave us both so much pleasure. I'm glad indeed to hear that things are not as bad as they might be. I wish it were possible to imagine what sort of a world was going to emerge from this extraordinary and nightmarish Alice-in-Wonderland activity. My brother Julian, whom we are expecting to see in a few days, seems to anticipate a federated Europe, flowing with beer and skittles: but the difficulty is to discover enough people, among politicians and the masses of men-in-streets, who want a federated Europe enough to wish to give up the habits, sentiments, and, for some, economic advantages associated with national sovereignty.

I was interested in what you said about my book. The "powder," as you call it, is something which obviously nobody will swallow who feels satisfied with what a tolerably comfortable human life can offer. In some curious way I have always felt that it couldn't give enough—that even its best offerings, like the finest works of art, the most ingenious speculations, the intensest pleasures, were inadequate. Nothing now seems to me adequate except freedom, in the psychological sense—the kind of consciousness that is intensely aware of things, but is in no way dependent upon them, in no way at their mercy. The difficulties in the way of achieving freedom are obviously enormous; but the attempt seems to be worth making as nothing else is worth doing. Incidentally, it seems clear that the ordinary condition of non-freedom is a condition of self-styled suffocation, and that the pleasures associated with it are the heads of a sixpence, whose reverse is the sort of thing that is happening now in Europe and China, and that has happened through all the periods of even the most flourishing civilization.

My most interesting news concerns my eyes, which I am re-educating, by means of a technique of training which all orthodox oculists denounce without having tried it, as useless and even harmful. The results are remarkable. I now read and go about without glasses; and the scar tissue which covered my right eye is slowly but surely growing thinner, so that I can actually read fair-sized print with it. The method, which is a combination of physical and mental exercise, is extremely interesting (quite apart from what it has done for me) in its psychological and even philosophical applications. Chris Wood[6] has also been taking lessons, with the result that his very myopic eyes are now practically normal—(all he complains of is that he still can't see boys' faces very clearly at a distance, by artificial light, in a restaurant!)

In the intervals I have been doing a screen version of "Pride and Prejudice," trying to prevent the worst happening—probably without much success. It is tiresome, fiddling work; but they pay one, while it lasts, as though one were a Lord Chancellor.

I've been reading little lately except books about language and books about the philosophy of science—both immensely important subjects which, for some odd reason, are almost completely neglected in schools and universities where people learn a given science without any idea of what they're doing or how they should interpret their findings, and where the nearest they get to linguistics is the formal grammar invented by the Greeks, developed by the Romans and preserved, in a fossil condition, in contemporary text-books.

Maria sends her best love, as do I, and as I'm sure Gerald would if he were here.

Yours,
Aldous

---

[6] Christopher Wood. Gerald Heard's companion. They accompanied the Huxley family on their trip to the United States aboard the *SS Normandie* in 1937.

TO EDDY SACKVILLE-WEST

701 S. Amalfi Drive,
Pacific Palisades, Calif.
9 January 1940

My dear Eddy,

I wish your last letter had brought us better news of you; but, alas, good news is more than can be expected, nowadays, from anybody. The only substantial piece of good news I know concerns this system of eye training, which has made it possible for me to pass, within a year, from reading, with increasing difficulty, with the aid of cataract glasses of fifteen diopters of magnification, to reading without glasses and (since I know how to recognise it the moment any sign of it appears) without strain. At the same time my blind eye, which was covered with scar tissue and which could distinguish only light and darkness, is now able in favourable conditions, to read large print.

The existence of such techniques whereby anyone who knows the right methods and is prepared to take sufficient trouble, can make himself in some measure the master of circumstances to which he was previously the slave, is always, to me extremely cheering. A number of these techniques have been independently developed—techniques for improving sight, hearing and the other special senses; for correcting posture and thereby improving general health; for securing muscular relaxation consciously, and thereby curing and avoiding many physical and psychological ills. All are good as far as they go, but of course none goes far enough; for each applies to a limited field and there is no correlating principle. All are merely secondary to, and on the periphery of the fundamental, central technique, which is that of obtaining a more general control of circumstances, by altering one's point of view about them. This central technique is, of course, the thing that Gerald [Heard] is talking about—the thing you describe as merely opium. (Incidentally, this is a false analogy. Opium provides temporary escape from enslavement to unpleasant circumstances, but only at the price of a worse enslavement. A technique for consciously altering the point of view towards circumstances enables the person who practises it to obtain a high degree of independence from those circumstances.)

Like all techniques, from piano playing to tightrope walking, the great central technique is effective only for those who are capable of practising it and, of the capable, only for those who wish to take the trouble. Those who are too weak, or too stupid, or too much preoccupied with other things to be able to bother, will obviously derive no benefit from it—just as they derive no benefit from the technical proficiency of concert pianists or tightrope walkers. Your statement that you will believe in the validity of Gerald's ideas only when you see an improvement in Hollywood films takes no cognizance of the obvious fact that no technique can do any good to anyone who fails to practise it. I might as well say that I shall never believe that your interest in and practice of music have no value until I see that the inhabitants of London cease being interested in jazz and take to Bach.

You say that you can't accept any system that doesn't save everybody. But this is precisely the attitude of the Communists, whom you condemn. They, like the Fascists, have worked out systems to save everybody—by force, if necessary. The result has been progressive enslavement, progressive dis-enlightenment, progressive bellicosity. The best that any large-scale system imposed from without can achieve is to diminish the individual's opportunities for behaving badly. Anything beyond this must, in the nature of things, come from the individual himself and take place within his own consciousness. He must wish, and have the capacity, to make some positive achievement in the way of controlling his circumstances. But experience shows that many people are incapable of achieving more than a very little, while, among the capable, many are unwilling to make the necessary effort. This is true of particular spheres of human activity, no less than in that of conduct at large. For example, many people are unmusical while many musical people are unwilling to cultivate their gift by hard work. In the same way many people are incapable of achieving independence from circumstances by means of that change in point of view which results from the substitution of what may be called theocentrism for egocentrism; and many more are too content with the pleasures of egocentrism (in spite of its attendant pains) to wish to change their point of view. The truth is that there is no system that can automatically and from outside, save everyone. Certain social systems diminish the opportunities for bad behaviour more than others. To discover what such social systems are is a matter of research and trial. Meanwhile the individual can only do his best to ameliorate that particular corner of the universe over which he has a certain amount of control—his own mind and physical organism, together with the circumstances which immediately surround him and which are also the circumstances of his neighbours. During times of disaster, like those through which Europe is now passing, even this may become exceedingly difficult for any given individual to accomplish.

I have read little of late, beyond some philosophical books on the methodology of science and the nature of language. The latter is particularly fascinating. The more one looks into language, the more clearly one sees that a considerable proportion of human ineptitudes and crimes are directly correlated with the fact that we use a language embodying false metaphysics and having a form radically different from the form of the world about us, as revealed by observation and experience. We can never think except in unsuitable and misleading terms. God knows what the remedy is. Perhaps there is none. Maria sends her love, as do I.

Ever yours affectionately,
Aldous

Since the studio pays him "like a Lord Chancellor," even on half-pay after February, the Huxleys are able to send food parcels to their family in Europe. Aldous is in poor health during the spring of 1940.

TO SUZANNE NICOLAS

701 S. Amalfi Dr.
Pacific Palisades, Calif
22 mai 1940

Chère Suzanne,
Maria m'a lu ta lettre d'il y a quelques jours. Après tout ce qui est arrivé en Hollande, tout ce qui est arrivé en Belgique, tout ce qu'on craint pour la France et l'Angleterre, je comprends trop bien ton boulversement. Il est bien difficile de ne pas se laisser abattre par le poids du mal et du malheur. On se sent aussi un peu dur, impitoyable et en même temps injustement privilégié par le sort si on ne permet pas à sa sympathie d'aller jusqu'au point où on souffre d'une souffrance égale ou comparable à celle des malheureux de l'Europe. Pourtant il me semble qu'un de nos devoirs les plus impératifs est de résister à cette tendance très naturelle de se laisser aller aux extremes de la sympathie. Devenir malade de sympathie et d'inquiétude c'est d'une certaine façon d'élargir le champ de la guerre—c'est de porter la dévastation dans une region qui, physiquement, était épargnée. On fait du mal à soi-même et à ceux de son entourage, et on ne fait pas de bien a ceux qui souffrent là-bas. Le Christ a dit—je cite les mots dans la traduction anglaise—"Sufficient

*unto the day is the evil thereof." C'est une condamnation de l'anticipa-
tion anxieuse du mal. Ce qu'il a appliqué au temps peut-être appliqué
également à l'espace. "Sufficient unto the place is the evil thereof." Il ne
faut pas étendre, par l'action de son esprit et ses émotions, le champ
d'un mal local. La possibilité de remédier à ce mal dépend de notre force
au moment ou l'occasion d'intervenir est offerte. Il est donc absolument
nécessaire d'épargner et augmenter cette force, de ne pas la dissiper en
permettant à sa sympathie de miner, inutilement, sa santé et son morale.
Le monde actuel offre, par le moyen des journaux, de la radio, du cinema, des moyens horriblement efficaces pour l'extension à l'infini d'un
mal en son origine limité. Il est, je crois, absolument nécessaire de s'im-
poser un régime de nouvelles et de commentaires–de n'en prendre
qu'une ou deux doses par jour, de rationner strictement ces stimulants
de l'esprit; car les stimulants de ce genre provoquent des émotions qui,
faute de la possibilité d'action directe et bienfaisante, bouleversent l'or-
ganisme qui les sent.*

*Maria vous apportera, à toi et à Joep et aux enfants, my best love.
En attendant, je t'embrasse bien affectueusement.*

Aldous

[Dear Suzanne,
Maria has read me your letter of a few days ago. After all that has happened in Holland, all that's happened in Belgium, all that one fears for
France and England, I understand only too well your dismay. It is very
difficult not to let yourself be laid low by the weight of evil and misfortune. One also feels oneself a bit hard, pitiless and at the same time
unduly privileged by destiny if one doesn't feel oneself, through sympathy, to be suffering as much as those unfortunates of Europe. Still, it
seems to me that one of our most important duties is to resist this natural tendency to give way to these extremes of sympathy. To make oneself sick through sympathy and worry is, in a way, to widen the field of
war—it is to bring devastation into a region that physically has been
spared. One does harm to oneself and one's circle, and one does no
good to those who suffer over there. Christ said—I quote the English
translation—"Sufficient unto the day is the evil thereof." It is a con-
demnation of the anxious expectation of evil. What he applied to time
perhaps applies also to space. "Sufficient unto the place is the evil
thereof." One must not extend, through the action of one's mind and
emotions, the field of a localized evil. The possible cure for this evil depends on our strength when the opportunity to intervene presents itself.

It is, therefore, absolutely necessary to save and add to this strength, not to dissipate it by allowing our sympathy to undermine our health and morale. Today's world offers, through the press, the radio, the cinema, horribly effective means to extend infinitely an evil, which in its origins, is limited. It is, I believe, absolutely necessary to ration one's intake of news and commentary, to take only one or two daily doses, to ration strictly these mental stimulants, because stimulants of this type provoke emotions which, for lack of possibility to act upon them, overthrow the organism which feels them.

Maria will bring my best love to you, Joep and the children. Meanwhile, I send affectionate kisses.]

TO EUGENE F. SAXTON

701 S. Amalfi Drive
Pacific Palisades, Cal.
6 August 1940

My dear Gene,
Thank you for your letter. I shall be interested to look at the book when it comes. The project of which Gerald [Heard] writes is still a bit vague. My part is to take the form of a brief philosophic summary.

Other activities have got into a temporary tangle, and I think I shall have to leave my projected Utopia book for a time just as, last year, I left a much more elaborate scheme—nearly a quarter executed—to do *After Many a Summer.* I have a notion that I shall do a semi-biographical, semi-speculative book instead, if I can get hold of the necessary documentation, which is proving rather difficult here. The subject will be Father Joseph, the advisor of Richelieu, a most extraordinary and highly significant figure, around whom one can crystallize a great deal of important material. If things turn out as I hope, this should get done pretty quickly.

We enjoyed seeing Mark and Josephine. I suppose they're back now. Our love to you all.

Yours,
Aldous

After abandoning a utopian novel in August 1940, Huxley begins, at the suggestion of Gerald Heard, to research Grey Eminence, *the historical work mentioned above, in August/September 1940 and to*

*write it in October 1940, completing the semi-biographical work in
May 1941.*

TO JAKE ZEITLIN[7]

701 S. Amalfi
Pacific Palisades, Calif.
5 May 1941

Dear Jake,

I enclose a word on Montagu's[8] pamphlet, which I hope is the sort of
thing you want. We had a beautiful trip in the desert; but I'm still very
busy with my MS for a few days more.

Yours,
Aldous H.

Whenever Aldous Huxley writes
A novel that delights
His followers,
His brother Julian
At once indites
A learned work
On Coprolites
For scholoars.

Ashley Montagu

*Huxley begins work doctoring a Charles Morgan script at Twentieth
Century Fox in July 1941 and in November starts work on the novel
Time Must Have a Stop.*

TO EUGENE F. SAXTON

701 S. Amalfi Drive
Pacific Palisades, Cal.
17 November 1941

My dear Gene,

I owe you an answer to two letters—an answer which has not been
forthcoming until today, owing to the fact that for some weeks I have

---

[7] Jacob Zeitlin (1883–1937). Professor, translator of Montaigne's essays, and Los Angeles
antiquarian bookdealer.
[8] Ashley Montagu (1905–1999). British anthropologist.

been kept incessantly busy, trying to finish off my script for the movies. Now it is done—or at least they think for the moment that it is done—and I am free to deal with accumulated correspondence.

It is good of you to offer to deal with the translation rights for the South American countries; and of course it will be more convenient in many ways to deal with them here. The trouble is, as Harold Raymond has pointed out in a recent letter to me, that there is a network of past commitments and options which cannot be dealt with except in the light of the papers handed over to Chattos by Pinker. These I am reluctant to have sent over in existing circumstances; for we should be in an awful stew if they got lost on the way. The present arrangements are responsible for considerable delays; but on the whole I think it best to let them stand for the time being, all the more so as there is no prospect of any large number of books being involved, seeing that the more popular of the old ones have already been translated into Spanish and Portuguese, while the supply of new ones can hardly in the nature of things exceed one per annum.

I was interested in the figures contained in your most recent letter. It looks as though the total sale will not exceed five thousand. Which isn't very much, considering that this is, in some ways, the best book I have written. But then, of course, the subject matter is not one with any wide popular appeal, so that perhaps we should be glad the book is doing as well as it has done. I am thinking now of getting down to work on the fantasy, of which I think I wrote you some time back—a narrative of three interconnected adventures in the manner of *Gulliver's Travels*, the first two comic and fantastic, the third, a sketch of Utopia, where all the stress is on psychology rather than mechanics. The notions are still pretty vague in my head, but they will clarify themselves as I get to work on them.

Our news from France is fairly satisfactory. The American visa has been given, and Maria's mother and sister are now waiting for the Portuguese visa, which depends on the fixing of a date by Pan-American airways, who have been cabled to from New York. So that, at the moment, it seems to be merely a question of waiting—but of waiting with a reasonable hope that something will come of it.

Our love to you both.

Ever yours,
Aldous

In December 1941 the Huxleys purchase a Mojave Desert retreat at Llano del Rio, giving up their 701 Amalfi Road home in February 1942. He stops work on his novel Time Must Have a Stop *and begins* The Art of Seeing *in April 1942, finishing the book in July. In November, partly because of the war and his diminished hopes for a more decentralized society, he turns increasingly to "non-dogmatic religious mysticism . . . the only common element . . . in the religions of the world."*

TO RAYMOND MORTIMER

As from Llano, Calif.
22 December 1941

Dear Raymond,

Maria read me your warm and friendly letter, which gave us both a great deal of pleasure.

Yes, I would agree with you now that there has been a good deal of wishful thinking among pacifists. But then non-pacifists seem to be even more guilty in this respect. They think, because they hope and wish, that they can neglect the advice of pacifists in peace-time and still get away with it—either by somehow stabilizing existing evil and so avoiding war, or else by getting into war and achieving some good thereby. But all history shows that evil can't be stabilized at a moderate pitch for more than quite short periods—that it always tends to become worse unless actively corrected. There is a tide in the affairs of men—and if evil is not dealt with in time, the situation arises in which every attempted solution is disastrous. The neglected cancer case dies on the table if operated. Off it if not operated. It is the same in politics. If the advice of pacifists is neglected (and pacifists alas, are wishful thinkers to suppose that it will be taken) then a situation arises where the choice is between yielding and war. Both alternatives are catastrophic—which more so than the other we can never judge since they cannot both be tried and compared. The non-wishful thinking about these matters seems to me to be that stated or implied in *Grey Eminence*—that the workings of the human ego in individual or, projected, in nations, create a vast mechanism of necessity in which men have to go on working as in a treadmill, grinding out— what? More necessity to commit further evil and madness in the future. From this horrible machinery there is no escape except by contact with the reality outside man's home-made universe—contact which permits people to perform free creative acts within that universe and thus in some measure to mitigate the prevailing misery. The number of people able to make free creative acts in any consistent way is probably very small at any given time, though many can occasionally achieve such freedom. Pacifists, I am afraid, have been wishful thinkers in over-estimating the numbers of consistently free persons. Non-pacifists have believed no less wishfully that the evil mechanism of necessity could be so manipulated as to turn out something other than its own self-perpetuation. The universe sets us a task of almost infinite difficulty, for it is, I believe, quite literally true that we are "Born under one law, to another bound; / Vainly begot, and yet forbidden vanity, / Created sick, commanded to be sound."

Meanwhile, our news is good. Maria seems to have found a regimen which enables her body to contribute a little to the output of energy that used to depend entirely on the will. After having been sickly in a half-hearted way with a low infection that kept me from ever being quite well, I seem to be emerging at last, while my lessons in the art of seeing are bearing gradual fruit in an improving condition of the eyes. (Incidentally, this is a really extraordinary technique which deserves to be spread far and wide among the countless sufferers from different forms of eye trouble.) I am trying to push it as much as possible—but have to proceed with immense caution, since the doctors and optometrists have a hatred of it, born of prejudice and a fear of competition in their own special preserve. If I can succeed in getting it recognized, I shall feel I have achieved something of real importance. News from France is scanty and we begin to fear that M's mother, sister and small niece may not be able to get over now, in spite of visas and clipper tickets. Well, our best love and God bless you.

Ever yours,
Aldous

TO EUGENE F. SAXTON

701 S. Amalfi Drive
Pacific Palisades, Calif.
30 December 1941

My dear Gene,
Thank you so much for the Christmas parcel of books, an admirably interesting selection which I look forward to reading in the course of the next few weeks. It was really very sweet of you to send it.

There is not much news here, except that we are a bit concerned over Matthew's health. He came back very much run down from college, and the doctor is not too pleased with him. We are advised to take precautionary measures to prevent worse happening, and I think we shall help him for the next few months at the little ranch on the desert which we have recently acquired. Meanwhile, there is still no news from France, and I am very much afraid that, given the present situation, there is very little hope that Maria's mother and sister will be able to get out.

Since writing to you last, I have changed my literary plans. The post Gulliverian stories have turned out once more (for I tried my hand at them last summer) to be refractory; and I am turning now to another project, which I won't describe to you until I am well under way with it and can see what it is like. This too has been difficult to get started; but I believe I have now found the right approach. How soon I can get it done, I don't yet know, but will report on it later. I am sorry to be so vague; but it is very difficult to forecast the progress of composition. Sometimes everything goes smoothly and quickly; sometimes there are the most frightful and unexpected traffic jams. It is impossible to tell in advance.

Maria joins with me in sending affectionate good wishes to you both and to the boys, for the coming year.

Ever yours,
Aldous H.

TO JULIAN HUXLEY[9]

140 S. Canon Drive
Beverly Hills, Calif.
2 April 1942

Dearest J,
I have only just seen, very belatedly, the paragraph in *Time* about the Zoo committee and your secretaryship. It sounds the most stinking, underhanded **sort of** affair. I can't tell you how sorry I am about it. I suppose you will have to make all kinds of new plans—not to mention the finding of new living quarters.

---

[9] While on a government-sponsored lecture tour in America, Julian learned that he had been fired from his post as director of the London Zoo, ostensibly for his liberal opinions and unwelcome innovations.

I will write to you at length when I am less frenziedly busy than I am at present.

Meanwhile, let me hear a word about your present projects and present doings.

Ever your affectionate,
Aldous

TO L. P. JACKS

Dear Dr. Jacks,
Your letter of January 21st got put away in a box as I was moving house, and has remained there ever since—to emerge only now. I am so sorry to have left it so long unanswered.

Surely the answer to your question is that Prometheus, if he goes far enough, finds by direct experience that reality is not evil—though, of course, there may be many subsidiary manifestations of reality, the Zeuses, the eagles and so forth, which are evil, presumably because they have somehow rebelled against the ultimate reality. Fr. Joseph somehow confused one of these subsidiary manifestations with the real thing. And of course most power politicians don't even know that there is a real thing, but are convinced that the local Zeus, or Nature red in tooth and claw, is reality and that there's nothing else.

Bérulle[1] would never have said that the soul merged in ultimate reality got dyed black—for he knew the older mystics and revered them. His Christocentric religion was strictly not mystical theology, but a kind of Pauline devotion with a mystical form. The doctrine of the Trinity and the hypostatic union made it theoretically possible to pass from his pseudo-mysticism to the real thing. But in fact it wasn't possible, since the activity of the imagination, necessary in Christocentrism, excludes the possibility of imageless contemplation. (There are good things on this subject in Abbot Chapman's "Spiritual Letters.")

Mystical practices may be employed to secure a merging of the soul with the most horrifying projections of human crime and madness, and perhaps with non-human powers of evil, if such exist. But they can also be used, if there is right knowledge and right will, to achieve union

---

[1] Pierre Bérulle (1575–1629). French cardinal and statesman.

with something which, as a matter of empirical experience is not evil—and perhaps not good either—but a form of pure existence which cannot be approached except through goodness. ("God is not good," said Eckhart, "I am good.")

Yours very sincerely,
Aldous Huxley

TO MARY HUTCHINSON

Llano, Calif.
2 November 1942

My dear Mary,
Your sad news reached us yesterday. There are no consolations. Nothing can replace or make up for the person, the shared experiences, the habits of thinking and feeling in common. The experience of bereavement is one of the extreme cases of that death in life which Tennyson writes of—the death in life to which all human experience, even the most triumphant, owes its strange poignancy and its incompleteness.

I did not see Jack during his illness, and so I think of him always as he was at the height of his powers overflowing with life and surrounded, as it were, by the aura of his pungent commentary on the world. It is hard to imagine the extinction of so much quickness and humour, such an intensity of personality.

Will you go on living at Cambridge, I wonder? Or move back to London? Or into the country somewhere?

There is not much news here. Matthew got a great deal better during the months he was here—but suddenly, two weeks ago, got appendicitis and had to be operated on at an hour's notice. He has done well, and I hope he'll soon be back at the point he had reached before the operation. Maria is very busy with work around the house and orchard, but is well—as am I, thanks to the stringent meatless, milkless, sugarless and saltless diet on which I have been placed by my excellent and rather crazy Viennese doctor. Meanwhile, one writes and one does what infinitesimally little one can to help in alleviating the misery of the world. Of books I don't read much outside the field of mystical religion, which is what now interests me beyond anything else and in which, I believe, lies the sole hope of the world. For obviously the world isn't going to be preserved from future wars by the seven-ocean navies and five-continent air-forces, of which there is talk here, but only by some sort of common belief, the holding of which makes people reluctant to embark on these enormous suicides. And seeing that all the world is now involved, not merely Europe and what remains of Christendom, it's clear that the belief cannot be associated with a given set of dogmas (themselves, as a matter of history, associated with imperialism), but must be based on something that all people can experience, and that has a place in all the existing religious traditions. Mysticism is the only thing that meets the requirements, the only theory and praxis capable of mitigating from within, and at the psychological source, the violence and ruthlessness which will, I am afraid, survive the present outburst and manifest themselves in goodness knows what fresh brutalities. One of these days, no doubt, some spiritual and ethical genius will make his incalculable appearance; but meanwhile there is plenty of preparatory work to be done.

Please give my love to Barbara and to Victor, to Jeremy too if you see him or write to him. We both have very affectionate recollections of his visit.

Goodbye, dear Mary.

Ever your affectionate,
Aldous

TO MARGUERITE BALTUS NYS

Beverly Wilshire Hotel
Beverly Hills, California
14 décembre 1942

Chère Mère,
Grâce à mes dix jours de travail chez Fox, je me sens (ce qui est très à propos à cette saison) un peu riche. Je vous prie donc d'accepter ce petit cadeau du Père Noel cinématographique, et j'espère que vous trouverez quelque chose de joli pour pendre a votre Christmas Tree ou pour mettre dans le bas des autres.

Affectueusement,
Aldous

[Dear Mère,
Thanks to my ten days of work at Fox, I'm feeling rather rich (which is very appropriate for this season). So I'd like you to accept this little gift from filmdom's Father Christmas, and I hope you will find

something pretty to put under your tree or to put in the stockings of others.]

Affectionately,
Aldous]

In March 1942 Huxley works on Jane Eyre *for Twentieth Century Fox and resumes work on* Time Must Have a Stop. *In the same month Matthew Huxley serves in the U.S. Army Medical Corps but is invalided out of the army in June 1942 after a serious illness.*

TO JAKE ZEITLIN

Llano, Calif.
25 April 1943

My dear Jake,
Thank you for your letter and article, which is full of sound sense on a subject which seems to drive most people into paroxysms of silliness. The most spectacularly imbecile planning is, I think, the planning of amateur strategists. I remember last year picking up *Look* or *Pic* or one of those papers in my dentist's waiting room and seeing an elaborately illustrated article on planning for victory. There were a series of maps covered with arrows representing a land route from America to Germany via central America and Brazil, with a hop to Dakar, then by puff-puff and road to Egypt and on via Syria and Asia Minor to Greece, Hungary and—final destination of the arrows—to Berlin. It looked simply splendid on the map, and I suppose the people who thought up the idea must have taken it seriously.

One thing which most planners seem to leave out of account is population trends. By 1961, one person out of six in Great Britain will be over sixty, and within the next decade there will be a considerable fall in gross population. America will reach an analogous position about fifteen years after England. Most of the countries of Western Europe will go the same way about the same time. But Eastern Europe and Russia are still in an upswing of population, and so is Asia. The questions raised by these facts are mildly disquieting, to say the least, and make complete nonsense of any long-range political plan envisaging permanent policing of the world by the English-speaking powers, with or without the help of such Western European nations as France. Nevertheless, people merrily go on formulating such plans.

383

How odd that the MS of *Grey Eminence* should have been offered to you! I gave it to one of the Civil Liberties organizations to be sold on behalf of a fund to defend those unfortunate booksellers who were arrested in Oklahoma for carrying copies of Marx's *Capital* and similar light reading. I suppose the buyer is getting rid of it again.

The books you mention on your post cards aren't of any special use to me. But if it isn't a bother to you, keep me posted on anything that turns up in that line.

Yours,
Aldous Huxley

TO MARTHA SAXTON

Trabuco Ranch
Trabuco Canyon P.O., Calif.
5 July 1943

My Dear Martha,
I have been away from home, and the news about Gene reached me only today. As I think about him now, I realize with surprise how few in all these years were the occasions on which I was with him, and how brief— and yet I always thought of him as one among the best of my friends. It was as though he possessed some quality stronger than absence and distance—an essential loveableness and reliability and warmth that continued to affect one in spite of the obstacles interposed by space and time. In a curious, hardly analysable way Gene was, for me, a living proof of the triumph of character over matter—physically almost always absent, and yet firmly present in my mind as a trusted friend, to whom I knew I could turn in any crisis without fear of disappointment.

And to you, dear Martha, what can I possibly say? There are no consolations that can be administered from without—only the mitigations of grief that come with time, and perhaps one's own tentative answers to the agonizing questions of life and death.

Ever yours affectionately,
Aldous

Huxley stays briefly with Gerald Heard at his "monastery" in Trabuco Canyon, July 1943, and in October 1943 the Huxleys take a pied-à-terre at 145½ South Doheny Drive in Beverly Hills. In February 1944 Huxley finishes Time Must Have a Stop, *the novel he later considers his best. In May he begins* The Perennial Philosophy, *completing it in March 1945.*

TO GEORGE CATLIN

Llano, Calif.
13 May 1945

Dear Catlin,
Your letter was forwarded to me here. Unfortunately I don't expect to be in town for some weeks, and gasoline rationing makes a casual trip impossible as this place is about eighty miles from Los Angeles, in the desert, between Palmdale and Victorville, with no bus service.

I was interested in a review you wrote same months ago of Hayek's book in *Nature*, with its suggestion that the only solution might be some kind of revived agrarian, decentralist form of society. To my mind, this conclusion seems more and more certain; for I cannot see how one is to have personal or political liberty in a world where industry, finance and even agriculture together with population, are highly centralized, and where the capitalistic or governmental few control the lives of the majority.

Unhappily most people don't want decentralism—at any rate yet awhile. And in Europe, of course, the fact that many millions will emerge from the war without a house, tools or the most elementary personal possessions will inevitably make them absolutely dependent for many years to come upon the central government with the result that liberty and democratic institutions will be absolutely out of the question. You cannot have freedom in barracks—and in barracks and upon government rations, millions and millions of Europeans will be living (if they contrive to live at all) for a generation to come.

Yours sincerely,
Aldous Huxley

In June 1945 Matthew becomes a U.S. citizen, and the Huxleys purchase a chalet in Wrightwood, California, where Aldous begins Science, Liberty and Peace. *On 19 November 1945 the* Los Angeles Times *reports that "Walt Disney has taken definite steps toward realizing his 23-year old dream of filming* Alice's Adventures in Wonderland *by signing Aldous Huxley, distinguished novelist and authority on Lewis Carroll, to work out the details" for a film which* *would combine a cartoon version of John Tenniel's drawings and Carroll's story together with an episode from the life of the Reverend Charles Dodgson (Lewis Carroll). Huxley's contract of October 1945 stipulates a payment of $2,500 for agreeing to write a treatment of* Alice in Wonderland *and a further $5,000 upon delivery of the treatment by 15 January 1946. He eventually produces a lengthy synopsis, but his work on the project comes to nothing and his name is absent from the credits when the entirely animated film is released in 1951.*

TO ELIAS GILLMAN

Llano, Calif.
24 June 1945

Dear Mr. Gillman,
Thank you for your interesting letter. Why the universe should be of such a nature that, as you say, "it is always easier to do harm than good" (because so enormously difficult to "die to self"), is indeed mysterious. But that is what in fact the world is like, all the masters of the spiritual life—those whose purity of heart permits them to have insight into reality and to see God—are agreed. Many are called, few chosen. One can only suppose that this immensely stringent intelligence test is, in one way or another, on one level of existence or another, continued indefinitely until, as the Mahayana Buddhists insist, all sentient beings shall at last have chosen to be liberated from selfhood into the knowledge of the divine Ground.

Yours sincerely,
Aldous Huxley

TO WALT DISNEY

Wrightwood, Cal.
23 November 1945

Dear Mr. Disney,
Herewith the synopsis, with the new passages more fully developed. I think the story is becoming more closely knit, smooth and dramatic than it was, and it should soon be ready to be worked out more fully.
I will ring up on Monday to see when we can get together again.
Yours very sincerely,
Aldous Huxley

TO SYBILLE BEDFORD

145½ Doheny Drive
Los Angeles, California 36
7 February 1946

My dear Sybille,
I have undertaken, rather rashly, to compile for the Encyclopaedia Britannica people an anthology of Essays and Criticism.[2] There will be a predominance of English material—but we need characteristic specimens from other literatures. So I should be most grateful if you could give me some help on the German side—not to mention any other language in which you can think of interesting material. I have not started systematically on the foreign stuff yet, and so far have only some bits of Nietzsche, an essay of Schopenhauer, two essays of Heine, some fragments of Goethe and an essay of Thomas Mann's lined up. I need some more Goethe; some Schiller (I had thought of something from those letters on Aesthetics, or whatever they are called, which I remember reading with interest years ago); some Lessing, I suppose; some Rilke—and perhaps half a dozen others to make up the quota. I'd be very grateful if you could give me some hints in regard to the most interesting item in any field from aesthetics to personal essay. The items must be reasonably short (or else reducible in length) and already translated into English.

Also if you have any special favourites in French (translated), do let me know, in case I may be ignorant of them or have overlooked them. And ditto with Italian, Spanish, Russian etc.

I hope you flourish. We are pretty well, I am glad to say. I am working on a movie version of *Brave New World*, which is rather interesting as well as fearfully topical, as I think the next phase of totalitarianism, when biology and psychology will be used instead of clubs and guns to regiment people and to make them like their servitude, is very close at hand—not 600 years away as in *B.N.W.*, but (if we escape the Bomb) about 100 or 200.

Our best love to you.

Ever yours,
Aldous

---

[2] Huxley worked until the mid-fifties on this long-lost anthology, a draft of which has recently been discovered among Huxley's papers in Hollywood. Many short pieces on the great essayists, as well as his 30,000-word overview of the history of the essay have been found. *EB* paid Huxley $1,200 for his labors, but decided not to go forward with the anthology, which would have exceeded 600,000 words.

1946

TO HAROLD RAYMOND[3]

Llano, Cal.
10 February 1946

Dear Harold,

Not much news here, except that the adaptation of *Brave New World* for the screen, which I was to have begun in January, has been held up because the man [Louis Walinsky] who made a play from it wants to be bribed before promising he won't hold up production by bringing some kind of frivolous case. He has, of course, no rights in the film version; but he could bring an injunction on the score of plagiarism, or what not, which (though it would likely be turned down by the courts) would effectively hold up production and cost the company a fortune.

Unfortunately I cannot lay my hands on the original contract with him. It is not in the papers I got from Eric Pinker and I understand that the representative of the William Morris agency, who handles my film business here, was told by you that there was no trace of it in London. One can forgive the Pinkers for being dishonest; but pure gratuitous inefficiency, resulting in the disappearance of a document, is another matter. It is the sort of thing I might do—but I don't expect it and can't excuse it in people whose business is business! Someday I suppose, the egregious Mr Walinsky,[4] the holder of the dramatic rights, may be bullied or bribed into giving the company a clear title. Meanwhile nothing can be done, which is a great bore.

Ever yours,
Aldous Huxley

TO JULIAN HUXLEY

Llano, Calif.
26 May 1946

Dearest J,

Your post card from Havana has just arrived. You certainly seem to be getting around a bit. I rather enjoyed Caracas when we there thirteen years ago—the fabulous elegance of the oil millionaires' wives and con-

---

[3] Harold Raymond. One of the senior partners (with Charles Prentice) at the British publisher Chatto and Windus.
[4] Walinsky's stage adaption of *Brave New World* was mounted by the English Players in Paris in September 1938. It had been banned from the English stage.

cubines, the elliptical dome of the capital with the life-sized fresco of the entire Battle of Carabobo, the house of Bolivar, and the almost perpendicular trip down to the port of la Guyara with its population of all the possible permutations and commutations of negro, white, Chinese, Red Indian, Hindu, such as one sees in its perfection of Trinidad—but dressed, not in the unutterably dowdy style of British colonies, but in cheap versions of the very latest French fashions. But I suppose, as in Brazil, syphilis is endemic and malaria all but universal—the kind of malaria that in South America is called "el economico," because it kills so quickly and so certainly that it is pure waste of money to send for the doctor.

I am afraid there is no hope of my getting to New York while you are there. I am involved in two jobs with time limits on them, one of which requires me to be on the spot, conferring and discussing. And anyhow the travel situation is such that one has to be Louis B. Mayer himself, in order to get a place on a train or a plane, or a room in a hotel. Let us hope that we shall have better luck next time.

Matthew is still at Berkeley studying Latin American history, economics, politics and languages, with a view of doing some sort of good neighbour job when he gets through his courses next autumn. I think he will do this sort of thing very well, for he is an excellent public relations man, as he discovered during last summer's film strike.

Best love from us both.

Ever your affectionate,
Aldous

TO JEANNE NEVEUX

Wrightwood, Cal.
29 July 1946

My dear Jeanne,
A few lines about old English plays which might do for adaptation. It is many years since I read Beaumont and Fletcher. But try the following. *The Maid's Tragedy*—a good specimen of the romantic poetic drama. Then look at *The Knight of the Burning Pestle*, which is a parody of the romantic drama in the form of a play within a play—the actor of the romantic play breaking off to talk with a man and woman in the audience, a bourgeois couple to whom he is apprenticed. I have seen this on the stage several times and it is amusing. As a whole Beaumont and Fletcher are better in individual scenes than in the whole

plays. You can almost always find something beautiful and touching in their place; but the pieces lack strength to stand up as wholes.

Then look at Ben Jonson's *Bartholomew Fair*, the whole action of which takes place in the booths and tents of the great Bartholomew Day fair, which used to be an important feature of London life. It is like a Breughel painting done in dramatic form. I think that, with skilful adaptation, this might be very interesting.

Have you looked at Webster? His *Duchess of Malfi* and *White Devil* are poor in construction, but they have wonderful poetry in them and the picture of renaissance Italian life in its more sinister aspects is wonderfully vivid. And then there is John Ford, whose *'Tis Pity She's a Whore* is a splendid play. Massinger is also interesting; but it is so long since I have read him, that I forget the individual plays.

Then there are the comedies of the Restoration, such as Wycherley's *Country Wife*, extremely indecent and harsh, but with a kind of brilliancy. Later there is Congreve, who is exquisitely witty; but perhaps his plays are already too French, in certain respects, to seem very new or striking to a French audience. Sheridan's *School for Scandal* is an admirable comedy. There must be existing translations, since Mme de Stael was writing about it enthusiastically 140 years ago. But it is well worth considering. You might also look at Goldsmith's *She Stoops to Conquer*. I know nothing about the contemporary theatre, not having been to a play for years.

Maria will tell you our news—which is nothing very spectacular. I am very busy doing a screenplay of my old short story, "The Gioconda Smile." Matthew is still at the university, doing very well, it seems. We expect Suzanne and family in a few days.

Our love to you all.

Ever yours,
Aldous

P.S. Two tips for relieving eyestrain when reading or doing close work: turn the book, or any other piece of printed material, upside down, so that you're not tempted to try to read it, and alternately bring it close to your nose and take it away to arm's length, watching how the white spaces between the lines grow larger as they approach and smaller as they recede. Do this several times slowly, then quickly, then slowly. It stimulates the eyes and makes them adaptable. Two: take a piece of wood or cardboard say 75 cm. long, or even 1 m., and mark the edge with parallel lines about half a centimeter apart in ink. On the opposite edge draw fine lines closer together. Hold the piece of wood immediately in front of your nose and sweep your eyes from left to right and right to left across the lines, moving the wood in the opposite direction as you do so. This gets the eyes shifting very rapidly and is a great rest and relief. Begin with the thicker lines and finish with the fine, close lines.

TO GRAHAM GREENE

Llano, Cal.
5 November 1946

Dear Graham Greene,
Thank you for your letter and the invitation to contribute an intro-duction to *The First Men in the Moon*. I don't, unfortunately, feel qual-ified for this, as I am not very well up in Wells and, except for the sci-entific romances, don't get much pleasure out of his novels. I found the re-reading of *Tono Bungay* a few years ago such a sad experience that I decided to make no further explorations in the Wellsian field. And to talk about *The First Men in the Moon* without discussing, however briefly, the other books would hardly be feasible.

Yours sincerely,
Aldous Huxley

TO ANITA LOOS

Wrightwood
[ca April 1947]

Dearest Anita,
Thank you for your good letter. Since writing last I have heard that Cornell[5] has finally received a copy of the play and didn't want it. Also it has been seen by Evelyn, who feels like she doesn't want to do an-other psychological melodrama—but has not, I gather, altogether turned it down. Ruth Gordon[6] also seems to have seen it, and doesn't like it. Meanwhile a copy is to go to Garson Kanin (or however his name is spelt) in Hollywood. Helen said she was giving a copy to Rodgers and Hammerstein, but I've not heard what their reactions are. Meanwhile no news from Jed Harris.[7] The outlook doesn't seem too good up to the present; but perhaps something will turn up in time.

[5] Katherine Cornell (1893–1974). American stage and screen actress.
[6] Ruth Gordon (1896–1985). American actress and screenwriting partner of her husband, Garson Kanin (1912–1999).
[7] Jed Harris (1900–1979). American producer-director.

About my affairs with Morris[8]—I don't quite know what to say. After the initial blunder of not looking into the affair of the potential claims of Crane Wilbur[9] last summer, they have handled things pretty efficiently. I'm expecting Halsey[1] to bring the final papers out here for my signature tomorrow; and if everything is now OK, I would be inclined to let the matter go. I will let you know in a few days whether the thing has actually come through according to schedule. Compared with my troubles, yours seem to be really monstrous. First the hanky-panky with Hydes, and then the business about the annuity.

I am glad you liked Suzanne and Claire and Bobby.[2] We were quite delighted with the whole family when they were out here last year.

I have thought a little about the idea, of which I spoke to you one day before you left—the story of the soap opera writer, like Elaine Carrington.[3] I think it should follow the classic fairy-tale pattern of the three wishes. We should see her first, a poor clergyman widow, like Mrs. Barclay of *The Rosary*, who prays earnestly for money to give away in good works. The next scene shows her in more than oriental luxury, the author of bestsellers and now permanently employed in the soap opera trade at a gigantic salary. She now prays for personal happiness and is at once proposed to by her manager, a handsome gigolo with an eye to the main chance. The next prayer is for the happiness of her daughter, who has lost her husband, or something of the kind, and this is fulfilled by the elopement of her own young gigolo with the girl. Other complications would be happening all the time—the daughter's first husband turning out to be a crook, the gigolo trying to rob her of her money etc., and as a counterpoint to the sordid real-life story, the soap operas would go on all the time, pouring out sweetness and light from twenty millions of loudspeakers. One can never go wrong with a classical motif such as the three wishes (see the admirable use of it in W. W. Jacobs' "The Monkey's Paw"): the problem is to find the proper incidents to group around the central motif.

Maria sends her best love, as do I.

Ever your affectionate,
Aldous

---

[8] William Morris Agency. Huxley's literary agency.

[9] Crane Wilbur (1886–1973). Film writer and director.

[1] Reece Halsey (1915–1980). Head of Morris's West Coast agency.

[2] Suzanne Nicolas, Maria's sister. Claire Nicolas White, daughter of Suzanne and Joep Nicolas. Robert Winthrop White, Claire's artist husband.

[3] Elaine Carrington (1891–1958). Successful radio scriptwriter, known as the "Queen of Soaps."

TO ANITA LOOS

145½ S. Doheny Drive
Los Angeles 36, California
22 April 1947

Dearest Anita,

Lacking the accomplishments of Yvonne, I can't play "Happy Birthday" and must content myself with writing and thinking it. This brings you all affectionate good wishes.

There have been some interesting developments in regard to my play. It seems that Shumlin[4] (is that how you spell his name?) is very much interested in and would like to put it on, provided he can get certain financial backing from Universal, who are going to do the picture. I know nothing of the New York theatre, but am told that he knows his business and has a round of successes. So, if the Morris people can get around Messrs Goetz and Spitz,[5] the twin brothers of Universal, something might begin to happen. Meanwhile I have just heard that Charles Boyer[6] is very anxious to play the leading man in the picture, provided some small changes can be made to boost his character a little (they all feel that the woman outshines them!). I expect to hear what the changes are today; and if they are not destructive—which I gather they are not—they can probably be inserted without much difficulty, and we shall have the advantage of getting a box-office magnet, as well as a good actor. If the Boyer deal goes through, I gather that shooting will begin within six weeks—which will mean immediate work on revision and final touches. I expect to hear what the plans are within the next day or two.

Meanwhile I'm delighted that you like the Carrington story. When the basic plot is worked out, we shall have to think up a soap opera, which will, of course, move in exactly the opposite direction. We shall follow the outlines of the soap opera plot in a succession of Wurlitzer-accompanied outbursts on the radio and by fragments which we hear the authoress talking into her Dictaphone. One reason for the estrangement between her and her husband is her habit of dictating in bed. (Like Mrs. Shandy, in Sterne, she is apt to interrupt at the most critical moments in order to record new inspiration.)

Yours affectionately,
Aldous

---

[4] Herman Shumlin (1898–1979). Hollywood director.
[5] William Goetz (1903–1969) and Leo Spitz took over production in the newly merged Universal-International studios after 1946.
[6] Charles Boyer (1897–1978). French-born leading man, starred in *A Woman's Vengeance* (1947), the film version of Huxley's story "The Gioconda Smile" (1921).

P.S. I hope you will like the little letter-head of ocean, hand and grunion. In his small way, the man who does the woodcuts has a remarkable gift.

TO GILBERT PERLEBERG

Dear Mr. Perleberg,

Thank you for your letter and the article, which I return herewith. Borelius is, of course quite right in feeling cynical about the claims of Geist as a force in history, working directly on the historical, collective level, as Hegel seemed to have envisaged it—Marxians, hypostatizing history as a kind of secular providence, still envisage it, albeit in terms which exclude the use of the word "Geist." He is wrong, as Jennsen points out, in denying Geist's existence and efficacy in relation to the individual. We have tended in the last century or so to imagine that there is a collective salvation produced by collective means. It is like saying that there can be collective pain or collective satisfaction of hunger. But when you prick your finger or eat dinner, it is not *I* who feel the pain or have my stomach filled, even under the best of possible social regimes. The most complete communion between men is a communion of solitude and the nature of things is such that we cannot get out of our solitude except in achieving the intuitive knowledge of God.

Yours sincerely,
Aldous Huxley

TO MATTHEW HUXLEY

Dearest M,

We were both delighted with your good letter. I am so glad that your British accent has not excluded you from Brooklyn and that you can do the questioning work which must be extremely curious and interesting. (Incidentally, one could make a very funny movie out of the adventures of a pollster. To my knowledge this has not been done. You should think of the possibilities.) The intestinal intimacies evoked by Serutan are as nothing compared with those elicited by Professor Kinsey about the sexual habits of the population. I have not yet seen his book, which I shall certainly get, but there was a very good article on his findings in last month's *Harpers Magazine*. If you haven't read it, do. One always knew that people's sexual habits were odd; but the full statistical record of the oddity is really most extraordinary. For example, I didn't know, in my innocence, that about twenty-five percent of children have sexual intercourse before the age of puberty; that one out of every six farm boys has affairs with animals; that a third of the male population has at one time or another indulged in homosexuality. And there are fascinating correlations between ability to profit by higher education and pre-marital sexual activity. Only two out of three college students have pre-marital intercourse; whereas ninety-eight per cent of those who never went to college have it. And then there is the very interesting fact that these patterns of sex behaviour don't appear to have changed—that things were just the same in grandpa's day as they are now—the only difference being, apparently, that we talk more in mixed company than our forefather did.

I have read the population book you mentioned in your previous letter. It came out several years ago in another and less available edition, which I got out of the library. As a supplement to it, read the book by Fairfield Osborn—which C [Canfield] has sent you in typescript. It sums it up very clearly the most significant facts about mankind's ignorant and wanton destruction of the basic natural resources upon which civilization and life itself depend. The more I read on the subject, the clearer it seems to be that we must all get together on a world conservation policy upon which the various nations can possibly agree, because having enough to eat is the one thing that interests everybody equally.

About Michael Hunter, I don't imagine there is anything that can be done about the picture, which is to be released in February. But anyhow, Hunter or no Hunter, why don't you get in touch with Zoltan [Korda], who is staying at the St Regis in New York, having some medical treatments for his arthritis, before coming back here. I am sure he will be glad to see you, and he will probably have many things of interest to say about the movie situation in England and on the continent. So far as I can make out from his rather vague letters, he wants to work on a script from my old short story, "The Rest Cure," with a view to shooting it in Italy this summer. If I can get my book finished by the end of February, which I hope, there should be time to get the script ready for summer production. I don't know what his and his brother's intentions about *Point Counter Point* now are. Maybe you could tactfully discover.

Denver Lindley[7] came here a few days ago in company with a new wife—not a very prepossessing one, but I dare say she's all right. Anyhow Denver looks a good deal less strained and unhappy than usual. For the rest things go on smoothly and uneventfully, with amazingly good weather on the surface and, beneath, a drought that is threatening to become catastrophic.

All best love,
Aldous

TO SYLVIA NICOLAS[8]

Wrightwood, Cal.
1 February 1948

My dear Sylvia,

I expect Maria has already written to thank you for your Christmas letter from Pittsburgh which arrived almost at the same time as the other from Islip, announcing that you had decided not to go back to your hermitage; so I will just add these few lines by way of supplement. I'm sure your decision will turn out to be a good one, provided always that you remember a few distressingly inescapable facts. First, you can't escape from the exasperation and troubles of life into solitude, into Europe-with-a-sleeping bag, into any set of external circumstances. The thing is to carry about with you what Catherine of Siena called "the cell of self-knowledge"—a portable and subjective hermitage suitable for all climates and occasions. Second, one has to practice all the virtues in relation to one's art if one wants to be a good artist, however remiss one may be outside the aesthetic field. Patience, prudence, fortitude—and a lot of humility. For even the greatest and most original talents have always begun by submitting themselves to the asinine procedure of practicing, over and over again, and to the disciplining of teachers much less gifted than themselves, boring people who possessed the merit, however, of knowing their stuff, and being able to teach—which gifted artists very often are not. So if you get the chance, supplement the inspiration which Joep can give you with the dreary but, surely, necessary routine of an art school. You don't, I seem to have noticed, suffer fools gladly. Neither do I. But I have dis-

---

[7] Denver Lindley (1906–1982). Magazine and book editor. He translated works by Mann, Remarque, and Maurois into English.
[8] Sylvia Nicolas was Maria's niece.

covered (a) that fools are often non-fools in certain respects and that non-fools, including oneself, are just as foolish in their own way as the fools (b) that one can greatly profit, intellectually and morally, from contrast with persons who seem rather dull and boring and lacking in the sprightlier kind of accomplishments. As the anonymous Victorian poet put it so well:—The good are so hard on the clever, and the clever so rude to the good.

So have the charity, if you are good, not to be hard and, if you're clever, not to be rude—together with the humility that is ready to accept the salutary disciplines of common life (so much more searching and more profitable, as Saint Teresa remarks, than any deliberately chosen self-mortification) or penance and the dull but useful and indispensable teachings of conventional schools.

Our best love to you all.

Your affectionate,
Aldous

TO BARONESS ZGLINITZKI[9]

Wrightwood, Cal.
20 March 1948

Dear Baroness Zglinitzki,
Thank you for your letter, with its news of Roy Campbell, whom I have not heard of these many years.

I was never more than a visitor at Trabuco, which was presided over by Gerald Heard. He has now left, and the college is under other trustees, being used, I believe, for somewhat different purposes from those which were being pursued when Heard was running it. There is at Santa Barbara a branch of the Los Angeles Vedanta Society, where you might hear lectures on the spiritual life which you would find of interest and help. The address is

Vedanta Society
Ladera Lane
Santa Barbara

Yours very truly,
Aldous Huxley

---

[9] Nicholson, Helen, Baroness de Zglinitzki (b. 1885–1954). American author of *Death in the Morning* (1937), a memoir of life in Spain at the onset of the Civil War.

The London stage version of The Gioconda Smile, *directed by Jack De Leon, opens in June 1948 for a nine-month run—Huxley's only successful play. From 29 June to 8 July 1948 the Huxleys stay with Maria's brother-in-law, Georges Neveux, in Paris. Huxley and Neveux work on the French version of* Le sourire de la Joconde, *which begins a moderately successful run in Paris in February 1949. In July/August 1948 Huxley works on the film version of his story "The Rest Cure" in Siena, Italy, for the Kordas.*

TO RICHARD ALDINGTON

Hotel de la Ville
Rome
18 August 1948

Dear Aldington,

Thank you for your letter of the ninth. I am glad to hear that you are going to do a non-feminine life of Lawrence. It is high time for just such a book. In regard to your questions.

1. Yes, by all means make use of the Preface to the *Letters* as you think fit.

2. It seems to me that the strangest and most significant thing about Lawrence was the intrinsic contradictoriness of his attitude. It is illustrated very clearly in *The Plumed Serpent*, where he alternately invites everyone to plunge into the ocean of blood and darkness and expresses his horror of the Mexicans who live in that ocean. The contradiction is never resolved by him. I have a feeling that, if he had lived he might have found a solution along some kind of Taoist lines—in the conception of an indwelling divinity operating on all levels from the inanimate and the physiological to the purely spiritual, a *Logos* with which it is man's business to co-operate on all these levels.

3. Presumably the explanation of Luhan's account of L's plot to destroy her is to be found in the fact that Lawrence often used very intemperate language, which he had no intention of translating into action. I often heard him say that he would like to kill so and so; but it was quite obviously a figure of speech.

4. I know nothing of the episode in the Café Royal and never heard either Lawrence or Heseltine talk about it. Perhaps Arlen could throw some light?

5. I think you are right about the perversity. He hated the obviously undesirable aspect of science and technology, therefore condemned the

whole thing, lock stock and barrel. This was rather his intemperance of language than his perversity. The latter came in, as you say, when he found himself in contact with a person who held views different from his own. In those cases he employed a mixture of bear-baiting, Socratic shock treatment and a kind of disinterested naughtiness.

With all good wishes for the success of your venture, I am

Yours very sincerely,
Aldous Huxley

TO MARY HUTCHINSON

Warwick Hotel
New York
23 November 1948

Dearest Mary,
May I ask you to send on the enclosed article and photograph to Cyril Connolly, whose address, at home and at *Horizon*, I don't seem to have. I'm sorry to bother you in this way.

Maria is already in California; but I have stayed on here for a bit in order to take a series of treatments for my eyes from a celebrated German doctor [Gustav Erlanger], who uses iontophoresis on eyes— introduction of drugs by means of a very mild galvanic current. I think the treatment has had some slight effect in clearing up the opacities. But probably it should be continued for a long time in view of the fact that they are of such long standing. The results on certain eye conditions are quite extraordinary—diabetic cataract, for example, clears up sometimes in a matter of weeks, making operation unnecessary and restoring practically normal vision.

Meanwhile I have seen some old friends—Ted, for example, and Marion (who seems to be drinking less, thank goodness); Osbert and Edith, who are the great lions of the moment and are lecturing at a thousand dollars an appearance. With Tom I have only corresponded and I doubt whether I shall see him before my departure on Thursday.

For the rest I have done a little work, nursed a cold and conferred with Fairfield Osborn, the zoologist, on the strategy of getting the problem of food-population-soil conservation into the centre of international politics—which is its proper place not only because of its intrinsic importance, but also because it is the only subject on which it might be possible to get peaceful co-operation. There seems quite a hope of getting something done. Too late, as usual. But perhaps in time to do some good and introduce some element of realism and sanity into political thought. Why mankind should do everything in its power to destroy itself is a mystery. Perhaps possession by devils is the most plausible explanation after all.

Peggy [Ashcroft] will bring you more of our news. But meanwhile this brings you my love. It was wonderful to find such a warmth of affection after all these years. Bless you, dear Mary.

Ever your affectionate,
Aldous

TO ANITA LOOS

Sage and Sun
Palm Desert, California
14 February 1949

My dear Anita,

I've been working on some additional scenes for the dramatization of *Ape and Essence*—scenes which will, I think, have the double advantage of increasing the playing time and heightening the drama and comedy. These are now nearly finished, and I am anxious to incorporate them into the script. Would you, therefore, be very kind and return the copy I sent you? I have only the rough draft here and would like to have a fair copy with all the additions.

Reece Halsey forwarded a note from Albert Taylor,[1] saying that he liked the first version and hoped to sell it as a piece with incidental music and ballet. Which may be a good idea. Meanwhile there seems to be a possibility *The Gioconda Smile* may finally be put on in New York. We are keeping all our fingers crossed.

I hope all goes well with you and your projects. It is beginning to look like television may soon kill not only the theatre and the movies, but radio, books, magazines, newspapers, and finally articulate speech and all the processes of ratiocination. Talk of the barbarian invasions—the fifth century was nothing to the twentieth.

We had Grace and Edwin staying with us for three days last week. Both in good form, and Edwin full of enthusiasm over the first photographs taken by the two-hundred inch telescope. The thing does all that was hoped for it, and the first sample shot revealed two entirely new and unsuspected kinds of nebulae, with faint images of nebulae

---

[1] Albert Taylor. A producer of *Damn Yankees*.

going on and on in undiminished numbers to a billion light years into space. So he is as happy as a king.

Best love from us both.

Yours affectionately,
Aldous

In late November 1948 Huxley goes to Palm Desert on doctor's orders and works there on English and French stage versions of Ape and Essence, *staying until the end of February 1949. From March to May 1949 Huxley works at his Beverly Hills home on a book about the French philosopher Maine de Biran, which later anchors his* Themes and Variations. *In May the Huxleys purchase a home at 740 North Kings Road, Los Angeles, and think of selling the Wrightwood chalet. They move to Kings Road in October 1949. In December, Matthew becomes engaged to Ellen Hovde; they marry in April 1950.*

TO GEORGES NEVEUX

Sage and Sun
Palm Desert, Cal.
24 February 1949

Cher Georges,
Voici la traduction de la pièce[2]—*un peu rustique, mais fidèle. La version actuelle n'est pas définitive, et je vous serai reconnaissant pour toute critique et suggestion.*

[Jack] De Leon, qui a vu une version antérieure, voudrait supprimer le Narrateur, en quoi, il me semble, il a tort. La pièce doit être non-réaliste, et le Narrateur contribue à cette fin. D'un autre homme de théâtre j'ai eu un conseil qui me semble meilleur. C'est de faire voir les cérémonies de la seconde acte en forme de ballet (à travers un mur de fond que serait en gaze). Ceci aurait l'avantage d'accentuer le non-réalisme de la pièce, de faire voir aux spectateurs des choses qui ne sont actuellement que d'écrite et entendues, et d'abréger le temps des discussions entre Poole et l'Archi-Vicaire—trop longues dans cette version. Un ballet avec une musique appropriée pourrait être très beau. Qu'en pensez-vous?

---

[2] *Ape and Essence.* Huxley's apt French title was *Le vice du vase,* from Montaigne's essay "Du Pédantisme." In 1603 John Florio nicely rendered the sense of Montaigne's phrase "*le vice du vase*" into English: "Knowledge is an excellent drug, but no drug is sufficiently strong to preserve it selfe without alteration or corruption, according to the fault of the vessel [*le vide du vase*] that contained it."

Au commencement de l'Acte j'ai l'intention d'ajouter une scène entre Loola et Flossie avant l'arrivée de Poole. Flossie sortira et ce sera grâce à elle, plus tard que l'Archi-Vicaire reviendra surprendre les amants. On a dit qu'il est inadmissible, à la fin, de faire enfermer l'acteur principale dans un placard. Il sera donc attaché à une chaise et assistera, en maudissant, au départ des amants.

De Leon veut diviser l'Acte II et III en 2 scènes séparées chacune, séparées par descente du rideau. Mais je n'en vois pas la nécéssité. Qu'en pensez-vous?

Nous attendons avec impatience les nouvelles de la Gioconde.

Tendresses à Jeanne et à Noele.

Bien amicalement,
Aldous

[Dear George,

Here is the translation of the play—a bit rough but accurate. The present version is not definitive, and I would be grateful for any criticisms and suggestions.

[Jack] De Leon, who saw a previous version, wanted to suppress the Narrator, about which I think he is wrong. The play must be non-realistic, and the Narrator contributes to this end. From another man-of-the theatre, I had some advice which seems to me better. It is to show the ceremonies of the second act in ballet form (through a background wall of gauze), which would have the advantage of accentuating the non-realism of the play, letting the spectators see things which are now merely written and heard, as well as to cut the length of the discussions between Poole and the Arch-Vicar—too long in the present version.

A ballet with appropriate music could be very beautiful. What do you think?

At the beginning of the act, I intend to add a scene between Loola and Flossie before Poole's arrival. Flossie will leave, and later, it will be because of her that the Arch-Vicar returns to surprise the lovers.

They say it won't work at the end to lock the lead actor into a closet; so he will be tied to a chair and will be present, cursing, as the lovers exit.

De Leon wants to divide Acts 2 and 3 into two separate scenes each, separated by a curtain, but I don't see the need. What do you think?

We impatiently await news about [*Le Sourire de*] *la Joconde* [their translation of Huxley's play, *The Gioconda Smile*].

Love to Jeanne and Noële . . .]

TO MRS. LOOMIS[3]

Wrightwood, Cal.
25 February 1949

Dear Mrs. Loomis,

Thank you for your letter. It is impossible for me to make any commitments in regard to a review of Mr Borsodi's book. Owing to defective sight, I have to ration my reading to what is strictly necessary to me at the moment, and as I have a lot of work immediately in front of me, it may be some time before I can get to the book. It may happen that I shall do something on it later on; but I can't undertake a publication date review.

I am concerned to hear that Mr Borsodi is losing his eyesight. As a fellow sufferer, I can offer two suggestions which may prove helpful. First, to get in touch with a competent teacher of the Bates Method of visual re-education and learn to use the eyes properly instead of improperly, so that bad functioning may not produce an organic impairment. The second suggestion relates to a man whose acquaintance I made this autumn in New York, Dr Gustav Erlanger, a German oculist of very high reputation, who was driven out by Hitler, and who uses Iontophoresis upon the eyes with remarkable effectiveness in many very difficult and apparently hopeless cases of cataract, retinitis, detached retina, atrophy of the optic nerve, etc. He is a very able man, has done much work in experimental physiology as well as in medicine and, after considerable opposition from his colleagues here, is now achieving deserved recognition, being now the President of the Iontophoretic Society. His address is 20 West 77th St, New York City—at least I think it is; but anyhow he is in the telephone book. I think his chemical treatment combined with Bates training in the proper use of the seeing apparatus, mental no less than physical, should be of great help to almost anyone whose eyes are in bad shape.

Yours sincerely,
Aldous Huxley

PS Addresses of good Bates teachers in different parts of the country can be obtained from the Corbett School of Eyesight Training, 1560 South St Andrews Place, Los Angeles, Cal.

---

[3] Mildred Loomis (1905–2000). Author, educator, and activist who taught at Ralph Borsodi's School of Living in New York state.

TO EDWIN HUBBLE

My dear Edwin,

The news of your mishap was forwarded to us by Anita from New York. I do hope that by this time the enforced rest will have given the *vis medicatrix naturae* a chance to get busy and that you will soon be up again and about. Meanwhile do let us know if there is anything in the way of books you would like—for I don't imagine that Grand Junction is precisely the Athens of the West. Oddly enough I was talking of Grand Junction only the day before the news of your being there reached us. Gerald Heard was describing his trip to Aspen, to see Schweitzer and celebrate Goethe and spoke of Grand Junction as a place he had stayed en route. Gerald gave a very amusing description of that strange performance in the mountains: a huge circus tent, interminable speeches about the great man (of whom Schweitzer privately remarked, "After all, he isn't as great as all that!"), concerts by Rubinstein and the Minneapolis orchestra, with Hutchins brooding upon the waters like the Holy Spirit of it all. I confess I agree with Schweitzer and have never been able to work up any great enthusiasm for Goethe, except as the author of some wonderful lyric poetry. Faust seems to me a mess and intolerably literary and Wardour-Streetish. Wilhelm Meister strikes me as the most monstrous monument to a serene and self-satisfied egotism in the whole of literature. Werther and the Elective Affinities one can't take seriously. Perhaps the supreme greatness appears in all the other things, which I have never read.

There is not much news here. We are moving into the new house—740 N. Kings Road, LA 46 is the address, Webster 3 0455 the phone number) in the intervals of being up here where I am working on a long study of Maine de Biran, a study which is turning into a consideration of life in general as exemplified by what a particular man and thinker did, felt and thought, and also by what he didn't do and feel or think—for what is left undone is often as significant in a biography as what is done. If the thing could be done well enough, and I don't know whether I can do it well enough, it might indicate a new and more satisfactory method of philosophical exposition—philosophy through the particular existent, abstractions in terms of a concrete experience. I have become fascinated by the problems of the individual's relations with history and culture—the extent to which a man is in history and out of it, like an iceberg in water. And why on earth are certain problems simply not touched, certain classes of facts, perfectly well known, not incorporated into systems of thought?

Biran, for example, was concerned all his life with the problems of psychology in relation to those of metaphysics. He had an acquaintance with the history of animal magnetism, was personally associated with some of the most reliable and honest magnetists of the generation after Mesmer, believed in the reality of reported cases of thought transference and even of pre-vision—and yet never thought of incorporating the data of magnetism into his theory of human nature and the universe. And yet one would have thought, on the face of it, that these magnetic phenomena cast a good deal of fresh light on psychology and, if telepathy and pre-vision be accepted, on the nature of the universe. Another very odd lacuna. Biran was a close friend of Ampère, with whom he interminably talked and corresponded about psychological problems. But Ampère was one of the two calculating boys (the other was Gauss) who developed into a man of genius in later life. And yet neither Biran nor Ampère ever discuss this fact of the latter's personal experience. And yet one would have thought that the existence of calculating children was pretty significant in the construction of a psychological system. Herschel at the same date perceived this for in writing about his own gift of seeing elaborate geometrical figures with the mind's eye, he remarks that the seeing is evidently done not by what he would ordinarily call himself, but by somebody not himself inhabiting his mind-body at a lower level than the conscious. One cannot help feeling that in Biran's case, as well as in the cases of many other philosophers, there is a certain reluctance to consider the full implications of facts which seem to lessen the importance of the conscious ego in the total psychic organization.

Our love to Grace and to you, dear Edwin, all best wishes for a speedy resurgence.

Ever yours,
Aldous

TO ANITA LOOS

Wrightwood, California
5 August 1949

Dearest Anita,
Thank you for the telegram of good wishes. It was sweet of you to remember. But how sad that the telegram should be followed by the

letter about Edwin. The situation doesn't sound too good, I'm afraid, and at best one can't hope for more than a very restricted existence. It would be a real tragedy if now, when the dream of so many years has come true, poor Edwin were not able to go up to Palomar and use the two-hundred-inch telescope.

Betty tells us that you are on the verge of rehearsal, so I suppose you are wildly busy. Ditto here, as I am trying to finish a long philosophical study, which is to take its place in a volume of essays, by a deadline in September.

In this fourth year of drought everything is horribly parched, the streams dry, the oaks losing their leaves, even the pine trees unhappy. A few more seasons of this kind of thing, and the whole of Southern California will have gone back to the coyotes. Which might be quite a good thing, perhaps.

Wrightwood is being rent by civil war. The present proprietor of the Wrightwood company is a dumb crook, who is too stupid to make money honestly, so tries to make it by shady ways and is again too stupid to succeed even dishonestly. His latest effort has been to build an enormous fence round the lake which since time immemorial has been a free swimming hole for everybody; and to charge an enormous fee. Result; boycotting of the lake, departure of infuriated visitors, nocturnal sabotage in the form of sacks of manure tossed into the water etc. It is amusing in one way, but very sad and deplorable in another; for the whole atmosphere of the village has changed for the worse; moreover, if the fool goes on as he is doing at present, he will ruin not only himself but the entire community and all the owners of property here. It could be made the subject of quite an interesting comedy—for the situation has been complicated by our proprietor having corruptly wangled a cocktail bar into the village, in the teeth of opposition by the majority of the inhabitants and above all the nuns and Methodists, who have youth camps in the mountains here. So it is all turning into a kind of farcical situation, full of the clash of principles and the conflicts of social forces.

All good wishes for *Blondes*.

Yours affectionately,
Aldous

TO LUDWIG BERTALANFFY[4]

740 North Kings Road
Los Angeles 46, California
30 October 1949

Dear Dr. von Bertalanffy:
Please excuse this long delay in thanking you for the gift of your book and for the very kind things you say in your letter and dedication. I delayed my answer hoping that I should be able to read the book before replying; but work on a long essay, not exactly *on*, but around the French philosopher Maine de Biran took so much more time than I anticipated that I was unable to do more than glance at it; and since I do not wish to appear rude, I must delay this letter no longer, thanking you retrospectively for your kindness and in anticipation only for the profit which I am sure I shall derive from your book.

You are one of those stratifically placed thinkers whose knowledge in many fields permits them to strike at the joints between the various academic disciplines—biology, philosophy, literature and the like—and so to penetrate to the quick of the living reality in a way which the specialist, however learned and gifted, can never do. If I had been able to go through with the biological and medical education, which was interrupted in my youth by a period of near blindness, this is what I should have liked to become—a fully gratified striker at the joints between the separate armour-plates of organized knowledge. But fate decreed otherwise, and I have had to be content to be an essayist, disguised from time to time as a novelist.

I did not know that you had written on Nicholas of Cusa[5]—a man who interests me very much, though I have read only a few of his writings and only two studies, English and French, of his thought.

Thank your once again for your greatly appreciated gift and letter.

Yours very sincerely,
Aldous Huxley

---

[4] Ludwig Bertalanffy (1901–1972). Vienna-educated theoretical biologist.
[5] Nicholas of Cusa (1401–1464). German cardinal and philosopher.

TO LAWRENCE POWELL

3 November 1949

Thank you for your letter. No, I never translated any Lucian—and don't recall ever having written anything about the dialogues, tho' I greatly admire them.

Sincerely,
Aldous Huxley

TO AMIYA CHAKRAVARTY[6]

740 North Kings Road
Los Angeles 46, California
5 November 1949

Dear Amiya Chakravarty,
I saw Gerald Heard this afternoon, and he gave me your letter, which had, I am afraid, been with him for several days. Hence the long delay in answering, for which I am very sorry. I greatly appreciate the honor of your invitation, and wish I could accept it. But unfortunately the thing is simply not feasible at this time. My wife and I hope to be in Europe next summer, and perhaps an opportunity for visiting India may present itself in the autumn of 1950. Meanwhile I wish you and the Pacifist Congress all success.

Thank you for the Pound translation. I used to see him during and just after the First World War, with Tom Eliot. He is not mad, of course; but has always suffered from an intense vanity, which manifested itself in being consistently "agin the government." This agin the governmentness took the form of espousing the unpopular cause of fascism, in the teeth of the "liberalism" of his old friends. The most nearly crazy thing about him was his phobia of Jews. There are passages in some of the radio talks he made from Italy, which display an anti-Semitism that is simply pathological. He is being horribly punished for foibles and crotchets rather than crimes. And the trouble is, of course, that, not being under the law, but under medicine, there is no legal redress. And whether medical redress is likely to come from psychiatrists who, in the main, are Jewish, seems very doubtful.

---

[6] Amiya Chakravarty (1901–1986). Indian critic, poet; literary secretary to Rabindranath Tagore, 1924–1933. Senior research fellow at Oxford, 1937–1940.

I must also thank you for the volume by Schroedinger,[7] which you very kindly sent me some weeks ago. I read the book when it came out and liked it very much. Someone "borrowed" my copy; so your most kind gift was extremely welcome.

Yours sincerely,
Aldous Huxley

TO AMIYA CHAKRAVARTY

740 North Kings Rd.
Los Angeles 46
25 November 1949

Dear Chakravarty,
Many thanks for your letter from Midway and for the copy of [D. T.] Suzuki's latest book. I look forward very much to reading this; for Zen interests me more and more. I like it for the purity of its doctrine, for the fact that it has never succumbed to the temptations of superstition, always associated with Bhakti-marga, to which, as you were telling me when you were here, the Ramakrishna people seem to be succumbing. Another valuable feature is its recognition of art as an indispensable means of expression and of nature as a manifestation of the divine. The great danger of Zen lies in its insistence on the reconciliation of opposites in the transcendent neutrality of Mind. This has meant, in practice, that it has come to terms with the fighting samurai spirit and, later, with the nationalism of modern Japan. I understand that Japanese officers used to be sent to Zen monasteries for training in self-control, so that they could become more efficient at their job of destruction. This problem of the reconciliation of opposites is a very grave one. Because God sends his rain upon the just and the unjust, it does not follow that men must regard justice and injustice with an equal eye. And yet, as a matter of empirical fact, strong feelings of approval and disapproval are impediments in the way of realization. The solution, I suppose, must be sought in the pursuit of what is rationally recognized as the good, without affect. It is a very hard problem, and a wrong solution of it leads to the Arjuna situation in the Gita.

In recent weeks I have been in correspondence with a French doctor, who has written a very interesting book, correlating psycho-analysis

---

[7] Erwin Schroedinger (1887–1961). Austrian Nobel Prize–winning physicist, interested in Vedanta.

with the doctrine of pure Vedanta and Zen—showing where Freud was right, where wrong, and how modern western psychology can be completely extended, made adequate to reality in its totality. He has recently sent me MS material on psychology aimed at realization, or *satori*, but without the employment of the Koran, as in modern Zen. He writes in an obscure and abstract style; but what he says seems to be of great value. I need hardly add that nobody paid the slightest attention to his book.

I am enclosing a brief foreword to your essay and hope that it will serve your purpose. Having been suddenly called upon to produce, at a day's notice, something for "Vedanta and the West," I am sending it to be printed there. I hope you do not mind. The circulation of V and W is so small that I don't think it can make much difference. ("It was only a little one," as the servant girl in Marryat's novel said, when excusing her illegitimate baby!)[8]

I hope the Congress has been interesting and profitable and that you are not too much exhausted by whizzing round the world in eighty hours.

Yours very sincerely,
Aldous Huxley

TO AMIYA CHAKRAVARTY

740 North Kings Road
Los Angeles 46, California
7 March 1950

My dear Chakravarty,
I thank you for a shower of presents from the Orient and for a letter from Brussels, announcing your return to Washington—where I presume you now are. I much enjoyed Suzuki's "Living by Zen," which you so kindly sent me, and the book on Soto, which I take to be a kind of Zen without koans. Of great profit to me has been the reading of Suzuki's "Zen doctrine of No-Mind," published last year by Ryder in London. This contains a great deal of hitherto untranslated material and which, though Suzuki himself (who came to see us the other day and whom I liked enormously) regards it as an unfinished book, strikes me as being the fullest and clearest exposition of Zen psychology yet made. No-mind is the divine aspect of the unconscious, and enlighten-

---

[8] Capt. Frederick Marryat (1792–1848). The novel in question is *Mr. Midshipman Easy*.

ment is the result of becoming conscious of this unconscious, of living consciously according to its laws. And here, of course, lies the basic problem of life: to get out of the home-made world of compensatory fancies and "ideals" and to live the life of the divine Life Force as it manifests itself on every plane from the inanimate through the physiological to the spiritual. If we open ourselves up to the divine Life Force in its physical and spiritual manifestations we are all right, as individuals and as societies of individuals. If, on the contrary, we turn our backs on the God-made universe and insist on living in the home-made, verbal universe of fancies and ideals, imagining that we can improve on nature and make God in our own image, then we ruin our private lives, physically and spiritually, and create societies such as we live in today. Our habit of doing most of our living in a home-made world of words, fancies and illusions is so deeply ingrained that it requires hard work with special techniques to "get back to where we have always been"— that is to say, to the given reality of Nature and Grace, to things as they really are, in themselves, and not to *quoad nos*, in relation to our egos. Zen may be defined as a method for proving Kant wrong. Kant said that we can never know the thing in itself—which is quite true so long as "we" stands for the unregenerate ego. Zen shows how the unregenerate ego can be dissipated, so that "we," in the sense of our undistorted consciousness, can become aware of reality as it is in itself.

We expect to be in New York at the end of the first week in April, and I hope very much that we may have a chance of meeting in the East before we sail for Europe on May 9th.

Yours very sincerely,
Aldous Huxley

Aldous and Maria sail for Europe on 9 May 1950, staying until September.

TO BASIL RATHBONE

The Warwick
New York
1 May 1950

Dear Basil,
Forgive this very small-sized note paper—the only thing I can lay my hands on—and let me thank you for your very kind and understanding

letter, as well as for the dream of Holmes (one of my favorite figures of mythology) which I return herewith. In case I don't catch you on the phone before you go, I will tell you now that I have made the change you suggested in the scene between Hutton and Janet after the storm. I also mentioned the possibility of dividing the play [*The Gioconda Smile*] after Act II, scene I. Traube says that it would not be feasible mechanically, since the prison-cum-Spence-sitting-room scene of Act III will require some minutes to prepare. Incidentally, the device he and his designer have worked out for this sounds as though it would be extraordinarily effective. He will tell you about the mechanics of it more authoritatively than I can do.

Please give my kindest regards to Mrs. Rathbone and believe me,

Yours very sincerely,
Aldous H.

TO AMIYA CHAKRAVARTY

The Warwick
65 W. 54th St., New York
6 May 1950

Dear Chakravarty,

Thank you for your letter. I was sorry indeed to have missed you on your passage through New York, and hope that there will be a chance of seeing you on our return in October—or late September, if I can get our sailing date changed, so that we can be back in time for the opening of my play on Broadway.

Your friend has just rung up; but these last days are so frenziedly busy that there was no spare moment for a meeting.

What you say about Einstein having been offended by my use of his name in *Ape and Essence* distresses me very much. I thought that I had made it perfectly clear that I was using him—just as I had used Faraday and Pasteur—as an embodiment of science. I could, as in the medieval allegory, have called them Sir Physics or Lady Biologia. But it seemed easier and more vivid to take the name of a real scientific pioneer to represent his science and to show—what is, alas, sufficiently obvious—that the labours of disinterested truth-seekers are constantly used to serve the purposes of the lowest human passions. In other words, "Ends are ape-chosen, only the means are man's." The purely allegorical nature of my Einstein figures is clearly indicated, first, by the fact that there are two of them, one in servitude to each army, and, second, by the Narrator's remark, after quoting Pascal on the idolatrous nature of the worship of truth without charity, that the death of the two Einsteins is in fact the suicide of modern science. Einstein as a person never enters into the book; his name is employed exclusively as a symbol and personification of Modern Physics.

Yours sincerely,
Aldous Huxley

TO BASIL RATHBONE

31 Pond Street
Hampstead, N.W.3
ca June 1950

Dear Basil,

I hope that all goes well, in spite of the miserable state of the world at large, with you and your family. London is a good deal more cheerful than it was two years ago, when I was here last; and one prays that the respite from war and the improvement in conditions may continue for a while longer. Meanwhile I have seen Valerie Taylor and talked with her about the play, gaining some useful ideas about it from the Janet's-eye point of view. She made two points which I thought were good. The first was that, when she played the part with Clive Brook, she felt that Hutton was insufficiently the amorist, that it wasn't made sufficiently clear that he had wantonly and as it were scientifically, as a matter of experiment, played with Janet's emotions to the point when she had become filled with a blind, almost physical passion for him, such a passion being the only force strong enough to drive her to murder. The stuff about the talented children is used by her as a justification and rationalization of this blind desire, after the event. A great deal of Hutton's experimental and vivisecting amorism must necessarily be suggested in the acting. But to help matters, I have added a few lines in the scene immediately preceding the poisoning of the coffee (see accompanying page). These should provide an opportunity for putting across, at a crucial moment of the story, what has to be expressed—namely, Hutton's gratuitous and wanton scientific arousing of Janet's emotions; Janet's taking this seriously as a manifestation of genuine love; and Hutton's uneasy realization that he may have set in motion forces which he cannot control. I don't think we shall have to lengthen this scene, and it would be best if it remained brief and unspecific—the hint and not a statement. The statement and explanation will come later, in the thunderstorm scene and in the condemned cell scenes. In the first act we don't explain, but merely show something in action.

The other point Valerie Taylor raised was one we have all been worried about—the finding of the weed killer by the nurse. To mitigate its obviousness she suggests that the nurse should find a whole collection of gardening equipment, of which the weed killer would be one item. This will, I think, do something to take the curse off the situation, and I have modified the text and stage directions accordingly.

With all good wishes to you both, I am

Yours very sincerely,
Aldous Huxley

TO GEORGES NEVEUX

67 bis Boulevard Lannes
Paris 16ième
[September 1950]

Cher Georges,
Combien nous regrettons le soleil et la verdure, les chasses aux champignons et les diners autour de la table de cuisine: Coufontaine absum, hélas, et non adsum; la Maison de Joyet est devenue un souvenir—mais un souvenir reconfortant et très beau, dont je vous remercie,

A bientôt.
Aldous

[Dear Georges,
How much we miss the sunshine and verdure, the hunts for mushrooms and the dinners around the kitchen table: Caufontaine[9] *ab*sum,[1] alas, not adsum; La Maison de Joyet[2] has become a memory, albeit a very beautiful comforting memory, for which I thank you.]

---

[9] A reference to Paul Claudel's (1868–1955) dramatic trilogy about the aristocratic Coûfontaine family, *L'Otage* (1911), *Le pain dur* (1918), and *Le père humilié* (1920). Huxley attended a performance of Claudel's *L'Otage* at the Comédie Française with Neveu, 30 May 1950.
[1] Absum/adsum: I am absent / I am there.
[2] On 26 June 1950, Huxley visited Maison Joyet, a sixteenth-century mansion, now the site of the town hall of the Burgundian city of Paray-Le-Monial.

On 3 October 1950 The Gioconda Smile *opens on Broadway for a five-week run. Aldous and Maria drive back to Los Angeles, visiting Frieda Lawrence en route.*

TO SHEPARD TRAUB

740 North Kings Road
Los Angeles 46, Cal.
28 October 1950

Dear Shepard,
We arrived last night, to find your letter waiting for me. I hope the play may still be nursed through a shaky convalescence into full health. Perhaps Maria's astrological witch may turn out to be right, when she said that after six weeks or two months, it would settle down into being a success. Valerie told me—which I hadn't realized before—that the same thing happened in London. A difficult and precarious beginning, then, after seven or eight weeks, full houses.

Meanwhile I am very willing to accept your suggested sliding scale for royalties. I will write Jerrow to this effect.

We had a good journey so far as weather was concerned, interrupted by a stay in Taos, New Mexico, to see our old friend, Frieda Lawrence, the widow of D. H. Lawrence.

All good wishes to Mildred and the infants.

Yours,
Aldous

TO SHEPARD TRAUB

740 North Kings Road
Los Angeles, Cal.
18 November 1950

Dear Shepard,
Thank you for your two letters. Well, the poor lady is dead and buried, and it's fruitless to spend time discussing the causes of the demise. Hutton could have been easier, the nurse more believable and the last act would have been more effective and the individual scenes would have seemed less long if the revolving stage had permitted us to stick to the original structure of the play. But it may be that even in the best of circumstances, the critics would have been hostile, the public cagy and the costs excessive.

All good wishes for your next venture, and love from us both to all of you.

Ever yours,
Aldous

TO JEANNE NEVEUX

740 North Kings Road
Los Angeles 46
30 December 1950

Dearest Jeanne,

No accents on this typewriter, so I write in English. Your last letter announced that you were going out of town for the Christmas holidays. Does this mean, I wonder, that you have been looking for something—house or apartment—in the neighbourhood of Brive? I rather hope so; for I think it would be a good thing for all of you, if you had a country retreat. Also I feel that it would be wise to make use of the Sanary money, now in the Westminster Bank, in some more fruitful way than leaving it where it is. If you think of getting something, do make use of it. If, on the other hand, you don't want to buy anything in the country, then I think we should consider the best means of transferring the sum over here. I imagine that there must be some way of doing this. Someone like Paul-Louis Weiller[3] would probably know how to set about it. I will not consult him, however, until I hear what you have decided about Brive. All I am concerned about is to get the sum unblocked and put it to some useful work, either in the French countryside or else over here.

We have been experimenting with Dianetics. Up to the present I have proved to be completely resistant—there is no way of getting me onto the time track or making the subconscious produce engrams. Furthermore I find that there is a complete shutting off of certain areas of childhood memory, due, no doubt, to what the dianeticians call a "daemon circuit," an engrammatic command in the nature of "don't tell," "keep quiet" etc. Whether I shall ever get anywhere, I don't know. Maria, meanwhile, has had some success in contacting and working off engrams and has been back repeatedly into what the subconscious says is the pre-natal state. Whether because of Dianetics or for some other reason, she is well and very free from tension. But she is rather disappointed

---

[3] Paul-Louis Weiller (1893–1993). French financier and patron of the arts.

that there are not other and more spectacular results. In any case the thing seems to be worth looking into and making experiments with. Hubbard, the author of the book, is a very queer fellow—very clever, rather immature, far from being a "clear" himself (he says he has never had time to undergo a thorough auditing) and in some ways rather pathetic; for he is curiously repellent physically and is probably always conscious of the fact, even in the midst of his successes. When one watches the auditing of a good case, all the phenomena described in the book—the revived pains and emotions, the re-seeing and re-hearing of events in very early childhood and even in the pre-natal condition, even as far back as conception (and apparently before conception in certain cases, with the implication of some kind of persisting consciousness)—can be observed. It is most curious to watch.

Best love to you all and a happy new year, in spite of everything.

Your affectionate,
Aldous

After the play closes in New York, Basil Rathbone appears in a production of The Gioconda Smile *at John Lane's Ogunquit Playhouse in southern Maine in 1951.*

TO BASIL RATHBONE

740 North Kings Rd.
Los Angeles 46, Cal.
6 March 1951

Dear Basil,
Well, I am up again, but still wambly on the legs—and the infection has affected my eyes so that I can't do any close work for the time being. So I take this opportunity of writing to you frankly what I think of the whole situation.

First of all I note with considerable astonishment that you write of the play, and have handled it, as though it were something still untried and experimental. But please remember that it ran in London for a year, that now, more than two years later, it is still playing in the English provinces, that it has been put on all over Europe, in South America, in South Africa, in Australia—generally with very good success. Now, what you are doing is to perform a major operation—to perform it blindly (for you will not have a chance to try out which of the two versions, yours or mine, is the better—on a theatrical property which has proved itself, financially and dramatically, before a remarkably wide variety of audiences, from the most cultivated to the most rustic and colonial. Is this sensible? Is this prudent? On one side is your opinion; on the other is the fact that, when acted by a competent all-round cast, in the form in which I wrote it, the play has worked well with audiences from London to Rio and from Oslo to Sydney. True, it failed to work well in New York. But that, I think, was due to poor direction, bad casting (particularly in the case of the nurse, who is a figure of cardinal importance) and, last but not least, the revolving stage which made it necessary to depart from the form which I had given to the last act by telescoping the scenes together instead of playing them in rapid alternation. Now you propose to do something even more drastic to the last act. Much of the force of that "conflict at a distance," which (as I explained in a letter I wrote you last autumn) is the essence of that act, will be removed by the reduction in the number of scenes and the bundling of an action originally conceived of as covering several days into a matter of hours. For the sake of exploring character and developing dramatic possibilities, we need first to show Hutton in despair—then to leave him there, so that the audience can imaginatively feel that his abjection lasts for a long time, while we shift to Janet and Libbard in the afternoon scene. Then, when we have shown the downward grade in Janet, we must go back to Hutton to show the beginning of the upward grade. Then back to Janet, to show a deeper level in the descent; then back to the prison and so on to the end. In this succession of alternating scenes it is obvious that more footage will have to be given to Janet than to Hutton—for the obvious reason that, in life, a mad person is a harder nut to crack than a sane one, even in a state of despair. This extra footage does not imply greater importance for the character of Janet than for that of Hutton. It merely means that Janet is a character for whom the long-drawn and searching treatment accorded to Raskolnikov in *Crime and Punishment* is dramatically right and necessary; while for Hutton it is not. So far as I know no objection to the greater length of Janet's scenes was ever raised by any of the male leads in the play—and these included such very well known actors as Raymond Rouleau in Paris and Clive Brooke in London. I cannot imagine that your following among summer stock audiences will feel any disappointment in seeing you perform in the last act as I wrote it. Quantitatively the scenes may be relatively short; but qualitatively they give you every opportunity for being eminently yourself and giving a performance they will long remember.

To me, all this is merely self-evident. But it may not be to you. And if you still believe that summer stock audiences will prefer to my play another play that is less true to life, less dramatic and worse-constructed, then I'm ready to allow the experiment to be made. In no circumstances, however, would I consider making the present paste-and-scissor recension of the last act a permanent acting version.

Yours,

Aldous

PS. If you decide to do the play, I believe it would be worthwhile to let your cast see a showing of the film version of the story ("A Woman's Vengeance," Universal). There is a beautiful performance by Hardwicke as the doctor, by Jessica Tandy as Janet, by Mildred Natwick as the nurse. Ann Blythe was quite good as Doris and, though it was absurd to cast a Frenchman in the role of an English country gentleman, Boyer had some very good moments as Hutton.

TO MATTHEW HUXLEY

740 North Kings Road
Los Angeles 46, Cal.
16 April 1951

Dearest M,

Many happy returns of the day! And here is a small gift. Let it serve as a contribution towards the electro-magnetic brakes of the jet-propelled perambulator which Ellen tells us you are designing in view of the impending and most blessed event.[4] (*Your* perambulator, I might add, was man propelled. I remember having shoved the damned thing around Kensington Gardens for hours at a stretch, and being commiserated with, one day, by old Sydney Schiff, that Maecenas of advanced art and letters, whose German-American origins made it necessary for him to overact the part of the English gentleman to the point of appearing at dinner in a hunting pink; on which occasion Walter Sickert remarked: "Hearts of oak are our Schiffs.") Meanwhile I hope we shall see you out here before the blessed event occurs. By the time you get here, the new bathroom should be ready—though only just, at the present rate of progress, which is reduced for weeks at a stretch to zero by the failure of the building inspectors to inspect. We have already had about six inspections—including one of the chicken wire on which the plaster is

---

[4] Matthew and Ellen's son, Mark Trevenen, was born on 20 October 1951.

laid—and are now waiting for another, this time on the first coat of the plaster. I suppose it is all very necessary; but in the meantime it is extremely exasperating.

Life goes on as usual, though at a slightly lower than average level of efficiency, owing to the after-effects of the flu we both had at the beginning of March. We are both a bit tired, and I am still plagued with recurrent flare-ups of inflammation of the right eye, which was affected during the period of high fever. I have begun a course of cortisone drops, which the specialist says is helpful in acute conjunctivitis and sometimes does marvels for even long-standing corneal opacities. Let us hope they work; for the eye trouble interferes with reading, and my historical book requires a great deal of reading. And how odd any historical period looks when you get down to the details of individual lives! The majestic generalizations of Toynbee and Spengler disappear and you find nothing but individual squalors and sublimities and eccentricities. I shall introduce as much as possible of this particularized queerness; for, after all, it is with particulars that we do our day to day living, not with generalizations and trends and abstractions, which exist only for large numbers and over long durations, not for individual Toms and Dicks and Harries. What people actually live with is always the personal fact of health, sickness, good or bad humour, desire or aversion, all experienced within the framework of current notions. And what astonishing things the current notions could make people do! One of the exorcists at Loudun expelled a devil lodged in the Mother Superior's body by having the apothecary come and give her an enema of holy water. The operation was completely successful, and Asmodeus came forth—not without dust and heat, as Milton would say. Molière, one sees, was not exaggerating; rather he was understating. Indeed, the doctors are uniformly sublime. One of their great triumphs at this time was the Perpetual Pill—a marble of metallic antimony which was swallowed, set up reactions with the juices of the stomach—reactions which had a purgative effect—passed through the intestines and was recovered in the stools, to be used again, *ad infinitum*. Perpetual Pills were left as heirlooms by parents to their children. And when the doctors abandoned a case as hopeless, they allowed charlatans and village healers to be called in. When Richelieu was dying and the doctors had given him up, an old woman was sent for, who made him drink a decoction of horse dung in white wine. Even after death the fantastic game went on. Most distinguished people were subjected to an autopsy and frequently cut up and buried piecemeal—the head here, the heart there. Sometimes the embalming was so badly done that extraordinary accidents would occur—as when the entrails of La Grande Mademoiselle, Louis XIV's first cousin, fermented in their porphyry urn and exploded with an enormous bang in the middle of the funeral service. . . . Never a dull moment.

Our best love to you both.

Ever your affectionate,
Aldous

TO MARY HUTCHINSON

740 North Kings Road,
Los Angeles 46, California
9 May 1951

Dearest Mary,
The Piero della Francesca book arrived a few days ago, and I was deeply touched by your thought of me. Thank you so very much. And what a splendid book! I have not yet been able to read Kenneth Clarke's text, as I have been bothered, ever since having an attack of flu two months ago, with recurrent attacks of inflammation in one of my eyes, and so have been compelled to cut down on all reading. However the trouble seems now to be wearing off and I hope to sit down to the introduction very soon. K.C. is always worth reading, and I expect to derive much pleasure and profit from what he says. Incidentally, I understand we are both to give a series of lectures on art at the Washington National Gallery—he next year, or the year after, and I in 1954. I haven't yet definitely decided on the subjects for my series—except that I mean to deal with various phases of the relationship between art and the other aspects of human life. (A most difficult problem, incidentally; for in many cases there doesn't seem to be any obvious connection between painting, say, and the rest of life. Painting develops according to the logic of its own history, not according to the logic of social history—except, of course, when a dictator comes along and orders a manifestation of Socialist Realism or Nordic Race-Spirit.)

There is not much news to report. We expect to become grandparents next autumn, and meanwhile Matthew and Ellen seem to be exceedingly happy, not merely at home but also at their respective jobs. So all is well there. Meanwhile we are both tolerably well. I am deeply immersed in the book I am writing on and around Urbain Grandier, the Nuns and Devils of Loudun and Jean-Joseph Surin, their exorcist, who himself became possessed and re-emerged only after twenty years of frightful psychological suffering. An extraordinary story, very copiously documented with *procès verbaux*, autobiographies, letters, medical reports—and with the seventeenth century in the background, half scientific, half mediaevally superstitious; in part deeply concerned with spirituality, in part mundane and cynical to an astonishing degree; having all the superhuman pretentions of absolute monarchy and all the grotesque squalor of pre-modern inefficiency. (The entrails of La Grande Mademoiselle were so badly embalmed that they fermented in their porphyry urn and blew up, in the middle of the funeral service, with a deafening report. And all the time her cousin, the King, was trying to pretend that he was a demi-god.) I have written about half the book and hope to get the whole thing done, if I stick close to my work, by the later part of the autumn. God knows, of course, what the lunatics in control will have done to the world by then. I imagine that Russian strategy calls for no global war, but plenty of small-scale action in the Far East with an intensive effort to dislodge Britain and the U.S. from the Middle Eastern oil-fields by the arousing of nationalistic sentiment against foreigners. If they succeed in cutting off Persian and Arabian oil for sufficiently long, they will have won without firing a shot. For Europe can't function without that. After which I suppose it's either A-bombs and H-bombs or Communist regimes everywhere.

How is Barbara? And the new infant? And Jeremy, and Peggy? Give them our love, but keep a great deal for yourself.

Ever your affectionate,
Aldous

TO MATTHEW AND ELLEN HUXLEY

740 North Kings Road
Los Angeles 46, Cal.
[July or August 1951]

Dearest M and E,

Thank you for your good letters and sympathy in this very tiresome affliction [iritis], which is not only uncomfortable, but incapacitating, since I can't do any work involving looking. (Hence the doubtless number of mistakes in this uncorrected letter.) It is oddly tiring—for the dragging pain and consequent nervous tension seem to take a great deal out of me, even though I sleep and lie down a good deal. The condition is better than at its worst, but remains more or less stationary in a half and half condition, now seeming decidedly better, now relapsing again. Evidently this is the usual course of the disease; but meanwhile it is a great bore. Thanks to a suggestion from Mrs. Corbett [a Los Angeles Bates Method practitioner] I have been able, since yesterday, to avoid the interminable neuralgic pains in the neck which had plagued me for some time and which were due, it seems, to the right eye having slipped off focus to the outside—exophoric squint—setting up nerve strain. A simple little exercise of drawing circles in the air over the nose and, with closed eyes, paying attention to them and imagining one sees them has been enough to draw the eye in and out and end the pain. This is one of those simple and beneficent things which no doctor, apparently, would ever deign to think of, preferring instead to numb the pain with codeine. Meanwhile I am taking a course of terramycin, which seems to be clearing up the remains of chronic bronchitis at the base of the right lung. And this may, if the low infection was acting as a focus, help the eyes. But one never knows.

I agree with you about Gerald [Heard]'s article and book. Both were very badly put together. Nevertheless the recorded facts remain very queer. The navy's balloons account for some sightings, but not for all, even in this country—and for none of the numerous sightings in England, continental Europe and Africa. Two remarkable men came to see me the other day, and I asked Gerald in to meet them. Both are physicists, products of Cal Tech. The elder has been working as a physicist for the navy since 1930, did many projects for them and headed their radar school during the war. He has recently been working in a laboratory placed at his disposal in the Pearl Harbour Navy Yard. He belongs to a rich family which has kept a foundation going for the last twenty-five years on problems of gravitation. It appears— and we saw the photos and had a lot of technical explanation—that he has now evolved a model disk, which can make use of a wholly new form of electro-gravitational energy. There is a metal disk, surrounded by one of the new dielectrics, incomparably more non-conducting than any available until recent years. A wire on the leading edge of the dielectric, is given an electric charge of very high voltage, which is positive. A corresponding negative charge is given to a wire on the trailing edge. The result: creation of a gravitational gradient, which causes the disk to advance. The reason, it seems, why this simple device was not discovered before was the lack of high K dielectrics. They are negotiating for the large-scale development of the apparatus and, meanwhile, are planning a recording device for picking up electro-gravitational radiations. They have also applied a similar device for stimulating the growth of plants. Both of these men—who were exceptionally able and level headed—regarded the disk saucers as real and were very much interested in the detailed descriptions which Gerald was able to provide from his files. Many of these descriptions correspond with methods for generating high-voltage current by introducing ions into a jet of flame playing against a metallic surface (I think I have got this right) which they envisage as the source of the high potentials necessary to create the gravitational gradient in a large disk. Altogether I was greatly impressed and hope, when I can go out again, to visit these people and see their miniature saucers. So, in spite of Gerald's bad writing, there may be something there after all. I have no settled opinions so far, but keep my trap shut and wait.

The reason why, if the saucers exist and are manned by Martians, we don't get their radar signals is simple: they are not using radar, but electro-gravitational waves, which will not be picked up until the suitable instrument exists. Incidentally, the man who had been head of the radar school, was saying how odd some of the anomalies of the radar are. Things appear on the screen which look as though they were made by solid bodies, when in fact there were no solid bodies present. Some of these, he told us, would be half the size of a battleship, if they were solid.

Much love to you both.

Your affectionate,
Aldous

TO MATTHEW HUXLEY

740 North Kings Road
Los Angeles 46, Cal.
1 July 1951

Dearest M,
Cocola tells me that you are floored for a name for the cub. Seeing that we embarked on the Evangelists with you, might not Mark be a possibility in the case of a boy? In the case of a girl, there is something to be said for Margaret—except that Miss Truman got there first. Something, too, for Frances, which was my mother's second name, as also the name of Matthew Arnold's youngest sister, who was alive when you were born and wrote me a letter to say how pleased she was

that you had been called Matthew. My mother's first name, Julia, is also good. So is Elizabeth—only it shortens to Lizzie, which is less satisfactory. Alternatively, you might try something Scandinavian, without, however, going for too much of the Icelandic Saga atmosphere. Or perhaps you had better do what was done in the case of the royal children in France—they were not named at all until a state baptism at five years old. Till then the Dauphin was called Monsieur, the elder daughter Madame, the second daughter Petite Madame, and the second son Monsieur d'Orleans. (We know all this as we are reading aloud a charming book, made up mainly of quotations from the day-to-day journal of Jean Héroard, the resident Physician of Louis XIII from his birth onwards. It gives a fascinating picture of nursery and adult life at the beginning of the seventeenth century. One of the charms of the situation was that Louis and his sisters were brought up with all his father's bastards, whose numbers were continually being augmented—as were also the numbers of the legitimate. He was aware of the distinction between bastards and the others before he could even talk, and at four was already drawing the line at eating at the same table with them.)

When you are next at a newsstand, invest fifteen cents in a copy of the latest "See" magazine—September 1951. There is an article by Gerald embedded in the midst of twenty-six (I counted them) nearly naked women, whose photographs constitute the rest of the magazine. Gerald's bearded image sits there like St Anthony in the midst of all his temptations—or is it a prevision of the homosexual's purgatory, innumerable bosoms and not a boy in view?

Our best love to you both.

Aldous

TO MATTHEW HUXLEY

740 North Kings Road
Los Angeles 46, Cal.
21 August 1951

Dearest M,

I forgot in my last letter to ask how it stood financially in regard to the blessed event. Please remember that, if you should need anything to cope with the emergency, I shall be only too proud and happy to advance it. This is merely to say that you must feel no hesitation in asking.

I have been thinking more about names and asking myself why, in the event of the cub's masculinity, we shouldn't think of my brother Trev. Trevenen has the defect of being a bit out of the ordinary, but the merit of being euphonious and of commemorating a very rare being, whom we all loved. And incidentally, talking of this name, I wish you would look into the Public Library next time you pass and examine a book called "Trevenen," which came out this spring or maybe last winter. I saw it briefly reviewed in the spring issue of the Journal of Parapsychology. It is the record of sittings with a medium undertaken by some clergyman—Dean of Detroit Cathedral, or something of the kind. The book is published by some rather obscure house, and I have not yet succeeded in getting hold of it, though Epstein of the Pickwick took my order at least six weeks ago. I am curious to know how the name came to be attached to this particular record of mediumistic communications. Probably it has nothing whatsoever to do with our Trev; but in these odd matters one never knows. I have mislaid the exact reference to the book, but I remember now it was mentioned in the Bulletin of Parapsychology, not the Journal—about May or June, I suppose.

My eye seems at last to have taken a turn for the better, and I am hoping that the improvement will be continued without serious setback.

Much love to you both.

Your affectionate,
Aldous

TO IGOR STRAVINSKY

740 N. Kings Rd.
Los Angeles 46, Cal.
22 August 1951

Cher ami,
Tardivement, mais avec quelle douleur, je viens d'apprendre la nouvelle de votre maladie et du bouleversement de tous vos projets. Que dire? J'ose seulment exprimer l'espérance que (comme cela arrive si souvent et si providentiellement) de cet échec apparent émergera un bien ultérieur plus grand. Avant votre depart j'ai été indigné de la façon à la fois imbécile et cavalière dont on a traité votre oeuvre et vous-même. Peut-être le malheur présent vous épargnera des difficultés et des déceptions plus accablantes, dues à la bêtise mêlée de mauvaise volonté dont vous avez été la victime. En tout cas, nous pensons à vous, Maria et moi, avec la plus grande affection et toute la force de notre sympa-

thie. J'espère que Véra [Mrs. Stravinsky] se porte bien. Our best love to her, *ainsi qu' à Bob [Craft].*

Avec mes souhaits et toute mon affectueuse admiration je suis, cher ami, bien cordialement vôtre,

Aldous Huxley

[Tardily, but with what pain, I have just learned the news of your illness and the upsetting of all your projects. What to say? I dare only to express the hope that (as happens so often and providentially) from this apparent setback a greater good will emerge later. Before your departure I was indignant over the idiotic and cavalier way your work and yourself were treated. Perhaps the present misfortune will save you from more oppressive future difficulties and disappointments due to the stupidity and bad will of which you have been the victim. In any case, Maria and I are thinking of you with the greatest affection and sympathy. I hope that Vera is well. Our best love to her and also to Bob Craft. With my best wishes and affectionate admiration, I am, dear friend,

Cordially yours,]

TO MATTHEW HUXLEY

740 North Kings Road
Los Angeles 46, Cal.
27 September 1951

Dearest M,
As I wrote in my last letter, I'm only too happy to help finance the cub. So I send a cheque for $500, which is the equivalent of your bonds plus practical nurse's salary for a couple of weeks. In case of acute crisis for either one of us, the bonds will be there to fall back on—increasing in value, albeit at a considerably slower rate than inflation causes them to decrease—but that is one of those things!

I was happy to hear that Ellen is so well, and hope that news of your financial concerns will be as good. We are to see some high-ups at Ford next week, I believe. The contacts may come in useful later. Nobody has words bad enough for [Robert M.] Hutchins and [Paul G.] Hoffman—the latter's autocratic madness has made him very unpopular in Pasadena and the former is regarded as unreliable. Which seems a pity, in view of the scope and potential importance of the Foundation.

Reactions to the play have been favourable on the whole—tho' producers are afraid of investing in a sardonic fairy-tale. Good advice came from George Cukor, who liked it very much but thought the character of Stoyte should be strengthened and enlarged—also from George Kaufman, who felt that the change-over from Stoyte as principal character to the Fifth Earl was all right in the book, but dangerous on the stage. Rose is working on a scheme to meet both these criticisms—a scheme to enlarge Stoyte and tie him in more closely with the Fifth Earl throughout the whole of the 2nd act. I don't know if we shall even find a producer—tho' several have expressed a liking for the play. The piece is essentially the same as those old tales in Grimm—about the man who is granted the right to get his wishes fulfilled and, before he knows it, has wished a sausage on to the end of his house. This ancient wisdom has become unpopular now, as one can see from the tone and substance of our modern fairy-tales, the comic strips.

Much love to you both.

Aldous

TO MATTHEW AND ELLEN HUXLEY

740 North Kings Road
Los Angeles 46, Cal.
21 October 1951

Dearest M and E,
I'm suddenly reminded of the letter I wrote to Arnold Bennett thirty-one years ago, in response to a note of his about Matthew's arrival—a letter in which I remarked that we literary gents might talk about our creative efforts, but that after all these creative efforts were pretty feeble in comparison with what our wives and le Bon Dieu contrived between them, to achieve! Best love to all three of you.

Your affectionate,
Aldous

TO JULIAN HUXLEY

740 North Kings Road,
Los Angeles 46, California
9 December 1951

Dearest J,
This is to wish you all the merriest Christmas and the happiest New Year compatible with diplomatic deadlocks, armament races, inflation and nationalism. Are you both well? And what news of Francis?

We flourish in a modest way. As I told you in my last letter, I am over the iritis which hit so hard this summer, and back to normal in regard to work—but conscious of a certain susceptibleness in the eyes and having to take care in consequence. At all costs I don't want to have a relapse—which is of frequent occurrence in iritis.

My historical book [*The Devils of Loudun*] is nearing its end, thank goodness—for it has entailed more research than I bargained for or is entirely good for the eyes. It is coming out rather long, but I hope will be interesting, both for the intrinsic strangeness of the events recorded and for the commentaries provoked by those events. After I have finished, I shall have to try and make some money—possibly by working on a film about Gandhi, which is projected by that curious character, Gabriel Pascal,[5] the man who was given the rights to make films of Shaw's plays. If the thing comes off, it will be an interesting job, but also an exceedingly difficult one.

How goes your project? I had a letter from Senton-Jones, who is, I gather, working with you on it. He enclosed a project for a Junior University—excellent, I thought. But who will put up with Casta?

News from Matthew and Ellen is good—tho' both seem to be a little exhausted by the energy of youngster.

Best love to you from us both.

Yours,
Aldous

David Dunaway cites Huxley's unpublished letter to Pascal, December 16, 1951:

India presents two dangers so far as my eyes are concerned—dust as a direct irritant and as a possible source of allergic symptoms which can bring on iritis . . . , for the condition often arises as a reaction to trouble somewhere else in the system. All this may sound very fussy and timorous; but I have had this eye handicap for more than forty years now, and know on what an exceedingly narrow margin I operate. This summer's experience proved how very little it takes to abolish that margin altogether and reduce me to complete incapacity (Huxley in Hollywood, p. 274).

Citing a June 1952 letter to Matthew, Huxley complains, "After wasting four months of my time, Pascal, on my demand that he

[5] Gabriel Pascal (1894–1954). Hungarian-born film director and producer.

compensate me for the loss by doubling his initial payment, has
called off the Gandhi business."

For his part, Pascal says, *"I'm afraid Aldous can't do a script on*
Gandhi. He approaches spirituality like a scientist, with his mind, not
with his heart. Just as his mysticism is more of a mental curiosity: it's
a laboratory mysticism. He is cold and embarrassed by emotion. I
don't think he understands that the dynamic force which moved
Gandhi was his all-prevailing love." (The Disciple and His Devil *by*
Valerie Pascal, p. 231). The project comes to nothing.

TO AMIYA CHAKRAVARTY

740 North Kings Road
Los Angeles 46, California
27 January 1952

Dear Chakravarty,
Thank you for your most interesting and helpful letter. The problem
which has to be solved first of all is the problem of storytelling,
dramatization and character. Once we have those, the rest (Gandhi's
message) will follow almost of itself. We only have to let him speak
the words he actually used and do some of the things he actually did.
But he must speak and do in living relation to a set of well delineated
and judiciously selected characters. If the framework is not interesting
and alive, the Mahatma's words and actions, however faithfully
recorded, will lose almost all their power to move and interest an audience.

Moreover, we have to remember three fundamental facts about
movies. One: the show lasts 100 minutes, during which it is possible
to speak less than 20,000 words. Two: spectators get hopelessly confused if the episodes of the film are too short and unrelated—as is necessarily the case with the episodes of a full-scale biography, where a
man is shown going from one thing to another and meeting a succession of dramatically unrelated people. Three: spectators cannot bear
repetition—and a man of principle is constantly doing the same sort
of thing in different contexts. From this it follows that we must (a)
confine ourselves to the most important aspects of the Mahatma's
message; (b) must arrange that our characters, though few in number
and present throughout the film, shall dramatically represent the
problems with which Gandhi dealt; and (c) that we must cover a rel-

atively short period (say, the last ten or fifteen years of Gandhi's life), during which we see only a few examples of his activity, each developed, however, to the limit of expressiveness.

Here are a few concrete problems in relation to the characters. Persons corresponding to Motilal and Jawaharlal Nehru are dramatically perfect. Now, what about the wife and mother? For dramatic purposes I feel that she should be (a) a representative of extreme Brahmin orthodoxy, for whom the acceptance of the untouchables is terribly difficult (though it is ultimately achieved under Gandhi's influence); (b) a timid respecter of the status quo, for whom her husband's and son's activities are acts of distressing folly.

This family has to be related (a) to the English, (b) to the untouchables, (c) to the Moslems. Perhaps our Motilal character can be an old friend of an English judge, whose duty it is at a later stage of the picture, to send the son and Gandhi to prison—making, as he does so, the remarkable speech which was made by the presiding magistrate at the time of Gandhi's first conviction.

In regard to the untouchables. I suppose we can see a family of them, of whom the father does the dirty work at the Brahmin household, while the daughter is adopted by Gandhi and goes around with him as the girl you describe actually did. (The episode of the water asked for and refused if not also given to the untouchable is wonderful and must be brought in).

The Moslem family. Does this, perhaps, consist of a Jinnah-like father, using communal politics to satisfy a personal ambition and of a son who throws himself into Gandhi's movement? This would be dramatically the best solution; but perhaps it might be unduly controversial.

We next have to consider the place where all these people live. It has to be some town where in fact Gandhi often came. It would be good to have a large industrial city, whose unspeakable proletarian slums could be contrasted with the poor, but relatively decent village life which Gandhi was trying to improve and consolidate.

And finally we have to decide on the principal historical episodes to be represented. The salt march will come somewhere near the beginning—very photogenic and useful in as much as it can be made to yield the rich documentary harvest on Indian life. Towards the end we shall have the old man's wanderings in the Eastern Bengal. Political activities (negotiations with viceroys etc.) must be kept to a minimum. The necessary historical background can be supplied by a narrator's voice. I think, perhaps, Gandhi should be shown in England—talking to cotton operatives, thrown out of work by the boycott; and maybe entering Buckingham Palace—to provide contrast with a subsequent scene in jail.

In the horrible communal fighting towards the end we must make full use of our fictional characters. E.g. the son of the Moslem family may be shown losing his life while protecting a Hindu family from the violence of his co-religionists.

I have set down a few notions more or less at random and should be most grateful if you would comment on them, making any suggestions from your own experience and knowledge which might give them dramatic truth and documentary authenticity. Our families have to be real Indian families, with their virtues and their faults, their customs, manners, idiosyncrasies. And overall there rests the problem of language. Everyone will have to speak English—but in the case of those who have not been educated in Europe (and do not in fact speak English) the English will have to be English-with-a-flavor, English in some way archaic and alien, so as to indicate, by a dramatic symbol, that, though on the screen they are speaking English, in life there actually speaking Hindi or Gujarati or Bengali.

How many problems!

Yours very sincerely,
Aldous Huxley

TO MATTHEW AND ELLEN HUXLEY

740 North Kings Road
Los Angeles 46, Cal.
13 February 1952

Dearest E and M,
The Hubbles (who have just read it) are forwarding to you the typescript of "The Devils of Loudun." Read it at your leisure and then pass it on to my agent, Jacques Chambrun, 745 Fifth Avenue, NYC. He may be able to sell bits of the book in serial form.

All goes well here. Cocola is still taking things easily; but is steadily gaining strength. Gandhi is still in abeyance, as Pascal is in Washington momentarily and, permanently, in a mess with Howard Hughes over *Androcles*. We have not yet seen Hoffman; but it will happen in due course.

I hope Trev flourishes. Stravinsky calls him The UNOUK, which is Russian for grandson. A good name—and when he gets too obstreperous he can be called Baby Onouks.

Love to you all.

Aldous

TO LAWRENCE POWELL

740 N. Kings Rd.
L.A. 46, Cal.
7 September 1952

Dear Larry,

Thank you for your letter and invitation. Alas, I feel wholly unqualified to talk about Shaw, whom I don't know at all well—perhaps because I have never found him very interesting. Did he, after all, ever know anything about human beings?

Next time I come into the library I hope to see you.

Yours truly,
Aldous

TO AMIYA CHAKRAVARTY

8 October 1952

Dear Chakravarty,

I was very sorry to learn of your accident. This matter of pain is a great mystery. Why should we be capable of a physical suffering so enormously beyond our biological needs, so utterly incommensurable with the utilitarian purposes of an organism which has to be warned when it is in danger and reminded, while the *vis medicatrix Naturae* is at work, to keep quiet and out of harm's way? It is hard to see why, in the courses of evolutionary history, living creatures have not developed some self-terminating mechanism by which pain would be automatically cut off as soon as it had served its biological purpose. In the spiritual sphere it can be made to serve the purpose of what the older pharmacologists used to call an "alterative"—as something which can change the percipient's state of being and open him up to another kind of experience. That it can contribute to the achievement of all kinds of *siddhis* and psychic states seems beyond question. Hence the widespread use of self-inflicted pain among the not quite highest types of the religious. Some of these (like the Curé d'Ars, who began by using pain for the sake of getting answers to his prayers, or like the man I have recently written about, J. J. Surin, who tortured himself in order to have such "extradorinary graces" as visions), have gone on to a pure and unalloyed spirituality. Others have remained on the lower level. In many cases there is evidence that the saints—e.g. Ramakrishna and the Maharishi—made use of the pain of their last illness for spiritual purposes and did not try to get rid of it by any form of control of the secondary nervous system, a control which was probably within their power to display. When we next meet, I hope you will tell me more of your own experiences with this terrible not-self, and the ways in which it opened the way for the other Not-self.

I am returning the little foreword, minus the passage about Kashmir, plus a long footnote, whose citation from A. V. Hill's Presidential Address to the British Association brings it right up to date. (Incidentally, I recommend a reading of Hill's address in full. It is published in *Nature* for September 6, 1952. It comes to no conclusions, but at least poses all the ethical dilemmas in which the man of science and the general public, which applies, or enjoys the applications of, science, at present find themselves.)

About your essay—I think this is excellent in regard to the ground it covers. But I think it would be well to add, for the sake of completeness, some account of Kautilya and the other theorists of Indian politics. I know no more about this than is contained in Zimmer's *Philosophies of India*; but you, of course, must be well acquainted with the original texts. It seems to me important that the teachings of the saints should be set against their historical background—the teachings (and the practice derived from those teachings) of the so-called practical man. Zimmer speaks of the blank pessimism of the Indian philosophy of politics, untouched as it is by any hope or idea of progress and improvement." But he also speaks of the practical ideal of "mutual goodwill, forbearance and cooperation" within each sovereign nation; and of the "ancient mythical ideal" of the virtuous world-monarch—whose title (is it not?) is your own name. And there is an interesting passage about the geometry of power politics—the series of concentric rings representing the "balance of power between sovereign states". At its best, I suppose the system of balances worked as well in India as it did with us in the eighteenth century, when Europe was governed by a caste of gentlemen who had sufficient fellow feeling, one with another, to make them reluctant to push violence to its logical conclusion. It was not an exalted ideal; but at least it "took the shine out of patriotism" (in Toynbee's words) and permitted only limited warfare. And that, I suppose, is about as much as we can hope for in an Age of Iron.

I don't know whether this suggestion is a good one; but would think that, just as it is important to see the Quakers against their theoretical and practical background—Hobbes, Cromwell, Louis XIV—so it is valuable to see Jainism and Buddhism and the doctrine of *ahimsa* against the background of Kautilya and the history of the Indian kingdoms.

I do not know what our plans are to be. Perhaps we shall stay here all through the winter, perhaps we may go to New York. It depends on a variety of factors. But if you should come out here, please let us know in advance.

Yours very sincerely,
Aldous Huxley

TO MARY HUTCHINSON

740 North Kings Road,
Los Angeles 46, California
2 November 1952

Dearest Mary,
Thank you so much for your letter and postcard. It was good to hear from you, and that you are well, and the rest of the family likewise. As one advances in years, one has overwhelmingly numerous occasions to confirm the immemorial estimates of old age as the time of physical and psychological misery—and this in spite of the mitigating effects of modern medicine and pensions. It is a comfort to hear some good news for a change.

Here all goes tolerably well. Maria got over her operation of last winter very satisfactorily, but remains with only a very narrow margin of safety on which to operate. If she doesn't do too much, if she isn't too hard pressed, all goes well. Unfortunately, in recent months, her mother has been troubled increasingly with arthritic pains, which produce spells of physical helplessness and engender states of mind which are very hard to deal with. The result is that M has been under more pressure than is good for her; and the problem remains and is hard to solve.

I am glad you liked the book. It represents, I think, the most successful of a series of attempts to carry on the process of thinking, not in abstractions, not in generalizations, but in terms of a particular case, a concrete situation, a series of individualized characters. Because they ignore the particular case, the facts of individual life in a body, science, philosophy and philosophical history are always inadequate to reality as we know it by direct experience. The supreme literary problem is this: how can one express the general in the particular, the abstract in the concrete, the spiritual in the material, the eternal in the temporal? The answer, of course, is that, unless you happen to be Shakespeare, you can never hope to do it adequately. But even if you have only a modest talent, you can take a shot at the target, knowing in advance that you won't hit the bull's eye, but content if you score something higher than zero.

At the moment I am writing some essays—on, around or tangential to the Far Western scene: the desert, the fantastically expanding population and economy, the brief and wildly improbable history. Soon, if all goes well, I shall be working on adaptations of some of my old stories for screen and television, for Leigh and Olivier and perhaps Ethel Barrymore. If it works, and if the next Depression holds off long enough, there might be some money in it. It would be welcome! Give my love to Barbara and Jeremy and their respective spouses, and to yourself the enduring fact of an old but faithful and unimpaired affection.

Yours,
Aldous

TO CYRIL CLEMENS

740 N. Kings Rd
Los Angeles 46, Cal.
25 November 1952

Dear Mr Clemens,
Thank you for your note and for the honor confirmed upon me by your society.

I knew Santayana very little—saw him once or twice in England and again while we were both staying at Cortina d'Ampezzo in the Dolomites. I remember him there among the mountains dressed as always in black, from top to toe, and taking his daily walk along a path which followed a contour line, and so permitted him to move in the midst of precipices without rising or falling, as though he were in Holland. It was a small but triumphant illustration of the Life of Reason.

Sincerely,
Aldous Huxley

TO CAMILLE R. HONIG

740 N. Kings Rd.
Los Angeles 46, Cal.
11 December 1952

Dear Dr. Honig,

Forgive the delay in thanking you for the gift of *Secret Tibet*, which we have just started reading aloud. We used to know Fosco Maraini[6] as a small red-headed boy, more than 25 years ago. His mother and father[7] were good friends of ours when we were living in Florence in the twenties.

I am engulfed in work at the moment—trying to write a script for a popular-scientific film about the Sun, against a deadline.[8] At the same time we are busy with preparations for the coming, early next week, of the grandchild and his parents—hiring cribs and play-pens, arranging for diaper service etc. All this encroaches upon the hours for walking and talking. Later on, I hope to have more leisure. But meanwhile I hope that you and your wife can find time to come here between 4 and 8 on December 27, when various friends will be drifting in and out for tea or sherry.

Yours very sincerely,
Aldous Huxley

TO ANITA LOOS

740 North Kings Road
Los Angeles 46, California
2 January 1953

Dearest Anita,

The picture is a thing of wonderful charm and beauty. I cannot thank you enough for it. You have really spoiled us. I think it will finally hang

---

[6] Fosco Maraini (1912–2004). Italian ethnologist and photographer.
[7] Yoi Crosse, English-born writer, and Antonio Maraini, sculptor.
[8] Frank Capra (1897–1991) commissioned Huxley to write a one-hour television program about the sun, neglecting to tell him he had paid Willy Ley $5,000 for a similar treatment—all the while writing his own script, which was eventually the one chosen by the studio.

in the dining room, where there are wall-spaces of just the right proportion for it. (My study has no wall space—only books; and the living room doesn't offer a suitable place for it.)

Christmas and the New Year have been made cheerful by the presence of Matthew, Ellen, and the little boy. It is a very happy family, with no cloud except the unconscionable delay in the materialization of Matthew's job at the UN. I do hope it will come soon; for the waiting is nerve-wracking and depressing for both of them.

We saw Clifford, Mary, and Richard[9] the other day—Clifford not too well, I thought, but active as ever in the party-going line; Mary looking hale and matronly looking, and very excited about the prospect of going to Spain to make pictures. Richard described one of the stories he is to do, and I listened in awed amazement. If only I could think of that sort of thing! But, alas, I can't! That is why I have to be content with such paltry assignments as the one I am on now—a movie about the sun. Popular science for T.V. and schools, with Frank Capra directing and producing. I hope we may turn out something of interest—but can't yet be sure. Meanwhile I have had to go back to school and learn some elementary astronomy.

How are your projects turning out? Better, I hope, than the play which was adapted from my *After Many a Summer* and which I think is rather good—but which nobody so far has wanted to produce. Maybe it will ultimately get put on; but meanwhile I am glad not to have to depend on anything so profoundly undependable as the theatre.

Love from us all and a very happy and very successful New Year to you, dearest Anita.

Yours affectionately,
Aldous

TO GEORGE SARTON

740 N. Kings Rd.
Los Angeles 46
14 January 1953

Dear Dr. Sarton,
Thank you for your very kind letter. I hope you did not find too many blunders in my temerarious excursions into the history of medicine

---

[9] Dr. Clifford Loos was Anita's brother. Mary, Anita's niece, was married to actor-producer Richard Sale.

and psychology. A little knowledge of the subject proved so fascinating that I found myself rushing in where angels fear to tread. The really interesting fact is that people were always good intuitive psychologists, even when their psychological science was manifestly inadequate. (Conversely, of course, the most learned and scientific psychologists may be without the smallest intuitive grasp of other people's thoughts, feelings and motives. I touched on this in an essay on Maine de Biran which I published two years ago in *Themes and Variations* and the same thought kept recurring while I was working on *The Devils*.) And presumably they were good intuitive psychologists even at times when there was no overt interest in psychology. E.g., Boccaccio was probably a good intuitive psychologist; but one looks in vain in *The Decameron* for any theoretical or even literary concern with psychology. Indeed the only 14th century psychologist of letters is Chaucer, whose work, it seems to me, is quite astounding in its modernity in this respect.

Very sincerely yours,
Aldous Huxley

TO WALTER HARDING[1]

740 N. Kings Road
Los Angeles 46, Cal.
14 January 1953

Dear Mr Harding,
Digging down through the almost fossilized accumulations on my desk, I have just found your letter of last August. This apology comes, I dare to hope, better late than never. There is no excuse, merely the deplorable fact and a tardy acknowledgement of the offence.

Some day I might write something about Thoreau—but I would have to re-read him first; and at the moment that is out of the question for me. T. is one of those authors one likes even when he is being rather dull—like Gilbert White of Selborne, who is always wonderful because of the very flatness of his unvarnished statements.

Sincerely,
Aldous Huxley

---

[1] Walter Harding (1917–1996). Distinguished American Thoreau scholar.

TO AMIYA CHAKRAVARTY

740 N. Kings Rd
LA 46, Cal.
28 March 1953

Dear Chakravarty,
Thank you for your good letter and for Northrop's book, which I hope to be able to read in the fairly near future. (My sight makes it necessary for me to ration my reading; so it may be a little while before I can return it.)

In regard to Dilip Roy[2] and Swami there has been a slight comedy of errors. Swami started by being all for him (though not accepting the reality of the Mira communications) and was distressed by any criticism of him. Then suddenly he called on the phone to say that he had found something in R's book on his relations with Sri Aurobindo,[3] which had deeply shocked him—something that implied that he, Roy, had gone in for the kind of Tantrik sexual exercises, of which he spoke, when you were here. I don't know what happened after that, as we have been out of town since then; but I imagine that Swami must have withdrawn anything in the nature of a sponsorship. Meanwhile I wish poor Roy could be induced to stop talking. But I suppose that can never be. The need to pour forth is clearly compulsive—a disease, and chronic, like diabetes or arthritis.

I am reading—or dipping into—Blyth's four volumes of translations, with commentaries, of Japanese *Haikus*. Most extraordinary and the nearest approach to an adequate expression of the kind of mystical experience which perceives *samsara* and *nirvana*, relative and absolute as identical. The brevity of the seventeen-syllable poems gives them, at their best, the quality of timeless instantaneity. They are punctiform, not linear.

It was good indeed to have had a chance of seeing you, and I hope the opportunity will soon present itself again.

Yours,
Aldous Huxley

---

[2] Dilip Kumal Roy (1897–1980). Musician and writer who in 1953 gave a series of music lectures in the United States sponsored by the Indian government. He was a disciple of Sri Aurobindo.

[3] Sri Aurobindo (1872–1950). Indian writer on yoga and nationalist poet active in trying to free India from British rule. Huxley thought highly of his *Life Divine*.

TO ANITA LOOS

740 North Kings Road
Los Angeles 46, California
24 April 1953

Dearest Anita,
Bonne fête, happy birthday! May 1953 be filled with happiness and (despite the sinister menace of peace!) prosperity. Meanwhile I hope all goes well and that your projects mature satisfactorily.

Here projects have had to be changed—for I found that the research entailed in preparing the lectures I was to give next year at the National Gallery in Washington was too much for my eyes. (It wasn't so much the reading as the poring over photographs). So I have had to call the whole thing off, and am feeling my way towards an alternative—perhaps essays, perhaps stories, perhaps both!

We saw Mary and Richard the other night at the showing of Charlie Brackett's film about the Titanic—Richard so olympianly the Great Director that he could hardly make himself aware of the existence of ordinary insects like ourselves; but Mary very sweet and full of a childlike optimism about the baby and all the money she and Richard were going to make in Europe. Well, I hope they will. But it doesn't grow on trees, even there.

Matthew, poor boy, is still out of a job. I do hope he will find something satisfactory soon; for it is a discouraging and depressing situation for them both. He gave us rather gloomy news about poor old Constance [Collier] in a recent letter—almost totally blind now. But she's wonderfully gallant, evidently, in spite of everything.

Do you ever plan to come out here? It isn't so bad, after all; so perhaps you'll bring yourself to take the westward plunge. In the meantime this brings you all our love.

Affectionately,
Aldous

P.S. Your picture hangs in my room. It is a constant reminder of you.

TO CASS CANFIELD[4]

740 North Kings Road
Los Angeles 46, California
29 April 1953

Dear Cass,

Thank you for your letters. I am glad the Paris book is finally arranged for, though sorry that the pages should take so long to be delivered.

I have had to cancel, or at least postpone, my Mellon lectures. The research, with its poring over photographs and reproductions, was too much for my eyes and, after two months work, I have had to call the thing off. Perhaps in some future year, if I can contrive to do the work by easy stages, I may give the lectures. Meanwhile I think I shall finish off a volume of essays mainly arising out of Western themes. Several have been completed already, and I have others in mind.

Have you, I wonder, seen Matthew since your return from Europe? He is still out of a job—the U.N. as vague and remote as ever, and alternatives either falling through or not materializing. I would be grateful indeed if you could give us the benefit of your practical wisdom. It is clear that, in many fields, Matthew's lack of a specialized education is a handicap, and I think that he ought, whether he gets the job immediately or doesn't, to go back to school and take some degree specifically aimed at providing the kind of Open Sesame which is now required. In his last letters he has made no further mention of these courses—he had something in mind at NY University. And I hope that, if you see him—and if, of course, you think the idea a good one—you will urge him to go on with the project. In any case it would be very kind on your part, if you could give him an hour of your time, find out what he is doing and why he isn't getting anywhere, and give him a little advice—and me, your frank opinion of the situation in general. The whole business is becoming disturbing. Matthew, I feel, is growing increasingly frustrated and discouraged; and of course the financial aspect of the situation is worrying.

Yours,
Aldous

PS Do you happen to know anything about Jacques Chambrun, the literary agent? He has done some work for me, selling stray articles and stories, and I have been quite satisfied with what he has done. But re-

---

[4] After the death of Saxton in 1943, Cass Canfield took over the correspondence with Huxley.

cently I can get no answers to my letters and payments for several small items which he has sold are long overdue. Do you know if anything has happened to Chambrun personally, or to his organization—which was quite a large one when I went to his office a couple of years ago? In future I don't think I shall make use of his services. But at least I want my current business with him straightened out.

TO JULIAN HUXLEY

740 North Kings Road
Los Angeles 46, California
30 June 1953

Dearest J,

What good news! First, that we shall be seeing you and, second, about the prize[5]—handsome in itself and a nice acknowledgement of work well done.

About arrangements. We will meet you at the airport on September 6th and bring you back here. About an hour's drive.) Then you can wash, rest and be prepared, by lunch time, to do whatever you wish or have to do. Would you like me to get Bob Hutchins over for dinner that evening? It would certainly be more agreeable to make him do the driving than to go traipsing over to Pasadena to see him. Incidentally, I have the impression—and it grows stronger and stronger—that poor Bob is the prisoner of his organization. They appointed a lot of academic fossils as heads of departments and, within six months, the whole Foundation looked like something in a Museum of Palaeontology. Then, to make matters worse, the trustees—i.e. young Ford, the executives of the Ford Motor Co and some other assorted tycoons—became greatly alarmed over such faint displays of independence and energy as the Foundation was able to make. Hoffmann was forced to resign, and I don't imagine that Hutchins will last very long. After which the Foundation will settle down to giving every professor in the country five thousand dollars to go on doing exactly what he is doing now. And that will be the end of that. It is a great pity, as I know of several deserving projects which almost certainly won't be supported by the FF. I earnestly hope you may have some luck with them, before petrifaction becomes complete.

---

[5] Julian was the recipient in 1953 of the Kalinga Prize for the Popularization of Science, a UNESCO-sponsored award created in 1952 by India's Kalinga Foundation Trust.

It looks as though Matthew were going to Harvard School of Public Health to take a Master's degree in Hygiene, as a preliminary to working first for a Health Insurance group and then, better armed, going on to the UN or some other international agency. The scheme sounds good. I think they will still be in NY when you come through—but they will presumably have to move back to Boston in the autumn.

Thank Juliette for her letter. I am so happy you have had news from Francis. Surely it's time he left the cannibals to their own devices. They will probably be happier without him, and he will certainly be happier without them!

Love to you both from both of us.

Ever your affectionate,
Aldous

TO MATTHEW HUXLEY

740 *North Kings Road*
Los Angeles 46, Cal.
16 July 1953

Dearest M,

We were made so happy by your good news of last night.[6] To be given more than one asks for—it is not merely the pleasantest of surprises, but also the sincerest of compliments.

Hutchins, who was dining with us, had said to Cocola earlier in the evening that he felt rather guilty in regard to you and the failure of the FF to make use of you. But when he heard what it was you were now embarked on, he was emphatic in saying that it had been all for the best—for this was something intrinsically more important, and with a better, more useful future than would have been your work on the FF. (Incidentally, Mr Davis, whom you interviewed this spring, has just resigned in a huff because nobody paid any attention to him!) Practically everyone else of importance in the Foundation has gone to New York, where Ford will occupy eleven floors of the skyscraper now being built on the site of the Ritz, and Hutchins is all alone in a vast air-conditioned office in Pasadena, trying to promote his scheme of a kind of GHQ for intellectual discussion, a genuinely Platonic and Socratic university, but not, I would guess, getting anywhere. I tried to sell him a project by our young psychiatrist friends, Dr Osmond and his associates in Canada,

---

[6] Matthew's Harvard fellowship led to a master's degree in public health and a successful career in health administration.

for investigating systematically the effects of mescalin on selected persons of high special abilities—a project, incidentally, which might throw a very great deal of light on the human mind and its place in the universe. He seemed interested, took Osmond's project and my own essay on the mescalin experience with him to read; but whether he can persuade the all too academic Dr [Bernard] Berelson, of the Behavioral Psychology Dept, to share his interest is another question. Maybe, when you have got into Medical Administration, you may be able to push some of these fundamental enquiries. I hope so. I also tried to sell Hutchins on looking into Samuel Renshaw's work on training of memory and the special senses. He had never heard of it, of course. Like most professional educators, he thinks of education only on the verbal level, and has never looked into the problem of developing the human being on the basic, vital, non-verbal levels of his mind-body. If Ford does something about either of these things, I feel I shall have achieved something of considerable importance.

I suppose you will now have to go house-hunting in Boston. If the situation there is as bad as in most other places, it will be a rather trying adventure. All we can do is to wish you all possible luck.

Love to Ellen and Trev. And to yourself, along with congratulations and every possible good wish for the new career.

Ever your affectionate,
Aldous

TO VICTOR GOLLANCZ

740 Kings Road
Los Angeles 46, Cal.
19 July 1953

Dear Gollancz,
This reply to your kind letter of last winter is six months overdue. I was waiting for a chance to read the whole of your book before sitting down to thank you. But owing to the fact that I read slowly and have so much that I must read as a matter of business, I haven't yet read more than a part of your memoirs.

So I had better get this letter written without further delay. It was kind indeed of you to send me your book and your comments on *The Devils*. (P. Toynbee's intense and one felt personal animus against them and me was very odd. I don't know him and am unfamiliar with his work, and my nearest approach to him is an acquaintance with his mother and Gilbert Murray. So what I ever did to make him feel so extremely bitter, I can't imagine.)

I liked your anthology, which contained many things with which I was unacquainted. The problem of twentieth-century religion, it seems to me, is the problem of finding an answer to the question implicit in Blake's remark: "If the doors of perception were cleansed, anything would appear to Man as it is, infinite."

But how to cleanse the doors? The problem is partly a moral one; partly also a problem in the realm of proper education in what must be called the non-verbal humanities—the education of man as a perceiving, feeling, intuiting mind-body. Much interesting work is being done in this direction by some of the Gestalt psychologists here—notably Dr Samuel Renshaw of Ohio State University, who has devised methods for enormously heightening the acuity and extending the range of the special senses, and of improving the memory. Needless to say, none of the professional educators have perceived the immense importance of these discoveries. Having gone through a purely verbal education, they can't think of educating other people except on the verbal level—with occasional concessions to man as a non-verbal creature, in the form of Swedish drill, clay modelling and games. Any idea of teaching boys and girls to be more widely and more intensely aware of the outer world is hardly thinkable by these people. Still less thinkable is the idea of training them to become more aware of the inner world and of establishing some slight measure of control over the autonomic nervous system, on which so much of our human destiny depends. I am preparing to write some essays on these themes and, in the interval, keep prodding away at such educators and officials of the great Foundations as I meet. In another twenty years, perhaps, something may begin to be done about education in the non-verbal humanities. Till then we must expect that educators will leave children to grow up in a verbal universe so dreary (for it consists of advertising slogans and popular science commonplaces) that, in mere self-preservation, they have to turn to television, alcohol, and political excitement.

With all good wishes, I am

Yours very sincerely,
Aldous Huxley

In July 1953 Huxley begins writing The Doors of Perception, *his best-known book after* Brave New World, *and which suggests the name of the rock band* The Doors. *On 28 September his old friend Edwin Hubble dies, and in October his granddaughter Tessa is born. On 3 November the Huxleys present themselves for examination as part of the application process for American citizenship. Proceedings are ultimately adjourned as a result of Huxley's scruples regarding the "bearing of arms" clause. Cass Canfield seeks legal advice on behalf of the Huxleys, but in the end they decide against pursuing the application and remain "resident aliens."*

TO CASS CANFIELD

740 North Kings Road
Los Angeles, California
7 November 1953

Dear Cass,

May I ask your advice on a practical problem which has turned up within the last few days. Maria and I decided two years ago to take out our first papers. We were *de facto* Californians, and it seemed the proper thing to become *de jure* Americans. We put in our final petition last spring and came up for examination this week. Our knowledge of the Constitution was sufficient; but a question has arisen in regard to the bearing of arms. In the final petition we were required to answer a questionnaire. This contained, among others, three questions: (a) Are you prepared to serve in the armed forces? (b) Are you prepared to do non-combatant service in the armed forces? (c) Are you prepared to do work of national importance under civilian control? We answered No to the first two and Yes to the third, knowing that there had been a Supreme Court decision (in 1946, I think) to the effect that a person objecting to bearing arms might none the less become a citizen. I assumed that in answering the third question in the affirmative, we were taking a legally acceptable course. But when we came up for examination, it turned out that this was not the case. So far as I can make out, the McCarran Act has been interpreted in such a way as to make the Supreme Court decision inoperative. That Act is now a law of the land, so that the Supreme Court decision in regard to an earlier law is now beside the point. The current situation, so far as we are concerned, is as follows. We shall be called up for further examination, probably within three or four weeks. If the examiner finds our position acceptable, we shall be allowed to proceed with our naturalization; if not, the petition will be rejected.

If it is rejected, we shall, I suppose, return to the status of resident alien. But in practice it will be difficult, perhaps impossible, to return to this country if we should ever leave it. Now I have various engagements in Europe next spring and do not wish to cancel them. Moreover the situation of not being wanted and not being able to come and go at will is one I would not be prepared to accept. So if the petition is rejected, I should feel bound, albeit with great reluctance, to wind up our affairs here and leave the country.

What I would like to know from you is this. Do you have any legal friends who are familiar with cases of this kind? (Recent cases—for the situation is different from what it was before the passing of the McCarran Act.) Do they know anything about the official thinking on the subject and the official attitude towards resident aliens who have been rejected, go abroad and would like to return? And finally what do they advise us to do? Our friends here are doubtful whether it would be wise to try to use influence, since the intervention of an outsider, however eminent or well-meaning, might merely serve to annoy civil servants, whose business it is to administer a law according to current procedures. Should the result of the coming examination be unfavourable, I believe I could take the case to court—but this is something which I would not, in any circumstances, wish to do.

I should be most grateful if you could make enquiries at your end. Discreet enquiries; for publicity could do nothing but harm. The whole business has its absurd side, since it hardly seems probable that the armed forces could be very keen on having either Maria or myself in their midst. However, a law is a law.

I'm sorry to trouble you in this way and would not do so if I didn't feel great need of your practical wisdom and some good advice.

> As ever,
> Aldous

TO CASS CANFIELD

740 North Kings Road
Los Angeles 46, California
8 January 1954

Dear Cass,

Thank you so much for the books, which I took away with me over Christmas. The Sitwell collection was mostly familiar; but the George Sand book was entirely new, and I enjoyed it hugely. The woman is so much more remarkable than the writer; for the novels—such at least as I have looked at, again in recent years—have become unreadable. (And yet, they were the great liberating influence of early Victorian days. Matthew Arnold, for example, read them with passion and felt that she stood for everything that his own society repressed. He even made a pilgrimage to see her in 1846.)

Thank you too for the book by Mrs Bedford, which I already know. (The author is an old friend of ours.) It is remarkably acute, delicate and vivid. I hope it will do well—though I fear that it may not be guide-booky enough to sell extensively. Books about Mexico almost have to be self-help books for the traveler; otherwise, like my own essay in this field, they don't seem to appeal to more than a very small public.

We are still waiting to hear what the naturalization officials have decided. We are now in the hands of a lawyer who is reputed to be the best in the field, and who is also a very important personage (a police commissioner of the city of Los Angeles) and a personal friend of the department heads here. Satisfactory legal precedents have also turned up; so let us hope all will now go smoothly. And if it doesn't, we will have the whole thing postponed to another season, when we get back from Europe.

We are supposed to sail on April 7th and expect to be in the East for two or three weeks before that. I may be giving a reading at the Po-etry Center sometime during that period, and I am wondering whether, to cover hotel expenses, it might be possible to deliver a lecture which was a great success when I gave it this autumn at Mills College and again at Palo Alto. Would you advise me to try to arrange for this through Colston Leigh? (I don't much like the man, who seems to me a real crocodile; but he presumably knows his business as a lecture agent.) Or is there someone else you know of who could do the thing on a less ambitiously professional level than Leigh? The lecture was en-titled, "Education in the Non-Verbal Humanities." But this is a bit for-midable.

So perhaps "The Training of the Psycho-Physical Instrument" would be better. Anyhow that, precisely, is what it is about—the edu-cation, universally neglected, of the mind-body which is the instrument we use in what currently passes for education as well as in doing our day-to-day living. I was paid $400 at Mills and $500 at Palo Alto, and would like to clear a similar or greater sum if I gave the lecture in or near New York. So should you know of someone who could arrange the thing with some interested institution, between March 15th and

April 7th—for a fee, of course, or a commission—I would be grateful if you would put him or her in touch with me.

Please give our New Year's greetings to Jane.

Yours as ever,
Aldous

In March 1954 Huxley starts work on The Genius and the Goddess. *On 7 April he and Maria sail for France, later that month attending Eileen Garrett's symposium on parapsychology and unorthodox methods of healing in the south of France. From 2 May until 15 May the Huxleys stay with Dr. and Mrs. Godel in Ismailia. Later Huxley gathers material for a book of essays,* Adonis and the Alphabet, *by visiting Cairo, Jerusalem, Beirut, and Cyprus; in June, Athens and Rome, spending July with the Neveux in Dieulefit and Vaison-la-Romaine; August they spend in London with Julian Huxley, sailing to New York on 21 August, and on 7 September they return to Los Angeles. He completes* The Genius and the Goddess *in October, and in November begins a stage version.*

TO PASTOR KNEBEL

Cunard Line
RMS Queen Elizabeth
11 April 1954

Dear Pastor Knebel,

Thank you for your kind and most interesting letter. To my mind the guiding principle in politics, sociology, economics and religion is summed up in the gospel sentence: "Seek ye first the kingdom of God and His righteousness, and all the rest shall be added." The kingdom of God is the given universe of Nature and Spirit. To seek God's righteousness in Nature is to collaborate with natural forces, not exploit the soil, destroy the forests, pollute the rivers, render the planet uninhabitable for future generations. It is also, it seems to me, to adjust, in a rational way, the human species (with its immense capacity for multiplication) to planetary resources. What is the good of talking about progress, peace and higher standards of living for all while the species adds 30 millions to its number every year and diminishes its fertile land, by exploitative farming, to the tune of about the same number of acres?

So much for seeking the Kingdom in the world of Nature. But there is also the Kingdom in the world of Spirit. We are much more than we generally think we are—more than an ego with a personal sub-conscious. We are also a part of Mind at large—and that includes the visionary world of poets and painters, and the world of pure spirit seen by the mystics and prophets. Let us seek these greater not-selves associated with our selves—and let us learn (there are many empirically valid techniques) to permit the physiological not-self, which runs our body (Aristotle's Entelechy, the Vegetative Soul of the Scholastics) to do its work without interference from our ego, which can never produce health, only psycho-somatic disorder.

If we first sought those two aspects of the Kingdom, then the rest (the strictly human world of law, political and economic arrangements, social relationships) would be added in the best possible form. But so long as we begin with the rest, so long as we try to settle things by power politics and power economics, whether capitalistic or communistic, then the Kingdom will certainly never get itself realized, and we shall have what we have now—what men, alas, have had during almost the whole course of their splendid and appalling history.

Sincerely,
Aldous Huxley

TO JULIAN HUXLEY

Hotel St. Georges
Beyrouth
22 May 1954

Dearest J,
We missed you here by a bare two weeks! I wish we had known about your movements in advance and not, as now, after the events from Maurice Shehab.

Meanwhile we are having a delightful time seeing the sights—mostly with Emir Maurice and his wife, and being entertained almost *too* hospitably by all manner of bigwigs from the ex-President to H.B.M. [Her Brittanic Majesty's] ambassador.

We spent two weeks in the S. of France at a congress of philosophers discussing parapsychology and of psychologists and doctors discussing unorthodox healing. Very interesting, and there were some remarkable people present. After it was over we flew to Egypt, spent 10 days on the canal with Roger and Alice Godel, then went to Cairo for the sights. The more I see of Roger, the more I like and admire him. I went round the wards with him every day, disguised as a doctor in a white gown. It was a liberal education in applied psychology and philosophy to see Roger at work on his patients—putting Socratic questions to the psycho-somatic and getting them to discover the most fundamental truths about their own nature.

Cairo was a great revelation. One really can form no idea of Egyptian art without seeing it in situ and in the mass. And the Coptic and Arabic stuff is also fascinating.

We hope to take a brief look at Damascus on Monday, then go on to Istambul, Athens (where we will meet the Godels again) and Rome for a couple of weeks from about June 5.

(c/o S. Roth, 13 Villa Ruoffo, Roma)

After that Paris and a stay somewhere in France with Jeanne and George Neveux. What are you doing this summer? I hope you will be in England late in August or early in September. Or else in France in July?

Love from us both to Juliette and yourself, and to Francis who wrote me a very nice letter not long since.

Matthew has been at Harvard since last autumn taking a Master's Degree in Public Health—which should be a very useful pass-key to many types of activity. Is Francis going to the B.M? And what of Arthur's domestic affairs?

Ever your affectionate,
Aldous

TO JULIAN HUXLEY

Rome
19 June 1954

Dearest J,

Thank you for your letter. Hutchins' address is The Ford Foundation, 914 East Green St, Pasadena, Cal. I forwarded the letter you enclosed in your first note immediately on my receipt of it—about three weeks or more ago.

Rome is still wonderfully beautiful—but the noise, the hazards of walking in mediaeval streets incompatible with the cars, bikes and motor scooters by which they are overrun! And a thousand or more new vehicles are added every month, along with heaven knows how many thousands of unemployed persons looking for work—so that the problem can only become more hopelessly insolvable as time goes on. What the place will be like in 10 years from now I cannot imagine.

We leave for Paris this afternoon and for a house in the country, somewhere in the Drôme, towards the end of the month. There, I hope to be able to so some work: for which I shall be glad—for one grows restless under the regime of idleness enforced by travelling; and meanwhile the wolves have to be kept from the door.

In principle we shall sail for NY towards the end of September; but it is possible that we may leave earlier or later. In any case I will keep you posted—and shall look forward to seeing you in England some time in August or September. We shall not stay long in New York and should be back in Los Angeles by mid-October.

I'm so glad to hear that the book is doing well and look forward to reading it with an interest that will be heightened by the fact that the subject matter is now not wholly unfamiliar.

Our love to you both.

Your affectionate,
Aldous

TO VICTOR FRANKL[7]

Pont Royal Hotel
Paris
23 June 1954

Dear Dr. Frankl,
Thank you for your very kind letter. I was much interested in your account of [Kurt] Lewin, who must have been a most remarkable man.

My friend, Dr. Humphry Osmond, of the Saskatchewan Mental Hospital, Weyburn, Sask., Canada is experimenting with mescalin and with other little known drugs. If you have any information regarding the psychological effects of tropical plants, I know he would be very happy to receive it.

Sincerely,
Aldous Huxley

---

[7] Victor Frankl (1905–1997). Austrian psychiatrist.

TO JULIAN HUXLEY

La Combe
Dieulefit (Drôme)
10 July 1954

Dearest J,

Thank you and thank Juliette for your kind letters. September 6th is an excellent date for me, and I hope to see you both then.

Meanwhile about Bob Hutchins. He has just written a letter announcing his resignation from the FF and his presidency of the Ford-financed Fund to the Republic—a new venture supposed to be dedicated to the defense of civil liberties and free speech. I don't know what it will actually achieve—but it has 15 million bucks!

Poor Hutchins has been *persona non grata* on the FF for the last two years, and I have the impression that everything he sponsored was automatically turned down. Whether you will get anywhere by starting afresh with FF, I don't know. Dr. Berelson, the head of "Behavioural Psychology," is a professional bottle who believes, principally, in obstructing everything that he finds unfamiliar. So heaven knows what will be your best course now.

This is lovely country, on the border line between Provence and Dauphine, with elements of both. But the weather is poor—tho' better, to judge by the papers, than anything in the rest of Europe.

Matthew's address is 186 Sullivan Sq, NYC. His Harvard stint is finished and for the next few months he does practical work in NY.

Love to you both.

Yours,
Aldous

TO THE EDITOR, TIME MAGAZINE

30 August 1954

Sir,

You inform your readers that in my last book [*The Doors of Perception*], I "prescribe mescaline, a derivative of peyote, for all mankind as an alternative to cocktails." Snappiness, alas, is apt to be in inverse ratio to accuracy. In actual fact, I did not prescribe mescaline for all mankind. I merely suggested that it might be a good thing if psychologists, sociologists and pharmacologists were to get together and discuss the problem of a satisfactory drug for general consumption.

Mescaline, I said, would not do. But a chemical possessing the merits of mescaline without its drawbacks would certainly be preferable to alcohol.

Aldous Huxley
Hampstead, London

TO CLAIRE MYERS OWENS

740 North Kings Road
Los Angeles 46, California
12 September 1954

Dear Mrs. Owens,
In case my note to La Jolla doesn't reach you, this is to thank you for your interesting letter, to tell you that Sheldon[8] has forgotten—but I am a 1-2-7, not a 16, and that I may be in New York City for a day or so in early October, where I can be reached c/o

Matthew Huxley
186 Sullivan Street
New York City 12

If you are in New York City at that time, I shall be happy to talk with you about those strange and enormously important matters, and to learn from you some of your ideas on the subject.

Sincerely,
Aldous Huxley

TO HUNTINGTON CAIRNS[9]

740 North Kings Road
Los Angeles 46, Cal.
20 December 1954

Dear Huntington,
A merry Christmas to you, and may you be as happy in 1955 as this odd universe and its yet odder inhabitants will permit anyone to be!

---

[8] William H. Sheldon (1898–1977). American psychologist, author of *Varieties of Human Physique* (1940), whose ideas on classification of human body types—endomorphic, mesomorphic, and ectomorphic—influenced Huxley.
[9] Huntington Cairns (1904–1985). American author and secretary-treasurer of the National Gallery of Art.

I have been reading with pleasure and profit (for I know nothing about the subject) your *Philosophy of Law*. I admire its clarity and the way you have reduced such vast masses of material to order.

This has been a very busy autumn for me—a short novel finished and a volume of essays polished and added to, until now it is very nearly completed. After which I don't exactly know what I shall do. Ruminate for a little and then—what? Embark on either a fantasy or a long novel—time will show which. (I feel fairly certain that I can't undertake the art lectures now. I had to do a few weeks of work with reproductions in connection with one of my essays, and found it a big strain. So we'd better forget about it, at least for the time being.)

That young man we met in the asylum garden,[1] with poor old Ezra—Denis Goacher—has just written me from England urging me to try to do something on behalf of Ezra. He talks of a petition to the president. But surely that wouldn't do much good, would it? Seeing that the case is not a matter for *pardon*, but for *re-diagnosis*. How is he, by the way?

Yours,
Aldous H.

TO ARNOLD GINGRICH

740 North Kings Road
Los Angeles 46, Cal.
3 January 1955

Dear Mr. Gingrich,
I appreciate your kind letter very much and am sending you herewith copies of two hitherto unpublished essays, which will take their place in a volume to be published, I imagine, about a year from now—along with the sewage essay which appeared last year in *Esquire* and a number of others, some short, some long and more systematic. *Esquire* seems to be the only periodical which still publishes essays, and if essays of the discursive kind on anything and everything are what you want, I think I can undertake the assignment you suggest.

I would envisage the writing of pieces of varying lengths—some very short: in which case there might be three or four of them in a single issue; others long enough to fill the whole of the available space.

---

[1] Huxley met Pound at St. Elizabeth's Hospital, the asylum to which Pound was confined from 1945 to 1958. Denis Goacher (1925–1998) was a British writer who tried to secure Pound's release.

In many cases, of course, the piece would be more strictly confined to a single theme than is the case with these two essays, where I have been experimenting with a form of writing which I enjoy very much and would like to be able to practice in perfection—the essay which says everything at the same time, without sacrificing clarity, which reflects the multiplicity and total togetherness of the world and yet is not a chaos.

With all good wishes for 1955, I am

Yours very sincerely,
Aldous Huxley

TO ROBERT PICK

Los Angeles 46, Cal.
7 January 1955

Dear Mr. Pick,
Thank you for your letter and the enclosed copies of my own letters, in which I have corrected one or two slips of transcription—or perhaps they represent slips in my original typing. You are, of course, at liberty to print these letters in your edition of Broch's works.

I always regret that I never met Broch, who must have been a very remarkable man with a most subtle and penetrating mind. His masterpiece, it seems to me, was *The Sleepwalkers. The Death of Virgil* exhibited, in a rather different form, some of the artistic defects of Virginia Woolf's later novels—too much sculpture with too little flat surface, so that, as in certain Indian temples, the sculpture became almost invisible and one was aware, at last, only of a rich over-all texture.

Sincerely,
Aldous Huxley

TO ARNOLD GINGRICH

740 North Kings Road
Los Angeles 46, Cal.
16 January 1955

Dear Mr. Gingrich,
Thank you for your letter. Yes, I would like to go ahead on the basis you mention and will set myself the deadline you suggest—somewhere between thirteen and seven weeks. I have several things cooking—some nearly done, others still in preparation—and will get them into shape as

soon as may be. One is on the literature of violence—Spillane and the so-called Comics—which is a much odder subject than is commonly supposed and deserves to be treated in a broad psychological, historical and sociological context. Another would deal with the relationship—a real and effective one—between methods of disciplining and educating children and the fundamental conceptions of religion. Where there is much beating of children and adolescents, the deity is apt to be thought of as transcendent, terrible and arbitrary. This conception changes when education employs less brutal methods, and the deity tends to be seen as immanent rather than transcendent, as identical with the individual's Inner Light.

The various phases of the New Thought movement, which William James regarded as the great American contribution to religion, represent a notion of deity which would never have arisen in a society which flagellated its children.

About agents—I agree that there seems to be no good reason for bringing any into this picture. I have faded out of Mr. Chambrun's life, and now Helen Strauss, of the William Morris outfit, is looking after my literary work—as the Morris people out here look after my film work (which has been non-existent for some years!) and T.V. and radio rights. But Miss Strauss had no part in the present arrangement and I don't see why Morris should be made any richer than it is already.

Sincerely,
Aldous Huxley

TO MATTHEW AND ELLEN HUXLEY

740 North Kings Road
Los Angeles 46, Cal.
5 February 1955

Dearest Matthew and Ellen,
The news is very bad, I fear. Dr Mason (Hawkins' assistant), whom I saw at the hospital Friday, told me that the malignancy has suddenly, almost explosively, started to spread—is in the liver and the lungs, and probably in the spleen and intestines too.

Cocola is dreadfully weak as she can hardly eat, owing to the liver trouble and has had to be fed with glucose and vitamins intravenously. She comes home tomorrow and we have the same nurse who looked after her in '51, a very nice good woman, for whom she has a real affection. I shall try to give her as much hypnosis as possible and hope this may keep her comfortable, increase her rest and even, perhaps, improve function. Leslie will cooperate with this. I try not to cry when I see her, but it is difficult—after thirty-six years. If you, Matthew, want to fly out, wire or phone that you have been given an unexpected vacation. With the surface part of her mind Cocola still talks of her condition as being entirely due to radiation sickness following the X-ray treatments. But the deeper mind, I think, knows what is happening; and the two will coincide sooner or later. But meanwhile we mustn't make it seem that you are coming on purpose because she is so ill.

Love her and love me. She needs it and so do I.

Aldous

TO JULIAN AND JULIETTE HUXLEY

740 North Kings Road
Los Angeles 46, California
27 March 1955

Dearest Julian and Juliette,
Thank you for your letters. The final phase of the illness was mercifully short—only about two weeks after the first unmistakable symptoms of cancer of the liver appeared—and relatively painless. We brought her back from the hospital on the seventh and were fortunate in being able to get the nurse she had after her operation, four years ago, a very sweet gentle woman, who was most attached to Maria and for whom Maria felt a real affection. The worst trouble was persistent nausea which made it necessary, in hospital, to feed her intravenously, as she could not keep down even liquids. However I was able, by hypnotic suggestion, to get rid of the nausea, and she was able to take water and liquid nourishment, without having to undergo the discomforts of intravenous feeding. As well as suggestions for her physical comfort I gave her constant reminders of those visionary and even mystical experiences which had given direction and meaning to her life during the last fifteen years, and I went on doing this even when she no longer recognized anyone, speaking into her ear—for hearing remains unaffected long after the other senses have gone—up to the very end, which came with wonderful tranquility at about six on Saturday morning, the twelfth.

Matthew was a great tower of strength and so was Maria's sister Suzanne, who came from New York on the Wednesday. The mechanics of life have arranged themselves well enough. I have our nice French cook who comes in several hours most days of the week, and a friend of Matthew's from Dartington, a young woman, who comes and does secretarial work and drives me about three afternoons a week, with a young man, a friend of Gerald's, who drives me on the other three days. But it is a strange amputated existence. However I am doing a lot of work—writing a play, at the moment, based on a short novel which is coming out. I expect to cross the country by car, with M's sister Rose at the wheel, in the latter part of April, stay for some weeks in New York, where I have been lent a penthouse on Park Avenue by George Kaufman, the playwright, and then pass the hot weather with Ellen and the children somewhere on the New England coast, with Matthew either commuting to his new job in New Haven, where he is to report on June 21st, or coming up for weekends, if the distance is too great. If Francis comes over this spring or summer, I hope I shall see him. Tell him to let me know his plans. I hope Switzerland was restful and pleasant and that all goes well with you both.

Much love from your most affectionate,
Aldous

In the second volume of her memoir, An Emigré Life: Munich, Berlin, Sanary, Pacific Palisades, *Marta Feuchtwanger describes the "absolutely fantastic" and "efficient" manner in which Maria Huxley took charge of caring for her after a car accident in Sanary in October 1933. Maria called the doctor and also called Toulon for an ambulance, waiting with her until the ambulance arrived.*

TO LION FEUCHTWANGER

740 North Kings Road
L.A. 46, Cal.
18 April 1955

Dear Lion Feuchtwanger,
Thank you for your kind note. How far away that night at Sanary seems—the shooting stars and then your wife's accident! A long time during which two individuals grow almost into one organism, whose separation leaves the survivor feeling strangely amputated.

Very sincerely yours,
Aldous Huxley

Huxley spends the months after Maria's death on 12 February in his Los Angeles home, working on The Genius and the Goddess. *In April/May his sister-in-law, Rose, drives him to New York via the Southern states. He spends May and June at George S. Kaufman's New York apartment on Park Avenue and the summer with Matthew and Ellen at Guildford, Connecticut. There he finishes* Heaven and Hell. *He returns to Los Angeles in September 1955.*

TO JULIAN HUXLEY

The Round Table Foundation
Glen Cove, Maine
9 August 1955

Dearest J,

Your letter reached me here, where I am staying for a few days—a most beautiful place, where my young friend Dr. Puharich[2] heads this foundation for research into ESP and the physical, chemical, and psychological means whereby the psi faculties may be intensified. My plan is to take a night train from Portland on Saturday—arriving in New York at 7.00 A.M. Sunday. Shall go to the Warwick Hotel and phone you at a more godly hour. Matthew and Ellen will come down from Guildford in the morning and will return in the afternoon. I shall stay one or perhaps two nights in NY, where I must have a conference with the man who is going to direct my play. So between our various businesses, we may have chances to meet on Monday and perhaps Tuesday.

Love to you both.

Your affectionate,
Aldous

TO MAX EASTMAN[3]

740 Kings Road
Los Angeles 46
12 December 1955

Dear Mr. Eastman,

Thank you for your letter and the fine sonnet, whose only defect is that it is not as nightmarish as its subject. But then, I suppose, poetry couldn't

---

[2] Dr. Henry Puharich (1918–1995). American psychical researcher.
[3] Max Eastman (1883–1969). American socialist writer, editor of *The Masses*.

be as nightmarish. It can express tragedy—but not the fungoid proliferation that leads to self-stultification and universal despair.

I have just finished a piece, which will appear in *Esquire*, on the future, as seen by three scientists, Harrison Brown, Sir George Thomson, and Sir Charles Darwin—a piece in which, of course, the "hungry fungus" plays the leading part. Someone ought to persuade the U.N. to adopt a new motto: Copulation without Population: or alternatively, *E pluribus nihil*.

Yours very sincerely,
Aldous Huxley

TO MATTHEW AND ELLEN HUXLEY

740 North Kings Road
Los Angeles 46, Cal.
5 March 1956

Dearest Matthew and Ellen,
The enclosed turned up a day or so ago on the floor of the Oldsmobile, under the seats. I imagine that you will be thankful to get it back.

Spring is here—roses, narcissus, iris, fruit trees in blossom. It makes one long to get out into the country. But the town is growing so fast that there will soon be no country to go to. Latest figures released by UN—37 millions a year increase. Julian's article in this month's *Scientific American* (very good—have boys read it!) is already out of date since he speaks only of 34 millions annual increment! Bill Kiskadden is so worried that he spends all his spare time trying to devise way of getting condoms to India—he could begin with a bang-up documentary by Fred Zinnemann[4] (in the style, I hope, of *Oklahoma*) and proceed to mass distribution of the merchandise. I say they must prepare the way through religion—a new ritual, the cupping of the lingam with rubber. One jokes—but the juggernaut rolls on, remorselessly, towards utter misery and, on the way, the triumph of communism.

Love to you all,
Aldous

---

[4] On September 11, 1956, Dr. Kiskadden sent the first copy of Huxley's documentary typescript on overpopulation to Fred Zinnemann. The script is housed at the Center for Motion Picture Study, Beverly Hills, California.

TO JULIAN AND JULIETTE HUXLEY

Yuma, Arizona
19 March 1956

Dearest Julian and Juliette,
I had hoped to be the first to break the news, but the press got there first, in spite of all efforts to be private, and you will probably have already seen the report of my marriage in the paper.

Laura [Archera] is a young Italian woman—about 40—from Turin, was a concert violinist, then gave it up, feeling that the career of an executant was too devouring and left no room for living. Maria and I met her first about 10 years ago and have seen her at intervals here and in Italy since then. I have grown to be very fond of her in recent months and she of me. Hence our decision to come to this Gretna Green[5] where one can get married in 5 minutes flat. Life is a totality: the past enriches the present, the present commemorates the past, tenderness calls to tenderness.

Ever your affectionate,
Aldous

Huxley had been working on a musical-comedy version of Brave New World. *It was never produced, nor was the version by Franklin Lacey (lyrics) and Laurence Rosenthal (music). The typescript of Huxley's musical version was published in* Aldous Huxley Annual, *vol. 3 (2003).*

TO MATTHEW AND ELLEN HUXLEY

3276 Deronda Dr.,
Los Angeles 28, Cal.
19 December 1956

Dearest Ellen and Matthew,
The Dictionary arrived today, and I have already gone exploring among the abbesses, the dells, the oodles, the Roly Dunglases and the dry bobs. What a treasure! Thank you indeed.

I am very glad you liked the play and shall bear your suggestions, Ellen, in mind. I sent the thing to Goddard Lieberson, the head of

---

[5] Village in the south of Scotland, well known as a place where underage English elopers could marry.

Columbia Records, asking his advice—but have not yet heard from him. He is probably on vacation. I also sent it to Anita. Perhaps, if it is not too much trouble, you would phone her and find out what she thinks the next practical step should be. I showed it to Charlie Brackett, who liked it, but said it was too "mental" for Twentieth Century even to think about it. He advised sending a copy to Charles Lederer—who was interested in adapting and producing about 2 years ago. But Lederer, tho' a pleasant fellow, doesn't strike me as carrying enough weight. His only production was *Kismet*—than which (I understand) nothing worse was ever seen.

Give my love to Francis and thank him on my behalf for his book, which has just arrived and which I am beginning to read with much pleasure.

Good news about M's new job! But how frightful to make another move!

A merry Christmas to you all and a very happy New Year from us both.

Ever your affectionate,
Aldous

TO JULIAN AND JULIETTE HUXLEY

3276 Deronda Drive,
Los Angeles 28, Cal.
31 December 1956

Dearest Juliette and Julian,
This is to wish you a very happy and healthy New Year. I was sorry to hear of Juliette's illness and hope it has left no bad after-effects. I had a bout of the flu earlier this month and have come down to the desert for a few days to spend a slow convalescence—for this year's virus leaves one very low and listless for a long time after the crisis is over.

I was delighted by the news of the Darwin medal—well earned.

Things go on here as usual—Nothing but scribble, scribble, scribble, as the Royal Duke said to Edward Gibbon. I have written a musical comedy version of *Brave New World* and am now looking for a composer. I hope it will get put on, for it should make a very lively spectacle. In the intervals I do my usual monthly pieces for *Esquire*—the last one inspired by a book on the founding fathers of modern psychology, Freud, Adler, Jung and Otto Rank. What an extraordinary amount of nonsense they talked, along with the sense! And what enormous sins of omission they committed! Once one sets forth their shortcomings dispassionately, they seem quite extravagantly odd.

Much love from us both.

Ever your affectionate,
Aldous

TO MARGARET ISHERWOOD[6]

3276 Deronda Drive
Los Angeles 28, Cal.
9 February 1957

Dear Margaret,

Thank you for your interesting letter. I am glad to hear that Laban[7] is being taken notice of officially. It was a pity that old FM [Alexander] had such a one-track mind. For of course there is no panacea, and proper use of the self must be combined with proper diet, proper psychology etc. I was talking recently to a woman who had studied with pupils of Dr. Vittoz,[8] the serious psycho-therapist who treated neurasthenics, teaching people to have a more vivid sensory awareness. Very interesting.

All goes well here. We have moved house and now have a prodigious view from high up in the hills above Beachwood Drive (near where you were on Los Feliz, but a little to the west). I am trying a new therapy for the eyes, based on the use of a sulfur compound plus a diet—which jointly offers great things for corneal opacities and cataracts. In a few months I may get results: it would be a great thing for me if it worked.

Gerald flourishes. He and I have done two Mutt and Jeff performances on T.V. recently—with great *éclat.*

Yours,
Aldous

---

[6] Margaret Isherwood (d. 1984). Writer on education and religion, author of *The Root of the Matter* (1954).
[7] Rudolf Laban (1879–1958). Founded the Art of Movement studio in England.
[8] Roger Vittoz (1863–1925). Swiss therapist.

TO G. B. STERN[9]

3276 Deronda Drive
Los Angeles 28, Cal.
14 June 1957

Dear G. B. Stern,

Thank you for your letter. Yes, I remember that luncheon—across what gulfs of time, change and death! I like your account of it. How intolerable I was then—still am, no doubt! But you are very friendly and sympathetic. I have no objection, of course, to publication.

I see John van Druten from time to time—but not since his illness, which has left him, I understand, in a rather bad way. But I hope he is emerging now from the shadow.

Yours very sincerely,
Aldous Huxley

Aldous and Laura Huxley visit Latin America in August 1958. (Two memoirs of their visits to Brazil and Peru have recently been published. The posthumous memoir by Elizabeth Bishop, "A New Capital, Aldous Huxley, and Some Indians" appeared in the Yale Review *in 2006. Joseph R. Jones's "Huxley in Lima" appeared in the* Aldous Huxley Annual *for 2001.) From Latin America the Huxleys travel to Italy in September 1958. Aldous visits Julian in London during October, and in that month* Brave New World Revisited *is published. After visits to Paris and several Italian cities, the Huxleys return in December to their Deronda Drive home in Hollywood. In January, Huxley works on* Island, *his final novel, and takes up a visiting position (February to December 1959) at the University of California, Santa Barbara, lecturing on "The Human Situation." In May he receives the Award of Merit for the Novel from the American Academy of Arts and Letters, New York. In early 1960 Matthew and Ellen take steps to dissolve their marriage.*

---

[9] Gladys Bronwyn Stern (1890–1973) was a prolific writer. In her memoir *And Did He Stop and Speak to You?* (1958) she recalls her second meeting with Huxley, which took place at a luncheon in the garden of an *auberge* in southern France during the early thirties: "At this lunch my normal faculties were subdued in the company of a brain great enough to put all ours out of action; yet not too subdued for silent amusement at noticing how if one of the party brought up a topic with any personal implication, Huxley immediately cut the umbilical cord. . . . Provided a subject could be kept impersonal, however, he went into it with mathematical accuracy and precision."

TO VICTORIA OCAMPO

20 August 1958

Dear Victoria,
I got your wire this morning, after our return from the interior—Brasília the new capital, and a trip into the jungles of the northwest to visit the Indians, who are stark naked and extremely amiable.

Unfortunately I don't see how we can manage a trip to Buenos Aires; for we have to be in Italy before the end of the month and there are things arranged for us to do here and in Bahia during the intervening days, so that there is simply no interval of time long enough to get to B.A. and back, with a day or two between journeys. I regret this very much; for I had hoped to see you—and certainly should have done so if our trip had not been delayed. *En attendant on me traite ici avec une extrème gentillesse mais un peu comme si j'étais un monument historique.*

Affectueusement,
Aldous

TO GILBERT PERLEBERG

3276 Deronda Drive
Los Angeles, California
10 January 1959

Dear Mr. Perleberg,
Thank you for your interesting letter. The problem, it seems to me, is this: How far can individuals or small groups of individuals, who have opened themselves to the Good and feel impelled to work for an order of things that shall make the Good more accessible to move people, prevail against a system—Technology in every field of human activity, industrial, organizational, economic, political, psychological and mind-manipulative—which develops autonomously according to the laws of its own nature, and not at all according to the laws of human nature? This system now affects and regiments practically everybody, so that individuals find themselves pitted against vast numbers as well as the interrelated techniques in every field—techniques whose purpose is simply to increase efficiency by substituting calculation for spontaneity, centralized control for liberty, concentration on means for their own sake and not on ends outside the system, much less ends outside the material order.

If it remains in its present state of development the sytem will destroy itself or be destroyed by a rebellion of outraged humanity. But it will not remain in its present state; for the technicians are now devoting more and more of their energy to the techniques of man—the technique of mind-manipulation, the technique of inducing individuals to accept and even love their servitude. The development of such techniques may permit the system to survive, if not indefinitely, at least for a long time. Who knows? The difficulty of forecasting future developments in a world where technological and demographic change are so rapid and so revolutionary, is insuperably great.

Sincerely,
Aldous Huxley

TO JULIAN AND JULIETTE HUXLEY

3276 Deronda Drive
Los Angeles 28, Cal.
16 March 1959

Dearest Julian and Juliette,
I hope you are safely back, not too tired from so much travelling among so many Indians, and not too much afflicted by the change of climate. All goes well here, I am glad to say. My troubles of last autumn were evidently due to sheer fatigue, plus a slight recurrence of the chronic bronchial condition which occurred in Brazil. Now I am quite well again, eating everything with impunity and doing two jobs at once—lecturing and conducting a seminar during half the week at the University of California at Santa Barbara, and working on a book in the intervals.

Matthew was out here for ten days at the beginning of the month— very unhappy, poor fellow, over the situation that has developed. He still hopes that Ellen may ultimately come back to him and that they may be able to re-establish the family. He is quite intensely a family man, with a passion for roots and a settled pattern of life—a passion evoked, perhaps, by reaction to the fact that Maria and I lived in many places during his childhood, and that he suffered from a sense of rootlessness. Be that as it may, he longs for roots and a settled family life. Whereas Ellen is basically a career woman and doesn't feel satisfied with family life. She does a good job as a mother, but would like to do it on the side, as an avocation. The reverse of Matthew's medal is a certain pedantry and perfectionism, a desire things should be just so and not otherwise. This, coupled with the all-too Huxleyan trait of impatience, of not suffering gladly those whom he regards as fools, has evidently been a long-standing cause of friction and of exasperation on Ellen's part. Into this situation Francis supervened—the perfect nonfamily man, non-routiner, fascinatingly non-rooted. For Ellen it was the discovery of an elective affinity, the beginning of a grand passion (a passion incidentally, almost and probably exclusively mental). And there the matter now stands. What will happen in the ensuing months, I can't imagine. Will Ellen go back to Matthew and the original family pattern? Matthew hopes so and is taking psychological treatment in order to clear up his own inner mess and make himself fitter for the relationship. He hopes that Ellen will also go to a psychological counsellor. But I doubt if she will and am not inclined to think that she will go back to Matthew and the old life. Will she and Francis ultimately get married? Who knows? I am inclined to doubt it. Meanwhile what will be the effect of the break upon the children? What sort of working arrangement will be arrived at in the event of a permanent separation? Will Matthew be successful in making an adjustment to the new situation—which means, in practice, will he find another woman, a family woman this time? Goodness knows what the answer to all these questions will be. Meanwhile one can only stand by, ready to offer consolation and advice if they should be asked for. It is a sad bad job, and all one can hope for is that all concerned will somehow contrive to make the best of it, or at least not to make the worse. Laura sends her love, as do I.

Ever your affectionate,
Aldous

TO MALCOLM COWLEY

3276 Deronda Drive
Los Angeles 28, Cal.
8 November 1959

Dear Malcolm Cowley,
Thank you for the proofs of your very interesting essay and of the text of the first edition of *Leaves of Grass*. How curious that, in later life, Whitman should have forgotten what, at the beginning of it, he had been talking about. Your references to Tantra are particularly interesting and

to the point. Whitman was a born Tantrik—*anima naturaliter Tantrika*. And at the time he wrote he would have had to be naturally Tantrik; for practically nothing was known about Tantra in the West until considerably later. In fact the bulk of our knowledge dates from the present century and comes from Sir John Woodroffe (Arthur Avalon). So I don't suppose that even Thoreau and Emerson had any knowledge through books of the sacramental, world-accepting side of the *Tat tvam asi* philosophy except, of course, where it is partially expounded in the *Gita*—with its very disturbing justification of war for those who can break the *ahimsa* commandment in a spirit of detachment. (How odd and all too human it is that there should be everywhere a God of Battles and almost nowhere a God of Brothels,—that almost everyone has said that killing can be done in a holy way and is not incompatible with enlightenment, whereas only a very few Tantriks and Christian heretics, such as the Adamites, the Brethren of the Free Spirit and John Humphrey Noyes have ever maintained that enlightenment was compatible with love-making, or that love-making could be a yoga or spiritual exercise!)

In reading Whitman I have often been struck by the beautifully Zen-like character of some of the shorter pieces in *Specimen Days*—the pieces in which he describes his experiences in the woods or at the edge of ponds, when he was convalescing from his stroke in New Jersey. The best of these pieces are like expanded *haikus*—and they have a very quiet and intimate quality extremely rare in Whitman's writings. For the most part he speaks as though through a megaphone to an enormous multitude; in these pieces, we catch him talking *sotto voce* to himself. Just as the best Japanese *haiku* writers do.

Thank you again for sending me the proofs and thank you once more for the very kind things you said about me at the Academy function last spring.[1] The reference to Diderot touched me very much.

Yours very sincerely,
Aldous Huxley

[1] Cowley presented Huxley with the Award of Merit Medal for the Novel at the Ceremonial of the American Academy and the National Institute of Arts and Letters on 20 May 1959.

TO JULIAN HUXLEY

3276 Deronda Drive
Los Angeles 28, Cal.
29 November 1959

Dearest J,

You will, I imagine, have heard by this time from the CBC, in regard to their proposed double interview with Alistair Cooke[2]—to be followed in my case, apparently, with another solo interview on the subject of *Brave New World Revisited*. I have said yes, provisionally, for Dec. 21st—and I hope this will not be an imposition on you. Cooke is a good man, and I think the interview should be pleasant enough. So I won't make any other arrangement for the 21st. On the 22nd, I believe, we are invited to Disneyland—which I haven't even seen, but which is said to have a lot of charm, as well as being one of the major manifestations of 20th Century Culture and so deserving of our anthropological inspection. I hope this will amuse you.

Would you like to see George Beadle of Caltech? I met him the other day at Santa Barbara, where he gave an excellent lecture in the Darwin Centenary series. A nice man, I thought, and exceedingly bright in a quiet, unspectacular way. And if you like Harrison Brown, we could probably get him over one day—or alternatively go over to Pasadena to have a look at the goings-on in Caltech. Let me know what you feel about this.

Incidentally what is the date when you have to leave here for Washington? I don't want to make any arrangement that would interfere with any plans you may have when you are here—eg. to go to La Jolla or some other spot of zoological interest.

I remain revoltingly busy—every week at Santa Barbara, either lecturing myself or listening to Darwin lectures and providing panel discussions of them; and in the intervals working on my book and coping with correspondence. Laura too is very busy with her psycho-therapy, at which she is remarkably good. But Santa B. will be over a day or two before you arrive and the neurotics I trust, will cease from troubling at least for a few days at Christmas.

Our love to you both.

Your affectionate,
Aldous

---

[2] Alistair Cooke (1908–2004). Journalist and radio-television broadcaster. His double interview with Huxley on birth control aired on CBC (Canadian Broadcasting Corporation) on 10 April 1960.

TO MARJORIE WORTHINGTON

3276 Deronda Drive
Los Angeles 28
11 January 1960

Dear Marjorie,

This brings you best wishes for 1960 and along with them a strange question—which you may regard as impertinent (if so, ignore it). But what I would like to know—not for myself but for a psychiatrist friend of mine in Canada, who is doing research on the odder aspects of the mind—is this. What did poor Willy[3]—I think of him with sadness and affection—hope to elicit, and what in fact did he elicit, from the people whom, as I remember him once telling me, he encased in touch-proof, sound-proof, sight-proof leather garments? As you probably know, a good deal of work on "limited environment" has been done in recent years—and it has been shown that the cutting off of sensory stimuli results quite quickly in visionary experience is, sometimes of a rather frightful kind, sometimes of a positive nature. It would be interesting to know, in this context, where Willy got the idea of the outer-world-eclipsing garment, whether there was some kind of occult tradition about this and, if so, where this tradition was described. It would be further interesting to know if the effects produced by the leather suit were similar to those produced in the not too dissimilar conditions of the experiments conducted at McGill and the National Institute of Health. We know so little about the mind, that every scrap of out-of-the-way evidence is valuable and illuminating. So forgive me for asking you.

Yours,
Aldous

During 1960 Huxley lectures extensively in a number of institutions. He is also a visiting professor at the Menninger Foundation in Topeka, Kansas, in March/April, and from September to November a visiting professor at MIT. In May he is stricken with oral cancer, but after radium treatments in June and July he appears to recover.

[3] William Seabrook (1887–1945). American author and Worthington's husband.

TO MATTHEW HUXLEY

3276 Deronda Drive
Los Angeles 28, Cal.,
2 February 1960

Dearest M,

I'm beginning to make plans for my excursion to Topeka and am wondering if there would be a chance for you to fly out for some weekend while I am there—which will be from March 15th to about May 4th or 5th. I would love to have this chance of seeing you—and in the intervals you could surely find some interesting people to talk to and listen to about mental health. So please let me know what weekend will suit you best. I'd like to hear soon, since there will doubtless be many engagements coming up, as soon as I arrive—and I would like to have a fixed date around which I can constellate them. My only engagement away from Topeka will be April 5th at Lawrence, Kansas, and April 7th and 8th at Lake Forest, Ill.—all these on the inside of a week, tho' I fancy the 8th is a Friday.

Let me hear what is happening. I can only hope that even the saddest outcome can somehow be made the best of. My own strong feeling in all this unhappiness is that, for the children's sake and the adults' too, there must be a minimum of bitterness.

Ever your affectionate,
Aldous

TO JULIAN AND JULIETTE HUXLEY

100 Memorial Drive
Cambridge, Mass.
22 October 1960

Dearest J and J,

I should have written before to thank Juliette for her long and vivid letter about your African adventure. Wonderful but strenuous. I'm happy you got back in one piece.

I'm momentarily in NY, for Trev's and Tessa's joint birthday—but am for the time being a Visiting Professor at MIT, giving a public lecture a week and conducting seminars. Also meeting a number of interesting people and even trying, without, alas, too much success, to do a little writing. I have been around so long that everyone now treats me as a kind of historical monument, like Stonehenge or Ann Hathaway's cottage—which is at once gratifying and embarrassing.

Cass Canfield hinted that you, Julian, might be coming to NY in the near future. I hope this is true. If it is, let us try to meet either in New York or at Cambridge. I shall be in residence at MIT until near the end of November—I don't yet know the exact date of my departure: but I want to get away before it starts to get really cold. Laura will be coming out for a few days either next weekend (28th) or the weekend after.

Ever your affectionate,
Aldous

TO ESTHER McCOY[4]

3276 Deronda Dr.
L.A. 28, Cal.
4 December 1960

Dear Mrs. McCoy,
Thank you for your letter. Yes, by all means quote the passage you mention. As for the article on Mendelsohn[5]—I believe it appeared in *House and Garden*, for which (as for other Condé Nast publications) I did a lot of writing in the twenties. But I can't be sure of this.

Meanwhile the hygienic boys go on merrily producing buildings of the most amazing inconvenience and inefficiency. I have bumped my head and been roasted in Niemayer's Brazilian hotels[6]—low ceilings plus glass walls in a tropical climate. What idiocy. And from India I hear bitter complaints (from the Indian ambassador most recently) of Corbusier's entirely non-functional buildings in the new Punjabi capital.[7] And see a recent *Scientific American* article in which the author contrasts the wonderful "performance" of primitive architects using mud and sticks and leaves with the folly of the skyscraper builders of New York, whose glass walls leak and impose (because of the greenhouse effect) unbearable strains on the cooling systems—not to mention the people.

Sincerely,
Aldous Huxley

---

[4] Esther McCoy (1904–1989). Architectural historian, chiefly interested in southern California modern architecture.

[5] Huxley is probably referring to his article on the modern architect Erich Mendelsohn (1887–1953), "Puritanism in Art," *The Studio*, March 1930, 200–203; *Creative Art*, March 1930, 200–202.

[6] In 1958, Huxley visited the new capital of Brasília as a guest of the government. The major new buildings there were designed by Oscar Niemeyer (b. 1907).

[7] LeCorbusier (1887–1965). Swiss-French architect, designed Chandigarh, capital city of the Punjab from 1950–.

TO WESLEY HARTLEY

3276 Deronda Drive
LA 28, Cal.

Dear Mr. Hartley,
Excuse the very long delay in answering your letter, which got buried and is only just come again to the surface.

My school education was interrupted by blindness when I was sixteen and so is far from typical. It was important—but still more important was the self-education demanded by having to adjust to unfavourable conditions—learning Braille, learning to typewrite without seeing, learning to find my way about a half-seen world.

College, when I could see well enough to go to Oxford, was certainly valuable to me as a would-be writer. I made friends with other would-be writers, wrote much poetry, helped to publish a little magazine. Of even greater importance was the opportunity which came to me while I was an undergraduate of meeting, at the house of a lady living near Oxford, most of the eminent intellectual figures of the time—Bertrand Russell, J. M. Keynes, Katherine Mansfield, Virginia Woolf, Roger Fry, Clive Bell, Lytton Strachey. Talk with these people was the most liberal of educations.

Sincerely,
Aldous Huxley

TO ALLEN GINSBERG

8 January 1961

Dear Mr. Ginsberg,
Unfortunately I don't know Dr. Heim, who is an acquaintance of my brother's not of mine. (It was *a propos* of a letter from him to my brother that I brought up his name in conversation with Tim Leary). I don't know anyone in Paris who is working with LSD or psilocybin. I would think that Burroughs' best bet would be to write the discoverer of psilocybin, Dr. Albert Hofmann, c/o Sandoz Co., Basel, Switzerland, asking if he can arrange for him, as an imaginative author, to test the drug experimentally.

Very useful therapeutic work with LSD is being done by a group in Canada (Vancouver) and Seattle. Very large doses leading to deep-level self-discovery.

Sincerely,
Aldous Huxley

TO MARGARET SANGER

3276 Deronda Drive
Los Angeles 28, Cal.
4 March 1961

Dear Mrs. Sanger,
Thank you for your clear-sighted compassion. Thank you for your courage and for the indomitable goodwill that overcame so many obstacles and stood firm against such storms of calumny and abuse. And thank you for your decision, after nearly half a century of work and struggle, to forego your well-earned rest and carry on the fight.

With all my respect and admiration, I am
Yours very sincerely,
Aldous Huxley

TO MARTHA VOEGELI[8]

3276 Deronda Drive
Los Angeles 28, Cal.
3 May 1961

Dear Dr. Voegeli,
Thank you for your very interesting letter. To begin with Dr. Tillich[9]— I find him bewildering because he uses such ambiguous language that I don't know, very often, what he is talking about. Also he never cites a concrete case history and speaks only in vague generalizations. My own contribution to the panel discussion was an effort to be concrete about the subject. I took a case history of the old world-view (Sir Matthew Hale, who sentenced a witch to death in 1664 because her neighbor's clothes, after a quarrel with her, became infested with lice). And I pointed out that the word "man" is habitually used by theologians in several different senses, so that the subject of the colloquium (How has science changed man's view of himself?) remained very ambiguous. In the subsequent discussion I pointed out that human beings

---

[8]Martha Voegeli was a physician and birth-control advocate.
[9] Paul Tillich, Aldous Huxley, and Robert Oppenheimer took part in a centenary colloquium at MIT in early April 1961. Tillich's speech, "The Inner Aim," was reported in the 21 April issue of *Time*.
    The case history to which Huxley refers is described in the tract "A trial of witches at the assizes held at Bury St. Edmunds . . . on the tenth day of March, 1664." This tract was consulted by the judges at the Salem witch trials in 1692, as they needed precedents for witch trial procedure.

are very variable and that there is not one *Telos* (as Dr. Tillich maintained) but several. All the great religions have recognized this fact. Christianity talks of the way of Martha and the way of Mary: Hinduism of bhakti, Karma, and jnana-yoga. This Dr. T. found very disturbing, I don't know why.

The only kind of religion, so far as I can see, that is compatible with scientific thought is a religion of mystical experience—not of a Nirvana *outside* the world, but within it (as the Mahayana Buddhists and e.g., Meister Eckhart insist). The ethical corollary of mystical experience (which involves a sense of solidarity with all beings) is compassion and ultimately *ahimsa*, with the paradoxical combination of working for the cause of goodness and at the same time obeying the injunction of Jesus (and all mystics): "Judge not that ye be not judged." Mystical experience is no more incompatible with science than is aesthetic experience. Incompatibility arises when metaphysical interpretations are made.

Sincerely,
Aldous Huxley

TO MATTHEW HUXLEY

3276 Deronda Drive
Los Angeles 28, Cal.
17 May 1961

Dearest M,
Nothing much to report since our talk last Saturday. Literally nothing remains of the house or its contents and I am now a man without possessions and without a past. This last fact I regret as much for you as for myself; for what has gone is a piece of your life and heart and mind as well as of mine. But there is nothing to do except try to start again from scratch.

Inasmuch formalities are a nuisance and tho' we are fairly well insured, as far as insurance goes, the amount we get won't approach the real loss. The differences between insurance payments and real loss can, however, be taken off one's taxes.

I expect to go to stay with Gerald tomorrow and shall try to get my book finished there.

All my love.

Ever your affectionate,
Aldous

TO JULIAN AND JULIETTE HUXLEY

Palace Hotel
Gstaad, Switzerland
1 August 1961

Dearest Julian and Juliette,
The mountains are a bit rainy, but beautiful, and the air is good, and the regime very healthful—large meals, mild walks, plenty of sleep. Laura arrived yesterday, and we plan to stay here till the 7th, then (I think) go to Turin for a few days before flying up to Copenhagen on the 12th (Hotel Royal Copenhagen from 12th to 19th).

I wish I could report anything very concrete or encouraging about Francis. I talked with him about the necessity of self-commitment, about the art of life being the art of stepping into the traps of jobs, marriage, social position etc, and transforming the traps into spiritual homes and springboards for flights into freedom. He seemed to agree that this was indeed a necessity, and spoke of a possible career in making documentaries for T.V.—which might be interesting albeit not very substantial. But he doesn't like to talk about his problems, at any rate with me—and Eileen Garrett[1] found the same reluctance in him. His difficulties spring from some kind of alien presence in his subconscious, like a possession—and I don't know how it can be exorcised or by whom. I wish I could have been more helpful; but evidently I am not the predestined exorcist.

Laura joins me in sending love to you.

Yours,
Aldous

TO SYBILLE BEDFORD

Palace Hotel
Gstaad, Switzerland
4 August 1961

My dear Sybille,
Your letter caught up with me here, where I came, after a week at Le Piol and 4 days at Vaison, to meet Laura, breathe some fresh air and listen to Krishnamurti, who is giving a series of talks here. We leave next Monday for Italy, shall pass a few days at the seaside near Spotorno, then fly to Copenhagen where we shall be staying from the 12th

---

[1] Eileen Garrett (1893–1970). Well-known medium.

to the 19th at the Hotel Royal. Then back to Italy. After which I don't really know. We may stay in Europe until we go to India in late October. Or return to Cal, to see about rebuilding, and go on to India from there. In any case it doesn't look as tho' I would be in England again in the near future. It would have been nice to make a tour together—but, alas, things have arranged themselves otherwise.

Laura sends her love, as do I.

Yours,
Aldous

TO JULIAN HUXLEY

Royal Hotel
Copenhagen, Denmark
20 August 1961

Dearest J,
Dr. Christian Volf will be in London either the 28th or the 29th—or both days, and will contact you when there, if these dates are unsatisfactory, would you let him know?

Dr. Christian Volf
Sonderborg
Denmark

Or, by cable, Vibrasonic, Sonderborg. (Can you let him know by the 25th if these dates won't do.)

I hope he may be able to do something with his sound waves to help your head-aches.

We leave tomorrow for Zurich to see a sick friend; then take the train to Torre del Mare (Fabbricato D, 12 Torre del Mare, Savona).

Copenhagen has been pleasant, but rather rainy—and I have met a number of interesting people here, including old Niels Bohr, who is apt (since he can't stop talking) to turn into Niels Bore.

Love to you both from both of us.

Affectionately,
Aldous

1962

TO BERNARDINE FRITZ[2]

6233 Mulholland
LA 28, Cal.
24 January 1962

Dear Bernardine,
Thank you for your letter. I am distressed to learn that I can be so paralyzing to people—a defect attributable to a certain shyness and difficulty in personal communication which it has taken me a lifetime to reduce to its present level and which, I suppose, will never be entirely got rid of. But all the same I enjoyed myself and found much profit as well as pleasure in Dr. Giorgi's talk. What a remarkable woman and what a good doctor, I would guess—at once humane and knowledgeable, scientific and intuitive.

Yours,
Aldous

TO JULIAN HUXLEY

2533 Hillegass Ave.
Berkeley 4, Cal.
12 April 1962

Dearest J,
Thank you for your letter with its (slightly illegible for my poor eyes) list of dates.

I have to go down to LA on Saturday, so shall miss you at the Morains. However I shall be free of engagements next week and would like to fly up to Portland, let us say on Wednesday 18th, listen to your speech on the 19th, sit in, if they will allow it, on the Population Conference and move South again on Friday or Saturday. The trip to the Grand Coulee would have taken 2 full days, I think—so it hardly seems feasible. Bonneville dam is interesting only when salmon are running—which they may be doing at this season; I'm not sure. What you should see while at Seattle is the northern rain forest on the west side of The Olympic peninsula—150 inches of rain a year and a forest of conifer and ferns the like of which I never saw elsewhere. Quite as extraordinary in its own way, as the most luxuriant of equatorial jungles.

---

[2] Bernardine Fritz (d. 1982). American journalist who established a Hollywood *salon* in 1939.

Ask the Reed people to let me know—by telegram, or special delivery letter, or phone (Hollywood 4-8044) if it will be all right for me to come on the 18th and observe the conference. I will stay at some hotel in town and drive out to the college.

It will be wonderful to see you. *A bientôt.*

Affectionately,
Aldous

TO JULIAN HUXLEY

6233 Mulholland
L.A. 28, Cal.
17 June 1962

Dearest J,

Many happy returns! But, goodness! How venerable we are getting. Birthdays, now, make me think of the conversation between Falstaff and Justice Shallow. Shallow asks after their quondam friend, Jane Night-Work. "Old, Master Shallow, old." "Nay, she cannot choose but be old." We cannot choose but be old. But fortunately one can, at least to some extent, choose to ignore the fact and get on with one's work and enjoy one's leisure.

I wound up my work at Berkeley a week ago and am back here, working at the moment on a paper to be delivered next October at the PEN club meeting in Buenos Aires—on Literature and Science. The subject keeps ramifying out as I look at it. When this is done, I hope to do some other essays. Later on I might hop over to Europe—but am not yet at all certain about plans.

I hear from Betty Wendel that you saw *The Genius and the Goddess* at Golder's Green. I shall be curious to hear what you thought of the play. Hauser is trying to find a West End theatre for it—so far without success.

Our love to you both.

Ever yours affectionately,
Aldous

TO JULIAN AND JULIETTE HUXLEY

6233 Mulholland
L.A. 28, Cal.
9 August 1962

Dearest J and J,

Thank you for the birthday wishes. They found me busily working on two assignments—my literature and science piece for the PEN Club meeting at Buenos Aires in October, and a piece which the Great Ideas of Today people asked me to do on the question (marvelously vague and meaningless) "Has man's conquest of space increased or diminished his stature?" Also another short piece—an introduction to a volume of essays on human ecology. (How incomprehensibly odd it is that the great powers are prepared to spend anything from thirty to a hundred thousand million dollars to put a man on the moon and another man, in a few years, on Mars, but will hardly spend a penny on the problem of how the human species is to survive [to say nothing of making progress] on a planet which, like those stupid parasites that kill their hosts and so commit suicide, we are doing our best to render uninhabitable. All cultures, I suppose, have contained considerable elements of organized insanity. In our culture, the organization is much more efficient and the insanity more dangerous than ever before.)

I have been ruminating the possibility of writing a kind of contrapuntal phantasy. On one level there would be a kind of science fiction vision of what might be, if we used our resources with intelligence and good will. On another level would be an account of what is actually happening at the present time. And on a third level would be another science fiction vision of what may be expected to happen if we don't behave with intelligence and good will. I can't yet envisage the form of such a book; but if I find a satisfactory form and can work it out in an interesting way, the result might be significant and important. Meanwhile I must sit around receptively, waiting, like Mr. Micawber, for something to turn up—or, more romantically, like the scholar gipsy, for the spark from heaven to fall.

Well, the poor play had a bad time in London! What puzzles me is the enormous difference between the London and the provincial critics. The latter were almost all enthusiastic, the former contemptuous. There was a piece in "The Stage," which expressed the same sort of wonderment. After praising the play, with certain reservations for weaknesses, all of which had been introduced by directorial cutting, the critic went on to wonder why his colleagues had reacted so badly to what, in his view, was an excellent piece of work. But he had no good answer. Things would have gone better, I am sure, if the casting had been better—everyone agrees that the young girl was a disaster—and if the piece had been performed as written. But evidently this is expecting too much. I was reading some eighteenth-century complaint the other day in which the author (I can't remember who it was) speaks of the actors' dreadful habit of changing the text of the play. No doubt Aeschylus and Sophocles had the same kind of trouble with *their* breed of hams. Laura is very busy, trying to get her volume of Recipes for Living completed by the September 1st deadline set by the publishers. How is *your* book going, Juliette? Golly, what a nest of singing birds we are! Our best love to you all.

Ever your affectionate,
Aldous

TO JULIAN AND JULIETTE HUXLEY

6233 Mulholland
Los Angeles 28, California
15 August 1962

Dearest J and J,
Plans have changed and I expect, if all goes well, to go to Brussels for the meeting of The World Academy of Arts and Letters from August 29th to September 3rd. Will you be in London after September 3rd? If so, I hope I may see you there. Laura has to stay here, working on her book; and the idea is that we meet in Buenos Aires at the beginning of October, for the PEN club meeting! (But will there be a meeting if Argentina's troubles get worse or even remain what they now are? *Quien sabe?* Anyhow, I shall be in Europe during September—part of the time in London. So let me know when you intend to go to Ischia.

Much love,
Aldous

TO JULIAN HUXLEY

L.A. 28, Cal.
28 August 1962

Dearest J,
Thank you for your letter. I expect to be at Hotel Atlanta,

7 Boulevard Adolphe
Brussels

and look forward to coming over to London on or shortly after Sept 4th. Will let you know.

I wish I knew more about this World Academy affair—but except for one letter of invitation I have heard nothing. There is evidently *un po' di confusione,* as the Italians like to remark when everything has gone totally wrong. If the Clarkes can have me, I shall, of course, be delighted to come with you.

Love to Juliette,
Aldous

TO JULIAN AND JULIETTE

6233 Mulholland
L.A. 28, Cal.
27 November 1962

Dearest Julian and Juliette,
How are things with you? Here all goes tolerably well. Laura has got her book off to the publisher and expects the first proofs before Christmas. I am busy, enlarging and (I think) greatly improving my piece for Literature and Science. I have also written a paper for one of Hutchins's conferences at the Centre for the Study of Democratic Institutions—on the probable impact during the next 10 years of technology on democratic institutions. We go up to Santa Barbara at the end of this week for this conference, which promises to be interesting.

I did a trip through several Eastern states last month, lecturing here and there. Met Roger Williams at the U of Texas and had some good talks with him and a look at his pictures of human differences even on the gross anatomical level, e.g. the aorta. When you see the half dozen commonest variations you can hardly believe that you are looking at the same organ, the differences are so great. And the differences are probably highly significant in human terms. Someone born with a narrow-gauge carotid artery becomes mentally senile early—for as deposits constrict the artery, the brain gets inadequate supplies of blood. Berty Russell obviously has a very large carotid artery!

Before I forget, dear Julian, what about nightingales? I want to introduce them into my Lit-Science essay. Do they sing in order to warn others off their territory? And if so, why at night? And is any of the singing an affair of sexuality—courtship etc?

Our best love to you both.

Ever your affectionate,
Aldous

TO JULIAN HUXLEY

6233 Mulholland
L.A. 28, Cal.
16 December 1962

Dearest J,

Thank you for the nightingale information: it will come in very useful.

I don't know why the reports of my Santa Barbara paper were made out to be so doomful. What I said was that if we didn't pretty quickly start thinking of human problems in ecological terms rather than in terms of power politics we should soon be in a very bad way. Disaster is inevitable only if we choose to do the things that make it inevitable, and refuse to do the things which will permit us to avoid it. Which all seems fairly obvious.

The newspaper accounts of the Great Fog were hair-raising. I hope you both got through the ordeal without damage. Here we have nothing worse than the usual drought—but I hear horrible accounts of snow and icy temperatures from people in the East.

A very merry Christmas to you both and to all who may be gathered about your tree.

Ever your affectionate,
A

1963

TO GEORGE CUKOR

6233 Mulholland
LA 28, Cal.
1 January 1963

Dear George,

Thank you for the "100 Dollar Misunderstanding," and which I read with much amusement and no little instruction—for it is a mine of linguistic treasures. When you're through with "My Fair Lady" you might try your hand at turning it into a musical.

Meanwhile a very happy new year to you.

Ever yours,
Aldous

PS Herewith Doctor [Felix] Mann's book on the Chinese needles.

TO ROSAMUND LEHMANN

6233 Mulholland
Los Angeles 28, Cal.
20 February 1963

My dear Rosamund,

Alas, Persia in April is incompatible with a series of lectures during the same month on the Pacific Coast. The nearest I can come to Teheran will be Rome for a week or so in mid-March, when the FAO is having some sort of a meeting in London in June, where I hope to see you.

All goes quite well here. We have not re-built, but are living with Laura's old friend, Virginia Pfeiffer, (who was also burnt out) in the house she bought after the fire [at 6233 Mulholland]. It is one of those temporary arrangements which may end by becoming permanent.

I have just finished a long essay on *Literature and Science*, and am now ruminating a kind of novel. Laura, meanwhile, has taken to authorship and is busily correcting the proofs of a book on her psychotherapeutic methods—a series of "Recipes for Living and Loving." So, what with Juliette's book on Africa, Francis's on Haiti and my son Matthew's on Eastern Peru, we seem to be getting into the writing racket in a big way.

Meanwhile I hope you're well and busy. Phil Nichols's passing saddened me greatly. We were at Balliol together and tho' I saw more of Robert in later years (Phil was generally *en poste*) we remained close friends. One ages into progressive solitude and a curious state

486

of separation—as though one belonged to an alien minority group merely tolerated by the younger majority.

Yours affectionately,
Aldous

TO JULIAN AND JULIETTE HUXLEY

6233 Mulholland
L.A. 28, Cal.
28 June 1963

Dearest Julian and Juliette,
Time has slithered by so quickly of late that it is only today that I find myself realizing that June 22nd is past and that I failed to send my best birthday wishes. Better late, I hope, than never this brings them. Many many happy returns, dearest Julian, of last Saturday.

Now for plans. We hope to fly to Stockholm at the end of July for the meeting of the World Academy there. Laura will stay only three days and go on from there to her sister's in Italy. I shall stay on for a little and then, if this suits you, come to London. Will you be there from, say, August 4th or 5th onward? And can you put me up at 31 Pond St? It would be wonderful for me if you could.

Much love to you both.

Ever your affectionate,
Aldous

P.S. Later plans are still vague. Laura will probably come to England later in August, after which we might go to Paris for a bit. Meanwhile her book has climbed on to the Best Seller List, and continues to boom along in a phenomenal way!

TO MATTHEW HUXLEY

31 Pond Street
Hamstead, N.W.3
16 August 1963

Dearest Matthew,
Thank you for your letter, what a horrible disaster for poor Gruenberg![3] Let's hope he comes out of it with an intact mind. Here all goes fairly

---

[3] Louis Gruenberg (1884–1964). Operatic composer.

well—but we're all getting *old*. Gervas is recovering from a prostate operation, and I shan't be able to see him. Harold Nicholson has just had a stroke. E. M. Forster, who was to have come to a cocktail party yesterday, fell off a chair and is temporarily immobilized.

We go down to Dartington tomorrow, to stay with the Elmhirsts. Next week I leave for Italy, rejoining Laura in Torino—from which, I suppose, we shall go out in a car for a sightseeing tour.

As for literary lawyers—I know of none. Perhaps your best course would be to ring up the authors' League and ask for a good address—or maybe the League's lawyers might do the job.

Meanwhile thank you for all the photos which followed me here, and for the charming pose of Trev with cat. My love to you both.

Ever your affectionate,
Aldous

TO JULIAN AND JULIETTE HUXLEY

108 Corso Galileo Ferraris
Torino
24 August 1963

Dearest Julian and Juliet,
Here we are, in the apartment of L's sister, under blue skies, with the thermometer registering a pleasant 75° or so. I'm glad to be out of London's weather—but look back nostalgically to the private weather of Pond Street where—in spite of my recurrent remotenenesses (I slip into them all too easily nowadays)—it was always warm and welcoming. Thank you for all that affection and solicitude. Those days with you were a most precious time.

Tomorrow we shall probably drive up into the mountains—if the weather remains good—up the Val D'Aosta to Curmayeur or some other pleasant place. The only trouble is that there will be several hundred thousand other cars on the road.

Laura sends her love and along with it should come, in a day or two, extra copies of *You Are Not the Target*, Juliette.

Ever your affectionate,
Aldous

TO MATTHEW HUXLEY

6233 Mulholland
L.A. 28, Cal.
24 September 1963

Dearest Matthew,
All good wishes for the new house and the new job. I hope the move won't prove to be too exhausting and disrupting. Unfortunately I shall not be in the neighborhood of Washington this autumn; for I have had to cancel my lecture tour. I didn't tell you before—for there didn't seem to be any point in stirring up unnecessary worry—but the reason for this enforced change of plan is that I'm suffering from the delayed after-effects of a course of radiation treatment that I had to have last spring. The trouble began in 1960 when it was found that I had cancer of the tongue. The Memorial Hospital boys at the Good Samaritan wanted to cut out half the tongue and leave me incapable of speech. We fought them off, and went in to see my old friend, Dr. Max Cutler. After further consultation with the professor of radiology and of surgery at the U of C medical center in San Francisco, it was decided to treat the tumor with radium needles. (Cutler is one of the great experts in this field.) The treatment worked and there has been no recurrence of tongue trouble. But there has been an involvement of glands in the neck. I had one out in 1962 (and this spring another tumor appeared. It was treated with cobalt radiation). This left me very low—but I felt well enough to go to Europe. Since my return there has been a flare up of secondary inflammation—as often happens after radiation. This is painful and debilitating. Moreover the nerve leading to the right-hand vocal cord has been affected, so I have only half a voice and can't speak loud or high. Hence the cancellation of the lecture tour. This state of affairs will doubtless wear off in time. (I had an analogous trouble in my mouth a year after the original treatment with the radium needle— and it passed in due course.) So patience is the watchword. Meanwhile please keep this information as private as possible. It's appalling how quickly one's private affairs can get into the tabloids.
My love to you both.

Ever your affectionate,
Aldous

INDEX

Index

Index

Ginsberg, Allen, 475
The Gioconda Smile (Huxley), 398,
    415, 417; stage version of, 398,
    400, 412, 417–419
Glass, Douglas, 269–270
Goldman, Emma, 351
Goldring, Douglas, 95, 98, 248
Gollancz, Victor, 73, 445–446
Grant, Duncan, 20
Graves, Robert, 26, 37
Green, Russell, 106, 133–134
Greene, Graham, 391
Grey Eminence (Huxley), 374–375,
    377, 384
Guyilyov, Nikolay, 91

Haire, Norman, 314, 315, 316
Haldane, Naomi, 16, 16n3. *See also*
    Naomi Mitchison
Hamnett, Nina, 67, 90
Harding, Walter, 439
Hartley, L. P., 175
Hartley, Wesley, 475
Haynes, E. S. P., 99
Hawtry, Ralph, 46, 46n2
Heard, Gerald, 8, 337, 347, 349,
    384
Heaven and Hell (Huxley), 461
Hermann, Eva, 325–326, 344–345
Honig, Camille R., 437
Hovde, Ellen, 401
Hubbell, Jay, 337–338
Hubble, Edwin, 404–405; death of,
    447
Hutchinson, John, 90
Hutchinson, Mary, 4, 6, 111,
    112–113, 114, 115, 116, 117,
    118–119, 120–121, 122, 124,
    128–129, 131–132, 135–136,
    136–137, 137–138, 138–139,
    139–141, 141–143, 143–148,
    149–151, 151–153, 153–154,
    154–156, 156–159, 162,
163–164, 164–166, 166–168,
    169–170, 170–171, 172, 173,
    174–175, 176–177, 177–178,
    178–180, 181, 182–183, 183,
    184–185, 187–188, 190–191,
    193, 195–196, 196–198,
    202–204, 204–205, 205–206,
    207–208, 209–210, 211, 213,
    215–216, 218–219, 221–222,
    227–228, 229–230, 238, 240,
    241–242, 243–244, 244–245,
    251–252, 257–258, 262, 263,
    266–267, 275–276, 279–280,
    282–283, 284, 288–289, 291,
    292–293, 295–296, 298–300,
    303–304, 333–334, 347–349,
    381–382, 399–400, 421–422,
    435–436; bisexuality of, 5
Hutchins, Robert M., 427, 443, 444,
    445, 454
Hutchinson, St. John, 5
Huxley, Aldous, 4, 314, 315, 337,
    351, 372, 384, 411, 415, 429,
    450, 454–455, 461, 463, 466;
    alcohol, in American literature, as
    boring, 286; on America, 172,
    175, 189–190, 338–339, 344;
    America, move to, 7–8, 337;
    American citizenship, application
    for, 447, 448, 449; on Bates
    method, 351, 365, 369, 370, 403,
    423; on Arnold Bennett, 252,
    253; on British Empire,
    immensity of, 169; in California,
    347, 348, 351; on cars, feeling of
    superiority in, 300; on censorship,
    269, 269n7; on Central America,
    286–287; on cinematic method,
    79; on community, 342, 343; on
    cosmic consciousness, 352; death
    of, 3, 10; Dianetics,
    experimenting with, 416; on
    dreams, 308; on dying, 279; on

Index

Index

Index

A NOTE ON THE EDITOR

James Sexton was born in Vancouver, British Columbia, and studied at the University of British Columbia, the University of Oregon, and the University of Victoria, where he received a Ph.D. With Robert S. Baker, Mr. Sexton edited the six-volume edition of Aldous Huxley's *Complete Essays*. He teaches English at Camosun College in Victoria, British Columbia, where he lives.